Blessed Victors

Blessed Victors

Theology of Persecution in the Third-Century Church

Ruth Sutcliffe

LONDON • NEW YORK • OXFORD • NEW DELHI • SYDNEY

T&T CLARK

Bloomsbury Publishing Plc, 50 Bedford Square, London, WC1B 3DP, UK
Bloomsbury Publishing Inc, 1359 Broadway, New York, NY 10018, USA
Bloomsbury Publishing Ireland, 29 Earlsfort Terrace, Dublin 2, D02 AY28, Ireland

BLOOMSBURY, T&T CLARK and the T&T Clark logo are trademarks of
Bloomsbury Publishing Plc

First published in Great Britain 2024
Paperback edition published 2026

Copyright © Ruth Sutcliffe, 2024

Ruth Sutcliffe has asserted her right under the Copyright, Designs and Patents Act,
1988, to be identified as Author of this work.

For legal purposes the Acknowledgements on p. xiii constitute an extension of
this copyright page.

Cover design by Charlotte James
Cover image © Juanmonino / Getty Images

All rights reserved. No part of this publication may be: i) reproduced or transmitted in any form, electronic or mechanical, including photocopying, recording or by means of any information storage or retrieval system without prior permission in writing from the publishers; or ii) used or reproduced in any way for the training, development or operation of artificial intelligence (AI) technologies, including generative AI technologies. The rights holders expressly reserve this publication from the text and data mining exception as per Article 4(3) of the Digital Single Market Directive (EU) 2019/790.

Bloomsbury Publishing Plc does not have any control over, or responsibility for, any third-party websites referred to or in this book. All internet addresses given in this book were correct at the time of going to press. The author and publisher regret any inconvenience caused if addresses have changed or sites have ceased to exist, but can accept no responsibility for any such changes.

A catalogue record for this book is available from the British Library.

A catalog record for this book is available from the Library of Congress.

ISBN: HB: 978-0-5677-1074-1
PB: 978-0-5677-1078-9
ePDF: 978-0-5677-1075-8
eBook: 978-0-5677-1077-2

Typeset by RefineCatch Limited, Bungay, Suffolk

For product safety related questions contact productsafety@bloomsbury.com.

To find out more about our authors and books visit www.bloomsbury.com
and sign up for our newsletters.

To persecuted Christians, in continuity with the church of past ages

Contents

Figures and tables	ix
Preface	xi
Acknowledgements	xiii
Notes on texts and translations	xiv
Abbreviations	xv

1 Theologizing on persecution — 1
   Deriving a 'theology of persecution' — 4
   The scope and nature of early persecution — 13
   The scope and method of this study — 26
   Experiencing persecution — 29

2 Clement of Alexandria: Progression to perfection — 35
   Clement in his context — 35
   Not prohibited, but not permitted — 42
   The reason for persecution — 53
   The *telos* of persecution — 56
   The appropriate response to persecution — 60
   Conclusion — 71

3 Origen of Alexandria: Purposeful persecution — 73
   Origen in his context — 73
   Persecution: Permitted by God — 80
   Persecution in unity with Christ — 87
   The rewards of persecution — 92
   Responses to persecution — 100
   The church's response — 105
   Conclusions — 107

4 Tertullian of Carthage: Pedantic polemicist — 109
   Tertullian in context — 109
   Persecution comes from God — 117
   Persecution for the name: The cosmic arena — 124
   The good of persecution — 129

	The appropriate response to persecution	138
	The church and persecution	148
	Conclusions	154
5	Cyprian of Carthage: Pragmatic pastor	157
	Bishop Cyprian	157
	The good God is in control	165
	Persecution with purpose	168
	The good of persecution: The end in sight	174
	Pragmatic responses	180
	The persecuted church	191
	Conclusions	195
6	Summa diogmologica	197
	Five diogmological questions	198
	The relationship of questions 1–3 with questions 4 and 5	209
	Diogmology and the fathers' use of Scripture	215
	Making diogmological sense of different perspectives	222
	Concluding reflections	235

Bibliography	239
Primary sources	239
Secondary literature	242
Scripture index	257
Index of ancient sources	261
Index of topics	275

Figures and tables

Table 1.1	Hypothetical presentation of a spectrum of acceptability of responses to persecution	32
Figure 6.1	Diogmology question 1	199
Figure 6.2	Diogmology question 2	202
Figure 6.3	Diogmology question 3	205
Figure 6.4	Foundational diogmology	209
Figure 6.5	Diogmology question 4	211
Figure 6.6	Comparative diogmologies	217
Figure 6.7	Commonalities	218
Figure 6.8	Divergences	218

Preface

This book began life as a PhD thesis, which in turn arose from an interest in how the early church constructed its theology from Scripture. This interest was kindled by an examination of early theological discussion on the Trinity, which led to an appreciation of the distinctive situations and perspectives of the early Christian writers. A growing awareness of contemporary Christian persecution, and the biblical testimony to its inevitability for bearers of the name of Christ, invited an examination of the fathers' use of New Testament 'persecution passages' such as in Matthew 5 and 10 and 1 Peter. I felt that the early Christians, nearer in time to the New Testament and experiencing episodes of significant persecution, would have something worthwhile to say. Initially, I proposed to look at the earliest writings: the Apostolic Fathers, the Martyr Acts and the second-century apologies. But it was the late second and early to mid-third-century theologians that really drew my interest. It soon became clear that they offered significant and extensive theological reflection on persecution. This reflection was much broader and more highly developed than that of earlier writers.

My objective evolved as I read the works of Clement, Origen, Tertullian and Cyprian, with whom I had previously had only a passing acquaintance. The richness and complexity of their interaction with Scripture and the evident impact of the persecution experience invited detailed attention. As I explored some secondary literature, I was surprised to discover a significant gap; very little work had been done on the *theology* of persecution, and what done was focused on martyrdom. Hence my decision to explore these fathers' 'theology of persecution'.

It is my hope that a deeper understanding of how the ancient church thought theologically about persecution will contribute to the contemporary church's understanding of what is and is not persecution, and how best to respond to it.

Acknowledgements

I am, foremost, grateful to God for his abundant blessings and his equipping for this task, and for the treasure of Scripture that has inspired and continues to inspire theological reflection in his church through the ages.

My sincerest thanks are offered to my PhD supervisors, Rev Dr John McClean and Dr Edwina Murphy for their wise advice, tireless encouragement, honest critique and unending support. Also, I acknowledge the encouragement of Rev Dr Greg Goswell who encouraged my scholarly pursuits from the very beginning. I am grateful for the resources of numerous college librarians, particularly those at Christ College Sydney, St Andrews Greek Orthodox Theological College, Moore College, the Australian Catholic University and the Queensland Theology College. A Senior Fellowship from Anglican Deaconess Ministries has enabled me to dedicate sufficient time to the completion of this project. I also very much appreciate the support and encouragement of the ministers and members of Willows Presbyterian Church. Last but not least, this work would not have been possible without the support of my family, Michael, Sarah and Katie: thank you.

Soli Deo gloria.

Notes on texts and translations

The texts for the four fathers are the established corpus for each. For Clement and Origen, I have used the critical editions of *Sources Chrétiennes* (Paris: Editions du Cerf) where published and accessible to me. For Origen's *De principiis*, I have used the text in Behr,[1] and for Origen's *Exhortation to Martyrdom* that of Koetschau.[2] Otherwise, where noted I have resorted to *Patrologica Graeca* (Paris: J. P. Migne, Imprimerie Catholique). English translations of *De principiis* are also those of Behr. For Tertullian and Cyprian, I have used *Corpus Christianorum, Series Latina* (Turnhout: Brepols). English translations of Cyprian's letters are those of Clarke.[3]

Unless otherwise specified, all other English translations of the sources are my own. Scripture quotations, unless otherwise specified or contained within Patristic citations, are from *The ESV© Bible* (The Holy Bible, English Standard Version©), copyright © 2001 by Crossway, a publishing ministry of Good News Publishers. Used by permission. All rights reserved.

Formatting and abbreviations of ancient literary sources conform to convention in *The SBL Handbook of Style for Biblical Studies and Related Disciplines*, 2nd ed. (Atlanta: SBL, 2014).

---

[1] John Behr, *Origen, On First Principles*. Trans. and ed. John Behr (Oxford: Oxford University Press, 2017).

[2] Origenous. Εἰς μαρτύριον προτρεπτικός (*Exhortation to martyrdom*). P. Koetschau, ed. Origenes Werke I. Die Schrift vom Martyrium, Buch I–IV gegen Celsus (GCS 2) (Leipzig: J. C. Hinrichs'sche Buchhandlung, 1899), 3–47.

[3] Graeme W. Clarke, *The Letters of St. Cyprian of Carthage*, Ancient Christian Writers, vols 43, 44, 46, 47 (New York: Newman, 1984, 1984, 1986, 1989).

Abbreviations

Primary sources

Clement of Alexandria
   Paed.   Paedagogos
   Protr.   Proterepticus
   Quis div.   Quis dives salvetur
   Strom.   Stromateis
Cyprian
   Dem.   Ad Demetrianum
   Don.   Ad Donatum
   Eleem.   De opere et eleemosynis
   Fort.   Ad Fortunatum
   Laps.   De lapsis
   Mort.   De mortalitate
   Pat.   De bono patientiae
   Test.   Ad Quirinum testimonia adversus Judaeos
   Unit.   De catholicae ecclesiae unitate
   Zel. liv.   De zelo et livore
Eusebius
   H.E.   Historia ecclesiastica
Jerome
   Vir. ill.   De viris illustribus
Justin
   1 Apol.   Apologia I
   2 Apol.   Apologia 2
Lactantius
   Inst.   Divinarum institutionum
Origen
   Cels.   Contra Celsum
   Comm. Gen.   Commentarii in Genesim
   Comm. Jo.   Commentarii in evangelium Joannis
   Comm. Matt.   Commentarium in evangelium Matthaei
   Comm. Rom.   Commentarii in Romanos
   Dial.   Dialogus cum Heraclide
   Ep Afr.   Episula ad Africanum
   Ep. Greg.   Epistula ad Gregorium Thaumaturgum
   Exc. Ps.   Excerpta in Psalmos
   Hom. Exod.   Homiliae in Exodum
   Hom. Ezech   Homiliae in Ezechielem
   Hom. Gen.   Homiliae in Genesim
   Hom. Jer.   Homiliae in Jeremiam

Hom. Lev.	Homiliae in Leviticum
Hom. Luc.	Homiliae in Lucan
Hom. Num.	Homiliae in Numeros
Mart.	Exhortatio ad martyrium
Or.	De oratione
PEuch.	On the Pascha
Philoc.	Philocalia
Princ.	De principiis (Περι Αρχων)

Plato

Theaet.	Theaetetus
Tim.	Timaeus

Pliny the Younger

Ep.	Epistulae

Tacitus

Ann.	Annales

Tertullian

Adv. Jud.	Adversus Judaeos
An.	De anima
Apol.	Apologeticus
Bapt.	De baptismo
Carn. Chr.	De carne Christi
Cor.	*De corona militis*
Cult. fem.	De cultu feminarum
Exh. cast.	De exhortatione castitatis
Fug.	De fuga in persecutione
Herm.	Adversus Hermogenem
Idol.	De idolatria
Jej.	De jejunio adversus psychicos
Marc.	Adversus Marcionem
Mart.	Ad martyras
Mon.	De monogamia
Nat.	Ad nationes
Or.	De oratione
Paen.	De paenitentia
Pall.	De pallio
Pat.	De patientia
Praescr.	De praescriptione haereticorum
Prax.	Adversus Praxean
Pud.	De pudicitia
Res.	De resurrectione carnis
Scap.	Ad Scapulam
Scorp.	Scorpiace
Spect.	De spectaculis
Test.	De testimonio animae
Ux.	Ad uxorem
Val.	Adversus Valentinianos
Virg.	De virginibus velandis

Secondary sources

BDAG   Danker, Frederick William, editor. *A Greek-English Lexicon of the New Testament and other Early Christian Literature*, 3rd ed. Chicago: Chicago University Press, 2000.
StPatr   Studia Patristica

1

Theologizing on persecution

Blessed are you when others revile you and persecute you and utter all kinds of evil against you falsely on my account. Rejoice and be glad, for your reward is great in heaven, for so they persecuted the prophets who were before you.

Jesus, Matthew 5:11–12

You will be hated by all, yet you will be blessed.[1] The impact of this statement may be dampened by its familiarity, but it is an extraordinary expectation for a teacher to express to his disciples. Yet, for the pre-Constantinian church, Jesus' words described exactly what they claimed to experience.[2] The focus of Jesus' statement is Christological; believers suffer hatred, reviling and persecution for 'my name's sake', 'on my account', because Christ himself was hated and reviled. These words of Scripture persist through the subsequent centuries, demanding a response from all who would identify with Jesus, the founder of Christianity. All who seek to identify with Christ must come to terms with it, not only as a principle but, for so many, a lived experience.

This association between being 'Christian' and expecting persecution persists in the pages of Scripture, despite recent scholarly trends which minimize the extent and seriousness of early church persecution or its contemporary relevance.[3] The early church certainly regarded itself as persecuted, and at odds with the society in which it was growing.[4] The evidence for this is embedded in a diverse array of literary witness, not just the admittedly controversial martyr acts. It appears in apologies, polemics, treatises and letters, written in multiple locations over the span of nearly two centuries.

---

[1] Mt. 5:11; 10:22; Jn 15:20.
[2] Michael Mullins, *Called to be Saints: Christian Living in First Century Rome* (Dublin: Veritas, 1991), 329–33.
[3] Observed by Paul Middleton, *Radical Martyrdom and Cosmic Conflict in Early Christianity* (Edinburgh: T&T Clark, 2006), 1–2; Eric Rebillard, *The Early Martyr Narratives: Neither Authentic Accounts nor Forgeries* (Philadelphia: University of Pennsylvania, 2021), 3–4 and the argument of Candida Moss, *The Myth of Persecution: How the Early Christians Invented a Story of Martyrdom* (New York: HarperOne, 2013).
[4] Middleton, *Radical Martyrdom*, 2. Johan Leemans and Anthony Dupont, 'Scripture and Martyrdom', in *The Oxford Handbook of Early Christian Interpretation*, ed. Paul M. Blowers and Peter W. Martens (Oxford: University Press, 2019), 417; Éric Fournier, 'The Christian Discourse of Persecution in Late Antiquity: An introduction', in *Heirs of Roman Persecution: Studies on a Christian and Para-Christian Discourse in Late Antiquity*, ed. Éric Fournier and Wendy Mayer (London: Routledge, 2020), 5.

Although it is increasing recognized that 'persecution' was not the targeted, systematic, top-down violence once assumed, there is adequate evidence that at least some Christians truly suffered in this period.[5]

Much recent literature on early church persecution sits within the framework of socio-historical[6] and discursive[7] investigations. This book takes a different approach, by offering a theological perspective, and examining writings which have not commonly been explored at the nexus of both theology and persecution. Specifically, this book explores how four early Christian thinkers – Clement and Origen of Alexandria and Tertullian and Cyprian of Carthage – understood, theologically, the experience of suffering for their faith. Together, these 'four fathers' provide four different perspectives, dissimilar in broader theology and lived experiences.[8] This is therefore a comparative analysis, which will examine a common framework of 'theology of persecution' across their diverse writings. I am particularly interested in the interrelationships of this theology with other aspects of their theologies and their interpretations of Scripture. How will their conclusions regarding the reason for, and ultimate outcomes of, persecution directly inform their understanding of the appropriate response to it? How they agree and disagree, and why, is a fascinating focus of research which has been underrepresented in the literature.

This study is important for several reasons. Firstly, the pre-Constantinian period was critically formative for Christianity. Although the intricate deliberations on the nature of the Triune God and the two natures of Christ took place in a later period, the foundations were laid by apologists, polemicists and other early writers. In the second and third centuries, the church articulated its rule of faith against alternative interpretations of the sacred writings, and began considering which writings were 'inspired'.[9] In this same period, the church established a community structure for pastoral care, doctrinal discernment, discipline and organization.[10] From relatively

---

[5] James Corke-Webster, 'The Roman Persecutions', in *The Wiley Blackwell Companion to Christian Martyrdom*, ed. Paul Middleton (West Sussex UK: John Wiley & Sons, 2020), 47; Jonathan P. Conant, 'Memories of Trauma and the Formation of Christian Identity', in *Memories of Utopia: The Revision of Histories and Landscapes in Late Antiquity*, ed. Bronwen Neil and Kosta Simic (London: Routledge, 2020), 36–56.

[6] Paul Middleton, ed., *The Wiley Blackwell Companion to Christian Martyrdom* (West Sussex UK: Wiley Blackwell, 2020) provides extensive biographies and an overview of current opinions.

[7] For example, Éric Fournier and Wendy Mayer, eds, *Heirs of Roman Persecution: Studies on a Christian and Para-Christian Discourse in Late Antiquity* (London: Routledge, 2020); Moss, *Myth of Persecution*; Conant, 'Memories of Trauma'.

[8] For a definition of 'church fathers', see Hubertus R. Drobner, *The Fathers of the Church, A Comprehensive Introduction*, trans. Siegfried S. Schatzmann. (Peabody MS: Hendrickson, 2007), 4–5. Hereafter my unqualified references to the 'four fathers' should be taken to refer to Clement, Origen, Tertullian and Cyprian.

[9] For an overview of this process and details of the early canon lists, see Edmon L. Gallagher and John D. Meade, *The Biblical Canon Lists from Early Christianity: Texts and Analysis* (Oxford: Oxford University Press, 2017). For a detailed analysis of the process of canonization, see Lee Martin McDonald, *The Biblical Canon: Its Origin, Transmission and Authority* (Peabody MS: Hendrickson, 2007).

[10] Drobner, *Fathers of the Church,* 64; Donald K. McKim, *Theological Turning Points: Major Issues in Christian Thought* (Louisville: Westminster John Knox, 1988), 2; Everett Ferguson, *The Rule of Faith: A Guide* (Eugene OR: Cascade, 2015), 32, 68; Frances Young, *Biblical Exegesis and the Formation of Christian Culture* (Peabody MS: Hendrickson, 2002), 18, 29.

obscure origins, the great Christian communities of North Africa and Egypt emerged, grew, organized and developed distinctive theological perspectives and practices.[11] All this happened in the shadow of antagonism and misunderstanding by the wider society, which must have impacted the developing community's self-understanding.

Theology does not develop in a vacuum but arises from the faith and practice of a community.[12] As Migliore explains, confession of Christ takes place in specific historical and cultural contexts and the response to theological questions will be shaped by the contexts in which the questions arise.[13] The experience (or simply the threat) of persecution and martyrdom is such a context. This context is theologically significant because it presents a challenge which shapes views of God's goodness and providence, the origin of evil, eschatological hope and what it means to 'take up the cross and follow' Jesus.[14] For Christians, salvation itself is linked to Jesus' promise, 'everyone therefore who shall confess me before men, I will also confess him before my Father who is in heaven. But whoever shall deny me before men, I will also deny him before my Father who is in heaven.'[15] Furthermore, only those who 'endure to the end' will be saved.[16] Given that persecution, which follows from external opposition to the confessional 'mark', presents a challenge in terms of the consequences of that confession, it is a reasonable assumption that it would promote theological reflection on the nature of confession.

This relationship between theology and experience was bidirectional; early Christians looked to the Scriptures, to the apostolic tradition and to the church's praxis to understand why they suffered and how they should respond.[17] Conversely, how they interpreted biblical texts that spoke of God's goodness, providence, promises and eschatological plan would be influenced by what they experienced. As Migliore further observes, theological questions arise with particular force in situations of crisis.[18] Persecution for one's faith is such a crisis. It tests understanding of and commitment to a worldview and practice that provokes suffering and death. The early fathers' opinions are often sought on matters of early theology, polemic, apology and praxis.[19] Given their context within this period, and their reflection upon what they testify to seeing and experiencing, it makes sense that they would also offer theological insights into Christian persecution. This book extends an invitation to hear them.

---

[11] For detailed overviews of these developments, see J. Patout Burns and Robin M. Jensen, *Christianity in Roman Africa: the development of its practices and beliefs* (Grand Rapids: Eerdmans, 2014) and C. Wilfred Griggs, *Early Egyptian Christianity: From its Origins to 451 CE* (Leiden: Brill, 1990).

[12] Daniel L. Migliore, *Faith Seeking Understanding: An Introduction to Christian Theology*, 3rd ed. (Grand Rapids: Eerdmans, 2014), xvi.

[13] Migliore, *Faith Seeking Understanding*, 205.

[14] Mt. 16:24.

[15] Mt. 10:32–33, NAS.

[16] Mt. 10:22.

[17] For an overview of the New Testament's presentation of the church as a persecuted community, see Paul Middleton, 'Martyrdom and Persecution in the New Testament', in *The Wiley Blackwell Companion to Christian Martyrdom*, ed. Paul Middleton (West Sussex UK: John Wiley & Sons, 2020), 51–71.

[18] Migliore, *Faith Seeking Understanding*, 4.

[19] For discussion of the potential contribution of patristics to contemporary social issues, see Andrew J. Prince, *Contextualization of the Gospel: Towards an Evangelical Approach in Light of Scripture and the Church Fathers* (Eugene OR: Wipf & Stock, 2017), 116–23.

Deriving a 'theology of persecution'

Definitions

Any consideration of a 'theology of persecution' first encounters the vexed question of what constitutes 'persecution'. Fournier considers it 'a malleable rhetorical label in late antique discourse, whose meaning shifted depending on the viewpoint of the authors who used it'.[20] The word used in the New Testament is the Greek διωγμός, defined by Danker as 'a program or process designed to harass and oppress someone'.[21] The term may be considered a discursive construct,[22] and indeed it was later deployed as such beyond the era of 'Roman' persecution.[23] It may be defined from the perspective of the intent of the alleged 'persecutor', which requires a motivation of hatred and injustice, as Moss asserts,[24] rendering questionable any alleged 'persecution' performed in ignorance or for legitimate socio-political reasons. Against this, Tertullian claimed that hatred and injustice toward Christians arises out of ignorance.[25] Too narrow a definition based on the motives of the 'persecutor' risks undermining and delegitimizing the actual effects on those who were the object of 'legitimate' opposition, making those in power the arbiters of what is good and right.

Alternatively, persecution may be considered from the perspective of the one who perceives themselves to be 'persecuted'.[26] It begs the question of the historical extent and degree of suffering actually experienced by early Christians that could be construed as 'persecution', which has led to questioning as to whether it was an objective reality.[27] For the purposes of the present study, the four fathers' perception that Christians were the subjects of persecution is accepted. Provided there is an allowance within a 'minimalist' perspective of some degree of persecution,[28] whether state-sponsored or locally driven, this will suffice, because it is the fathers' perspectives that I seek to elucidate. Therefore, my working definition of persecution is 'antagonism or opposition experienced by Christians as a consequence of profession of allegiance to Christ',

---

[20] Fournier, *Heirs of Roman Persecution*, 2.
[21] Frederick William Danker, ed. *A Greek-English Lexicon of the New Testament and other Early Christian Literature*, (BDAG) 3rd ed. (Chicago: Chicago University Press, 2000), 253.
[22] Reviewed by Wendy Mayer, 'Heirs of Roman Persecution: Common threads in discursive strategies across Late Antiquity', in *Heirs of Roman Persecution: Studies on a Christian and Para-Christian Discourse in Late Antiquity*, ed. Éric Fournier and Wendy Mayer (London: Routledge, 2020), 317–39. Judith Perkins, *The Suffering Self: Pain and Narrative Representation in the Early Christian Era* (London: Routledge, 1995), 214, concludes that 'Christianity did not produce its suffering subject alone, but that this subjectivity was under construction and emanated from a number of different locations in the Graeco-Roman cultural world'. See also L. Stephanie Cobb, *Divine Deliverance: Pain and Painlessness in Early Christian Martyr Texts* (Oakland: University of California Press, 2017), 122–3. The four fathers do not emphasize the martyrologies' depiction of painless torture that is Cobb's particular focus.
[23] Leemans and Dupont, 'Scripture and Martyrdom', 434; Fournier, 'Discourse of Persecution', 2.
[24] Moss, *Myth of Persecution*, 164.
[25] *Apol.* 1 (CCSL 1:85–7)
[26] Leemans and Dupont, 'Scripture and Martyrdom', 417.
[27] Recent pushback against 'extreme' minimalism, by scholars who accept the central conclusions of minimalism, is noted by Paul Middleton, *Companion to Christian Martyrdom*, 3.
[28] Which is in turn dependent on one's definition of persecution, as noted by James Corke-Webster, 'Roman Persecutions', 47.

without requiring a distinction between 'legitimate' and irrational antagonism, or between what is perceived and what is objectively verifiable.

Another vexed question is the definition of 'martyr', which has received much more recent attention because of contemporary ascriptions of 'martyr' to suicide bombers and the like.[29] As Middleton observes, agreement on a definitive and consistent definition of 'martyr' is elusive.[30] He resists the urge to provide a definition of martyrdom, holding to his initial stance that martyrs are 'made' or constructed by the stories told about their deaths. 'Essentially, attempts to define martyrdom are ultimately ways to distinguish between deaths of which the narrator or reporters approve and those they do not.'[31] Similarly, Kotzé summarizes current consensus: 'martyrdom is a complex and elusive concept, a construct that was created through discourse. It is something that had to be *made* and it could be *remade*.'[32]

My working definition of a Christian martyr, for present purposes, is based on what the four fathers whose writings I examine 'made' it to be. A particular outcome of my investigation is the connection between confession and martyrdom in the writings of the fathers.[33] Therefore, pre-empting these findings, a martyr is 'one whose confession of allegiance to Christ results in the imposition of death'. This definition is deliberately broad, to encompass subsequent discussion of so called 'voluntary' martyrs and those who died as a consequence of imprisonment or other suffering, as well as those directly executed.

For the purposes of this study, then, a 'theology of persecution' is 'the Christian reflection on the experience of suffering as a consequence of participation in the Christian faith and its relation to God and his ways'. It is the *theologian's* integrated description of the origin of, reason for and ultimate *telos* of persecution, and the appropriate response to persecution by Christians. As a shorthand label for this specific definition, perhaps rather presumptuously, I propose the neologism 'diogmology' for 'theology of persecution'. It seems in keeping with other 'ologies' identifying elements of theology, thus emphasizing its theological focus. It is to be understood as a theological locus, not merely a discursive tool. In this sense it differs from 'martyrology', which in practice focuses on writings about martyrs.

By way of comparison, de Wet introduces the neologism *douology* as a term for the *discourse* of slavery from the Greek *doulos* (slave) and *logos* (word, argument, discourse).[34] The term stems from de Wet's confessed challenge to 'develop a new

---

[29] Paul Middleton, 'Creating and Contesting Christian Martyrdom', in *The Wiley Blackwell Companion to Christian Martyrdom*, ed. Paul Middleton (West Sussex UK: John Wiley & Sons, 2020), 25.
[30] Middleton, *Radical Martyrdom*, 9–10.
[31] Middleton, 'Creating and Contesting', 25.
[32] Annemaré Kotzé, 'Augustine and the Remaking of Martyrdom', in *The Wiley Blackwell Companion to Christian Martyrdom,* ed. Paul Middleton (West Sussex UK: John Wiley & Sons, 2020), 135 (original emphases).
[33] Consistent with the general observation of L Stephanie Cobb, 'Martyrdom in Roman Context', in *The Wiley Blackwell Companion to Christian Martyrdom*, ed. Paul Middleton (West Sussex UK: John Wiley & Sons, 2020), 89, that *martys*, originally meaning 'witness' in a legal sense, came to be used by Christians to designate those killed for confessions of faith.
[34] Chris L de Wet, *Preaching Bondage: John Chrysostom and the Discourse of Slavery in Early Christianity* (Oakland: University of California Press, 2015).

analytical language for speaking about slavery, a language that would assist in laying bare the *discursivity* of slavery'.[35] He took as a relevant precedent Elizabeth Schüssler Fiorenza's coining of 'kyriarchy' and 'kyriarchization', as appellations for the intersectional structures of domination, and draws on the study of discourse as promoted by the French philosopher Michel Foucault.[36] In contrast, my study is theological, an attempt to systematize the theological reflection of four ancient theological writers on the experience of persecution as they perceived it, through the lens of other theological loci, the other dimensions of the *-ology*. This is appropriate, since these loci are represented by the five theological questions which I will use to frame the fathers' 'diogmologies'.

The scope of 'diogmology'

Diogmology, as I have defined it, should be distinguished from theodicy. Theodicy examines the relationship between God and 'evil',[37] which embraces many forms of suffering that do not necessarily relate to being Christian. Diogmology relates to the particular sufferings of Christians for being Christian.[38] Theodicy may be viewed as the defence of the providence of a good and omnipotent God towards all creation, whereas persecution presents a challenge in relation to God's providence toward his own people, specifically. Providence is certainly a point of connection between diogmology and theodicy, because of the tension between God's superintendence of evil and the free actions of those who perform it.[39]

Although studies of persecution, including its socio-historical basis, discursive construction and ideology/theology, often focus on martyrdom,[40] a thorough treatment of diogmology must not be limited to martyrdom. It must rather situate martyrdom within the context of persecution. Persecution and suffering also encompass threatening, imprisonment, torture, exile, slave labour, loss of property and economic opportunity, as well as vilification, slander and discrimination. All of these could be

---

[35] de Wet, *Preaching Bondage*, 3 (his italics).
[36] Ibid., 4. Specifically, de Wet utilizes critical theoretical approaches, within the wider context of cultural historiography, to reveal the discourse of slavery embedded in Chrysostom's homilies by examining how these works enunciate the slave body (p. 41).
[37] S. A. Oliver, 'Theodicy', *New Dictionary of Theology*, ed. Martin Davie et al., 2nd ed. (Downers Grove: IVP, 2016), 897–900.
[38] M. A. Rae, 'Suffering', *New Dictionary of Theology*, ed. Martin Davie et al., 2nd ed. (Downers Grove: IVP, 2016), 878.
[39] Mark S. M. Scott, *Journey Back to God: Origen on the Problem of Evil* (Oxford: Oxford University Press, 2012), 1–2; N. M. P. Helm, 'Providence', *New Dictionary of Theology*, ed. Martin Davie et al., 2nd ed. (Downers Grove: IVP, 2016), 714–15.
[40] For example, Hans von Campenhausen, *Die Idee des Martyriums in der alten Kirche* (Göttingen: Vandenhoeck & Ruprecht, 1964); W. H. C. Frend, *Martyrdom and Persecution in the Early Church* (Oxford: Blackwell, 1965; Cambridge: James Clarke, 2008); Theofrid Baumeister, *Die Anfänge der Theologie des Martyriums* (Münster: Aschendorf, 1980); Glen W. Bowersock, *Martyrdom and Rome* (Cambridge: Cambridge University Press, 1995); Daniel Boyarin, *Dying for God: Martyrdom and the Making of Christianity and Judaism* (Stanford: Stanford University Press, 1999); Rebillard, *Early Martyr Narratives*; Moss, *Myth of Persecution*; Leemans and Dupont, 'Scripture and Martyrdom', Middleton, *Companion to Christian Martyrdom*.

considered as 'suffering for the name'.[41] Although the early Christians' actions could be perceived as politically or socially subversive, this was not their stated motivation.[42] Nor should diverse forms of suffering be indiscriminately termed 'martyrdom', which has expanded beyond its original connection to μάρτυς as 'witness', to embrace many forms of dying or extreme suffering by one who claims to have a faith or purpose, however defined or relevant.[43]

My working definition of a Christian martyr anticipates the connection I will demonstrate between martyrdom and confession: one who suffers death as a consequence of professed allegiance to, and unwillingness to renounce, the name of Christ, and the faith and practices that attend such confession. Even though it was a relatively rare consequence of ancient 'persecution', martyrdom cannot be ignored. An important part of the investigation is to locate it within the whole framework of persecution, which I will argue is centred, in the minds of the fathers, on the concept of 'confession'. Should a Christian who publicly confesses Christ expect to be martyred, perhaps even desire it, or are there equally valid expressions of confessing Christianity and enduring to the end? The diverse writings of the early church exhibit different answers to this question. Clement is 'moderately supportive of the idea of martyrdom, but not at all exhortative',[44] whereas Tertullian has rightly been characterized as 'an enthusiastic proponent of martyrdom'.[45] One objective of this study is to determine the basis of this diversity, and the attendant issue of so-called 'voluntary martyrdom'.

To reiterate, this book presents a study of comparative historical theology. Whilst it contributes to understanding patristic theology in its social context, it is not an attempt to add knowledge about that social context. Just as the study of theodicy cuts across disciplinary boundaries,[46] so too diogmology should be derived in relationship to its place within other theological schema. 'Theology' in its broadest sense encompasses all Christian doctrine, the various loci of which are interconnected.[47] Consequently, my intent is to explore the fathers' theologizing on persecution within the framework of five fundamental questions, each relating to one or more loci of broader theology: the doctrines of God himself, Christology, eschatology, soteriology and ecclesiology.

Describing the fathers' theology of persecution requires engagement with a range of their writings. The church fathers wrote about the nature, person and character of God, explored ideas of God as Trinity, the work and person of Christ and the Holy Spirit, the nature of humankind, demons and angels, the purpose and organization of the church, and expounded (often speculatively) on the afterlife. Nevertheless, the extant writings

---

[41] Mt. 5:11; 39–41; 10:22, 25; Lk. 6:22; Acts 5:41; 2 Cor. 4:8–9; 12:10; 1 Pet. 2:12.
[42] Robert L. Wilken, *The Christians as the Romans Saw Them*, 2nd ed. (Newhaven: Yale University Press, 2003), xvii, highlights the importance of appreciating the differences in perception between pagans and Christians.
[43] The misappropriation of martyr terminology in contemporary politico-religious debate as rightly critiqued by Moss, *Myth of Persecution*, 8–13, is acknowledged by the present author. However, Moss's solution, to downplay or discount the early church's persecution experience, is misdirected.
[44] Annewies van den Hoek, 'Clement of Alexandria on Martyrdom', *StPatr* 26 (1993): 324–41, at 340.
[45] Middleton, *Radical Martyrdom*, 19.
[46] Scott, *Journey*, xiv
[47] Migliore, *Faith Seeking Understanding*, 12–13.

of the second and third centuries are not systematic theologies.[48] Often, a theological position was articulated in response to an inappropriate or heretical perspective.[49] As with other aspects of theology, such as soteriology and ecclesiology, the fathers' diogmologies must be pieced together from diverse works, not just those focusing on persecution.[50]

Constructing a diogmology entails investigating the bidirectional influence and interconnectedness between persecution and other theological loci within each father's oeuvre. For example, conclusions about the origin of persecution must account for the writer's perspective on the goodness and providence of God and his ultimate purpose for his people. Careful attention must also be paid to the context, genre and purpose of a given work and the arguments within it, especially when extracting a smaller discussion from a wider. Failure to do so will misrepresent the writer's intentions.[51] Additionally, as Hall emphasizes, 'the fathers never split theology off from spirituality, as though theology was an academic, mental exercise ... theology and spirituality, the Christian mind and heart, worship and reflection are an inseparable whole'.[52]

The fathers' theology was grounded in their reading of unified Scripture.[53] Whilst an awareness of extra-biblical influences such as Greek philosophy is important – Baur asserts that 'a correct understanding of the development of the truths of the faith is not possible without taking the influence of the philosophical schools into account'[54] – this book focuses on how the fathers derived their theology of persecution from the biblical literature, primarily the New Testament. Each of the four claimed to write as Christians, with Scripture as their primary source of truth. This invites the use of Scripture as a basis for comparison, being their claimed common ground. By comparing which passages each father uses when writing about persecution, and how they exegete the same or similar passages, I will show the relationship between their biblical interpretation and their diogmologies. The method will be to examine the fathers' engagement with certain 'benchmark' passages, which are utilized by three or more of them. A similar exercise was undertaken by Paul Hartog, who examines martyrdom themes across five primary sources which 'exhort to martyrdom', and their use of common scriptural passages.[55] Hartog's study utilizes three of the large corpus of texts

---

[48] Drobner, *Fathers of the Church*, 72; however, John Behr, introduction to *Origen, On First Principles*, trans. and ed. John Behr (Oxford: Oxford University Press, 2017) xx, regards Origen's *De principiis* as the first attempt at a systematic theology.

[49] Basil Studer and Anelo Di Berardino, eds, *History of Theology*, vol. 1, *The Patristic Period*, trans. Matthew J. O'Connell, (Collegeville MN: Liturgical, 1997), 8.

[50] Such as the Exhortations to Martyrdom, Tertullian's *Scorpiace* and *De fuga*, Cyprian's *De lapsis* and *Ad Demetrianum*.

[51] Basil Studer and Anelo Di Berardino, eds, trans. Matthew J. O'Connell, *The Patristic Period*, vol. 1 of *History of Theology*, 9.

[52] Christopher A. Hall, *Learning Theology with the Church Fathers* (Downers Grove: IVP, 2002), 10.

[53] Young, *Biblical Exegesis*, 10, 29; John J. O'Keefe and Russell R. Reno, *Sanctified Vision: An Introduction to Early Christian Interpretation of the Bible* (Baltimore: Johns Hopkins, 2005), 12.

[54] Ferdinand C. Bauer, *History of Christian Dogma*, ed. Peter C. Hodgson, trans. Robert F. Brown and Peter C. Hodgson (Oxford: Oxford University Press, 2014), 58.

[55] Paul A Hartog, 'Themes and Intertextualities in Pre-Nicene Exhortations to Martyrdom', in *The Wiley Companion to Christian Martyrdom*, ed. Paul Middleton (West Sussex UK: John Wiley & Sons, 2020). My research was conducted independently of Hartog's.

I interrogate, and his focus is on martyrdom, so his findings are narrower in scope than mine. Nevertheless, there are common themes and common biblical passages identified across both studies. Hartog concludes:

> The broader analysis of common themes and common interpretive traditions within all five of these works extolling martyrdom is a fascinating and fruitful study in and of itself. The frequent themes, recurring images, and common interpretive traditions with such exhortative works are windows that illuminate our appreciation of the theological understanding and rhetorical construction of martyrdom within an array of early Christian texts.[56]

A final influence, the importance of which should not be underestimated, is the fathers' diverse personal experiences of persecution, within their social and intellectual milieus.[57] Clement and Origen were teachers.[58] Tertullian was a polemicist and prominent in his church community.[59] Cyprian was a bishop.[60] Origen and Cyprian experienced the Decian persecution first hand and personally knew confessors and martyrs.[61] Clement and Tertullian wrote more at arm's length, although both testified to witnessing persecution.[62] Clement, Origen and Cyprian withdrew, Tertullian apparently did not.[63] Alexandria and Carthage were different intellectual and cultural environments, their ideas expressed in different languages.

If these diverse thinkers, writing under such different circumstances, reach similar conclusions, it strengthens the argument for a common diogmology, especially if they each appropriate Scripture similarly in expressing it. Conversely, if the different fathers' thoughts are found to be conflicting, their conclusions at variance, the exercise will nevertheless be worthwhile as a demonstrating the primacy of individual factors in the fathers' theologizing. Kannengiesser has issued the challenge for engagement of patristic scholarship with theology on a broader systematic level, investigating how their hermeneutic applied to life within their culture.[64] This book addresses this need with respect to an important aspect of the early fathers' claimed experiences.

---

[56] Hartog, 'Themes and Intertextualities', 115.
[57] Frend, *Martyrdom and Persecution*, 362. David Wilhite has done extensive work on the North African context of Tertullian and Cyprian: David E. Wilhite, *Tertullian the African: An Anthropological Reading of Tertullian's Context and Identities*, Millennium-Studien, 14 (Berlin- Boston: De Gruyter, 2007); David E. Wilhite, *Ancient African Christianity: An introduction to a unique context and tradition* (New York: Routledge, 2017).
[58] Annewies van den Hoek, 'The Catechetical School of Early Christian Alexandria and its Philonic Heritage', *Harvard Theological Review* 90, no. 1 (1997): 59–87, at 85–6.
[59] Tertullian, *Anim.* 9.4 (CCSL 2:792) involves him in interviewing a sister in receipt of visions. Geoffrey D. Dunn, *Tertullian* (New York: Routledge, 2004), 9–10; Éric Rebillard, *Christians and their Many Identities in Late Antiquity: North Africa 200–450 CE* (Ithaca: Cornell University Press, 2012), 10.
[60] The seminal work on his episcopate is J. Patout Burns, *Cyprian the Bishop* (London: Routledge, 2002).
[61] As evidenced by Origen's *Exhortation to Martyrdom* and Cyprian's *Ad Fortunatum* and letters.
[62] *Strom.* 2.20 (PG 8:1069); *Scorp.* 1.11–13 (CCSL 2:1070–1).
[63] See Ruth Sutcliffe, 'To Flee or Not to Flee? Matthew 10:23 and Third Century Flight in Persecution', *Scrinium* 14 (2018): 133–60, at 133.
[64] Charles Kannengiesser, 'A Key for the Future of Patristics: The "Senses" of Scripture', in *In Dominico Eoquio, In Lordly Eloquence, Essays on Patristic Exegesis in Honour of Robert Wilken*, ed. Paul M. Blowers et al. (Grand Rapids: Eerdmans, 2002), 99.

Scholarship in context

The field of early Christian studies is massive; socio-historical studies, literary studies, patristic theology and exegesis are sizeable disciplines in their own right. It is a difficult task to demonstrate 'absence' of coverage of a topic such as 'diogmology' in such a vast body of literature. Each area of scholarship could be mined for what has and has not been elucidated in the context of persecution. The following discussion is necessarily tailored to demonstrating how aspects of these disciplines overlap, surround and inform the present study.

Socio-historical investigations of the nature and extent of early Christian persecution provide an essential background to the topic. They address the milieu and experiences which the fathers encountered in the Graeco-Roman world.[65] Important insights, from an 'external' perspective, have been gained regarding the social, political and religious factors contributing to persecution.[66] Their remit obviously does not encompass the Christians' own theological evaluation. Significant attention has been and continues to be given to the literary discourse of persecution and martyrdom and its shaping of Christian identity,[67] and to religious violence and conflict.[68] Whilst I hope to offer a theological contribution to the discussion of Christian identity, this book does not constitute a discussion of the literary or rhetorical construction of that identity. The socio-historical and discursive scholarship does, however, raise the important issue of the reliability of the patristic sources as historical documents. As Fournier notes:

> One significant challenge for the historian interested in the subject of persecution is to adequately walk the line between taking our ancient sources seriously and accepting our texts at face value ... Our emphasis on the rhetorical nature of many claims of persecution should not tempt us to distinguish between the false binary of 'real' or 'false' persecution. In most cases it is impossible to determine whether claims of persecution 'really happened' or how severe they 'really were.'[69]

---

[65] Examples include Everett Ferguson, *Backgrounds of Early Christianity* (Grand Rapids: Eerdmans, 2003); Burns and Jensen, *Christianity in Roman Africa*; Griggs, *Early Egyptian Christianity* and older works such as Jean Daniélou, *The origins of Latin Christianity*, vol. 3 of *A History of Early Christian Doctrine Before the Council of Nicaea* (London: Westminster, 1977); Frend, *Martyrdom and Persecution*.

[66] For example, Robert L. Wilken, *The Christians as the Romans Saw Them*, 2nd ed. (Newhaven: Yale University Press, 2003); Timothy D. Barnes, 'Pagan Perceptions of Christianity', in *Early Christianity: Origins and Evolution to AD 600*, ed. Ian Hazlett (London: SPCK, 1991), 231–41.

[67] A seminal work is Judith M. Lieu, *Christian Identity in the Jewish and Graeco-Roman World* (Oxford: Oxford University Press, 2004). See also Candida Moss, 'The Discourse of Voluntary Martyrdom: Ancient and Modern', *Church History* 81 (2012): 531–51 and the rider by Matthew Recla, 'Martyrdom and the Creation of Christian Identity', in *The Wiley Blackwell Companion to Christian Martyrdom*, ed. Paul Middleton (West Sussex UK: John Wiley & Sons, 2020), 199–206.

[68] Jitse H. F. Dijkstra, 'Religious Violence in late antique Egypt reconsidered: The cases of Alexandria, Panopolis, and Philae', in *Reconceiving Religious Conflict: New Views from the Formative Centuries of Christianity*. ed. Wendy Mayer and Chris de Wets (New York: Routledge, 2018), 211–33, at 211, considers religious violence to be one of the most hotly debated issues currently in Late Antique studies. Wendy Mayer, 'Re-theorizing Religious Conflict', pp. 3–29 in the same volume, calls for a fresh set of theoretical foundations for the study of religious conflict that incorporate a neuroscientific approach.

[69] Fournier, 'Christian Discourse of Persecution', 5.

Literary analysis examines the claims themselves and how they functioned discursively. In contrast, my interest is how they functioned theologically. Obviously, some historical reconstruction is necessary, and will be provided in due course.

In studies of patristic theology, in contrast to literary and historical studies, persecution generally forms, at most, a backdrop. For example, Ashwin-Siejkowski examines Clement's work through the lens of his journey to perfection or likeness to God.[70] This theme undoubtedly underpins Clement's diogmology, however the author scarcely mentions persecution. Scott sets Origen's broader theology within the framework of his theodicy, and the journey of fallen souls back to God, but excludes explicit discussion of persecution. This is despite claiming that 'Origen's adult life was punctuated by profound experiences of persecution' and 'he would live in the shadow of his father's martyrdom'.[71] Barnes' influential work on Tertullian[72] includes a historical analysis of persecution, but confines discussion of Tertullian's theological perspective to martyrdom.[73] Osborn only briefly references persecution in his treatise on Tertullian's theology.[74] Cyprianic studies are the notable exception, as the bishop's writings are so heavily contextualized to the Decian persecution and its aftermath. However, the focus (appropriately) is on what I would term his applied diogmology: the individual and communal responses to persecution, and his developed ecclesiology.[75] Even this brief survey invites a fuller study of the fathers' theology of persecution. Studies of patristic theology, whether extensive surveys[76] or investigation of specific loci,[77] help to identify the necessary theological framework and foundational assumptions with which any diogmology must engage, and my indebtedness will be acknowledged throughout this project. There is, nevertheless, a lacuna with respect to theology of persecution as a discrete locus.

One focused consideration is Tabbernee's examination of Eusebius' 'theology of persecution', which he traces through revised editions of the *Historia ecclesiastica*. Tabbernee explores how Eusebius transitions from initially considering persecution as the demonic attempt to frustrate the Logos' message, to viewing emperors as God's instruments for chastening the church, and ultimately views Constantine as a Christ-

---

[70] Piotr Ashwin-Siejkowski, *Clement of Alexandria: A Project of Christian Perfection* (London: T&T Clark, 2008).
[71] Scott, *Journey*, 1.
[72] Timothy D. Barnes, *Tertullian: A Historical and Literary Study* (Oxford: Clarendon, 2005).
[73] Barnes' chapter on Martyrdom, *Tertullian*, 164–86, certainly presents Tertullian's theology of martyrdom, but largely attributes Tertullian's thought development to Montanism, which is now considered simplistic.
[74] Eric Osborn, *Tertullian: First Theologian of the West* (Cambridge: Cambridge University Press, 2003), 236.
[75] E.g. Geoffrey D. Dunn 'Cyprian and Women in a Time of Persecution', *Journal of Ecclesiastical History* 57, no. 2 (2006), 205–25.
[76] Such as J. N. D. Kelly, *Early Christian Doctrines*, 5th ed. (London: Continuum, 1977); Walter Bauer, *Orthodoxy and Heresy in Earliest Christianity* (London: SCM, 1972); Henry Chadwick, *Heresy and Orthodoxy in the Early Church* (Aldershot: Variorum, 1991); David E. Wilhite, ed., *The Cambridge Companion to Early Christian Theology* (Cambridge: Cambridge University Press, forthcoming).
[77] E.g. Brian E. Daley, *The Hope of the Early Church, A Handbook of Patristic Eschatology* (Peabody MS: Hendrickson, 2003), on eschatology. There is a wealth of material on Trinitarian thought and the later Christological controversies.

like saviour of persecuted Christians.[78] Leeman and Dupont conclude that 'the early church had a coherent theology of martyrdom as well as a systematic overview of scriptural material supporting it'.[79] They base this conclusion on a consideration of martyr acts and the apostolic fathers, particularly Ignatius, and focus on the theological concept of *imitatio Christi*. Candida Moss has also thoroughly explored *imitatio Christi* in the early martyrological literature, as distinct from the writings of the fathers.[80] Imitation of Christ is certainly an aspect of a theology of persecution and is developed in much greater depth in the four fathers. I suggest that it should be more definitively centred on the centrality of confession of the name of Christ. I have elsewhere argued that the second-century writers did not have a fully developed 'theology of persecution', although there were certainly themes in common with the four fathers.[81] Hartog identified several themes common to Tertullian's, Origen's and Cyprian's 'exhortations to martyrdom', as well as Ignatius' *Epistle to the Romans* and in Pseudo-Cyprian.[82] One of these themes is imitating Christ in suffering.

Jane McLarty provides an overview of early Christian theologies of martyrdom.[83] She acknowledges that martyrdom was 'created through narrative', and examines how martyrdom as a concept was theologically constructed, to make sense of the suffering Christians anticipated and witnessed.[84] Her focus is martyrdom and the martyrological literature, but she does engage to some extent with the four fathers. McLarty posits that we can speak only of 'theologies', rather than one overarching theology of martyrdom.[85] I shall show, however, that a study inclusive of the broader theology of persecution will reveal some foundational common ground between ancient writers. McLarty situates the common theological motif (or attitude) of the martyrological texts she examines in 'a sense of *emotional* connection: a sense of loyalty to the savior God and solidarity with fellow-believers and sufferers'.[86] The focus in the four fathers is more specific than this, but the themes of martyrdom which McLarty identifies in her study nevertheless resonate with my conclusions: the expression of Christian identity, loyalty to the personal relationship with God through the person of Jesus, the imitation of and participation in Christ's suffering, the defeat of Satan and communal effect, and the eschatological hope. This congruence is interesting in a more restricted study in which the author advises she has 'only been able to give a flavour of the richness of theological themes and imagery in the various martyrdom texts from the first Christian centuries'.[87]

---

[78] William Tabbernee, 'Eusebius' "Theology of Persecution": As seen in the various editions of his *Church History*', *Journal of Early Christian Studies* 5, no. 3 (1997): 319–34.
[79] Leeman and Dupont, 'Scripture and Martyrdom', 420.
[80] Candida R. Moss, *The Other Christs: Imitating Jesus in Ancient Christian Ideologies of Martyrdom* (Oxford: Oxford University Press, 2010), vii.
[81] Ruth Sutcliffe, 'No Need to Apologise? Tertullian and the Paradox of Polemic Against Persecution', *StPatr.* 126 (2021), 267–78.
[82] Hartog, 'Themes and Intertextualities', 104.
[83] Jane D. McLarty, 'Early Christian Theologies of Martyrdom', in *The Wiley Blackwell Companion to Christian Martyrdom*, ed. Paul Middleton (West Sussex UK: John Wiley & Sons, 2020), 120–134.
[84] Ibid., 120.
[85] Ibid., 121.
[86] Ibid., 121.
[87] Ibid., 131.

The above examples illustrate that scholarly exploration and analysis of theologizing about persecution, when it does occur, tends to be focused on martyrdom. However, because martyrdom was relatively infrequent, prioritizing it risks downplaying the impact of persecution overall, and may disengage it from the majority experience.[88] Exploring the fathers' theology of persecution more broadly is a 'gap' worthy of filling, because it speaks to broader, timeless concerns and the wider experience of the church.

The scope and nature of early persecution

The recent trajectory of scholarship on early persecution has been characterized by minimalism, away from the assumption of continuous, widespread, legal persecution, towards a more sporadic, populist-driven series of local outbreaks. This is well summarized by Corke-Webster, who observes that 'most scholars today accept that the steps Roman authorities took against Christians in this period were far more limited in both chronological and geographical extent than many early Christian accounts would have us believe.'[89] Nevertheless, Corke-Webster does not deny that Christians genuinely suffered; he offers the basis of a different scholarly trajectory that he recommends be more comprehensively pursued; that of persecution as a locally contextualized or 'bottom-up' phenomenon. This is also my assumption for this present study, as it reflects the observations of the four fathers.

The works of the second- and third-century apologists, Eusebius' *Historia ecclesiastica*, the martyr acts and subsequent late antique and medieval ecclesiastical martyr cults may give the impression of persistent and vicious 'official' persecution until Constantine.[90] Fisher may be considered typical of the late nineteenth- to early twentieth-century 'maximalist' perspective which assumed a fairly consistent, high level of persecution initiated in significant part by the emperors themselves, between the late first and early fourth centuries.[91] Likewise, Gwatkin regarded persecution as 'the policy of the state', from the Flavian period.[92] Against this, Gibbon[93] had previously proposed that the persecutions occurred under 'temperate Roman policy' and the church 'enjoyed many intervals of peace and tranquillity'.[94] A series of challenges to the idea of pre-Decian imperial proscription of Christianity began with the work of Theodore Mommsen in 1890, as described by Corke-Webster.[95]

---

[88] Recla, 'Creation of Christian Identity', 199, cautions against basing an understanding of Christian identity formation on the theology of martyrdom, an experience of only a minority of Christians.
[89] James Corke-Webster, 'Roman Persecutions', 33.
[90] Keith Hopkins, 'Christian Number and its Implications', *Journal of Early Christian Studies* 6, no. 2 (1998): 185–226; Andrew Louth, 'Hagiography', in *The Cambridge History of Early Christian Literature*, ed. Frances Young, Lewis Ayers, and Andrew Louth (Cambridge: Cambridge University Press, 2004), 358–61; Moss, *Myth of Persecution*, 7–8, 15, 18.
[91] George Park Fisher, *History of the Christian Church* (London: Hodder and Stoughton, 1898), 47–9.
[92] Henry Melvill Gwatkin, *Early Church History to A.D. 313*, vol. 1 (London: MacMillan & Co., 1912), 95.
[93] Edward Gibbon, *The Decline and Fall of the Roman Empire* (Edinburgh: Ballantyne, 1903), 2:82.
[94] Gibbon, *Roman Empire*, 2:94. Notwithstanding significant differences between eighteenth- and twenty-first-century measures of what might constitute 'moderate punishment', Gibbon's opinion is in line with the current consensus.
[95] Corke-Webster, 'Roman Persecutions', 33–4.

Frend's seminal overview of early Christian persecution and martyrdom drew on a large range of extant patristic and ancient secular literature, resulting in what could be termed an 'intermediate view' of imperial involvement. Whilst recognizing that persecution was not continuous, Frend does attribute some awareness of and antagonism towards Christians to emperors such as Domitian, Trajan, Marcus Aurelius and Severus.[96] He attributes both popular and imperial animosity toward Christians to the charge of atheism and lack of distinction between Christianity and Judaism in the second century.[97] Frend recognizes an ambiguous situation, with no general edict proscribing Christians and yet asserts that 'open profession of Christianity had been and continued to be an offence'.[98] Corke-Webster regards this traditional view of specific 'persecuting' emperors as reliant on selective reading of independent pieces of evidence, which he systematically dismantles.[99]

Geoffrey de Ste. Croix introduced the important distinction between the motivations of ordinary pagans and that of the imperial government in the persecution of Christians.[100] He rightly rejects the centrality of 'emperor worship', situating devotional acts within the broader context of sacrificing to the gods.[101] De Ste. Croix concludes that although many Christians doubtless suffered persecution in diverse ways, there were also significant periods of peace. Persecution occurred sporadically, regardless of who the emperor was, with public opinion and the provincial governors playing the key roles.[102] 'We know of no general persecution until that of Decius. Between 64 and 250 there were only isolated, local persecutions; and even if the total number of victims was quite considerable ... most individual outbreaks must usually have been quite brief.'[103] Barnes concurs; although 'the Christian could never feel permanently safe', actual persecution was 'local, sporadic, almost random'.[104]

Recent literature, accepting of this more limited extent of persecution, has further investigated the social and religious causes of negative interactions between Christians and pagan Roman society. Wilken reconstructs contemporary pagans' views of the early church, explaining what aspects of the two worldviews would have led to misunderstanding and conflict, and why.[105] Ferguson likewise considers Christianity's classification as a *superstitio*, the imputation of *flagitia* and undesirable social attributes, popular ridicule, and the unacceptability of Christian teachings as factors in its unpopularity.[106]

---

[96] Frend, *Martyrdom and Persecution*, 210–14, 217, 237, 240, 268–70, 320–1.
[97] Ibid., 240, 255–260, 274, 279–80.
[98] Ibid., 220.
[99] Corke-Webster, 'Roman Persecutions', 35–45.
[100] Geoffrey E. M. de Ste. Croix, 'Why were the Early Christians Persecuted?' in *Christian Persecution, Martyrdom and Orthodoxy*, ed. Michael Whitby and Joseph Streeter (Oxford: Oxford University Press, 2006), 106.
[101] Ibid., 112.
[102] Ibid., 121.
[103] Ibid., 107.
[104] Barnes, *Tertullian*, 161.
[105] Wilken, *As the Romans Saw Them*.
[106] Ferguson, *Backgrounds of Early Christianity*, 593–609.

Kreider postulates that the early church was a community of patient perseverance, whose ethos and lifestyle permitted a consistent 'fermenting' growth despite adverse circumstances.[107] Despite criticisms of his method and assumptions,[108] there is significant congruence between Kreider's ideas and the fathers' diogmology.[109] Works such as these assume a sporadic level of persecution driven predominantly from local tensions. Corke-Webster summarizes:

> For most of the 300-year period before the accession of Constantine, Rome did not target Christians. When it did, the persecution was not long and systematic but rather brief and uneven. The traditional model relies upon the framework of Christian authors who were determined to fit Roman treatment of Christians into standard schema of benevolent emperors and tyrants inherited from early Greco-Roman historiography. To that framework modern scholars have pinned independent pieces of evidence that often cannot carry such interpretive weight, and when considered independently either do not suggest targeted action against Christians, or do so only in the most vague of terms.[110]

Nevertheless, Corke-Webster affirms that Christians did indeed suffer and that this suffering needs to be taken seriously. Its reality may in fact have been obscured by the misdirected emphasis on the extent of 'top-down' official activity against Christians. Persecution commonly took the form of delation, the identification of Christians to the authorities by their neighbours and associates, and therefore 'must be rooted in local contexts'.[111]

Candida Moss may be regarded as adopting an extreme minimalist approach, arguing that actual Christian persecution was rare and martyrdom a myth invented and perpetuated by Christians.[112] Moss has, appropriately, been criticized for overstating the case for dismissing the entire tradition of early Christian persecution.[113] Her introductory premise appears congruent with the minimalist approach of most current scholarship: 'although prejudice against Christians was fairly widespread, the prosecution of Christians was rare, and the persecution of Christians was limited to no more than a handful of years'.[114]

---

[107] Alan Kreider, *The Patient Ferment of the Early Church: The Improbable Rise of Christianity in the Roman Empire* (Grand Rapids: Baker, 2016), 6.

[108] Bradley J. Daugherty, review of *The Patient Ferment of the Early Church*, by Alan Kreider, *Fides et Historia* 50, no. 2 (2018): 165–7; W. Brian Shelton, review of *The Patient Ferment of the Early Church*, by Alan Kreider, *Journal of Theological Studies* 68, no. 2 (2017): 772–4; Litfin, 'Was the Early Church "Patient"?' (Gospel Coalition, October 31, 2016) https://www.thegospelcoalition.org/reviews/patient-ferment-of-the-early-church/

[109] See discussion in Chapter 6.

[110] Corke-Webster, 'Roman Persecutions', 47.

[111] Ibid.

[112] Moss, *Myth of Persecution*.

[113] James R. Harrison, 'The Persecutions of Christians from Nero to Hadrian', in *Into all the World: Emergent Christianity in its Jewish and Greco-Roman Context*, ed. Mark Harding and Alanna Nobbs (Grand Rapids: Eerdmans, 2017), 266–300, at 266–7; Paul Hartog, 'The Maltreatment of early Christians, Refinement and Response', *Southern Baptist Journal of Theology* 18, no.1 (2014): 49–79; W. Brian Shelton, review of *The Myth of Persecution* by Candida Moss, *Journal of the Evangelical Theological Society* 57, no. 1 (2014): 210–14, at 14.

[114] Moss, *Myth of Persecution*, 15.

However, sometimes she fails to adequately distinguish between arguments against 'continuous' persecution (which are widely accepted) and assertions or implications that there was no persecution at all, merely 'prosecution'. Her definition of persecution is malleable and somewhat vague, primarily described in terms of what it is 'not'.[115] As Shelton notes, Moss's definition of martyrdom remains unclear initially, eventually emerging as narrower than the traditional meaning of any form of suffering leading to death.[116] Moss finds the perception of 'prosecution' as 'persecution' illegitimate,[117] but this downplays the importance of delators and other 'bottom-up' drivers of detention and interrogation. Christians were first 'persecuted' (by local conflict and delation) before coming to the attention of the authorities and being 'prosecuted'.

Moss consistently describes martyrdom and persecution as 'myth', 'invented', 'story', and 'shrill rhetoric'. One can certainly appreciate Moss's concerns about historical and contemporary misappropriation of the account of early Christian persecution, without dismissing all persecution as mythical. In what seems an unresolved tension in the work, Moss herself acknowledges that Christians were actively disliked, arrested and executed.[118] Primarily, it is the discourse of martyrdom from the fourth century onwards that Moss finds illegitimate.[119] Ultimately, she upholds a minimalist perspective in arguing that the Romans did not persecute Christians as Christians, and whilst Christians experienced this opposition as 'persecution', the subsequent narrative of persecution and its appropriation should be challenged. It is important to note that Moss primarily draws on martyrologies and apocryphal accounts, which are widely acknowledged to be late and redacted. She provides little engagement with third-century writers such as the theologians in my study, whilst acknowledging that Tertullian, at least, might have something more to offer.[120]

As previously noted, early Christians, such as the four fathers, certainly perceived themselves to be persecuted. Such a perception is not incongruent with a 'minimalist' position on the extent and nature of the persecution 'experience'. The position taken in this book is minimalist, and persecution is understood in the 'bottom-up' rather than 'top-down' sense, as advocated by Corke-Webster.[121] Persecution predominantly arose from local conflict and animosity, resulting in Christians coming to the attention of authorities and being prosecuted. Nevertheless, as Middleton observes, although persecution 'was for the most part local, the Christians 'imperialized' their suffering'.[122]

---

[115] This malleability is particularly evident in the use of the word 'persecution' in *Myth of Persecution*, 154–60. Moss provides no initial definition of the broader concept of 'persecution', even under 'definitions' (*pp.* 25–29). Persecution is eventually defined on *p.* 164 in very narrow terms: a certain group 'unfairly targeted for attack and condemnation, usually because of blind hatred'. Throughout the work, martyrdom and persecution seem interchangeable, with the evidence against the former sometimes applied indiscriminately to conclusions about the latter.
[116] Shelton, review of *Myth of Persecution*, 211.
[117] Moss, *Myth of Persecution*, 159–164.
[118] Ibid., 129, 143, 145.
[119] Ibid., 244–246.
[120] Ibid., 260.
[121] Corke-Webster, 'Roman Persecutions', 46.
[122] Middleton, *Radical Martyrdom*, 40.

Crucially, in the trial of Christians, both the Christian and the 'authorized' Roman realities were reinforced. The confession, ἐγώ χριστιανός εἰμί, which the Christian longed to make, was heard by Roman ears as a confession of being a member of a seditious, obstinate, stubborn and superstitious cult that threatened the very fabric of reality ... The Christians, in contrast, saw an opportunity to assert their own loyalty to God through the means by which one was ultimately called: to suffer for the Name.[123]

The latter perspective, that of the Christian experiencing persecution, I suggest can only be fully understood from a theological perspective. As Barnes observes, 'The most serious result of the persecutions was not so much the deaths of Christians as an atmosphere of emotional tension, which profoundly affected corporate life and the development of Christian thought'.[124]

Graeco-Roman references to Christians provide evidence that popular animosity was no figment of the Christian imagination.[125] Even though martyr acts doubtless contain later editorial enhancements,[126] the case for a total dismissal of their evidence is unconvincing.[127] The value of second-century apologies as reliable testimonies to events has been questioned,[128] yet the identification of ideological biases does not rule out an underlying historicity. The extent to which persecution permeates the diverse writings of third-century fathers testifies to its impact, however this has primarily been explored where it pertains specifically to martyrdom.[129] By demonstrating common, coherent elements of the four fathers' 'diogmology', the present study provides an additional line of evidence from their writings that persecution was indeed a present and affective reality for them, which concerns about historical and contemporary misappropriation should not overshadow.

---

[123] Ibid., 70.
[124] Barnes, *Tertullian*, 163.
[125] Tacitus, *Annales* 15.44 (Loeb 322:282–4); Seutonius, *Nero* 16 (Loeb 38:110); and see Wilken, *As the Romans Saw Them*, 50; Stephen Benko, 'Pagan Criticism of Christianity during the First Two Centuries AD', *Aufstieg und Niedergang der römischen Welt Asbury* 23, no. 2 (1980): 1054–1118; Pierre de Labriolle, *La Réaction Païenne: Étude sur la polémique antichrétienne du Ier au VIe siècle*. 2nd ed. (Paris: L'Artisan du Livre, 1948).
[126] E.g. the Quintus pericope in the *Martyrdom of Polycarp*; Middleton, *Radical Martyrdom*, 26–27, and the extensive examples discussed by Moss, *Myth of Persecution*.
[127] For a recent assessment, see Rebillard, *Early Martyr Narratives*.
[128] Lorraine Buck has been particularly critical of their form and regards them as literary fictions rather than the addresses they purport to be: P. Lorraine Buck, 'Athenagoras' *Embassy*: A Literary fiction', *Harvard Theological Review* 89, no. 3 (1996): 209–26, at 220–2; she is even more critical of Justin: P. Lorraine Buck, 'Justin Martyr's Apologies: Their Number, Destination, and Form', *Journal of Theological Studies* 54, no. 1 (2003): 45–59. 45–59.
[129] One work which dismisses the reliability of a patristic witness is Carly Daniel-Hughes and Maia Kotrosits, 'Tertullian of Carthage and the Fantasy Life of Power: On Martyrs, Christians and Other Attachments to Juridicial Scenes', *Journal of Early Christian Studies* 28, no. 1 (2020): 1–31. For a response, see Chapter 4 of this book.

Martyrology and apologetic studies

Two major extant types of literature pertaining to the second and third centuries are martyr acts and apologies. There is general recognition that the extant martyr acts are redacted versions from the post-Constantinian era, which means that their historicity must be open to question.[130] Their theology is therefore almost certainly influenced by concerns and emphases of the later period.[131] Nevertheless, to acknowledge them as redacted accounts or even 'narrative fiction' based on probable events, and to mine them for their theological contribution (albeit reflective of a later period) is still a legitimate exercise.[132]

Frend utilizes martyrologies and apologetic literature to contrast orthodox, Gnostic and Montanist perspectives on martyrdom, but his account is primarily historical rather than theological.[133] Middleton draws on martyr acts, Jewish intertestamental literature and the third-century fathers to present a 'cosmic conflict' theology of radical martyrdom.[134] Both Middleton and Frend incorporate some third-century fathers' writings, but the focus is intentionally on martyrdom rather than persecution more broadly.

The martyrologies, obviously, focus on martyrdom and were particularly instrumental in shaping Christian identity.[135] They address the zenith of the diogmological discourse, the final outcome for many – but not all. Given that persecution encompasses more than martyrdom, we must look at a broader field, whilst acknowledging any congruency or disparity with the message of these *Acta*. Martyrologies emphasize the righteousness of the martyr and martyrdom as a glorious end. They demonstrate a diogmology of cosmic conflict and victory, confession

---

[130] Moss, *Myth of Persecution*, 91–125 is correct in her appraisal that the historicity of the martyr acts is questionable in its detail. Rebillard, *Early Martyr Narratives*, concludes that reading martyr acts for historicity is misdirected.

[131] The Donatists, particularly, adopted a martyr/persecution perspective, which Augustine countered with his own theme of martyrdom as a doctrinal identity marker: Leemans and Dupont, 'Scripture and Martyrdom', 434. Kotzé, 'Augustine and the Remaking of Martyrdom', 135, considers Augustine to have remade martyrdom into something which every Christian could still experience in daily life. Moss, *Myth of Persecution*, 234, notes the 'explosion of martyrdom stories, and hagiographic literature in general' that occurred in the post-Constantinian era, and how Eusebius and others appropriate the 'true' martyr to the cause of orthodoxy against heresy. See also the collected essays in Fournier and Mayer, *Heirs of Roman Persecution*.

[132] As demonstrated by McLarty, 'Theologies of Martyrdom'.

[133] Frend, *Martyrdom and Persecution*, 293; Frend's position is typical of an older view of the Gnostic and Montanist perspectives, now deemed simplistic. For current overviews see Birger A. Pearson, *Ancient Gnosticism, Traditions and Literature* (Minneapolis: Fortress, 2007); Christine Trevett, *Montanism: Gender, Authority and the New Prophecy* (Cambridge: Cambridge University Press, 2002) and William Tabbernee, 'Early Montanism and Voluntary Martyrdom', *Colloquium* 17, no. 2 (1985), 33–44; William Tabbernee, 'Montanism and the Cult of the Martyrs in Roman North Africa: Reassessing the Literary', in *Text and the Material World: Essays in Honour of Graeme Clarke*, Studies in Mediterranean Archaeology and Literature 185, ed. Elizabeth Minchin and Heather Jackson, (Uppsala: Astrom Editions, 2017), 299–313.

[134] Middleton, *Radical Martyrdom*.

[135] Lieu, *Christian Identity*, 253–259; also Judith M. Lieu, 'The audience of apologetics: the problem of the Martyr Acts', in *Contextualising Early Christian Martyrdom*, ed. Engberg, Uffe Holmsgaard Eriksen, and Anders Klostergaard Petersen (Frankfurt am Main: Peter Lang, 2011), 205–23.

of Christ before the representatives of demonic paganism, and glorification by death.

The second-century Christians reset their experiences of suffering in the context of an apocalyptic contest. They participated in Christ's battle with Satan. They claimed their place as Christ's warriors by holding fast to the Name, refusing to choose physical life and deny. By holding to their confession, they bought life through death. Their deaths were inspirational models for other Christians to follow.[136]

In contrast, the second-century apologies argue *against* persecution. They emphasize the innocence of the Christians and the injustice of punishment for the bearing of a name, in the absence of identifiable crimes. The extensive literature on the extant early apologies evaluates the nature, causes and extent of persecution from the Christian perspective, and their contribution to doctrinal development.[137] The paucity of systematic consideration of the apologists' *theological* reflection on persecution is understandable, for two reasons. Firstly, apologies directed to pagans contain very few, if any, direct scriptural quotations or allusions, because of their pagan audience. Secondly, the second-century apologists do not demonstrate a developed and consistent diogmology.[138]

Apologetic alone is arguably insufficient for articulating a theology of persecution, because its very nature is to plead *against* persecution, or at least the injustice of it.[139] Apology therefore presents a tension which must be reckoned with in the fathers' theology of persecution, because a plea against persecution seems to be at odds with its inevitability and the copious exhortations to how the Christian must respond to it. How may one argue against what Christ has predicted and pronounced a blessing? This is another area which has received minimal attention. I will show that a coherent theology of persecution, specifically Tertullian's, provides a resolution of this tension, reconciling the essential messages of both martyr act and apologetic. For all these reasons, I have chosen to examine, not the martyrologies nor the second-century apologists' works, but the writings of the third-century fathers for a fresh perspective on a developed theology of martyrdom.

---

[136] Middleton, *Radical Martyrdom*, 101.
[137] For overviews, see J.A. Tixeront, *Handbook of Patrology*, trans. S. A. Raemers (St Lis: Herder, 1920), http://www.earlychristianwritings.com/tixeront/; Richard A. Norris Jr., 'The Apologists', in *The Cambridge History of Early Christian Literature*, ed. Frances Young, Lewis Ayers, and Andrew Louth (Cambridge: Cambridge University Press, 2004), 36–44; Robert M. Grant, *Greek Apologists of the Second Century* (Philadelphia: Westminster SCM, 1988); Avery Dulles, 'The Patristic Era', in *A History of Apologetics* (San Francisco: Ignatius, 2005).
[138] Sutcliffe, 'No Need to Apologise?
[139] Hopkins, 'Christian Number', 197–8, n. 27, argues for a Christian audience for the apologies, to justify their faith and celebrate their uniqueness.

Patristic exegesis and reception of Scripture

The fathers upheld Scripture as divine in origin and the primary source of truth.[140] The New Testament contains many references to persecution,[141] most of which the four fathers employed. As I shall demonstrate, not all of these passages were interpreted in the same way by the four. Some, which might appear very relevant to persecution, are omitted, or used in an entirely different context. Consequently, certain 'benchmark' passages can serve as a basis for comparison between the fathers' perspectives.[142] As Murphy predicts with respect to Cyprian's use of Paul, one can learn almost as much about a writer's theology and environment from the verses he ignores, as the passages used in common.[143]

The reception and exegesis of Scripture by the early fathers has been, and continues to be, the subject of extensive scholarship.[144] As Frances Young observes, this endeavour is not limited to an examination of commentaries and homilies, but an engagement with 'reading strategies' used to 'form the practice and belief of Christian people, individually and collectively ... the Bible was at the heart of the debate'.[145] She observes a consistency in which the Bible was employed across different genres, always with a relevance for spirituality and praxis. Therefore, whilst most of the patristic texts with which I engage are not strictly 'exegetical' in literary genre, they may be regarded as suitable subjects for assessment. Interpretation of Scripture is undoubtedly subsidiary to and in service of theological and apologetic aims, and those very theological aims are my focus. From the vast trove of scholarship on patristic exegesis, three aspects are relevant to the present study:

1. Scripture is to be read as a unity.
2. Theology may drive exegesis.
3. Use of Scripture is contextual.

---

[140] Clement, *Strom.* 7.16.95.3–97.2 (SC 428: 288-94); *Protr.* 8.1 (SC 2:143); Origen, *Princ.* 1.3.1; 4.1.1 (Behr 1:66; 2:458–60); Tertullian, *Test. An.* 6.1 (CCSL 1:182), Cyprian, *Ad Quirinum* I, Introduction; O'Keefe and Reno, *Sanctified Vision,* 12.

[141] Notably, Mt. 5:10–12, 39, 44–45; 10:16–40; 16:24–27; 23:34–36; 24:9–10; Mk 4:17; 8:29–38; 13:9–13; Lk. 6:22–32; 9:23–26; 11:4–12; 12:51–53; 21:12–19; Jn 7:7; 15:18–21; 16:1–3; 17:14–16; Acts 5:41; 9:4–5; Rom. 8:35–37; 12:14–21; 1 Cor. 4:10–13; 2 Cor. 4:7–11; 12:10; Gal. 6:12; 2 Thess. 1:4–7; Heb. 11:35–40; 13:12–14; 1 Pet. 1:6–7; 2:12–15, 19–23; 3:13–18; 4:12–19; 5:8–10; Rev. 2:9–13; 6:9–11; 16:6; 17:6; 18:24; 19:2.

[142] This approach was recently applied in a more limited context by Hartog, 'Themes and Intertextualities'.

[143] Edwina Murphy, *The Bishop and the Apostle: Cyprian's Pastoral Exegesis of Paul* (Berlin: de Gruyter, 2018), 2.

[144] For overviews of patristic exegesis see Rowan A. Greer and James L. Kugel, *Early Biblical Interpretation,* Library of Early Christianity 3. (Philadelphia: Westminster, 1986); Kannengiesser, *Handbook of Patristic Exegesis;* Ronald E. Heine, *Reading the Old Testament with the Ancient Church: Exploring the Formation of Early Christian Thought* (Grand Rapids: Baker, 2007); O'Keefe and Reno, *Sanctified Vision;* Stephen Westerholm and Martin Westerholm, *Reading Sacred Scripture: Voices from the History of Interpretation* (Grand Rapids: Eerdmans, 2016); and the foundational studies of Frances Young, particularly *Biblical Exegesis;* Paul M. Blowers and Peter W. Martens, eds, *The Oxford Handbook of Early Biblical Interpretation* (Oxford: Oxford University Press, 2019) presents the state of scholarship to that date.

[145] Young, *Biblical Exegesis,* 299.

Firstly, the fathers perceived Scripture as a unity, within a Christocentric framework encapsulated by the Rule of Faith.[146] The patristic sense of the Christological unity of Scripture led to a search for deeper meanings beyond the immediate sense;[147] this accounts for their typology, allegory and various conclusions which may be unexpected to a twenty-first-century interpreter. Therefore, the temptation to evaluate the fathers by contemporary criteria must be resisted.[148] What will be apparent through the fathers' use of 'persecution passages' is the interconnectedness of this Christocentricity with their diogmology. It is 'for the name' that the Christian is persecuted, and 'in Christ' that confession occurs. It enables the fathers, post-figuring Christ, to connect their experiences to the apostles and to the prophets, who prefigure him.[149] This relationship has been underutilized in debates about the direction of influences between 'Christian' and 'Jewish' ideas of martyrdom, which usually focus on Daniel and 4 Maccabees.[150]

Secondly, the fathers' theology, defined within the Rule of Faith, often drove their exegesis, rather than the other way around. Fairbairn's discussion of the Alexandrian-Antiochene debate demonstrates this well,[151] as does Torjesen's exposition of Origen's exegesis.[152] 'Instead of seeing possible correlation with modern methods of exegesis, allegorical method ought rather to be studied by examining interrelations between the method and the whole complex of theological understanding within which it is set.'[153] Young also identifies a need for work on 'the interrelationship between biblical material and theological thinking, the understanding of one undoubtedly affecting the other'.[154] This principle is evident in the writings of the third-century fathers, as they apply their individual interpretations to persecution passages. There is an interplay between text, context and theology, whereby Scripture is brought to bear on Christian thought and praxis, and the lived experience draws the exegete to derive applicable meaning from the text. I will pay particular attention to any correlation between divergent and convergent exegesis amongst the four, and any corresponding divergence and convergence in their theology, to identify the possible directions of influence.

---

[146] Young, *Biblical Exegesis*, 10, 16, 18; O'Keefe and Reno, *Sanctified Vision*, 69; Hartog, 'The "Rule of Faith" and Patristic Biblical Exegesis', *Trinity Journal* 28, no. 1 (2007): 65–86; Rowan A. Greer, 'The Christian Bible and Its Interpretation', in *Early Biblical Interpretation*, ed. James L. Kugel and Rowan A. Greer (Philadelphia: Westminster, 1986), 107–203.

[147] O'Keefe and Reno, *Sanctified Vision*, 73.

[148] Young, *Biblical Exegesis*, 4.

[149] O'Keefe and Reno, *Sanctified Vision*, 81–83. Moss, *Other Christs*, 19, 44, demonstrates the importance in the earliest Christian literature of rendering individual and corporate suffering meaningful by the concept of imitating Christ.

[150] For an overview of such discussion, see Jan Willem van Henten, 'Early Jewish and Christian Martyrdom', in *The Wiley Blackwell Companion to Christian Martyrdom*, ed. Paul Middleton (West Sussex UK: John Wiley & Sons, 2020), 76–8. Frend, *Martyrdom and Persecution*, 31–78, argues for influence of Jewish martyr narratives on Christians, in contrast to Bowersock, *Martyrdom and Rome*, 7, 26–7, 37. For an appraisal of these positions see also Middleton, *Radical Martyrdom*, 103–34.

[151] Donald Fairbairn, 'Patristic Exegesis and Theology: The Cart and the Horse', *Westminster Theological Journal* 69, no. 1 (2007), 1–19.

[152] Karen Jo Torjesen, *Hermeneutical Procedure and Theological Method in Origen's Exegesis*, Patristische Texte un Studien 28 (Berlin: De Gruyter, 1986).

[153] Torjesen, *Hermeneutical Procedure*, vii.

[154] Young, *Biblical Exegesis*, 4.

Thirdly, the fathers' use of Scripture varied with the purpose and audience of their writing. Young concludes that exegesis, in whatever context, served the development of the Christian life, and that 'there does not seem to be any evidence that particular "reading strategies" were confined to particular genres, or that distinct genres produced distinctive methodologies'.[155] Nevertheless, Scripture is employed to differing extents and purposes across genres. There is relatively little recourse to biblical quotation or allusion when writing to pagans compared with writing for Christians. Wilhite has shown that Cyprian uses Scripture differently according to his audience, as a rhetorical strategy.[156] Tertullian uses the same passages for different ends in different works, even with contradictory exegetical premises.[157] Failure to consider the context of a comment on persecution within a given work can lead to a biased interpretation. For example, if one only read Origen's *Exhortation to Martyrdom*, he could be seen as uncompromisingly pro-martyrdom, even exemplifying a 'martyrological, world-denying fervor'.[158] However, in that work, Origen writes to confessors already imprisoned, for whom the only alternatives are martyrdom or apostasy. When Origen's views on withdrawal and flight are examined in other works, he is seen to be much more circumspect. Similarly, Tertullian might be accused of blatant self-contradiction if his views on fleeing persecution in *De fuga* and *Ad uxorem* are compared without considering the different rhetorical objectives in these works.

It is beyond the scope of the present study to provide a detailed discussion of the fathers' use of exegetical strategies such as typology and allegory;[159] their relevance will be indicated in discussion of specific passages. Even Origen, the father most renowned for allegorizing, utilized no unique exegetical techniques that were not also found in prior works.[160] Both allegory and typology are legitimized in the context of the overarching Christological unity of Scripture; they are both means of interpreting Scripture in terms of the divine economy.[161]

Young observes that the fathers themselves did not distinguish between typology and allegory,[162] but she offers the following helpful descriptions. A type is a mimetic impress or figure in the narrative, prophetic in that it points to fulfilment. It impresses one narrative upon another, recapitulating, fulfilling and giving meaning. A type is autonomous, having its own meaning, yet mirrors another event or character.[163] Examples relevant to the present study include Old Testament martyrs such as Abel and Daniel's three friends, which prefigure persecuted Christians, and Moses' defeat of Pharaoh and his hoards at the Red Sea as a type of Christ's defeat of the Devil. Whereas

---

[155] Ibid., 247.
[156] David E. Wilhite, 'Cyprian's Scriptural Hermeneutic of Identity: The Laxist "Heresy"', *Horizons in Biblical Theology* 32, no. 1 (2010): 58–98, at 81.
[157] Geoffrey D. Dunn, 'Tertullian's Scriptural Exegesis in *De praescriptione haereticorum*', *Journal of Early Christian Studies* 14, no. 2 (2006): 141–55, at 146.
[158] As does L. Arik Greenberg, '*My Share of God's Reward*': *Exploring the roles and formulations of the afterlife in early Christian Martyrdom* (New York: Peter Lang, 2009), 134.
[159] See O'Keefe and Reno, *Sanctified Vision*.
[160] Young, *Patristic Exegesis*, 294.
[161] O'Keefe and Reno, *Sanctified Vision*, 90.
[162] Young, *Patristic Exegesis*, 153.
[163] Ibid., 152–4.

typology preserves the original narrative, allegory uses the words as symbols or tokens which refer to a deeper reality, the true meaning hidden in the text, translating the narrative into propositions.[164] An example would be Origen's allegorizing of texts which suggest an imminent *parousia* and irrevocable final judgement. As O'Keefe and Reno suggest, the difference lies in the effort the reader must put into interpretation. Typology brings two figures into association with a perceived fit. Allegory is a more intentional, explicit and potentially strained association, requiring significantly more interpretation.[165] For the purpose of this study, it will not be necessary to definitively determine whether an interpretation is strictly 'typological' or 'allegorical', but merely to ascertain that the writer is drawing out a perceived deeper or additional meaning to conform their exegesis to their wider, unified approach to Scripture, and to their theological perspective.

There has been little extensive treatment of patristic use of New Testament 'persecution passages' specifically. I propose that scriptural passages which reference persecution provide a basis for comparison of the fathers' theology of persecution. I will show that whilst the fathers often draw the same conclusions from some passages, at other times their interpretations vary, and this is attributable to the broader theologies and the objectives of their writing.

Social identity theory

A growing body of scholarship explores the concept of early Christian identity, both how they perceived themselves and how outsiders viewed them.[166] There is scope to contribute a theological perspective to the discussion of early Christian social identity in the context of persecution. Jensen recognizes that Christian confession is both a positive affirmation of identity and

> a refusal to accept alternative ways of finding and describing one's self by [other] means, even if that means suffering and death ... it is an offering of one's self up to the providence of God as it is evidenced in the life, death, resurrection and promised return of Jesus Christ. For the Christian, therefore, human purpose and identity are fulfilled – and vindication received in discipleship, even if discipleship results in martyrdom.[167]

Matthew Recla identifies the difficulty in considering 'martyrdom' as a critical part of Christian identity because, by definition, not all Christians were martyred. Rather, he perceives a substitution of the martyr's actual death with a theological construct, 'willingness to suffer'.[168] Once again, Recla's emphasis is on martyrdom rather than the

---

[164] Young, *Patristic Exegesis*, 161–2.
[165] O'Keefe and Reno, *Sanctified Vision*, 90.
[166] In particular, Lieu, *Christian Identity*; Philip A. Harland, *Dynamics of Identity in the World of the Early Christians* (New York: T&T Clark, 2009); Rebillard, *Many Identities*.
[167] Michael P. Jensen, *Martyrdom and Identity: The Self on Trial* (London: T&T Clark, 2010), 2–3.
[168] Matthew Recla, 'Creation of Christian Identity', 199.

broader category of persecution, but his discussion is valuable for our present purposes in terms of conclusions about the centrality of confession in the writings of the four fathers and whether it necessarily encompassed confession to the point of death. I will return to this in Chapter 6.

'Social identity theory' endeavours to explain group processes and intergroup relations.[169] This collective view of identity examines where boundaries are drawn between a group and the 'other'.[170] Baptism and readmission after penance were delineating boundaries between the world and the church in the third century.[171] Such social identity is acknowledged to be constructed and malleable, not 'primordial, ingrained or static', and individual identity is affected by or based on belonging to a particular group.[172] 'Identity theory' is more individual, stressing the interplay between the self and social structure. It examines identity variability, motivation and differentiation, particularly how identities manifest in different relationships and situations. Identities are seen as multiple and interrelated, able to be switched on and off. How one identifies oneself in terms of social, ethnic and other identities may shift from one situation to another, with the potential for blending and hybridisation.[173]

Lieu observes that texts play a central role, not only in documenting what it means to be Christian, but in actually shaping Christian identity.[174] Lieu's seminal study focuses on second-century extant texts and as both she and Harland note, this privileges the educated minority who wrote the texts.[175] Writers such as Clement, Origen, Tertullian and Cyprian may not be at all representative of their communities' attitudes, priorities and behaviours, however there is no doubt they seek to *form* them through their writings, which were doubtless heard (rather than read) by a wide audience.[176] The fathers sought to articulate the identity constructed by the central text of the faith, Scripture, and what that meant for confession of the faith in an adversarial world. They wanted to shape Christian behaviour in accordance with this scriptural identity. That endeavour is worthy of attention, irrespective of, or perhaps even because of, inconsistencies in how Christians were living out that identity. Lieu recognizes that literary texts seek to inculcate appropriate attitudes, even if their audience who share that identity do not necessarily hold them. Hence, they are persuasive and imperative rather than descriptive.[177]

---

[169] Michael A. Hogg, Deborah J. Terry and Katherine M. White, 'A Tale of Two Theories: A Critical Comparison of Identity Theory with Social Identity Theory', *Social Psychology Quarterly* 58, no. 4 (1995), 255–69, at 225.
[170] Harland, *Dynamics of Identity*, 6.
[171] Ruth Sutcliffe, 'Learning Not to Sin: Repentance in Tertullian and Cyprian' *Colloquium* 53, no. 1 (2021): 73–97.
[172] Harland, *Dynamics of Identity*, 6–7; Lieu, *Christian Identity*, 13.
[173] Harland, *Dynamics of Identity*, 8–9.
[174] Lieu, *Christian Identity*, 7.
[175] Lieu, *Christian Identity*, 8; Harland, *Dynamics of Identity*, 4.
[176] Lieu, *Christian Identity*, 10, 17, 29. Edwina Murphy, 'Cyprian, Scripture and Socialisation: Forming faith in the catechumenate and beyond', in *The Intellectual World of Christian Late Antiquity: Reshaping Classical Traditions, 100-600 CE*, ed. Lewis Ayres, Matthew R. Crawford and Michael Champion (Cambridge: Cambridge University Press, 2023), 153–65, at 164, illustrates how the catechumenate was intended to shape identity.
[177] Lieu, *Christian Identity*, 157.

As Rebillard explains, early Christians were neither homogenous nor consistent in their attitudes and behaviours. Individuals can have multiple identities or memberships, both within and across groups, which can be latent or activated in different situations.[178] Rebillard argues that binary oppositions between Christians and non-Christians (such as Tertullian portrays) are a discursive construct and that confessional identities were less important than such written sources convey.[179] He argues that religious adherence was only one of many early Christian identities, which they may or may not have chosen to activate in different circumstances.[180] This concept of malleable and competing identities is illustrated by the different responses to the Decian edict and the different portrayals of the church to insiders and outsiders in the fathers' writings.[181] I will offer a theological perspective on competing identities in terms of the fathers' perception of the Christian's central identity as confessors of the name of Christ.

Identity theory has been applied directly to the writings of the third-century fathers, but not from a diogmological perspective. Mullins Reeves and Thate explore Clement's portrayal of three different tiers of martyrdom as a potential definition of 'orthodoxy'.[182] Wilhite applies social identity theory to Tertullian and Cyprian,[183] noting that identities are constructed by differentiating oneself from others.[184] Tertullian, an indigenous African, rejects Roman colonizers as the Devil's puppets and sees persecution as evidence of the work of God-opposing cosmic forces.[185] Cyprian constructs social identity through his portrayal of a person or group's relationship to Scripture. The orthodox, aligned with the bishop, are scripturally informed and receive few quotations. The heretics and schismatics are scripturally ignorant and Cyprian quotes scripture to them copiously.[186]

This book explores theological perspectives rather than concepts of social identity *per se*, and as such will make a modest contribution to the discussion of early Christian social identity. I will examine the centrality of confession of Christ for the fathers' concept of Christian identity and show how that confession was variously understood in relation to martyrdom. The fathers recognized that Christians did not always behave in accordance with this identity, but they were nevertheless concerned to form it according to Scriptural ideals.

---

[178] Rebillard, *Many Identities*, 3–4.
[179] Ibid., 1.
[180] Ibid., 3, 7.
[181] Ibid., 50–1.
[182] Pamela Mullins Reeves, 'Multiple Martyrdoms and Christian Identity in Clement of Alexandria's *Stromateis*'. *StPatr* 46 (2013): 61–8; Michael J. Thate, 'Identity Construction as Resistance: Figuring Hegemony, Biopolitics and Martyrdom as an Approach to Clement of Alexandria'. *StPatr* 66 (2013): 69–85, at 72. I offer an interpretation of Clement's 'categories' in the next chapter.
[183] Wilhite, *Tertullian the African*; Wilhite, 'Hermeneutic of Identity', 58–98.
[184] Ibid., 41.
[185] Ibid., 59, 162.
[186] Wilhite, 'Hermeneutic of Identity', 58–9, 63, 79, 81–4.

Religious conflict literature

There is a significant body of research being currently published about religious conflict and violence, and how the discourse of violence is constructed.[187] It is certainly relevant to the distinction between persecution as a construct or discourse, against persecution as a historical or objective reality. Whilst it is recognized that the fathers' discussion of persecution is an 'elite' discourse undoubtedly aiming to form the identity and behaviour of 'ordinary' Christians, I do not propose to take the issue of objectivity versus discourse further in my presentation of the four fathers' theology, nor conduct a sociological or discursive analysis. Third-century persecution of Christians, as understood by the four fathers, certainly fits Mayer's definition of 'religious conflict',[188] and as she notes, 'until very recently, religious conflict per se has rarely been a topic of investigation with regard to the pre-Constantinian era and received little focused theological reflection'.[189]

The scope and method of this study

This book takes the reader on an investigative journey, along a path that intersects patristic theology, exegesis, history and social identity theory, a journey off the well-beaten paths of these disciplines. The objective is to determine how the fathers thought *theologically* about the experience of suffering for the faith, and how this informed (or was intended to inform) the Christian response to persecution. The map or guidebook for this journey of exploration will be a collection of specific 'persecution passages' in the New Testament, which will serve as benchmarks for comparison. To do all this effectively will necessitate an appreciation of each father's context in their third-century worlds.

As Sider notes, 'the perceptions of the early Christians can be understood and appreciated only when we have unravelled the intricately woven fabric of their experience'.[190] Recognition that the early fathers lived, thought and engaged in particular social, political, historical, religious, economic and cultural contexts provided impetus for Rankin to address a significant lack of interface between patristic and historical studies.[191] Harrison identifies a general failure 'to bring the New Testament documents into dialogue with the later Roman and Jewish sources for a richer

---

[187] Perkins, *The Suffering Self*; Wendy Mayer, 'Religious Conflict: Definitions, Problems and Theoretical Approaches', in *Religious Conflict from Early Christianity to the Rise of Islam,* ed. Wendy Mayer and Bronwyn Neil (Berlin: De Gruyter, 2013), 1–20; Cobb, *Divine Deliverance*; Wendy Mayer and Christ de Wet, eds, *Reconceiving Religious Conflict: New Views from the Formative Centuries of Christianity* (New York: Routledge, 2018); Fournier and Mayer, *Heirs of Roman Persecution;* Conant, 'Memories of Trauma'.
[188] Mayer, 'Religious Conflict', 5.
[189] Ibid., 9.
[190] Robert D. Sider, *Ancient Rhetoric and the Art of Tertullian* (London: Oxford University Press, 1971), 132.
[191] David I. Rankin, *From Clement to Origen: The Social and Historical Context of the Church Fathers* (Hampshire: Ashgate, 2006), 1.

understanding of the historical, social and ideological perspectives regarding persecution'.[192] The early Christian writings, with their heavy use of Scripture, provide another important medium for facilitating the contextual analysis of the New Testament's own 'theology of persecution'. Each of these extra-biblical sources contributes to the tapestry of understanding the intent and application of the New Testament's theology of persecution.

Why this time and these places? The period I have chosen for examination is 195–260 CE, for several reasons. The third century is a more fruitful locus of inquiry than the second, because of the larger number and greater diversity of extant writings. The late second through mid-third centuries hosted a spectrum of types and degrees of persecution; there were periods of relative peace, through episodes of local unrest and prosecution, up to the first 'state-sponsored' persecution and its aftermath. Greek and Latin theological writing developed distinctively in the third century and the numerous extant writings cover a variety of genres.

By the end of the second century, the church was established in major centres throughout the Roman world, some of which have been retrospectively identified with distinctive schools of thought.[193] It is reasonable to assume there would be regional variation in the experience of persecution and theological reflection on it. Candida Moss's interest in the shaping of Christian identity through discursive practices within different cultural settings leads her to explore the notion of regional ideologies of martyrdom.[194] She concludes that 'the influence of local religious, social, political, and economic structures on the articulation of martyrdom is a critically important and often overlooked feature of histories of martyrdom'.[195] Moss's study invites further regional comparisons with respect to third-century theological discourse on persecution more broadly. In this book I compare writings from two different times and two different socio-theological backgrounds to bring a cross section of patristic writings to bear on the questions of diogmology.

To achieve a balance between breadth and depth, the study has been restricted to four patristic writers: Clement and Origen of Alexandria, and Tertullian and Cyprian of Carthage. Tertullian and Clement wrote during the last decade of the second century through to the early second decade of the third. They witnessed the persecutions in the reign of Severus and the common experience of relative peace, punctuated by local outbursts of anti-Christian animosity during this period. Origen's writings extend through the second quarter of the third century, contemporary with Cyprian during the Decian persecution and its aftermath in the 250s. Clement and Origen are foundational to the Alexandrian Greek tradition, Tertullian and Cyprian to the Western Latin tradition. This study provides a four-way contrast between the theological and exegetical traditions, social milieu and persecution experiences in two eras.

Although I provide an analysis of the fathers' thought, this book is not a critique. Some ambiguities will be discovered, for which potential resolutions may be proposed,

---

[192] Harrison, 'Persecutions of Christians'.
[193] Fairbairn, 'Patristic Exegesis', 2–3; Burns and Jensen, *Roman Africa*, XLVI–XLVII.
[194] Moss, *Ancient Christian Martyrdom: Diverse Practices, Theologies and Traditions* (New Haven: Yale University Press, 2012).
[195] Ibid., 124.

but it is not my purpose to endorse or oppose their positions, nor to offer anachronistic explanations. Nor will I endeavour to 'prove' the historicity of what they claim to have observed and experienced. Not all of the fathers' writings are extant, a particular limitation with Origen, and care must be taken to not misrepresent their thoughts even as we work with what is available. My focus is their use of Scripture in the articulation of their theologies of persecution. Where an aspect of their thought appears to derive from extra-biblical ideas, this will be flagged and suggestions offered, without attempting detailed philosophical engagement.

Five diogmological questions

The idea behind 'diogmology' as a locus of theological investigation is that the elements of the fathers' theology of persecution can be explored systematically through a series of questions, each of which in turn relates to one or more loci of broader theology. These diogmological questions provide the framework for discussion in the following chapters, each chapter discussing a particular father.

Question one concerns the origin and oversight of persecution. Where does persecution come from and who governs it: God or the Devil? This is the *Theo*-logy perspective, based on the character and purposes of God and related to the question of theodicy. Question two addresses the reason for persecution, and whether it is inevitable. This issue is Christological and soteriological. The third question asks, what is the *telos* of persecution, its ultimate outcome? What then are the 'benefits' of persecution in this life and/or the next? Can persecution itself be considered 'good'? This is a soteriological and eschatological question.

Question four concerns the appropriate response(s) of the persecuted Christian, which depend on the answers to the first three questions. This is a discipleship question and it has a pneumatological aspect. The fifth question inquires, what should be the church's collective response to persecution? How should the church support the persecuted, in their different responses? How does persecution inform ecclesiology, and how should the church respond publicly to persecution?

This appears to be a novel approach to patristic writings. Tabbernee's exploration of Eusebius' theology of persecution concentrates on the issues raised by the first and second questions, but in an incidental manner as they unfold in Eusebius' revisions of the *Church History*. Analyses of the second-century apologies do not explore the arguments in this way.

A central focus in considering each father's 'answers' to the diogmological questions will be their use of Scripture. The fathers' own selection of Scriptures and their interpretation of them will drive the discussion. In the final chapter, key biblical passages which relate to the five questions, the majority from Matthew 5 and 10 and 1 Peter, will serve as points of comparison, or benchmarks.[196] I will determine whether the fathers use these passages to make a direct theological point (exegesis informing diogmology) or whether the passage is imported into a pre-formed argument

---

[196] Mt. 5:10–12, 44–45; 10:16–18, 19–20, 21–22, 23, 24–25, 26–31, 32–33 (Lk. 12:8–9); Mk 8:38 (Lk. 9:26); 1 Pet. 2:12–15, 19–20; 3:13–18; 4:12–14, 15–16; Rev. 6:9–11.

(diogmology informing exegesis). These benchmark passages will be engaged with as each father utilizes them, and then specifically addressed in Chapter 6 in their comparative role.

Experiencing persecution

The history of scholarship on the reasons for and extent of early Christian persecution has been well summarized by Harrison.[197] Although Christians were already unpopular in the first century,[198] and Nero's severe but local persecution may have set some precedent,[199] the legal position of Christians remained unchanged from the time of Nero to the mid-third century.[200] Individual outbreaks of persecution, prior to Decius, were brief and local, with periods of relative peace in between. Nevertheless, Christianity occupied a grey area of Roman law, neither legitimized nor definitively proscribed, which Williams describes as 'effectively illegal'.[201]

Neither Pliny nor Trajan dispute whether Christians deserve death; Pliny is concerned with whether the defendant was *currently* Christian. Only those who denied they were currently Christians were put to the test requiring them to invoke the gods, offer prayer, incense and wine to the emperor's image and curse Christ, to prove their denial. Extant accounts of Christian trials in the *Acta*, and complaints of apologists, affirm a charge of being 'Christian' and attempts to persuade the Christians to deny this identity, in an apparent reverse application of Pliny's procedure.[202] This later practice is confirmed by Clement, Origen and Tertullian.[203] Although the Pliny–Trajan correspondence cannot be held up as a lasting or universal policy beyond its original context in early second-century Bithynia-Pontus,[204] persecution for 'the name' of Christian was a central *theological* concept for the fathers, and was the lens through

---

[197] Harrison, 'Persecutions of Christians', 266–300.
[198] Tacitus, *Annals*, 15.44 (Loeb 322:282–4) calls Christianity a pernicious superstition (*exitiabilis superstitio*) and deserving of exemplary punishment. See also Birgit van der Lans and Jan N. Bremmer, 'Tactitus and the Persecution of the Christians: An Invention of Tradition?' *Eirene: Studia Graeca et Latinas* 53 (2017): 299–311.
[199] Travis B. Williams, *Persecution in 1 Peter: Differentiating and Contextualizing Early Christian Suffering*. Supp. *NovT* 145 (Leiden: Brill, 2012).
[200] Timothy D. Barnes, 'Legislation Against the Christians', in *Early Christianity and the Roman Empire*, Timothy D. Barnes (London: 1984), 32–50; Likewise, de Ste. Croix, 'Early Christians', 106; Corke-Webster, 'Roman Persecutions', 35.
[201] Williams, *Persecution in 1 Peter*, 225. This is consistent with Pliny, *Epp.* 10.96–97 (Loeb 59: 284–92), in which both Pliny and Trajan assume that Christians are worthy of punishment, yet Trajan states there is no general rule to serve as a fixed standard and commends Pliny for his discretion. See also James Corke-Webster, 'Trouble in Pontus: The Pliny-Trajan Correspondence on the Christians Reconsidered', *Transactions of the American Philological Association* 147, no. 2 (2017): 371–411.
[202] *Martyrs of Vienne and Lyon*, Eusebius, *H.E.* 5.1 (Loeb 153:406–36); *Acts of the Scillitan Martyrs*; *Passio Perpetuae*; Tertullian, *Nat.* 1.3–4; *Apol.* 2 and see de Ste. Croix, 'Early Christians', 110–11. See also Tertullian, *Scap.* 4.2 (CCSL 2:1130) and Cyprian, *Dem.* 13 (CCSL 3A:42–3).
[203] Clement, *Strom.* 4.6.28.3–4, 4.11.79.1–2 (SC 463: 102, 184–6); Origen, *Cels.* 2.13 (SC 132:320); Tertullian, *Nat.* 1.2 (CCSL 1:12–13); *Apol.* 2, 4, 6 (CCSL 1: 87–91, 92–4, 96–8).
[204] Corke-Webster, 'Trouble in Pontus;' and James Corke-Webster, 'The Early Reception of Pliny the Younger in Tertullian of Carthage and Eusebius of Caesarea', *The Classical Quarterly* 67, no. 1 (2017), 247–62.

which they viewed the persecution experience and understood the actions of governors against them.

Christians were tried by *cognitio extra ordinem* or special investigation, conducted by the provincial governor in various cities he visited on his assize tour of the province.[205] Only the governor could conduct a capital trial and he had broad discretionary power as to what cases were tried, how they were tried, and the punishment or acquittal prescribed. Nevertheless, Roman criminal law was rather arbitrary, with uncertainty as to the applicable legislation.[206] Although a malefactor or Christian might be brought in by local police under the *eirenarch*, perhaps because of a public disturbance,[207] in most cases the *cognitio* was on the basis of an accusation brought by a delator, with penalties for false accusations. The burden of proof lay with the delator, but the social status of the accused and the governor's inclination could be decisive.[208]

The most significant objection raised against Christians was their exclusive worship of their one God and consequent rejection of the entire Graeco-Roman pantheon, its attendant civic cult, and the traditional ancient religious beliefs and practices of the societies in which they lived. This branded them as 'atheists'.[209] It was widely believed that the divinely bestowed peace and prosperity of the Empire, or *pax deorum*, could be disrupted if the gods were not given due attention, or if certain sects were allowed to intrude. Such a *superstitio* would not receive recognition as *religio licita* and might be subjected to restrictions or even banned altogether.[210] Jan Bremmer has questioned the Enlightenment-derived assumption that polytheistic religions were more 'tolerant' of alternative religious sects than monotheistic religions.[211] The problem with the Christians was the *exclusivity* of their worship.

Although Christians were rumoured to be associated with immoral practices, this seems to be at least partially the result of the assumption that those who did not observe piety toward the gods must be morally deficient.[212] Perceived involvement in local unrest, or the delation of a person as 'Christian' to the authorities, could result in arrest. Christians so detained would be brought before the governor under the procedure of *cognitio extra ordinem*, the outcome of which was at the governor's discretion and could result in execution. Confirmation that the defendant was currently 'Christian', verbally or by refusal to sacrifice, was sufficient for conviction.

---

[205] For a detailed discussion of this procedure, see de Ste. Croix, 'Early Christians', 113–23; in the wider context of the Roman judicial arrangements in Asia Minor, see Williams, *Persecution in 1 Peter*, 138–76.
[206] de Ste. Croix, 'Early Christians', 117.
[207] As was the case in *Martyrdom of Polycarp*, 6–12 in *The Apostolic Fathers, Greek Texts and English Translations*, ed. and trans. Michael W. Holmes (Grand Rapids: Baker, 2004), 231–7.
[208] Williams, *Persecution in 1 Peter*, 170–6; Burns and Jensen, *Roman Africa*, 8.
[209] Tertullian, *Apol.* 24.6–10 (CCSL 1:134–5), *Prax.* 13.8 (CCSL 2:1175); de Ste. Croix, 'Early Christians', 133–7.
[210] Wilken, *As the Romans saw them*, 31–47.
[211] Jan Bremmer, 'Religious Violence and its Roots', in *Reconceiving Religious Conflict: New Views from the Formative Centuries of Christianity*, ed. Wendy Mayer and Chris de Wets (New York: Routledge: 2018), 30–42.
[212] McLarty, 'Theologies of Martyrdom', 124.

Until Valerian, it is more accurate to speak of persecution *under* a given emperor, than persecution *by* emperors. Emperors prior to Decius probably had little knowledge of, or interest in, the Christians and expressed different degrees of ambivalence toward them rather than directly initiating persecution. Nevertheless, Christians understandably perceived that the law did not help them, and their pleas to authorities went unheeded. The basis of Christian suffering was the animosity of the populace under varying circumstances, perhaps resulting in delation or mob action. When such 'persecution' brought them to the attention of the governor's court, they could be 'prosecuted'.[213] Therefore, the individual Christian's tenuous position was based on the good will of their neighbours, with public opinion and circumstances, and interpersonal tensions, varying from time to time.[214]

Tertullian argued that persecution of Christians arose from wilful ignorance.[215] It would take little disruption to arouse the hostility of the whole community and lead to mob action, with the intervention of police and local magistrates to keep the peace.[216] An individual governor might be positively or negatively disposed toward Christians at the time, with a trial leading to almost any outcome, adding to the tenuousness and uncertainty of their situation.[217]

Romans believed that right worship of the gods was important not only for the right ordering of society, but also for individual piety and morality. Hence, one who abjured religion and ancestral traditions would be considered morally deficient and socially irresponsible.[218] The secrecy surrounding Christian rites and practices made them vulnerable to accusations of *flagitia*, or abominable practices, such as cannibalism, infanticide and incest.[219] Intense public feeling for emperors at times of visitation (*parousia*), military triumph or anniversary celebrations, would single out Christians for their non-participation and disrespect. This might explain the persecutions during Severus' visit to Africa. Civic strife, wars, famine, plague, economic hardship and unrest would draw attention to those whose 'atheism' had angered and insulted the gods and disrupted the *pax deorum*.[220] 'Voluntary martyrdom' may have increased antagonism toward Christians, contributing to outbreaks and intensifying them once begun.[221]

Persecution, as Williams notes, was not 'an undifferentiated unity'.[222] Documented forms of persecution were economic oppression including confiscation of property

---

[213] Which does not eliminate 'persecution', rather than simply 'prosecution', contra Moss, *Myth of Persecution*, 14, 151.
[214] Wilken, *As the Romans saw them*, 16. Williams, *Persecution in 1 Peter*, 39–55, describes several probable sources of such conflict.
[215] *Apol.* 1 (CCSL 1:85–7).
[216] As with Polycarp's arrest and the mob outcry against the Christians of Vienne and Lyons; after the executions, peace was restored. See also Burns and Jensen, *Roman Africa*, 7, 17.
[217] Tertullian gives some examples of lenient governors in *Scap.* 4.3 (CCSL 2:1130).
[218] Wilken, *As the Romans saw them*, 48–67; Tertullian, *Spect.* 13 (CCSL 1:239).
[219] Tertullian, *Nat.* 1.7 (CCSL 1:17–21); *Apol.* 7–8 (CCSL 1:98–101); de Ste. Croix, 'Early Christians', 128–9, queries how seriously the government took accusations of *flagitia*, although they were presumably believed by the populace.
[220] Tertullian, *Apol.* 40.2 (CCSL 1:153); *Nat.* 1.9 (CCSL 1:22–4); *Apol.* 40–41 (CCSL 1:153–6). Cyprian, *Dem.* 3, 5, 10 (CCSL 3A:36, 37, 40–1).
[221] de Ste. Croix, 'Early Christians', 129–31; Middleton, *Radical Martyrdom*; Moss, *Myth of Persecution*, 94–104).
[222] Williams, *Persecution in 1 Peter*, 297. For a comprehensive overview, see Williams, 297–326.

and fines,[223] physical violence[224] and mob lynchings,[225] cursing and other spiritual affliction,[226] imprisonment often with hard labour and/or deprivation,[227] exile,[228] torture,[229] rape and consignment to brothels,[230] and execution by various means.[231]

Christian responses

The four fathers' writings, particularly Cyprian's, provide insight into the responses of early Christians to persecution, or the threat of it. These responses could *potentially* be considered as a spectrum (Table 1.1).

Table 1.1 Hypothetical presentation of a spectrum of acceptability of responses to persecution

Sacrificiati		*Libellatici*	*Stantes*	*Confessores* and *Martyras*	'Voluntary Martyrs'
Voluntarily apostatized, denied Christ and sacrificed	Caved under pressure or threat of torture; reluctantly apostatized	Directly or indirectly paid officials to get a certificate, but did not actually sacrifice	Did not openly come forward; hid. Probably suffered deprivation	Confessed when accused; accepted imprisonment, exile, torture and sometimes death, from deprivation or execution	Came forward or provoked their own martyrdom
Generally condemned	Opinions varied		Generally commended		Controversial: generally condemned?

Ideas of a 'spectrum' of responses with accompanying overtones of acceptability or condemnation are usually traced to Clement's three 'categories' of behaviour in *Stromateis* 4.4. Clement distinguishes between the genuine or 'gnostic martyr', who does not seek martyrdom but patiently accepts it if it comes, and those who flee it from cowardice or rush forward to embrace or even provoke it.[232] Middleton suggests that Clement was 'departing from a traditional, enthusiastic view of martyrdom' from the second century,[233] steering a middle course that was subsequently adopted as mainstream.[234]

---

[223] Origen, *Princ.* 4.1.2 (Behr 2:462); Williams, *Persecution in 1 Peter*, 133-4.
[224] Tertullian, *Cult. Fem.* 2.13.4 (CCSL 1:369–70); Williams, *Persecution in 1 Peter* 132–3.
[225] Tertullian, *Apol.* 49.4 (CCSL 1:169); Cyprian, *Epp.* 7.1; 20.1.2; 43.4.1 (CCSL 3B:38; 106–7; 204).
[226] Cyprian, *Ep.* 58.6.3 (CCSL 3C:328–9).
[227] Tertullian, *Res.* 8.5 (CCSL 2:931–2); *Jej.* 12.2 (CCSL 2:1270–1).
[228] Clement, *Strom.* 4:7.52.3 (SC 463:144); ἀτιμία τις περιβάλλῃ τούτων φυγῇ
[229] Origen, *Cels.* 8.54 (SC 150:296); Cyprian, *Dem.* 12 (CCSL 3A:42).
[230] Tertullian, *Apol.* 50.12 (CCSL 1:171); *Pud.* 1.14 (CCSL 2:1283).
[231] Clement, *Strom.* 2.20.178 (PG 8: 1069); Tertullian, *Mart.* 4.2 (CCSL 1:6), *Apol.* 50.3, 12 (CCSL 1:169, 171); *Spect.* 27.1 (CCSL 1:249); *Pat.* 13.8 (CCSL 1:314); *Scap.* 3.5 (CCSL 2:1129); Cyprian, *Dem.* 12 (CCSL 3A:42).
[232] *Strom.* 4.4 (SC 463:76–88).
[233] Middleton, *Radical Martyrdom*, 29.
[234] Ibid., 38–9.

The idea of a 'spectrum' of 'acceptability' was promoted by de Ste. Croix, who further subdivided martyrs into 'voluntary martyrs', 'quasi-volunteers', 'religious suicides' and 'ordinary martyrs'.[235] This categorizing, by imputing specific motives or intentions, oversteps the evidence. It has rightly been challenged by Nicholson, who argues it is 'not possible to provide a single definition of what early Christians meant by voluntary martyrdom any more than it is possible to identify a single spirit of the martyrs'.[236]

Middleton, following de Ste. Croix, argues that 'radical' or voluntary martyrdom was widely practised, even amongst the 'orthodox', and was not the hallmark of heretics such as Montanists,[237] although assumptions regarding the frequency of volunteerism have been challenged by Vincelette.[238] Moss argues that there is no clear evidence for the existence of a category of 'voluntary martyr' prior to Clement's writings, and that it emerged in the third century to support the legitimacy of flight.[239] Moss argues that the distinction, championed by de Ste. Croix, has its basis in nineteenth-century understandings of appropriate behaviour, rather than any discrete taxonomy of practice. Moss's argument for the distinction of volunteerism post-Clement rests significantly on her thesis that the martyr acts were heavily redacted and even composed much later than the events they purport to relate. They are, she alleges, third-century or later documents. Whilst Middleton also acknowledges that there were later redactions of the *Acta*, such as the Quintus pericope in the *Martyrdom of Polycarp*,[240] his argument draws predominantly on martyr acts as evidence of the early widespread practice and acceptance of 'radical martyrdom'. I will not engage with debate on the dating and legitimacy of the martyr acts,[241] except where they specifically impact the four fathers' arguments. However, I will revisit Clement's 'categories' and Tertullian's apparent promotion of volunteerism in their respective chapters, before drawing some overall conclusions in Chapter 6. Suffice it for now, that it does appear that even the most 'authentic' martyr narratives show evidence of later modification, and that none of the four fathers overtly draw on any *Acta*, apart from Tertullian's brief citation of a version of the *Passio* of Perpetua.[242]

I have argued elsewhere that flight from persecution does not fit neatly into these classifications but has its own theological trajectory.[243] Tertullian considers flight equivalent to apostasy,[244] whereas the other three fathers merge it with the *stantes*. Cyprian essentially ranks confessors who were spared death, *stantes* and those who

---

[235] Geoffrey E. M. de Ste. Croix, 'Voluntary Martyrdom in the Early Church', in *Christian Persecution, Martyrdom and Orthodoxy*, ed. Michael Whitby and Joseph Streeter (Oxford: Oxford University Press, 2006), 153–4.

[236] Oliver Nicholson, 'What Makes a Voluntary Martyr?' *StPatr* 45 (2013): 159–64, at 161. Likewise, Alan Vincelette, 'On the Frequency of Voluntary Martyrdom in the Patristic Era', *Journal of Theological Studies* 70, no. 2 (2019): 652–79, cautions against such subcategorizing.

[237] Middleton, *Radical Martyrdom*, 23–5.

[238] Vincelette, 'Frequency of Voluntary Martyrdom'.

[239] Moss, 'Discourse of Voluntary Martyrdom'.

[240] Middleton, *Radical Martyrdom*, 25–7.

[241] For a useful appraisal see Rebillard, *Early Martyr Narratives*.

[242] *Anim.* 55.4 (CCSL 2:862–3)

[243] Sutcliffe, 'To Flee or Not to Flee?'

[244] *Fug.* 5.1, 7.2 (CCSL 2:1141, 1144–5).

prudently withdrew, as equal in standing.[245] Tertullian appears to be pro-martyrdom to the extent of advocating volunteerism, whereas the others advocate avoidance. What are we to make of these disparities? The answer to that question will have to wait until the fathers' complete diogmologies are unpacked. The theological basis of the fathers' various opinions on volunteerism will contribute to the voluntary martyrdom/legitimacy of flight discussion by offering a fresh perspective on the 'radical martyr'.

---

[245] *Laps.* 3 (CCSL 3:222).

2

Clement of Alexandria

Progression to perfection

We must not think that God actively produces afflictions ... but we must be persuaded that he does not prevent those actively working to cause them but overrules for good the crimes of enemies.

Clement, *Stromateis* IV

If this book were a drama, Clement of Alexandria (c. 150–215) could be considered a foil for the main protagonists. He is somewhat an outlier, because his conclusions on certain points differ significantly from the other three fathers. It is appropriate to start with him, however, because his presentation of the gnostic martyr is considered a turning point in the theology and practice of martyrdom.[1] Yet he will turn out to represent neither the beginning nor end of a theological era with respect to persecution, but simply his own person. His diogmology is framed within his largely unique theological perspective, one aptly termed as 'a project of Christian perfection' by Piotr Ashwin-Siejkowski.[2]

Clement in his context

Clement's life and works

What little we know of Clement's life comes from hints in his extant works and Eusebius' scant biography.[3] The relationship between historical events, Clement's life experiences and his writings is opaque. He wrote wholly or predominantly during Septimius Severus' reign (193–211), his first book of *Stromateis* listing emperors to the death of Commodus in December 192.[4] The unreliable fourth-century *Historia Augusta* is the sole reference to a specific Severan edict of persecution, allegedly

---

[1] Paul Middleton, *Radical Martyrdom and Cosmic Conflict in Early Christianity* (Edinburgh: T&T Clark, 2006), 27; Candida Moss, 'The Discourse of Voluntary Martyrdom: Ancient and Modern'. *Church History* 81, no. 3 (2012): 531–51, at 542.
[2] Piotr Ashwin-Siejkowski, *Clement of Alexandria: A Project of Christian Perfection* (London: T&T Clark, 2008).
[3] Eusebius, *H.E.* 6.13–14 (Loeb 265:42–50). see also Ashwin-Siejkowski, *Christian Perfection*, 20–37; Eric Osborn, *Clement of Alexandria* (Cambridge: Cambridge University Press, 2005), and Eric Osborn, *The Philosophy of Clement of Alexandria* (Cambridge: Cambridge University Press, 1957).
[4] *Strom.* 1.21.146–7 (PG 8:881–4). Eusebius *H.E.* 6.6 (Loeb 265:26–8) confirms this.

forbidding conversion to Judaism or Christianity.[5] Nevertheless, the flight of catechists from Alexandria, and the martyrdom of Origen's father apparently occurred around this time.[6] Eusebius states that Severus incited persecution against the churches, especially in Alexandria, particularly in his tenth year (202–3). Griggs considers it likely that Alexandrian Christians did suffer in this period.[7] Clement himself laments: 'As for us, every day we observe with our own eyes abundant fountains of martyrs being half-roasted, ripped open, beheaded'.[8] Origen looked back on this period with some nostalgia for the perseverance of the church in the face of martyrdoms.[9] Whatever the details now lost to us, local outbreaks of persecution of Christians in the Severan era can certainly be acknowledged without the requirement for them being instigated by the emperor himself.

Clement's education evidently encompassed Stoicism, Platonism, Pythagoreanism and Judaism, as he draws in detail from these sources.[10] Following conversion to Christianity,[11] he became associated with the so-called Alexandrian 'school'.[12] Eusebius' account of a continuous, established catechetical 'school' successively under Pantaneus, Clement and Origen[13] is now considered simplistic and inaccurate, however.[14] Origen does not acknowledge any direct indebtedness to Clement. According to Griggs, Egyptian Christianity prior to the episcopate of Demetrius (189–232) was more diverse and broad-based in its literary and ecclesiastical traditions than the northern Mediterranean, with potentially greater Gnostic influences.[15] Clement, influenced by such an eclectic intellectual milieu,[16] wrote before this transition, leaving

---

[5] H. A. Sept. Sev. 16.8–17.1 (Loeb 139:392). For critiques, see Timothy D. Barnes, 'Legislation Against the Christians', *Journal of Roman Studies* 58 (1968): 32–50, at 40–1; Timothy D. Barnes, *Tertullian: A Historical and Literary Study* (Oxford: Clarendon, 2005), 31, 151; J. Patout Burns and Robin M. Jensen, *Christianity in Roman Africa: The Development of its Practices and Beliefs* (Grand Rapids: Eerdmans, 2014), 10 and James Corke-Webster, 'The Roman Persecutions', in *The Wiley Blackwell Companion to Christian Martyrdom*, ed. Paul Middleton (West Sussex UK: John Wiley & Sons, 2020), 40–1, who demonstrates the inconsistencies between the various scant references to a Severan 'persecution'.

[6] Eusebius, *H.E.* 6.1-2 (Loeb 265:8–14).

[7] C. Wilfred Griggs, *Early Egyptian Christianity: From its Origins to 451 CE* (Leiden: Brill, 1990), 61; also Barnes, *Tertullian*, 156.

[8] *Strom.* 2.20 (PG 8:1069) Ἡμῖν δὲ ἄφθονοι μαρτύρων πηγαὶ ἑκάστης ἡμέρας, ἐν ὀφθαλμοῖς ἡμῶν θεωρούμεναι, παροπτωμένων, ἀνασκινδαλευομένων, τὰς κεφαλὰς, ἀποτεμνομένων; and see Annewies van den Hoek, 'Clement of Alexandria on Martyrdom', *StPatr* 26 (1993): 324–41, at 325.

[9] Origen, *Hom. Jer.* 4.3.2 (SC 232:264) and see W. H. C. Frend, *Martyrdom and Persecution in the Early Church* (Cambridge: James Clarke, 2008), 322.

[10] Ashwin-Siejkowski, *Christian Perfection*, 39–41, 79–108.

[11] Ibid., 22.

[12] Annewies van den Hoek, 'The Catechetical School of Early Christian Alexandria and its Philonic Heritage', *Harvard Theological Review* 90, no. 1 (1997): 59–87; Ronald E. Heine, 'The Alexandrians', in *The Cambridge History of Early Christian Literature*, ed. Frances Young, Lewis Ayers, and Andrew Louth (Cambridge: Cambridge University Press, 2004), 117–130; Ashwin-Siejkowski, *Christian Perfection*, 31–7 and Stuart Rowley-Thomson, 'Apostolic Authority: Reading and writing legitimacy in Clement of Alexandria'. *StPatr* 46 (2013): 19–31.

[13] Eusebius, *H.E.* 5.11, 6.6 (Loeb 153:462–4; 265:26).

[14] Ashwin-Siejkowski, *Christian Perfection*, 31–4. Ronald E. Heine, *Origen: Scholarship in the Service of the Church*, Christian Theology in Context (Oxford: Oxford University Press, 2010), 49, regards it as Eusebius' own creation.

[15] Griggs' *Egyptian Christianity*, 34.

[16] Ashwin-Siejkowski, *Christian Perfection*, 22–23, 30–31.

Alexandria during the persecutions of 202–3, after which Origen supposedly took over catechesis.[17]

Ashwin-Siejkowski also describes a pluralistic intellectual Alexandrian community, with particular competition between the Great Church and hetero-Gnostics,[18] and a more institutionalized focus under Origen, appointee of Demetrius.[19] Thomson postulates that Clement was probably an educator acting as a conduit between the teaching of the *Logos* and the church hierarchy.[20] Similarly, Rizzi describes Clement as a self-identified professional teacher, 'fully integrated in the philosophical milieu of his time, who offers his services in the name of Christ on the public market of ideas to the wide audience of his fellow citizens'.[21] Ashwin-Siejkowski places Clement as a catechist and apologist in the evolving διδασκάλεῖον, pursuing his particular programme.[22] The consensus is that Clement was teaching Christianity, but was largely or wholly independent of the church hierarchy. His extant works were produced in Alexandria. After he departed, except for a commendation to the church in Antioch in 211,[23] he subsequently disappears from history. There is no evidence that he was martyred,[24] which is an argument from silence, but it seems certain that Eusebius and others would have mentioned his martyrdom, if it happened.

Clement and philosophy

Clement's relationship with Greek philosophy is complex, and the subject of scholarly dispute. Völker denies that Clement crossed a boundary to Hellenize Christianity: 'Clement never crossed the borderline in his method of connection ... It has always been said since the days of the Enlightenment, that the Christian church fathers through the use of philosophy Hellenized. I never believed that.'[25] Lilla argues that Clement exhibits a strong influence of Platonism, Jewish-Alexandrine philosophy and Egyptian Christian Gnosticism.[26] Floyd considers Clement to have 'Christianised' the largely Platonist thought world he 'inherited',[27] but is also comfortable labelling him a 'Christian Platonist'.[28] Lanzillotta considers Clement's 'positive and creative

---

[17] Eusebius, *H.E.* 6.3.1 (Loeb 265:16). Griggs, *Egyptian Christianity*, 57–8.
[18] Ashwin-Siejkowski, *Christian Perfection*, 34–5.
[19] Ashwin-Siejkowski, *Christian Perfection*, 36–7; Griggs, *Egyptian Christianity*, 28–34, 45–56.
[20] Rowley-Thomson, 'Apostolic Authority'.
[21] Marco Rizzi, 'The Work of Clement of Alexandria in the Light of his Contemporary Philosophical Teaching', *StPatr* 46 (2013): 11–17, at 11.
[22] Ashwin-Siejkowski, *Christian Perfection*, 35–7.
[23] Eusebius, *H.E.* 6.11 (Loeb 265:36–8); Ashwin-Siejkowski, *Christian Perfection*, 31.
[24] Eusebius, *H.E.* 6.14 (Loeb 265:48), cites a letter from Alexander to Origen, implying Clement's death.
[25] W. Völker, *Der wahre Gnostiker nach Clemens Alexandrinus*, Texte und Untersuchungen zur Geschichte der altchristlichen Literatur 57 (Berlin: n.p. 1952), 9, 32 (n. 3). 'Clemens bei seiner Methode der Anknüpfung nie die Grenzlinie überschritten hat ... Seit den Tagen der Aufklärung ist es immer behauptet worden, dass die Kirchenvater des Christentum durch die Verwendung der Philosophie hellenisiert hatten. Ich habe das nie geglaubt.'
[26] Salvatore R. Lilla, *Clement of Alexandria: A Study in Christian Platonism and Gnosticism* (Eugene OR: Wipf & Stock, 1971), 9–59, 142–89.
[27] W. E. G. Floyd, *Clement of Alexandria's Treatment of the Problem of Evil* (Oxford: Oxford University Press, 1971), xv, xviii.
[28] Floyd, *Problem of Evil*, xix.

appropriation of Greek philosophy' to be indisputable.²⁹ Certainly, Clement cites Greek philosophical writings more than other early fathers, exhibiting a detailed knowledge of them. Osborn attributes to Clement quotations of more than 300 different literary sources for more than 1,000 references to other writers, citing 348 different classical authors including Plato (600 times) and Philo (300 times) – but he also cites Scripture 5,121 times.³⁰ Clement respects philosophy as a proto-source of truth, providentially provided to the pagans as the Law was provided to the Jews.³¹ Gibbons examines how Clement's exploration of Mosaic influence on philosophy shaped his arguments.³² This dependency trope, that Plato received his philosophy from Moses, is found in a number of early Christian writers. Clement reconstitutes the fragments of truth contained in philosophy supposedly derived from Moses and reinterprets Moses as moral exemplar and philosopher.

Philo's influence is most evident in Clement's synthesis of Old Testament and Middle Platonist theology.³³ Ashwin-Siejkowski considers Clement 'a Christian philosopher, but with an obvious predilection for Plato and Pythagoras on one side, and with a strong inclination to allegorical interpretation of the Old Testament and the Jewish tradition (pseudepigrapha) on the other'.³⁴ Clement's respect for Plato is evident, particularly his theology of deification, *theosis* or attaining 'likeness to God as far as possible',³⁵ which Clement interprets in a Christian context. Van den Hoek concludes, 'he borrows from Platonic thought definitions of God, the reason for the deification of humans and that of the world of ideas'.³⁶

Nevertheless, Ashwin-Siejkowski rightly rejects simplistic characterizations of Clement as a Christian Platonist, arguing for a strong influence of Hellenistic Judaism, and concluding that 'it is difficult to assert that there was one dominant influence on Clement'.³⁷ Eric Osborn concludes that Clement's identification of the Bible as his final authority makes him a Platonizing Christian rather than a Christian Platonist, with a

---

²⁹ Lautaro Roig Lanzillotta, 'Greek Philosophy and the Problem of Evil in Clement of Alexandria and Origen'. *Estudios griegos e indoeuropeos* 23 (2013): 207–23, at 208, esp. n. 4.
³⁰ Osborn, *Clement of Alexandria*, 2, 5.
³¹ *Strom* 1.1.119–20 (PG 8:705–8) φιλοσοφίας καὶ τῆς ἄλλης προπαιδείας ... ἔργον προνοίας καὶ φιλοσοφίαν; *Strom* 1.5.121–2 (PG 8:717) ⟨ἐπαιδαγώγης⟩ γὰρ καὶ αὐτὴ τὸ Ἑλληνικὸν, ὡς ⟨ὁ νόμος⟩ τοὺς Ἑβραίους εἰς Χριστόν; *Strom*. 6.5.42.1; 6.6.44.1; 6.8.62.1, 67.1; 6.17.195.9 (SC 446:146; 148; 186; 196; 378–80); Ashwin-Siejkowski, *Christian Perfection*, 100.
³² Kathleen Gibbons, *The Moral Psychology of Clement of Alexandria*. (New York: Routledge, 2017).
³³ For perspectives, see Eric Osborn, 'Philo and Clement: Quiet Conversion and Noetic Exegesis', in *The Studia Philonica Annual* 10 (1988), 108–24; Annewies van den Hoek, *Clement of Alexandria and his use of Philo in the Stromateis: An early Christian reshaping of a Jewish model*. Supp. *Vigiliae Christianae* 3 (Leiden: Brill, 1988); Ashwin-Siejkowski, *Christian Perfection*, 43–67.
³⁴ Ashwin-Siejkowski, *Christian Perfection*, 30–1. For examples of Clement's use of Plato, see David I. Rankin, *From Clement to Origen: The Social and Historical Context of the Church Fathers* (Hampshire: Ashgate, 2006), 127–31.
³⁵ *Strom*. 1.19.173–4 (PG 8:1040, 1044) ὁμοίωσιν Θεῷ φησιν αὐτὴν εἶναι κατα το δυνατον; Henny Fiska Hagg, 'Deification in Clement of Alexandria with a Special Reference to his use of *Theaetetus* 176B', *StPatr* 46 (2010): 169–73.
³⁶ Annewies van den Hoek, Introduction to *Clément d'Alexandrie, Les Stromates, Stromate IV*, Sources Chrétiennes No. 463 (Paris: Cerf, 2001), 31. 'Il emprunte à la pensée platonicienne des définitions de Dieu, le motif de la divinisation des humains, et celui du monde des idées.'
³⁷ Ashwin-Siejkowski, *Christian Perfection*, 3–5.

'massive use and profound reverence for the Bible'.[38] Initially recognizing a significant Platonist influence in Clement's theology,[39] Osborn later acknowledged that emphasis on verbal parallels between Clement and Platonism 'provided a simple picture of Clement as a card-carrying Middle Platonist. This account has fallen apart.'[40] Rather, Osborn recommends, 'we simply ask what problems forced Clement to write and where he found Christian teaching in need of elucidation'.[41] This is helpful for understanding Clement's theology of persecution. The problem of how a 'good God' could preside over persecution was one such problem in need of elucidation. Clement finds he must draw on extra-biblical vocabulary and concepts to explain it, whilst staying true to the essential principles of Christian theology.

Clement uses prophecy and Plato to provide a biblical theology. He finds in Scripture the progress of the soul to God; the 'how' of this is the central problem he seeks to solve and it requires him to go beyond exegesis. He uses Platonic dialectic to handle theological complexity and bring coherence to it.[42] The influence of Stoicism is also evident,[43] particularly with respect to ὁ Λόγος as physician (ἰατρός), which bears strongly on his eschatology and hence his sense of the ultimate good end of persecution. Clement liberally mixes in his own thoughts, particularly in the *Stromateis*, in which Rankin perceives Clement endeavours to explain the faith to mature Christians by use of pagan wisdom to interpret true gnosis.[44] Perhaps the penultimate word goes to Catherine Osborne, who focuses on Clement's eclecticism, his discriminating approach which he likens to images of bees, gold-digging and pruning; the value of cutting out falsehood and harvesting the truth, gaining understanding through lesser mysteries that equip one to discern the deeper truths of Scripture.[45] The final word is from Clement himself: 'Our knowledge, and our spiritual garden, is the Saviour Himself.'[46]

Alexandria hosted multiple Gnostic sects, and their influence would have been noticeable. 'Gnosticism' is a disputed general term for a diverse group of sects influencing and intersecting with Judaism and Christianity, mainly from the late first through the fourth centuries. A dualist philosophy, it distanced the ultimate divinity from the evil world of matter and its creator, through a series of emanations, and held that salvation from evil matter was accomplished through *gnosis*, knowledge, imparted secretly by a redeemer figure.[47] Although Clement rejected aspects of Gnosticism,

---

[38] Osborn, *Clement*, 68, but see 68–80 for his full argument.
[39] Osborn, *Philosophy of Clement*, 78.
[40] Osborn, *Clement*, xii.
[41] Ibid., xiii.
[42] Ibid., 75.
[43] Ashwin-Siejkowski, *Christian Perfection*, 93–100.
[44] Rankin, *Clement to Origen*, 125.
[45] Catherine Osborne, 'Clement of Alexandria', in *The Cambridge History of Philosophy in Late Antiquity*, vol. 2, ed. Lloyd P. Gerson (Cambridge: Cambridge University Press, 2000), 270–82, at 272–3.
[46] *Strom.* 6.1.2.4 (SC 446:60) Ἡ γνῶσις δὲ ἡμῶν καὶ ὁ παράδεισος ὁ πνευματικὸς αὐτὸς ἡμῶν ὁ σωτὴρ ὑπάρχει.
[47] For overviews see Birger A. Pearson, *Ancient Gnosticism: Traditions and Literature* (Minneapolis: Fortress, 2007), who defends the term Gnosticism and identifies its Platonist and Judaistic roots; David Brakke, *The Gnostics: Myth, Ritual and Diversity in Early Christianity* (Cambridge: Harvard University Press, 2010); Bernard Simon, *The Essence of the Gnostics* (London: Arcturus, 2004); Karen L. King, *What Is Gnosticism?* (Cambridge: Harvard University Press, 2003), ch. 1 n. 7. I will refer to 'Gnostics' in this broad sense with a capital 'G'.

especially dualism and determinism, he incorporated and adapted Gnostic ideas.[48] Osborn notes elements of Gnostic gospels found in Clement, such as hidden mystery, secret knowledge and Christ as the one revealer.[49] The one aspiring to perfection (τελείωσις) is the *true* Christian 'gnostic',[50] ὁ γνῶστικός, whom Ashwin-Siejkowski defines as 'a Christian, either man or woman, who achieved ethical excellence, intellectual (philosophical) education and spiritual perfection. The gnostic integrated all theological (faith, hope and love) and cardinal virtues and was able to demonstrate his or her perfection through activities.'[51]

According to van den Hoek, 'imitation of God, within the limits of human capacity, is the task to which the Gnostic is called'.[52] Osborn regards Clement's gnostic as a sage or complete Christian, rather than representing a form of competitive Gnosticism. 'His own idea, the true gnostic or man of knowledge, was within the reach of all believers'.[53]

Through this lens, Clement sees the Christian life as developmental; the Christian gnostic is trained to live as a stranger in the world, free of the passions of embodiment.[54] Christianity is the true philosophy, and the true gnostic is inspired by the *Logos*, the divine teacher who instructs the gnostic on the path to perfection,[55] which only a Christian can achieve.[56] Clement therefore frames his discourse on the origin, purpose, consequences of and response to persecution in terms of this deification or progression toward perfection. This is important, because the persecution experience for an individual is only one possible step or phase in this journey.

Clement and Scripture

Ultimately, Clement must be recognized as a Christian, given his recourse to Scripture as his final authority, and the centrality of the work of the Christ-*Logos* in his theological scheme. Osborn, reviewing Clement's use of Scripture,[57] finds that despite Clement's adoption of Philo's allegorizing strategies, he nevertheless upheld the historical veracity of Scripture and the actual words and deeds of Jesus.[58] Ashwin-Siejkowski similarly concludes that Clement was a Christian biblical hermeneutist, who based his thought primarily within the scriptural framework of the Old and New Testaments, citing them

---

[48] Ashwin-Siejkowski, *Christian Perfection*, 8–9.
[49] Osborn, *Clement*, 77.
[50] *Strom.* 2.19.173 (PG 8:1040) Οὗτός ἐστιν ὁ κατ' εἰκόνα καὶ ὁμοίωσιν ὁ γνωστικὸς, ὁ μιμούμενος τὸν Θεὸν καθόσον οἷόν τε; *Strom.* 2.20.174, 178 (PG 8:1048–9, 1069). I will refer to Clement's 'gnostic' with a lower case 'g'.
[51] Ashwin-Siejkowski, *Christian Perfection*, 11, n. 38.
[52] van den Hoek, *Stromate IV*, SC 463:33; 'L'imitation de Dieu, dans les limites de la capacité humaine, est la tâche à laquelle est appelé le gnostique.'
[53] Osborn, *Clement*, 24–5.
[54] *Strom.* 2.19.173 (PG 8:1040–1); 2.20.178 (PG 8:1069) 3.5.190 (PG 8:1145); Brian E. Daley, *The Hope of the Early Church: A Handbook of Patristic Eschatology* (Peabody, MS: Hendrickson, 2003), 45.
[55] *Protrep.* 11.112.1–2 (SC 2.179–80); *Strom.* 8.1 (PG 9:357); *Paed.* 1.1.1.2, 4 (SC 70:108–10), identified with Christ in chs 2 and 7.
[56] Ashwin-Siejkowski, *Christian Perfection*, 81–4.
[57] Eric Osborn, 'Clement and the Bible', in *Origeniana sexta Origène et la Bible/ Origen and the Bible: Actes du Colloquium Origenianum Sextum Chantilly*, 30 aout–3 seprembre 1993 (1995), 121–32.
[58] Osborn, *Clement of Alexandria*, 75–80.

more extensively than many of his contemporaries.⁵⁹ Scripture is Clement's criterion for distinguishing truth and heresy.

> For we have, as the origin of teaching, the Lord, both through the prophets, through the Gospel, and through the blessed apostles, 'in many ways and at many times', leading from the beginning to the end of knowledge ...⁶⁰ He then, who of himself believes the Lord's Scripture and voice, which by the Lord works effectively for men, is regarded as trustworthy. Indeed we use it as a criterion to discover realities.⁶¹ ... But if it is not adequate to sincerely state an opinion, but what is said must be verified, we do not wait for the testimony of men, but by the voice of the Lord we verify the matter being examined, which is the surest of all demonstrations, and moreover is the only demonstration we experience.⁶²

Judith Kovacs views Clement as a pioneer Christian exegete, noting that he was one of the first to cite and allude to almost all books ultimately recognized as canon; his works 'constitute a crucial link in the tradition of Alexandrian exegesis that runs from Philo the Jew to Origen'.⁶³ Kovacs provides a useful overview of scholarship on Clement's exegesis, highlighting the work of Claude Mondésert and J. Carleton Paget.⁶⁴ In particular, she agrees that Clement expresses a high view of the law, and of Moses as the law incarnate, whose revelation is subordinated only to that in Christ, with the whole of the Old Testament as prophecy in the sense not only of future prediction but an expression of ancient philosophical truth.⁶⁵ Clement is clear that the Scriptures have a higher authority than philosophy.⁶⁶ For Clement, Scripture is the source of true philosophy and true theology. Scripture is necessarily enigmatic, because it treats of divine things which can only be spoken of symbolically, and because it is designed to encourage diligent study by those who have purified themselves and are devoted to God.⁶⁷ Clement's exegesis has much in common with that of Philo and later Origen,

---

⁵⁹ Ashwin-Siejkowski, *Christian Perfection*, 41–2, van den Hoek, *Clement and his Use of Philo*.
⁶⁰ *Strom.* 7.16.95.3 (SC 428:288) Ἔχομεν γὰρ τὴν ἀρχὴν τῆς διδασκαλίας, τὸν κύριον διά τε τῶν προφητῶν διά τε τοῦ εὐαγγελίου καὶ διὰ τῶν μακαρίων ἀποστόλων ⟨⟨πολυτρόπως καὶ πολυμερῶς⟩⟩ ἐξ ἀρχῆς εἰς τέλος ἡγούμενον τῆς γνώσεως.
⁶¹ *Strom.* 7.16.95.4-5 (SC 428:288) Ὁ μὲν οὖν ἐξ ἑαυτοῦ πιστὸς τῇ κυριακῇ γραφῇ τε καὶ φωνῇ ἀξιόπιστος εἰκότως ὡς ἂν διὰ τοῦ κυρίου πρὸς τὴν τῶν ἀνθρώπων εὐεργεσίαν ἐνεργουμένῃ· ἀμέλει πρὸς τὴν τῶν πραγμάτων εὕρεσιν αὐτῇ χρώμεθα κριτηρίῳ.
⁶² *Strom.* 7.16.95.8 (SC 428:290) Εἰ δ' οὐκ ἀρκεῖ μόνον ἁπλῶς εἰπεῖν τὸ δόξαν, ἀλλὰ πιστώσασθαι δεῖ τὸ λεχθέν, οὐ τὴν ἐξ ἀνθρώπων ἀναμένομεν μαρτυρίαν, ἀλλὰ τῇ τοῦ κυρίου φωνῇ πιστούμεθα τὸ ζητούμενον, ἣ πασῶν ἀποδείξεων ἐχεγγυωτέρα, μᾶλλον δὲ ἢ μόνη ἀπόδειξις οὖσα τυγχάνει.
⁶³ Judith L. Kovacs, 'Introduction: Clement as Scriptural Exegete: Overview of History and Research', in Veronika Cernuskova, Judith Kovacs and Jana Platova, eds, *Clement's Biblical Exegesis. Proceedings of the Colloquium on Clement of Alexandria* (Olomouc, Czech Republic, May 29–31, 2014) (Leiden: Brill, 2016), 1–37, at 1.
⁶⁴ Kovacs, 'Introduction', *Clement's Biblical Exegesis*, 2–3, citing Claude Mondésert, *Clément d'Alexandrie. Introduction à l'étude de a pensée religieuse à partir de l'Écriture* (Paris: Aubier, 1944); J. Carleton Paget, 'The Christian Exegesis of the Old Testament in the Alexandrian Tradition', in *Hebrew Bible/Old Testament. The History of its interpretation*, vol. 1, ed. M. Saebo, Ch. Brekelmans, and M. Haran (Göttingen: Vandenhoeck & Ruprecht, 1996), 478–542.
⁶⁵ Kovacs, Introduction, *Clement's Biblical Exegesis*, 2–3.
⁶⁶ Ibid., 9.
⁶⁷ Ibid., 11, citing *Strom.* 2.16.72; 4.19-21; 5.12.78.

although Clement's exegesis tends to involve accumulation of references from across Scripture to address a given topic, rather than a systematic commentary on a specific larger passage.[68] One notable example of intensive treatment of a biblical text of relevance to the present study is his exegesis of Matthew 10:32 and Luke 12:8 in *Stromateis* 4.9, to be discussed below.

Clement is critical of heretics who are selective and incomplete in their use of Scripture, taking passages out of context. 'But truth is not found by changing significations, for they will thus ruin all true teaching, but in establishing the teaching which belongs to and perfectly suits the Lord and Almighty God, establishing each thing demonstrated in scripture again from similar scriptures.'[69] Clement condemned heretics for selectively taking extracts from the prophets and stringing them together, interpreting in a literal sense what should be understood allegorically.[70] Pre-empting Origen, Clement believed that prophecies were spoken enigmatically, so that their meaning was hidden, except to advanced readers instructed by the *Logos*. They alone can receive the mysteries of the Christ hidden in the text.[71]

Clement mainly discusses persecution in *Stromateis* IV and a little in books II, VI and VII. Although these deserve detailed examination, his picture of the persecuted gnostic must be placed in the context of how he understands persecution. This in turn rests on his interpretation of God's goodness and providence gleaned from other writings, particularly the *Protrepticus* and *Paedagogus* I. Here Clement establishes the perspective unique amongst the four fathers, that God neither wills nor permits persecution. This colours his subsequent diogmology.

Not prohibited, but not permitted

The first diogmological question to pose to Clement is the origin of persecution: does he consider it to originate from God, or apart from God? It will be evident that Clement's conception of God's goodness and providence determines his conclusions regarding God's role in persecution, and becomes the basis for all that follows, including the lens through which he views certain Scriptures.

---

[68] Kovacs, 'Introduction', *Clement's Biblical Exegesis*, 12.
[69] *Strom.* 7.16.96.4 (SC 428:292) Ἡ ἀλήθεια δὲ οὐκ ἐν τῷ μετατιθέναι τὰ σημαινόμενα εὑρίσκεται, οὕτω μὲν γὰρ ἀνατρέψουσι πᾶσαν ἀληθῆ διδασκαλίαν, ἀλλ᾽ ἐν τῷ διδασκέψασθαι τί τῷ κυρίῳ καὶ τῷ παντοκράτορι Θεῷ τελέως οἰκεῖόν τε καὶ πρέπον, κἂν τῷ βεβαιοῦν ἕκαστον τῶν ἀποδεικνυμένων κατὰ τὰς γραφὰς ἐξ αὐτῶν πάλιν τῶν ὁμοίων γραφῶν.
[70] *Strom.* 3.4.189 (PG 8:1141).
[71] *Strom.* 5.9.57.1–2 (SC 278:116) οὐδὲ μὴν βεβήλοις τὰ τοῦ Λόγου μυστήρια διηγεῖσθαι; *Strom.* 5.10.66.2 (SC 278:134) regarding milk as catechesis and meat as the contemplation of the divine; *Strom.* 6.15 (SC 446:288–326).

Clement's picture of God

Clement recognizes that God is supremely righteous, and 'the only perfect and good God'.[72] He alone is truly God, exercising the providence of divine power.[73] God does good because he *is* good; goodness is intrinsic to God and he is the source of all goodness, not merely as the means to an end. 'The good, consequently, does good; for God is good, consequently God does good.'[74] According to Karavites, Clement considers God's goodness to be a defining attribute of his divine substance.[75]

Against dualist heresies, Clement maintained that God's goodness encompasses his justice rather than contradicting it; the one God is just *and* good.[76] God is good on his own account, but he is just on *our* account; and he is just *because he is good*.[77] God hates nothing that he has made, and since he made everything, he loves everything and therefore wishes it good.[78] God's justice, then, is good, and sometimes manifested as punishments and reproach. This is like the application of medicine or surgery which seek a cure, albeit by unpleasant means.[79] Karavites concludes:

> Since Clement begins with the premise that God is goodness and love, it follows that in meting out punishment God does not cease to be good and loving. To cease being so, would have implied that God changed His substance, something that is unthinkable. For God to have changed into something other than goodness and love would have made Him less than the perfect being He is. It is therefore sinful man who changes toward God rather than the reverse. God does not countenance evil nor is He responsible for evil and injustice.[80]

God afflicts punishments, not from hatred, wrath or vengeance, but for justice, to undermine sin.[81] He acts towards us as we do toward our children.[82] Punishment must result from love and leads to salvation in this life and restoration of the disturbed order in the next.[83] As Lanzillotta aptly summarizes, Clement's good God, to whom evil is totally alien, must necessarily save humanity. To this end, the divine *Logos* is a teacher, and even punishment and suffering have pedagogical value.[84]

---

[72] *Quis div.* 1.2 (SC 537:100) δοξάζειν τὸν μόνον τέλειον καὶ ἀγαθὸν θεόν.
[73] *Protr.* 10.103.1 (SC 2:170–1).
[74] *Paed.* 1.8.63.1 (SC 70:224) ὠφελεῖ ἄρα τὸ ἀγαθόν· ἀγαθὸς δὲ ὁ θεὸς ὁμολογεῖται, ὠφελεῖ ἄρα ὁ θεός.
[75] Peter Karavites, *Evil, Freedom & the Road to Perfection in Clement of Alexandria*. Supp. *Vigiliae Christianae* 43 (Leiden: Brill, 1999).
[76] *Paed.* 1.8.71.1 (SC 70:234) ἀγαθὸς ὁ θεός ... καὶ δίκαιος ὁ αὐτὸς θεός. *Paed.* 1.9.88.1 (SC 70:264) Καὶ ὁ αὐτὸς δίκαιος καὶ ἀγαθός, ὁ ὄντως θεός, ὁ ὢν αὐτὸς τὰ πάντα καὶ τὰ πάντα ὁ αὐτός, ὅτι αὐτὸς θεός, ὁ μόνος θεός.
[77] *Paed.* 1.9.88.2 (SC 70:266) Ὥστε ἀγαθὸς μὲν ὁ θεὸς δι' ἑαυτόν, δίκαιος δὲ ἤδη δι' ἡμᾶς, καὶ τοῦτο ὅτι ἀγαθός.
[78] *Paed.* 1.8.62.3–63.1 (SC 70:222–4).
[79] *Paed.* 1.8.64.4–65.1; 1.9.83.2 (SC 70:226, 258).
[80] Karavites, *Evil, Freedom*, 72.
[81] *Paed.* 1.8.66.1–2; 1.8.68.3 (SC 70:228, 232).
[82] *Paed.* 1.9.75.2 (SC 70:244) ὁ κύριος πρὸς ἡμᾶς, ὡς καὶ ἡμεῖς πρὸς τὰ τέκνα ἡμῶν.
[83] Karavites, *Evil, Freedom*, 72–3.
[84] Lanzillotta, 'Problem of Evil', 216.

Providence, πρόνοια, is an important concept for Clement. 'There being then a providence, it is impious to think that the whole of prophecy and the economy in reference to a Saviour did not take place in accordance with providence.'[85] Clement situates God's providential care for the world and its creatures in God's love for everything he made.[86] In contrast to determinism or fate, divine providence orders all things well, even martyrdom.[87] Indeed, there is a special, individual care or providence for those who accept the discipline and teaching of God. 'The souls of the righteous are in the hand of the Lord, and no plague shall touch them.'[88] Clement thus concludes God helps Christians in persecution by taking them to himself; they should not fear what men can do to them.

For Clement, providence does not mean God directly *causes* everything to occur. This is critical to his diogmology. Specifically, God is not the cause (το ἐνεργεῖν) of evil and suffering; he did not will (θελήματι) the suffering of Christ nor of the martyrs.[89] Clement's solution is not that such things happen outside of God's will, but that he does not actively prevent them.

> But nothing is without the will of the Lord of all ... such things happen, not being prevented by God; for this alone saves both the providence and the goodness of God. We must not therefore think that he actively produces afflictions (this thought be far from us!) but we must be persuaded that he does not prevent those actively working to cause them but overrules for good the crimes of enemies.[90]

Clement's view of providence in this context is therefore largely teleological; God works in all situations to bring about his own good ends. As Karavites explains, providence cannot allow evil to remain useless and more injurious; God's nature is not only to do good, 'but especially to ensure that what happens through evil may come to a good and useful issue'.[91] In particular, God works to prevent sin and to modify the effects of sin, but not by coercion. Clement upholds free will. The possibility of abuse of free will was intrinsic to man's freedom, but 'man's capacity to become virtuous was tantamount to his perfection'.[92] The greatest achievement of providence is to redirect evil for good.[93] The martyrs, for example, are not wronged; they are trained in endurance and released by death to go to the Lord.[94] The true guilt lies with the judge who freely

---

[85] *Strom.* 5.1.6.2 (SC 278:32) Προνοίας τοίνυν οὔσης, μὴ κατὰ πρόνοιαν γεγονέναι πᾶσαν τήν τε προφητείαν καὶ τὴν περὶ τὸν σωτῆρα οἰκονομίαν ἡγεῖσθαι ἀνόσιον.
[86] *Paed.* 1.8.62.3–4, 63.1–2 (SC 70:222–4).
[87] *Strom.* 4.7.52.4 (SC 463:144) καλῶς πάντα τὴν θείαν διοικεῖν πρόνοιαν.
[88] *Strom.* 4.11.80.5 (SC 463:188) citing Ps. 118:6.
[89] *Strom.* 4.12.86.2 (SC 463:198).
[90] *Strom.* 4.12.86.3–87.1 (SC 463:198) Ἀλλὰ μὴν οὐδὲν ἄνευ θελήματος τοῦ κυρίου τῶν ὅλων ... τὰ τοιαῦτα συμβαίνειν μὴ κωλύσαντος τοῦ Θεοῦ. τοῦτο γὰρ μόνον σῴζει καὶ τὴν πρόνοιαν καὶ τὴν ἀγαθότητα τοῦ Θεοῦ. Οὐ τὸ ἐνεργεῖν τοίνυν αὐτὸν τὰς θλίψεις οἴεσθαι χρή, μὴ γὰρ εἴη τοῦτο ἐννοεῖν, ἀλλὰ μὴ κωλύειν τοὺς ἐνεργοῦντας πεπεῖσθαι προσῆκεν καταχρήσασθαί τε εἰς καλὸν τοῖς τῶν ἐναντίων τολμήμασιν.
[91] Karavites, *Evil, Freedom*, 80–1.
[92] Ibid., 45.
[93] *Strom.* 1.17.134 (PG 8:801) and see Osborn, *Philosophy of Clement*, 74–5.
[94] *Strom.* 4.11.80.1 (SC 463:186).

condemns them.⁹⁵ Clement also sees providence as educational, the work of the Παιδαγωγός, encompassing providential discipline or punishment.⁹⁶ Humans need to freely choose to work with providence, which requires both individual choice and God's grace. Salvation is collaborative and one must assent to divine guidance.⁹⁷ One needs to learn how to make use of each situation, to be trained for eternal life.⁹⁸

Critically for Clement, God does not deliver (ἐκδίδωμι) Christians to such suffering, rather he foretold and predicted it would happen.

> Yes but, they say, 'if God cares for you, why then are you pursued and murdered? Has he delivered you to this?' But we do not suppose the Lord wills us to fall into calamities, but he predicted prophetically what was to happen to us, that we would be persecuted, murdered, impaled, on account of his name. Thus, he did not want us to be persecuted, but he indicated in advance what we would suffer, to exercise us, by prophecy of what would happen . . .⁹⁹

Clement's strict delineation of what a good God does and does not will shows some indebtedness to philosophy. Clement has shaped his understanding of God's goodness, perhaps in his attraction to transcendency, in such a way that God's goodness necessarily separates him completely from even permitting evil. As Karavites notes, 'with the aid of Plato Clement absolves God from any responsibility for evil. God is all goodness and this association with evil is a priori impossible'.¹⁰⁰

Kenney posits the attraction of Platonist transcendence for Christian thinkers; the true level of reality is the truly divine world, beyond which was the ultimate source of divinity and perfection, the One or Good itself, which exceeds all finitude and anthropomorphic description.¹⁰¹ By Clement's time, Plato's concept of the Good, presented in *The Republic*, was being merged with the One.¹⁰² Osborn argues that Clement's ideas of God's goodness can be largely traced to Platonism and Stoicism,¹⁰³ and that the two main influences on Clement's theodicy are persecution and Gnostic

---

[95] *Strom.* 4.11.78.2–79.1 (SC 463:184).
[96] *Paed.* 1.9.75.1 (SC 70:224); *Strom.* 5.1.7.8 (SC 278:36) ὁ σωτήρ, τῆς ἀγαθοῦ κτήσεως διδάσκαλός.
[97] *Strom.* 5.1.7.2–3 (SC 278:34) and see George Karamanolis, *The Philosophy of Early Christianity* (Durham: Acumen, 2013), 168.
[98] *Strom.* 4.6.32.1 (SC 463:108).
[99] *Strom.* 4.11.78.1–2 (SC 463:184) Ναί, φασίν, εἰ κήδεται ὑμῶν ὁ θεός, τί δήποτε διώκεσθε καὶ φονεύεσθε; Ἤ αὐτὸς ὑμᾶς εἰς τοῦτο ἐκδίδωσιν; Ἡμεῖς δὲ οὐχ οὕτως ὑπολαμβάνομεν τοῖς περιστατικοῖς περιπίπτειν ἡμᾶς τὸν κύριον βουληθῆναι, ἀλλὰ προφητικῶς τὰ συμβήσεσθαι μέλλοντα προειρηκέναι, ὡς διὰ τὸ ὄνομα αὐτοῦ διωχθησόμεθα, φονευθησόμεθα, ἀνασκινδυλευσόμεθα. Ὥστ' οὐ διώκεσθαι ἠθέλησεν ἡμᾶς, ἀλλ' ἃ πεισόμεθα προεμήνυσεν, διὰ τῆς τοῦ συμβήσεσθαι προαγορεύσεως . . .
[100] Karavites, *Evil, Freedom*, 175.
[101] John Peter Kenney, 'Platonism and Christianity in Late Antiquity', in *Christian Platonism, A History*, ed. Alexander J.B. Hampton and John Peter Kenney (Cambridge: Cambridge University Press, 2021), 162–82, at 168.
[102] Alexander J. B. Hampton and John Peter Kenney, eds, *Christian Platonism, A History*. (Cambridge: Cambridge University Press, 2021), 16–18. Regarding 'The Good', see Gerald A. Press, *Plato, A Guide for the Perplexed* (London: Continuum, 2007), 43, 221.
[103] Osborn, *Philosophy of Clement*, (1957), 78.

dualism.[104] The first questioned God's care for his people and the second his unity and goodness.[105] But these are more foils than influences. Certainly, persecution provides a challenge to simplistic concepts of God's goodness and providence, to which dualism is, in Clement's view, an erroneous response, for there is only one God.

Floyd considers Clement to be 'steeped in' his middle Platonist 'heritage' albeit framing his response from Scripture 'in the language of Stoic ethics and Platonic metaphysics'.[106] Floyd also argues that Clement's speculation on the problem of evil is largely dictated by his anti-Gnostic polemic, although he is not immune to the agonizing reality of evil, especially in the context of martyrdom.[107] We can certainly bear these influences in mind, whilst appreciating that Clement ultimately frames a Christian response to evil, albeit with what Lanzillotta terms a 'positive and creative appropriation of Greek philosophy'.[108] Osborn recognizes that 'Clement's Platonism is an expression of his theme of universal salvation by a good and gracious God'.[109] Lanzillotta also recognizes that Clement's view of evil is intrinsically bound to his theology of universal salvation. This concept 'ponders both the existence of evil and God's role and/or responsibility in its perpetuation in the form of punishment'.[110] Clement was the first to utilize Greek philosophy to argue for the necessity of salvation, based on his philosophical definition of God and the central place of the Logos.[111]

This definition of God, whilst fundamentally a description of the Creator God and Father of Christ and thus 'Christian', nevertheless appropriates vocabulary suggestive of Platonism: the One and the Good.[112] So-called Middle Platonism, which was the Alexandrian milieu in Clement's day, was a set of varying ideas resulting from the engagement of a diverse array of thinkers with Plato's texts. It was a set of problems rather than doctrines, a field of thought in which Clement browsed alongside others with whom he did not necessarily agree. In his perception of God, Clement evidently found the synthesis of the One and the Good to be palatable and appropriate for his needs.[113] This means that Clement, paradoxically, imposes a constraint on God's providence which he doubtless does not consider to be a limitation. Insisting that God does not permit, but only refrains from prohibiting evil, he effectively restricts God's providence to working around it, rather than through or with it. As I shall show, this premise is not shared by the other fathers.

---

[104] Ibid., 65–83.
[105] Ibid., 70–1. He maintains this position in, Osborn, *Clement of Alexandria*, 48–51.
[106] Floyd, *Problem of Evil*, xix–xx.
[107] Ibid., xix, 91, 95.
[108] Lanzillotta, 'Problem of Evil', 208. See Ashwin-Siejkowski, *Christian Perfection*, 81–2 for balance.
[109] Eric F. Osborn, 'Clement and Platonism', in *Origeniana octava: Origen and the Alexandrian tradition (Origene e la tradizione Alessandrina)* (papers of the 8th international Origen congress, Pisa, 21–27 August 2001), 419–27, at 419.
[110] Lanzillotta, 'Problem of Evil', 215.
[111] Ibid., 21.
[112] For further discussion see Kenney, 'Platonism and Christianity', 172.
[113] Floyd, *Problem of Evil*, xv.

The nature and origin of evil

Given that God is not in any way the source of evil, where then does Clement consider evil to originate, and how does he view it? One contemporary explanation was the dualist attribution of evil to the material world, the creation of which was attributed to a lesser deity, thus absolving the Supreme Being from evil. Clement opposed this, attributing evil to the disobedience and imperfection of created man, albeit man with the capacity to become virtuous.[114] Floyd asserts that Clement's speculation on evil is driven largely by his opposition to the Gnostic disparaging of matter and the helplessness of humans.[115]

Another question is whether Clement espoused a 'Platonist' privative view of evil, whereby evil does not substantively exist but is a privation of substance, form and goodness. If so, Clement anticipates the Neoplatonist Plotinus.[116] However, Clement does not describe evil in this way, but rather speaks of evil as opposing good, and as originating in actions and ideas.[117] As Karavites explains,

> Clement is not willing to accept that evil is an illusion and that those we call evil are not evil in our temporal world, though he was prepared to argue that evil has a utilitarian purpose. In his view evil is an activity contrary to the will of God; therefore it is not merely the privation of good, as Augustine contended. Evil is a bad activity or judgment springing from some error opposite to good.[118]

Karavites provides further definition. Evil for Clement is whatever is condemned by God, whatever opposes his laws.[119] It is a disposition of the soul which opposes reason.[120] It is less than the Platonist totality that is goodness.[121] It is doing what is against nature because it lacks what is in accordance with nature.[122]

> Everything sensible and intelligible is good but owing to its having been created it runs the risk of becoming nothing. It can be changed, altered, corrupted. This change, in its turn corruptive, is hamartia, evil. Evil has no hypostasis because it is not an object nor a being, the μή ὄν, but it can corrupt the essence of good... There is nothing hypostatically and naturally evil.[123]

Although evil is not a hypostasis, it is nevertheless real, 'an existential fact, an active refusal on man's part to be what he was made to be, the image and likeness of God'.[124]

---

[114] Karavites, *Evil, Freedom*, 45.
[115] Floyd, *Problem of Evil*, 91.
[116] Lloyd Gerson, 'Plotinus', *Stanford Encyclopedia of Philosophy* (2018), ed. Edward N. Zalta, https://plato.stanford.edu/archives/fall2018/entries/plotinus/, citing Plotinus, *Enneads*, I, 8.
[117] For Origen's perspective on evil as non-being, see Chapter 3.
[118] Karavites, *Evil, Freedom*, 83.
[119] Ibid., 46.
[120] Ibid., 29.
[121] Ibid., 32.
[122] Ibid., 34.
[123] Ibid., 34.
[124] Ibid., 35.

Evil is, essentially, action, and may be voluntary or involuntary. Evil is the product of ignorance. Involuntary evil is an irrational act, freely performed and the result of ignorance or weakness. Voluntary evil is a crime, ἁμαρτία or sin. κακία may be moral or physical. Both depend on humans because we do not learn, or we fail in self-restraint. In accordance with Plato, no one prefers evil for its own sake. But evil is contingent upon the existence of man and the physical world and has no meaning without such existence. Abstinence of evil in a man does not guarantee him goodness.[125] Clement does not think evil is necessary as a counterpoint to good, or that if there were no evil there could be no good either. Evil comes from disobedience.[126]

Clement blames the free will of the Devil and humans for the origin of evil, not God or an inferior deity. Evil is part of the finitude or weakness of matter,[127] but the world with all its limitations is exactly as God planned it. Evil is part of the natural balance and harmony and challenges humans to use their free will appropriately.[128] As Floyd recognizes, Clement defends the presence of evil teleologically; it is purposeful, not because God wills it, but because he uses it providentially.[129] Karavites concurs: 'Everything created was created good and only man's transgression is responsible for the introduction of evil. Once man lost his special status through his own fault, evil is used by God not as a counterpart of good but as a means to good.'[130]

This is certainly Clement's perception of persecution-related evil, as I shall elaborate below. It seems the most consistent interpretation, rather than an appeal to a privative view of evil, for which I find no clear evidence in Clement. Karavites identifies a flaw in Clement's reasoning at this point, because it seems to restrict God's power, because if God uses evil as a means to good, he is subject to a law of causality. Clement tries to eliminate this by making humans responsible for the introduction of evil; 'thereafter God only used evil to undo what man had foolishly incurred'.[131]

In common with other early fathers, Clement links evil and idolatry with the demonic world.[132] Karavites observes that humankind's fall is predicated on the prior fall of the Devil and angels which become the force opposing God. Clement perceives the Devil, unlike evil, to be a hypostasis, and the adversary of man.[133] Clement describes the Devil as 'that wicked tyrant and dragon' who 'draws aside and binds living men to idols with chains of superstition, burying them so they decompose together'.[134] The

---

[125] Ibid., 30, 42.
[126] Ibid., 83.
[127] *Strom*. 7.3.16.2 (SC 428:76) κακῶν δὲ αἰτίαν καὶ ὕλης ἄν τις ἀσθένειαν ὑπολάβοι.
[128] Floyd, *Problem of Evil*, 93–4.
[129] Ibid., 92, 95.
[130] Karavites, *Evil, Freedom*, 83.
[131] Ibid., 83.
[132] For an overview see Everett Ferguson, 'Demonology of the Early Christian World', Symposium series vol. 12. Lectures presented at the University of Mississippi, Feb 1980 (Lewiston NY: Edwin Mellen, 1984), 109–15. More recently, the comprehensive work of Eva Elm and Nicole Hartmann, eds, *Demons in Late Antiquity: Their perception and transformation in different literary genres*, Transformationen der Antike, 54 (Berlin, Boston: De Gruyter, 2020) examines Christian and non-Christian ideas of demons and intermediary beings.
[133] Karavites, *Evil, Freedom*, 43.
[134] *Protr*. 1.7.5 (SC 2:61) Ὁ γοῦν πονηρὸς οὑτοσὶ τύραννος καὶ δράκων … ζῶντας ἐπιφέρων συνέθαψεν αὐτούς, ἔστ᾽ ἂν καὶ συμφθαρῶσιν.

Devil's objectives are evident: 'The Devil tempting us, knowing what we are, but not knowing if we will endure, but wishing to crumble our faith, tempts [us] in order to bring us into subjection to himself.'[135]

The Devil originated idolatry, and lures humans into it. People whom the Devil has assimilated do the Devil's idolatrous work and are therefore at enmity with Christ and his people, who oppose idolatry.

> But the adversary is not the body,[136] as some will it, but the devil, and those assimilated to him, who walks together with us in men dedicated to his works in this earthly life. Inevitably, then, those who confess themselves to be of Christ, but find themselves in the midst of the devil's works, suffer the most hostile treatment.[137]

By situating evil with the demonic, Clement distances God from any causality. Clement's concept of God's goodness means God can in no way originate or permit evil.[138] Clement stresses that sin is an activity of humans, not a work of God; sinners are the enemies of God.[139] God has given humans freedom of choice, which in turn makes individuals accountable for virtue and for evil.[140] Clement denies that evil is the will of God; God merely abstains from preventing it. Good things are caused by God, whereas evil happens without God preventing it. What God does do is bring order and good to what is wrongly done.[141] 'We must not therefore think that he actively produces afflictions – this thought be far from us! – but we must be persuaded that he does not prevent those actively working to cause them but overrules for good the crimes of enemies.'[142] Furthermore, 'all things are arranged with a view to the salvation of the universe, both generally and particularly. It is then the function of the righteousness of salvation to improve everything as far as practicable.'[143]

Several questions remain. Firstly, has Clement really solved the problem or merely pushed it back a step? Secondly, how can God keep his hands clean, so to speak, in the interventions that turn evil to good? Must there not be some form of manipulation of the evildoer? Thirdly, has Clement made God so transcendent with respect to evil that he has removed any real assurance that a God who merely refrains from prohibiting can truly turn all things for good? Fourthly, is the Devil without restraint?

---

[135] *Strom.* 4.12.85.1 (SC 463: 194) Πειράζων γὰρ ὁ διάβολος εἰδὼς μὲν ὅ ἐσμεν, οὐκ εἰδὼς δὲ εἰ ὑπομενοῦμεν. ἀλλὰ ἀποσεῖσαι τῆς πίστεως ἡμᾶς βουλόμενος καὶ ὑπάγεσθαι ἑαυτῷ πειράζει.
[136] Contra some dualist/Gnostic views.
[137] *Strom.* 4.14.95.2–3 (SC 463: 214) ἀντίδικος δὲ οὐ τὸ σῶμα, ὥς τινες βούλονται, ἀλλ᾽ ὁ διάβολος καὶ οἱ τούτῳ ἐξομοιούμενοι, ὁ συνοδεύων ἡμῖν δι᾽ ἀνθρώπων τῶν ζηλούντων τὰ ἔργα αὐτοῦ ἐν τῷ ἐπιγείῳ τῷδε βίῳ. Οὐχ οἷόν τε οὖν μὴ παθεῖν τὰ ἔχθιστα τοὺς ὁμολογοῦντας μὲν ἑαυτοὺς εἶναι [τοῖς] τοῦ Χριστοῦ, ἐν δὲ τοῖς τοῦ διαβόλου καταγινομένους ἔργοις.
[138] *Strom.* 7.2.12.1 (SC 428:64) κακαίας δ᾽ αὖ πάντῃ πάντως ἀναίτιος.
[139] *Strom.* 4.13.93.3–94.1 (SC 463: 212) τὸ ἁμαρτάνειν ... οὐδὲ ἔργον Θεοῦ. Ἐχθροὶ δὲ οἱ ἁμαρτάνοντες εἴρηνται Θεοῦ.
[140] *Strom.* 4.19.124.2–3 (SC 463:262).
[141] Osborn, *Clement of Alexandria*, 49–51.
[142] *Strom.* 4.12.87.1 (SC 463:198) Οὐ τὸ ἐνεργεῖν τοίνυν αὐτὸν τὰς θλίψεις οἴεσθαι χρή, μὴ γὰρ εἴη τοῦτο ἐννοεῖν, ἀλλὰ μὴ χωλύειν τοὺς ἐνεργοῦντας πεπεῖσθαι προσῆκεν καταχρῆσθαί τε εἰς καλὸν τοῖς τῶν ἐναντίων τολμήμασιν.
[143] *Strom.* 7.2.12.2–3 (SC 428:64–6).

Floyd concludes that Clement's theodicy does not offer a solution to the problem of evil so much as a rationale for understanding it, because the problem of why God allowed the fall remains.[144] Osborn likewise identifies the weakness of Clement's position in merely pushing the problem back one stage, for God gave humans the freedom of will, which is the direct cause of evil.[145] These are valid observations; arguably, not preventing evil is indistinguishable from permitting it. But perhaps this is largely a problem for modern scholars, influenced by centuries of discussions of theodicy. As Ferguson observes, there was little uniformity in early Christian thought as to when, where and why demons rebelled, despite a consistent testimony to them being created good and rebelling of their free will.[146] It seems to be accepted, without any agonizing over why God permitted this rebellion, until Origen constructed his theology of the fall of rational creatures. It does not appear to be a problem for Clement, who distances God from any permissive involvement with demonic fall. McClymond observes that whilst emphasizing angelology, 'Clement was not particularly interested in the evil angels, and so he did not develop a theology of the demonic'.[147]

Clement does address the difference between causation and non-prevention, but in the context of Greek philosophers 'stealing' truth from the Hebrew prophets.[148] The thief did not have the good end in sight, but providence directed the theft to a useful outcome. Clement rejects the proposition that non-prevention equates to causation even if proper precautions were not taken. Rather than it being analogous to a ship's master being the cause of a shipwreck because he had power to prevent it by reefing the sail, but did not, Clement's preferred analogy is that one must blame the javelin, not the shield, for the wound incurred. As Karavites notes, Clement places the blame not with non-prevention but with 'execution, actualization and realization ... the act of not preventing something carries no blame'.[149] Clement has not really answered his detractors, however; he has merely mixed his metaphors. He maintains that prevention is active intervention; declining to prevent is not an action. However, God reserves the right, whilst not preventing evil, to judge those who act wickedly. Free will once again carries the load of responsibility for evil. Also, the good outcome to which providence directs the evil does not exonerate the perpetrator, a position which underpins Clement's aversion to being complicit in the persecutor's sin by provoking martyrdom.

Whilst acknowledging the ambiguities in Clement's position, I suggest Clement's theology of *persecution*-related evil is somewhat more satisfactory than his general theodicy, because of his teleological focus, and ultimately because of his broader diogmology. Persecution is not the same as other manifestations of malevolence. God knows the good that will come from the persecution experience, which he does not prohibit. God predicts and refrains from preventing persecution, even though it is not what he wants, because he nevertheless uses it for good. Clement's response as to why

---

[144] Floyd, *Problem of Evil*, 96–7.
[145] Osborn, *Philosophy of Clement*, 72–3.
[146] Ferguson, 'Demonology of the Early Christian World', 109.
[147] Michael McClymond, *The Devil's Redemption: A New History and Interpretation of Christian Universalism* (Grand Rapids: Baker 2018–19), 1:241.
[148] *Strom.* 1.17.133–4 (PG 8:796–7).
[149] Karavites, *Evil, Freedom*, 31.

God does not help the persecuted, is to point to the good which comes from persecution, not to testify that persecution is itself good (contra Tertullian). No wrong is done to those who are released by death to go to the Lord.[150] This will be explored in the remainder of the chapter.

God does not will or cause persecution

Clement uses the same arguments to describe God's relationship to persecution as to evil. 'He is absolutely not the cause of evil';[151] 'we must not think that he actively works afflictions';[152] 'neither does God will the persecuted be persecuted'.[153] If persecution is regarded as evil in this sense, then it is something a good God would not – could not – directly produce. It follows that it will have the same origin external to God, and Clement's diogmological arguments will be closely tied to theodicy.

Furthermore, Clement denies that even Christ's suffering was God's will, although God brought good from it. He argues that if God's people were persecuted by the will of God, that would either make persecution a good thing, or make the persecutors guiltless.[154] Nor does Clement entertain persecution being a just retribution for sin. He refutes Basilides' idea that martyrs' suffering must somehow equate to punishment for sins committed in a former life. It would make the faithful martyrs' confession cooperative in such a punishment, and see the denier rewarded. It would also imply that Jesus himself had been sinful.[155] Clement did not allow the innocence of persecutors, nor will he allow persecution itself to be good (despite potentially good outcomes) hence it cannot be God's will. This suggests an element of circular reasoning: is persecution evil, *therefore* God does not permit it, or does God not permit it, *therefore* it must be evil? Interestingly, Clement does not engage with texts such as Isaiah 53:10, Acts 2:23 or 1 Peter 3:17 which ascribe Christian suffering to God's will. His argument is *a priori* what a good God would 'will'.

Although Clement affirms that everything takes place through God's will, as van den Hoek notes, it is not through his will that persecutions and punishments take place, because they are the work of the Devil. God does not hinder the Devil's work but places the onus on the free will of the individual. 'This train of thought tries to save both God's providence and goodness and to leave freedom for human choice.'[156] In this way, Clement rationalizes the injustice of the persecution which he asserts that God does not prevent. The injustice of the judge who punishes innocent Christians does not affect the providence of God, because the judge is no puppet. He is responsible for his actions, and he is judged, as are we in respect of our choices and endurance.[157] Therefore,

---

[150] *Strom.* 4.11.80.1 (SC 463:186).
[151] *Strom.* 7.2.12.1 (SC 428:64) κακίας δ' αὖ πάντη πάντως ἀναίτιος.
[152] *Strom.* 4.12.87.1 (SC 463:198) Οὐ τὸ ἐνεργεῖν τοίνυν αὐτὸν τὰς θλίψεις οἴεσθαι χρή.
[153] *Strom.* 4.12.86.2 (SC 463:198) οὔθ' οἱ διωκόμενοι βουλήσει τοῦ Θεοῦ διώκονται.
[154] *Strom.* 4.12.86.2 (SC 463:198) Οὔτε γὰρ ὁ κύριος θελήματι ἔπαθεν τοῦ πατρὸς οὔθ' οἱ διωκόμενοι βουλήσει τοῦ Θεοῦ διώκονται, ἐπεὶ δυεῖν θάτερον, ἢ καλόν τι ἔσται διωγμὸς διὰ τὴν βούλησιν τοῦ Θεοῦ, ἢ ἀθῷοι οἱ διατιθέντες καὶ θλίβοντες.
[155] *Strom.* 4.12.85.1–3 (SC 463:194–6).
[156] van den Hoek, 'Clement of Alexandria on Martyrdom', 333.
[157] *Strom.* 4.11.79 (SC 463:184–6).

the one who offers himself for martyrdom contributes to the persecutor's sin.[158] Overall, because of the way Clement describes persecution and persecutors, it seems he starts from a premise that persecution is evil and hence not God's will. As shall be shown, this is the opposite conclusion from his contemporary Tertullian.

Clement anticipates the next obvious question, whether God is really in control of such situations. In defence of providence, he concludes that nothing happens without God's will, but such things happen without his prevention. He neither produces nor prevents afflictions but overrules the crimes of his enemies for good.[159] Clement does not definitively explain here what such overruling entails, yet he is certain it will happen, because of his confidence in God's providence and foreknowledge. Yet he stops short of the other fathers' acknowledgement that the Devil is under God's direct restraint and cannot work evil against God's people unless God gives him permission. That would involve permission rather than non-prohibition. Clement's Devil is not leashed, yet will certainly be defeated. Perhaps Clement has somewhat painted himself into a corner.

Clement distinguishes between the persecution itself, which is evil, from its outcomes, which can be good. Many pleasurable things are evil. Poverty is unpleasant but can focus the soul on essentials. Thirst is unpleasant but is the efficient cause of the pleasure of drinking. Likewise, persecution is the efficient cause of the martyr's reward. Because evil cannot be the efficient cause of good, persecution, like thirst, cannot be 'evil'.[160] This appears to contradict Clement's use of the same arguments for persecution as for evil,[161] but they are different arguments.

Clement defends his corner by distinguishing between persecution itself (ontological), and consequences which may attend it, which may be evil in the short term but ultimately good (teleological). The persecutors commit a crime and bear responsibility for their actions against the martyrs. This is borne out in Clement's interpretation of Matthew 10:23; Christ does not advise flight as if persecution were an 'evil' thing (κακός), nor to avoid death, but because he does not want us to abet 'evil' (κακός) and be a participator (συνεργός) in the 'evil' (πονηρία) of the persecutors.[162] This would be an immediately evil consequence. In the longer term, God transforms the evil he does not prevent, by turning it into good; by providence he corrects and benefits those who experience it.[163] Likewise, Clement determines that God does not 'punish', because punishment is retaliation for evil; rather, God corrects through chastisement, for good purpose, not vengeance. Such correction is educational and medicinal, a mark of good-will, not ill-will.[164] God does not chide men from hatred, because he suffered for us rather than destroy us.[165]

---

[158] *Strom.* 4.10.77.1 (SC 463:182).
[159] *Strom.* 4.12.87.1 (SC 463:198).
[160] *Strom.* 4.5.23.1 (SC 463:94).
[161] *Strom.* 4.12.86.2–87.1 (SC 463:198).
[162] *Strom.* 4.10.76.2, 77.1 (SC 463:180–2).
[163] *Strom.* 1.17.134 (PG 8:800).
[164] *Strom.* 7.16.102.5 (SC 428:308); *Paed.* 1.8.70.3; 1.9.75.1; 1.9.76.1 (SC 70:234, 244–6).
[165] *Paed.* 1.8.66.1–2 (SC 70:228).

If we step outside Clement's framework, his rather utilitarian justification of the evil of persecution by considering only the potential good which results seems inadequate. But rooted as it is in Clement's (likely Platonist-influenced) starting point, his understanding of what it means for God to be 'good', it makes sense for the preservation of God's goodness and providence.

The reason for persecution

If God foretold persecution and does not prevent it, it must be inevitable, and since God turns it to good, it must have a reason. Determining this reason is the second diogmological question, and here Clement turns definitively to Scripture.

The centrality of confession

Clement conceives of salvation as a process of deification, perfecting, *theosis* or likeness to God ὁμοίωσις Θεῷ, and returning to God. This process occurs continuously throughout this life and the next. To this end, Christ is a paedagogue and model.[166] Central to this progression is the participation in Christ's sufferings. Discussing 'gnostic' martyrdom, Clement quotes Philippians 1:29:

> But the apostle, writing to us about endurance of afflictions, says, 'And this is from God, that it is given to you on behalf of Christ, not only to believe on Him, but also to suffer for His sake, having the same conflict which ye saw in me, and now hear to be in me.'[167]

Clement also describes persecution as part of the war against the principalities of darkness; it is for Christ's sake we are persecuted and in him we are conquerors.[168] The adversary in this war is the Devil, and those who confess themselves as belonging to Christ find themselves in the midst of the Devil's works.[169] Persecution brings Christians to the ultimate choice: confession or denial, which determines Christ's response to them. Persecution therefore unites the principles of participation in Christ's suffering and confession of the name, which for Clement is consistent with being 'in Christ'.

An important concept for Clement is that those who confess or acknowledge Christ will in turn be acknowledged by him. The key Scriptural references are the parallel passages Matthew 10:32-33; Mark 8:38; Luke 9:26 and Luke 12:8-9, but they are not identical. Matthew 10:32-33 and Luke 12:8-9 share the language of acknowledgement

---

[166] *Strom.* 7.2.6.1 (SC 428:50) *Protr.* 12.120.3 (SC 2:190); 1.8.4 (SC 2:63); J. N. D. Kelly, *Early Christian Doctrines*, 5th ed. (London: Continuum, 1977), 184.
[167] *Strom.* 4:13.92.2 (SC 463:208–10) Ἀλλ᾽ ἡμῖν γε ὁ ἀπόστολος εἰς τὴν τῶν θλίψεων ὑπομονὴν γράψων, «καὶ τοῦτο, φησίν, ἀπὸ θεοῦ· ὅτι ὑμῖν ἐχαρίσθη τὸ ὑπὲρ Χριστοῦ, οὐ μόνον τὸ εἰς αὐτὸν πιστεύειν, ἀλλὰ καὶ τὸ ὑπὲρ αὐτοῦ πάσχειν.
[168] *Strom.* 4.7.47.2, 5 (SC 463:136) citing Eph. 6:12; 1 Pet. 4:12–13; Rom. 8:36–37.
[169] *Strom.* 4.12.95.3 (SC 463:214).

and denial in both the positive and negative senses.[170] Both pericopes include Jesus' encouragement to testify before Jewish and Gentile prosecutors, without being anxious about what to say, because the Holy Spirit will teach them in that hour. The word for confess/acknowledge is ὁμολογέω, which has a wide semantic range, encompassing committing oneself, being of one mind, conceding to the truth of something, publicly claiming or professing allegiance.[171] The word for deny is ἀρνέομαι, which, equally broadly, means to refuse, disdain, deny the truth of, repudiate, disown, disregard and renounce.[172] The semantic range of the words suggests something more than just verbal acknowledgement or denial. Indeed, Clement considers them to reflect a personal investment in the person, mission and message of Jesus, the trajectory of the gnostic life. The confession/denial is made 'before men',[173] who can only destroy the body, and are not to be feared. Matthew's Jesus will in turn confess/deny the person before the Father in heaven, who can destroy both body and soul; Luke's Jesus confesses before the angels of God.

Mark 8:38 and Luke 9:26 speak of those ashamed of Christ and he of them, in only the negative sense. Luke omits Mark's qualification, 'in this adulterous and sinful generation'. The word 'ashamed' in each case is ἐπαισχύνομαι, to experience a painful feeling or sense of loss of status because of something or someone.[174] The context for both is Peter's confession of Christ, followed by Jesus' announcement that the Son of Man must suffer, and is not connected with the Holy Spirit testifying. The word ashamed, in this context, is a challenge to those who find offense in the necessity of the Christ having to suffer and die.

Clement refers to these passages in *Stromateis* 4.9, describing them as the Lord's explicit sayings on martyrdom.[175] He brings together both the confess/deny and be-ashamed versions 'written in different places', along with the reference to the Holy Spirit's teaching what to say. Clement emphasizes the specific wording of the Greek texts, the fact that Christ speaks of the one who confesses ἐν ἐμοί, 'in me' (Mt. 10:32; Lk. 12:8) but denies simply με, 'me'. It is this version, rather than ἐπαισχυνθῇ με, 'be-ashamed-of me', that Clement proceeds to expound. In agreement with the Valentinian Heracleon, he states:

> [Christ] rightly used, with regard to those who confess, the term 'in me', and applied to those who deny him the word 'me', because these, although they confess him with the voice, do not confess him in their conduct. But only those who live in the confession and conduct according to him confess 'in him', in whom he also confesses, having received them and being possessed by them; for he can never

---

[170] Common to Matthew and Luke, postulated as the common source Q 12:8–9; James M. Robinson, Paul Hoffmann and John S. Kloppenborg, eds, *The Critical Edition of Q* (Leuven: Peeters, 2000), 304–7.
[171] BDAG 708–9.
[172] BDAG 132–3.
[173] ἐνώπιον τῶν ἀνθρώπων
[174] BDAG, 357.
[175] SC 463:170–80.

deny himself. But those deny him who are not in him. For he did not say, 'Who will deny' in me, but 'me'. For no one who is in him will ever deny him.[176]

Thus, only those who are 'in Christ', and in whom Christ also dwells, confess. Just as Christ cannot deny himself, neither can those 'in him' deny him. Their identity is mutual, in contrast to those who deny, who are not 'in him'. Clement brings together the concepts of participation in Christ and confession of his name.

Clement is less restrictive than Heracleon, however, as to the nature of that confession. To be called to confess at trial is outside our power; it is providential.[177] For some this testimony occurs at the close of life, even though they have not confessed Christ by their previous conduct; this will be accepted by God.[178] But it is preferable to confess consistently by one's actions in life, as well as by word before the tribunal. The true and perfect martyr, however, is the one who has ascended to love; this is the perfect confession, the objective of *theosis* and perfection.[179] The gnostic martyr confesses from love; confession at trial is, as it were, an optional extra, but valuable for obtaining forgiveness, especially if one's life-confession has been imperfect.

Inevitability and blessing

Persecution provides the ultimate context for confession and denial. It is inevitable, even if it is not God's 'will'. Clement states that Christianity was prophesied to be persecuted to the end, flourishing despite the prohibition by rulers and their attempts to exterminate it.[180] Christ's prediction of persecution and murder for the sake of his name serves to encourage endurance.[181]

Clement acknowledges the blessedness of the persecuted. The perfect man or gnostic loves the Lord sufficiently as to not fear death.[182] This is part of the righteousness required by the beatitudes; blessed are those who are persecuted for righteousness' sake, and hunger and thirst for righteousness, and weep and mourn for righteousness, and who wish to be poor for righteousness' sake.[183] This is martyrdom for love's sake; suffering for righteousness, which brings blessing.[184] Citing 1 Peter 3:15-17 and 4:12-14, Clement exhorts his readers to sanctify God in their hearts, be ready

---

[176] *Strom.* 4.9.72.1-3 (SC 463:174) Καὶ καλῶς ἐτὶ μὲν τῶν ὁμολογούντων « ἐν ἐμοὶ » εἶπεν, ἐτὶ δὲ τῶν ἀρνουμένων τὸ « ἐμὲ » προσέθηκεν. Οὗτοι γάρ, κἂν τῇ φωνῇ ὁμολογήσωσιν αὐτόν, ἀρνοῦνται αὐτόν, τῇ πράξει μὴ ὁμολογοῦντες. Μόνοι δ' ἐν αὐτῷ ὁμολογοῦσιν οἱ ἐν τῇ κατ' αὐτὸν ὁμολογίᾳ καὶ πράξει βιοῦντες, ἐν οἷς καὶ αὐτὸς ὁμολογεῖ ἐνειλημμένος αὐτοὺς καὶ ἐξόμενος ὑπὸ τούτων. Διόπερ « ἀρνήσασθαι ἑαυτὸν οὐδέποτε δύναται »· ἀρνοῦνται δὲ αὐτὸν οἱ μὴ ὄντες ἐν αὐτῷ. Οὐ γὰρ εἶπεν· ὃς ἀρνήσηται ἐν ἐμοί, ἀλλ' ἐμέ· οὐδεὶς γάρ ποτε ὢν ἐν αὐτῷ ἀρνεῖται αὐτόν.
[177] *Strom* 4.9.73.5, 4.9.74.1 (SC 463:176).
[178] *Strom.* 4.9.73.1-3; 4.9.74.3 (SC 463:176, 178).
[179] *Strom* 4.9.75.3-4 (CCSL 463:180).
[180] *Strom.* 6.18.167.4 (SC 446:396).
[181] *Strom.* 4.11.78.1-2 (SC 463:184) ὡς διὰ τὸ ὄνομα αὐτοῦ διωχθησόμεθα, φονευθησόμεθα, ἀνασκινδυλευθησόμεθα.
[182] *Strom.* 4.4.14.1 (SC 463:78).
[183] *Strom.* 4.6.25-27 (SC 463:98-102) Matt 5:3-12.
[184] *Strom.* 4.7.46.1 (SC 463:134) Ὁρᾷς δι' ἀγάπην διδασκομένην μαρτυρίαν.

to defend their hope in the knowledge that it is better to suffer for well-doing than for evil. They should not think it strange to suffer but rejoice in their participation in the sufferings of Christ. The gnostic's *telos* is not in the physical life.[185] Similarly, commenting on 1 Peter 4:13–14, Clement recalls that those who are righteous will suffer for righteousness' sake, as did Christ. Those through whom God is glorified are the glory of God.[186] Paul writes that for Christ's sake we are being killed, regarded as sheep to be slaughtered.[187] Clement interprets this suffering for Christ's sake as a source of rejoicing.[188]

Clement's interest in Matthew 5:10–12, throughout *Stromateis* 4.6, is in the application of the beatitudes to the gnostic life.[189] The blessedness of martyrdom, as with distributing goods to the poor, is the demonstration of love shown to Christ, which is the path of the gnostic Christian. We are to seek the true treasure in heaven, the narrow path, taking no thought for the things of the body, seeking the truth in word and deed. Those who are persecuted for righteousness' sake are blessed because from love of God they gnostically despise death. They do not hate their persecutors but use trial as an opportunity to testify.[190] Clement does not define Christians by their experience of martyrdom, but rather places martyrdom and other responses to persecution within his broader scheme of the gnostic life. This is important for understanding Clement's three potential responses to martyrdom and the reasoning behind his so-called 'middle way', discussed below.

The *telos* of persecution

Clement views this life in continuity with the next, working towards the *telos* of perfection. This perfection entails achieving likeness to God (ὁμοίωσις Θεῷ) as far as possible – deification.[191] The road to perfection has many stages, is a response to God's invitation and grace, and requires the tutoring of the Παιδαγωγός, Christ.[192] Only Christ is perfect. All other people begin according to the image (εἰκών) of God but are yet to obtain the likeness (ὁμοίωσις), which is a process of growth according to the model of Christ; γνῶσις is essential to this.[193] As Osborn notes, for Clement the hope of Christians is to be like Christ; life is a preparation, confessing the way of the cross in purity and obedience; God in his goodness uses discipline to train and sanctify, producing beneficial results even from the evil of persecutors.[194] Suffering for

---

[185] *Strom* 4.7.46.1–47.4, 52.2 (SC 463:134–6, 144).
[186] Frag. *1st Peter*, (PG 9:732) from the 6th C Latin translation of Cassiodorus.
[187] Rom. 8:36; Paul quotes Ps. 44:22, probably to show that the persecuted are in solidarity with, rather than rejected by Christ; so Robert Jewett, *Romans: Hermeneia – A Critical and Historical Commentary on the Bible* (Minneapolis: Fortress, 2007), 548.
[188] *Strom*. 4.7.47.4 (SC 463:136).
[189] SC 463:98–128.
[190] *Strom*. 4.6.41.1, 41.4 (SC 463:126, 128) τὸ δεῖν γνωστικώτερον δι' ἀγάπην τὴν πρὸς τὸν Θεὸν θανάτου καταφρονεῖν· . . . γινώσκοντες πρόφασιν εἶναι μαρτυρίου τὸν ὁντινοῦν πειρασμόν.
[191] Ashwin-Siejkowski, *Christian Perfection*; Hagg, 'Deification', 169–73.
[192] Ashwin-Siejkowski, *Christian Perfection*, 14.
[193] *Protr*. 12.122.4 (SC 2:192–3); Hagg, 'Deification', 171–2.
[194] Osborn, *Clement of Alexandria*, 226–8.

righteousness is part of this process; being met with adversity and doing good, not for reward or renown, but in hope of completing life in the image and likeness of God.[195] Clement sees God creating good outcomes of persecution in this life, in continuity with the next. As van den Hoek explains, 'The human soul must be purified by a life of observance, so that the simple martyr, man or woman, becomes a gnostic martyr during their lifetime. Gnostic martyrdom is then defined as a condition or a way of life that is based on the rule of faith leading to divine knowledge.'[196]

Discipline and medicine

Persecution is not without benefits in this life. Clement perceives that while God uses discipline to punish sinners, he also applies it to correct and improve his people, to provide examples for others and to purge post-baptismal sin.[197] Christ the Παιδαγωγός aims to improve the soul by training it for a virtuous life, but instruction must be preceded by healing, both of which he provides.[198] God is healer to the sick, guide to the blind, water for the thirsty, shepherd to the sheep and teacher to the child.[199] God is good, and he only does good. Therefore, he uses punishments to cure the passions; reproof is like surgery, cautery or purgative medicine, restoring the patient to healthy and true humanity.[200] Some of God's medicines are mild and some are astringent.[201]

The concept of healing in Clement is not restricted to the Παιδαγωγός, however. Emily Cain explains that Clement uses medical concepts of blindness and healing as a metaphor of salvation, bring together healing of both body and soul.[202] Each person is ill and in need of a doctor, is blind, and cannot learn until cured; the Word is both physician and educator. Clement links the eye of the body with the eye of the soul to describe vision and knowledge of God that is transformed through baptism, akin to cataract surgery. The baptized person becomes part of an elite group of people who are fundamentally and radically different from the rest of humanity through their deified eyes, which are enabled to see God.

For Clement, persecution affords opportunity to develop the patience, endurance, love and forgiveness of enemies, obedience and disconnection from the world that lead to perfection and which continue into the next life. It is not the sole opportunity but it

---

[195] *Strom.* 4.22.137.1–2 (SC 463:284).
[196] van den Hoek, *Stromate IV*, 15. 'L'âme humaine doit être purifiée par une vie d'observance, de sorte que le simple martyr, homme ou femme, devient un martyr gnostique durant le temps de sa vie. Le martyre gnostique est alors défini comme une condition ou un mode de vie qui est fondé sur la règle de foi conduisant vers la connaissance divine.'
[197] *Strom.* 4.24.153.5–154.2 (SC 463:312–14).
[198] *Paed.* 1.1.1.4; 1.1.3.3 (SC 70:110, 112).
[199] *Paed.* 1.9.83.3 (SC 70:258).
[200] *Paed.* 1.8.65.1 (SC 70:226).
[201] *Paed.* 1.9.83.2 (SC 70:258) ὁ δὲ οὐ μόνον τὰ ἤπια ἐπιπάσσει φάρμακα, ἀλλὰ καὶ τὰ στυπτικά.
[202] Emily Cain, 'Medically Modified Eyes: A baptismal cataract surgery in Clement of Alexandria', *Studies in Late Antiquity* 2.4 (2018), 491–511. See also Michael White, 'Moral Pathology: Passions, Progress and Protreptic in Clement of Alexandria', in *Passions and Moral Progress in Greco-Roman Thought*, ed. John T. Fitzgerald (London: Routledge, 2007), 284–387. White examines Clement's *Quis dives salvetur* through the lens of Clement's concept of disease, desire and passion as moral and medical conditions requiring a philosophical doctor of the soul.

is a rich one. Patience and endurance are especially developed under trial, as is the opportunity to forgive and thence be forgiven.[203] This idea is developed in *Stromateis* IV. The persecuted are blessed because they are persecuted for righteousness' sake (Matt 5:3–12). For Clement, the righteousness is the central issue, the true desire for which they are blessed. Persecution, like poverty and other hardships thus trains and enables the gnostic to live righteously in preparation for eternal life.[204] The source of all excellence is when the gnostic scorns death for the love of God, which is why persecution brings blessing.[205]

Clement teaches that the soul separates from the body in a process throughout life, in preparation for natural death. This process of crucifixion to the world (Gal. 6:14) makes it easy to relinquish life when the time comes.[206] By learning gnosis and being devoted to the good life in the body, one is sent on to the state of immortality.[207]

> Therefore, the gnostic's goal is not located in the soul, but it depends on him to always be happy and to be the blessed and royal friend of God. And if someone were to surround him with contempt, the condemnation to exile and the confiscation of his goods and even at death, he will never be separated from his freedom nor his fundamental love for God.[208]

This does not mean that Clement is a wholehearted advocate of martyrdom, however. For Clement, martyrdom is one path to perfection, but not the only one. Drawing on 2 Corinthians, he determines that perfection comes through a variety of virtues, but no one except Christ is perfect in all things at once.[209] We are made martyrs out of love by the commitment to righteousness, by right conduct, because it is right to do good.[210] True perfection will come not from martyrdom alone, although Clement earlier acknowledges that this can make up for a lifetime of inadequate confession.[211] Clement uses a collage of Pauline citations regarding godly sorrow and patience in afflictions, which he says serve as 'the preparatory exercises of gnostic discipline'.[212] We are to be as perfect as we can whilst still abiding in the flesh, and this may come by different paths, including martyrdom.[213] Martyrdom is thus almost of incidental value to Clement. As Mullins Reaves observes, 'Clement's prioritization of the self-sufficient,

---

[203] *Strom.* 2.20.174, 178 (PG 8:1048, 1069).
[204] *Strom.* 4.6.25.1–2 (SC 463:98).
[205] *Strom.* 4.6.41.1 (SC 463:126).
[206] *Strom.* 4.3.12.5 (SC 463:74–5).
[207] *Strom.* 4.4.18.3 (SC 463:88).
[208] *Strom.* 4.7.52.2–3 (SC 463:144) Οὔκουν ἐπὶ τῇ ψυχῇ τὸ τέλος ἕξει ποτὲ ὁ γνωστικὸς κείμενον, ἀλλ' ἐπ' αὐτὸ τὸ εὐδαιμονεῖν ἀεὶ καὶ τῷ μακαρίῳ εἶναι βασιλικῷ τε φίλῳ τοῦ Θεοῦ· κἂν ἀτιμίᾳ τις περιβάλλῃ τοῦτον φυγῇ τε καὶ δημεύσει καὶ ἐπὶ πᾶσι θανάτῳ, οὐκ ἀποσπασθήσεταί ποτε τῆς ἐλευθερίας καὶ κυριωτάτης πρὸς τὸν Θεὸν ἀγάπης.
[209] *Strom.* 4.21.130.1–2, 5; 132.2–133.3 (SC 463:270, 272, 276–8).
[210] *Strom.* 4.22.135.1–4 (SC 463:280).
[211] *Strom.* 4.9.73.2–3 (SC 463:176).
[212] *Strom.* 4.21.132.1 (SC 463:274) Ταῦτα γνωστικῆς ἀσκήσεως προγυμνάσματα.
[213] *Strom.* 4.21.131–134 (SC 463:272–80).

progressive gnostic lifestyle contributes significantly ... to his relative lack of enthusiasm for martyrdom by death'.[214]

Confession, rather than martyrdom, is the priority. Clement presents every trial as an occasion for testifying. Therefore we are not to detest our persecutors, but undergo punishments at their hands, even if the trial is more protracted that we hoped.[215] The Christian, the one who is 'in Christ', is obligated to confess 'in him', in order to be confessed by him.[216] In this sense Clement is very much an individualist.[217] Clement is primarily concerned with the individual confessor, and the value of confession by life, not just at trial. Oral confession is not universally necessary, because the Spirit chooses and enables the confessor at trial.[218] Those who confess by life and word are better than those who confess by word alone. The key issue is that the motivation is love, which makes the 'really blessed and true martyr'.[219]

Towards perfection

For Clement, the present life of the gnostic Christian is an education for the perfected life beyond death, its goal the eternal contemplation of and assimilation to God.[220] Clement does not regard the soul as intrinsically immortal, but progressively attaining to incorruption. This purifying, progressive transformation involves acquisition of gnosis and divesting oneself of passions,[221] and may also involve painful pre- and post-mortem discipline.[222] In Clement's hierarchical view of heaven, the more advanced tutor the lesser, and receive different degrees of glory according to their *gnosis*[223] – not their explicit sufferings or martyrdom. 'The more we are subjected to peril, the more *gnosis* of which we are counted worthy.'[224] Punishment after death, as in life, is medicinal and temporary, by which sinners are brought to repentance.[225]

For Clement, salvation is a process of perfecting and deification, rather than an 'eschatological crisis'.[226] Persecution and martyrdom present one possible pathway. 'The perfect inheritance pertains to the perfect man, the one who attains the image of God.'[227] Clement assigns different degrees of glory according to *gnosis*, the lifelong

---

[214] Pamela Mullins Reaves, 'Multiple Martyrdoms and Christian Identity in Clement of Alexandria's Stromateis', StPatr 46 (2013): 61–8, at 67.
[215] *Strom.* 4.6.41.4 (SC 463:128).
[216] *Strom.* 4.9.72.1–2 (SC 463:174).
[217] Mullins Reaves, 'Multiple Martyrdoms', recognizes this individualism, in terms of constructed identity, rather than the diomological context presented here, although they are not incompatible.
[218] *Strom.* 4.9.73.5–74.1 (SC 463:176).
[219] *Strom.* 4.9.75.3–4 (SC 463:180).
[220] *Strom.* 7.3.13.1–2 (SC 428:68–70).
[221] *Strom.* 6.13.105.1 (SC 446:270); 7.10–11 (SC 428:180–216) and summarized well by Ashwin-Siejkowski, *Christian Perfection*, 152–74.
[222] *Strom.* 6.14.109.3–6 (SC 446:278).
[223] *Strom.* 6.13–14 (SC 446:270–88).
[224] *Strom.* 4.17.110.5 (SC 463:238) ὅσῳ πλείονος κατηξιώθημεν γνώσεως τοσούτῳ ὑποκείμεθα μᾶλλον κινδύνῳ.
[225] *Strom.* 7.2.12.5 (SC 428:66).
[226] Daley, *Hope of the Early Church*, 44.
[227] *Strom.* 6.14.114.4 (SC 446:288) ἡ μὲν τελεία κληρονομία τῶν εἰς ἄνδρα τέλειον ἀφικνουμένων κατ' εἰκόνα τοῦ κυρίου; see also Daley, *Hope of the Early Church*, 45.

denial of self, rather than a single act of martyrdom. Since no salvific value is specifically assigned to martyrdom, it is not something that should be deliberately sought.[228] Rather, when required, martyrdom is perfection, not because a man ends his life as others, but because he has exhibited the perfect work of love.[229]

Although not a vigorous advocate of martyrdom, Clement still accords it value. God brings good out of it. Rather than it being a calamity and a punishment, the martyrs are in peace, dying in the hope of immortality. Martyrdom is a 'glorious purification'; they are chastened a little and thereby God proves them and finds them worthy of sonship.[230] The gnostic martyr is cleansed from the stains of the soul and knows it will be better for him after his departure.[231] In contrast to his contemporaries, Clement does not develop the idea of martyrdom as a second baptism for the cleansing of post-baptismal sin. He makes only the vague statement that the witness of confession 'appears to be the cleansing of sins with glory'.[232] Clement held that the second repentance, usually understood as the public penitential process, was available only for involuntary sins, committed in ignorance or under compulsion; wilful sin was not covered by further repentance.[233] Clement's emphasis is rather on medicinal and educative punishment; this process, rather than the act of martyrdom, seems to be his solution to post-baptismal sin.

Clement's account of martyrdom is therefore mainly individualistic. The benefits of persecution to the church come through God's choice of individuals. There is even less emphasis on the benefit of martyrdom as witness to those outside the church. Confession for Clement is primarily before God, but he acknowledges that heathen will be amazed, and some led to faith.[234] The gnostic beseeches that those who hate him will repent,[235] but this is in the context of the general beneficence of the gnostic towards others rather than the witness of the martyr as such.

The appropriate response to persecution

If persecution is not prevented by God; if God foreknew it and uses it for good, both in this life and the next, and if persecution enables confession of one's identity in Christ, then it should elicit a positive response. The nature of this response, individually and collectively, answers the final two diogmological questions.

Joy, love and patient endurance

Clement emphasizes the blessedness of the persecuted from the beatitudes and 1 Peter, interestingly without the corresponding imperative to 'rejoice'.[236] These passages situate

---

[228] *Strom.* 4.4.17.1; 4.21.130.1 (SC 463:84, 270); 7.11.66.3–67.1 (SC 428:208–10).
[229] *Strom.* 4.4.14.3 (SC 463:78).
[230] *Strom.* 4.16.103.3–104.1 (SC 463:228) κάθαρσιν ἔνδοξον.
[231] *Strom.* 7.13.83.1(SC 428:254).
[232] *Strom.* 4.9.74.3 (SC: 463:178) Ἔοικεν οὖν τὸ μαρτύριον ἀποκάθαρσις εἶναι ἁμαρτιῶν μετὰ δόξης.
[233] *Strom.* 2.13.166 (PG 8:993–7). And see David P. O'Brien, 'The Pastoral Function of the Second Repentance for Clement of Alexandria', *StPatr* 41 (2006): 219–24, at 221.
[234] *Strom.* 4.9.73.5 (SC 463:176).
[235] *Strom.* 7.12.74.5 (SC 428:230–2).
[236] *Strom.* 4.6.25.1; 4.6.41.2; 4.7.46.3 (SC 463:98, 126–8, 136) cf. Matt 5:12, 1 Pet 1:6, 4:13.

joy in persecution's affiliation with Christ's suffering and the promised reward. Clement does not understand joy as an emotional state of conjured happiness; indeed, the gnostic seeks to be ἀπαθής.[237] For Clement, passionlessness is the disciplined control of sensual impulses; not eradication of feelings but a silencing of the negatives and a strengthening of the positives, especially love.[238] As Pinckaers explains, joy is an active choice, 'a criterion on the moral life, allowing us to distinguish true virtue and to show us the way to happiness, the path that leads to God'.[239] Clement is focused on this path; the elect person is led away from life, thanking and blessing God for his departure, embracing the heavenly mansion.[240] The martyr chooses the joy that exists in prospect through present pain, as thirst is the precursor to the pleasure of drinking.[241] This enables Clement to emphasize the motivation of love and the blessedness of the martyr according to Christ's teaching and to quote Peter's exhortation to rejoice in suffering and reproach. He then paraphrases Plato's *Republic*, that 'the just man, though stretched on the rack, though his eyes are dug out', adding 'will be happy'.[242] In the original passage, Glaucon contrasts the unjust man who seems just, with the truly just man who, despite imputations of wickedness, holds to his justice unwaveringly even to death. Of these two, he concludes, 'we may judge which of them is the happier'.[243] Clement's paraphrase affirms that the latter example suits the martyr who is steadfast in righteousness. His understanding of joy, then, relates to the satisfaction of the righteous response.

'Love your enemies', quotes Clement, adding that the enemies are those who follow the Devil's lead in treating Christ's followers with particular hostility, knowing that nothing will separate the gnostic martyr from God's love.[244] Clement specifies that the gnostic Christian is characterized, not just as one who suffers wrongfully, as if unmindful of injuries, but who prays for those who do him wrong.[245] Even when the gnostic conducts himself rightly, becoming a martyr out of love, he is not perfected until the close of life, that the excellency of the power be of God, not us. The gnostic therefore perseveres, knowing he is troubled on every side but not perplexed, persecuted but not forsaken, cast down but not destroyed.[246]

Endurance is implied in Clement's conception of the true Christian gnostic's journey to perfection in the knowledge and love of God. Patience as modelled by Daniel and Jonah is an aspect of the Christian's daily living, not just under persecution. The gnostic establishes the habit of doing good.[247] For some Christians in Clement's day, the

---

[237] *Strom.* 4.23.147.1 (SC 463:300); van den Hoek, *Stromates IV*, 30.
[238] Ashwin-Seijkowski, *Christian Perfection*, 159.
[239] Servais Pinckaers, *Passions and Virtue*, trans. Benedict M Guevin (Washington DC: Catholic University of America Press, 2015), 43–4.
[240] *Strom.* 4.26.166.1 (SC 463:334).
[241] *Strom.* 4.5.23.1 (SC 463:94).
[242] *Strom* 4.7.46.3, 52.1 (SC 463:136, 144) 1 Pet 4:13–14.
[243] Plato, *Republic*, Book 2, 361–2 (Loeb 237:134) κρίνωνται ὁπότερος αὐτοῖν εὐδαιμονέστερος.
[244] *Strom.* 4.14.95–6 (SC 463:214–6).
[245] *Strom.* 7.14.84.5 (SC 428:260).
[246] *Strom.* 4.21.131.1 (SC 463:272) citing 2 Cor. 4:7–11.
[247] *Strom.* 7.12.80.1 (SC 428:244) and see Alan Kreider, The *Patient Ferment of the Early Church: The Improbable Rise of Christianity in the Roman Empire* (Grand Rapids: Baker, 2016), 17–18.

suffering was intense but brief. For others, deprivation, exile or imprisonment were prolonged. All faced perpetual uncertainty for their earthly future, whether short or long. Clement portrays the gnostic life as one of perseverance.[248] The gnostic is to be an example of love, faith and purity (1 Tim. 4:12), and to be content in all circumstances (Phil. 4:11–13). He cites Hebrews 10:36–39 regarding the endurance that comes through faith and the examples in Hebrews 11 of the faithful endurance of the martyrs.[249]

The gnostic confessor

Clement is, as van den Hoek observes, 'moderately supportive of the idea of martyrdom but not at all exhortative'.[250] Confession, which Clement insists is necessary, is a voluntary act of acknowledging one's adherence to Christ. Whilst provocative, it is not necessarily a deliberate request for or incitement to martyrdom, however. Not all confessors were martyred, although confession opened the possibility, even likelihood of martyrdom,[251] and undoubtedly many confessors desired it. So, there is a sense in which advocacy of confession with high likelihood of subsequent martyrdom is in fact an exhortation to voluntarily give one's life. But if a way to confess – or at least avoid denial – could be found that did not necessitate death, that might be acceptable.

Clement's aversion to voluntary martyrdom is in keeping with his conviction that God chooses the martyr.[252] Clement is comfortable with the idea of God providentially providing for the confessor's escape, provided this is not facilitated by denial. God does not want his people to aid or abet evil, by facilitating the sin of the persecutor.[253]

> If he who kills a man of God sins against God, he who presents himself before the judgment-seat also becomes guilty of his [own] death. Likewise, him who does not avoid persecution, but out of daring presents himself for capture. Such a one effectively becomes an accomplice in the crime of the persecutor. And if he also uses provocation, he is wholly guilty, challenging the wild beast. And similarly, if he affords any cause for conflict or punishment, or retribution or enmity, he gives occasion for persecution.[254]

Clement discerns more than one way of confessing Christ; by life and by word, and not necessarily at trial.[255] Although confession may indeed lead to death, true

---

[248] *Strom*. 4.21.131.1–132.1 (SC 463:272–6).
[249] *Strom*. 4.16.101.1–103.2 (SC 463:224–8).
[250] van den Hoek, 'Clement of Alexandria on Martyrdom', 340.
[251] *Strom* 2.20.178 (PG 8:1069) τὸ εὐλαβὲς καὶ δι' αἱμάτων ἐνδείκνυσθαι.
[252] *Strom*. 4.9.74.1 (SC 463:176).
[253] *Strom*. 4.10.76.2 (SC 463:180).
[254] *Strom*. 4.10. 77.1–2 (SC 463:182) Εἰ δὲ ὁ ἀναιρῶν ἄνθρωπον Θεοῦ εἰς Θεὸν ἁμαρτάνει, καὶ τοῦ ἀποκτειννύντος αὐτὸν ἔνοχος καθίσταται ὁ ἑαυτὸν προσάγων τῷ δικαστηρίῳ· οὗτος δ' ἂν εἴη ὁ μὴ περιστελλόμενος τὸν διωγμόν, ἁλώσιμον διὰ θράσος παρέχων ἑαυτόν. Οὗτος ἐστι τὸ ὅσον ἐφ' ἑαυτῷ ὁ συνεργὸς γινόμενος τῇ τοῦ διώκοντος πονηρίᾳ, εἰ δὲ καὶ συνερεθίζοι, τέλεον αἴτιος, ἐκκαλούμενος τὸ θηρίον. Ὡς δ' αὔτως κἂν αἰτίαν μάχης παράσχῃ τινὰ ἢ ζημίας ἢ ἔχθρας ἢ δίκης, ἀφορμὴν ἐγέννησε διωγμοῦ.
[255] *Strom*. 2.20.174 (PG 8:1048); 4.9.74.1 (SC 463:176).

martyrdom is more than death; it is a work of love, a work of perfection, the entire life of the gnostic.[256] Clement is quite supportive of alternatives to execution, provided one's 'confession', verbal or otherwise, is not impaired. In a Stoic sense, the event of martyrdom is almost a matter of 'indifference' to the attainment of gnosis and perfection.[257] But it also stems from Clement's conviction that God does not actively will persecution and martyrdom, but rather *uses* such circumstances for good, not being restricted to a single path.

The confessor is not abandoned in his or her fundamental responsibility to confess Christ. When Jesus promises persecution and requires confession, he also promises the Holy Spirit will enable and even formulate that confession (Mt. 10:18–20). Baptism removes the sin which obscures the Spirit's light, enabling contemplation of the Divine, the Holy Spirit flowing from above.[258] 'The spiritual man, the gnostic, is the disciple of the Holy Spirit abundantly supplied by God, which is the mind of Christ'.[259] The gnostic soul becomes a temple of the Holy Spirit, overcoming fear and trusting God in the face of punishment.[260] The Holy Spirit comes to the confessor's aid, imparting what should be said in defence before the synagogues, rulers and powers.[261] Although verbal confession is not always necessary, it is given to some to make it, and 'if the spirit of the Father testifies in us, how then are we hypocrites, who testify with the voice?'[262]

Constructing a middle way?

Clement famously describes three attitudes to martyrdom; the denigrator, the volunteer and the gnostic.[263] The first two are disparaged, and the gnostic is upheld as the true martyr. Frend calls this 'the first explicit statement of two contrasting views of martyrdom, both of which were henceforth to be at variance with orthodoxy'.[264] Ferguson considers it 'mainstream teaching' that one was not to volunteer for martyrdom,[265] and describes Clement's favoured position as 'the model which was commended as normative Christian conduct'.[266] Middleton posits that if the Quintus pericope is a later insertion to the *Martyrdom of Polycarp*, then Clement 'becomes the *first* voice tempering that of those who were enthusiastic for death'.[267] Gibbons observes that distinctions which certain ancient authors made between licit and illicit forms of martyrdom have sometimes coloured scholarly analyses, particularly the tendency to

---

[256] *Strom.* 4.4.14.3, 15.4 (SC 463:78, 80–2).
[257] As pain, poverty and wealth are *adiaphora;* van den Hoek, *Stromate IV*, 16.
[258] *Paed.* 1.6.28.1 (SC 70:160–2).
[259] *Strom.* 5.4.25.5 (SC 278:64) Πνευματικὸν γὰρ καὶ γνωστικὸν οἶδεν τὸν τοῦ ἁγίου πνεύματος μαθητὴν τοῦ ἐκ θεοῦ χορηγουμένον, ὅ ἐστι νοῦς Χριστοῦ.
[260] *Strom.* 7.11.64.6–7 (SC428:204).
[261] *Strom.* 4.9.70.4 (SC 463:172).
[262] *Strom.* 4.9.73.4 (SC 463:176) Εἰ δὲ « τὸ πνεῦμα τοῦ πατρὸς » ἐν ἡμῖν μαρτυρεῖ, πῶς ἔτι ὑποκριταί, οὓς φωνῇ μόνῃ μαρτυρεῖν εἴρηκεν;
[263] *Strom.* 4.4 (SC 463:76–88).
[264] Frend, *Martyrdom and Persecution*, 354.
[265] Everett Ferguson, 'Early Christian Martyrdom and Civil Disobedience', *Journal of Early Christian Studies* 1, no. 1 (1993), 73–83, at 75.
[266] Ibid., 81.
[267] Middleton, *Radical Martyrdom*, 27.

simplistically equate voluntary martyrs with the New Prophecy and reticence toward martyrdom with Gnostics. Exactly when early Christians started drawing distinctions between licit and illicit forms of martyrdom, and how prevalent those distinctions were, remains an open interpretive question.[268]

Moss, noting that there was no Greek or Latin term for a 'voluntary martyr', finds evidence for such a category only in texts which distinguish attitudes behind different forms of martyrdom, which are 'never neutral'. Moss considers this distinction to begin with Clement, whom she believes neither knew nor used the martyr acts, which were written later.[269] Clement, she argues, is 'creating meaning', positioning *himself* (one who fled to avoid martyrdom) as the *via media*.[270]

> Much has been made of the ways in which Clement is influenced by the positions of his opponents and takes a reasonable middle position between them. Much more should be made, however, of the ways in which Clement creates this middle position and sets himself firmly on it ... perhaps he is more constructive than descriptive.[271]

Given that Clement precedes the final versions of the martyr acts, the question is what Clement is trying to achieve. Moss's suggestion, that Clement creates and promotes the middle way which justifies his own flight from persecution, imputes a motive that must be weighed against Clement's broader diogmology. Clement's response to persecution – avoidance or prudent withdrawal provided one's confession is not compromised – is entirely consistent with his views on the origin of, reason for and ultimate *telos* of persecution. If his desire to flee persecution is made the starting point, as Moss implies, then his view of persecution as an evil and his interpretation of God's providence must be made subservient to that. It seems more likely that his internally consistent diogmology drives his behaviour rather than vice versa. The path of the Christian gnostic is central to Clement's theology and is coherent with his views of God's providential activity in the context of persecution, and with his 'middle' position.[272] The opposite starting point, affirming that God does cause persecution and martyrdom, would logically require it to *not* be avoided (as Tertullian argued).

Was Clement *establishing* orthodoxy? De Ste. Croix considers Clement's condemnation of Gnostic deprecators as a defence of the orthodox position, but does not think Clement regards volunteers as heretics.[273] Middleton, following de Ste. Croix,

---

[268] See Kathleen Gibbons, *The Moral Psychology of Clement of Alexandria* (New York: Routledge, 2017), 117.
[269] Moss, 'Discourse of Voluntary Martyrdom', 541.
[270] Ibid., 542.
[271] Ibid., 544.
[272] Gibbons, *Moral Psychology of Clement*, 116–22, situates Clement's arguments within the context of his larger theorization of the Mosaic Law. His construction of the true martyr (the gnostic) is as one who obeys the law, that is, having the proper attitude toward life and death. But true martyrdom is not first and foremost a matter of bodily life and death but achieving knowledge of God and living the life appropriate to the one who has acquired it; a nuanced, situational reasoning according to the principles of life bestowed by God and not excessive attachment to embodied existence and its pleasures.
[273] G. E. M. de Ste. Croix, 'Voluntary Martyrdom in the Early Church', in *Christian Persecution, Martyrdom and Orthodoxy*, ed. Michael Whitby and Joseph Streeter (Oxford: Oxford University Press, 2006), 153–200, at 158.

presents a case for the prevalence of voluntary martyrdom, as a phenomenon common to both orthodox Christians and heretics in the early church.²⁷⁴ Middleton proposes that willing martyrdom was initially regarded as a mark of orthodoxy, but by the third century this was changing, largely due to how Clement was understood.²⁷⁵ This was a departure from a view of martyrdom that no longer distinguished orthodox from heretic.²⁷⁶ Middleton suggests Clement must deny that heretics are true martyrs, so he uses his opponents' arguments and labels to decry both volunteerism and avoidance. Clement's 'middle way' subsequently became the orthodox position; as Middleton puts it, 'the baby of radical zeal for martyrdom was thrown out with the bath water of heresy'.²⁷⁷ Hyldahl also recognizes the third-century attempt to steer the community toward passive acquiescence in arrest and faithful confession rather than volunteerism, and likewise regards a distinction between actual behaviours of orthodox and heretic as unsubstantiated.²⁷⁸ Tite regards Clement's 'model' as misleading, and fundamentally a polemical device.²⁷⁹ This would fit with a third-century redaction of the *Martyrdom of Polycarp* to contrast Quintus the volunteer with Polycarp the orthodox martyr.²⁸⁰

Whilst Middleton and Hyldahl are correct in their assessment of how Clement was subsequently understood and utilized, I suggest that Clement does not *intend* to define Christian orthodoxy by attitudes to martyrdom. He does, however, contrast authentic 'gnostic' martyrdom with inappropriate alternatives. Although potentially Clement's volunteerist and abstentionist 'categories' may be aligned with certain heresies, this is a polemical device; his distinctions are based on motivation. For Clement, the characteristic mark of the faithful martyr is the good and gnostic life.²⁸¹ The gnostic martyr, who has divested himself of the affections of the body, and is faithful through love to the Lord will not depart from his doctrine through fear of death; this is the τέλειος.²⁸² When called, he 'obeys, easily, and gives up his body to the one asking';²⁸³ he 'avoids denying Christ through fear because of the command ... nor does he sell his faith in the hope of offered gifts prepared, but in love to the Lord he will most gladly be released from this life'.²⁸⁴ One inappropriate alternative is the avoidance of martyrdom:

---

²⁷⁴ Middleton, *Radical Martyrdom*; de Ste. Croix, 'Voluntary Martyrdom', 153; but contra Alan Vincelette, 'On the Frequency of Voluntary Martyrdom in the Patristic Era', *Journal of Theological Studies* 70, no. 2 (2019): 652–79.
²⁷⁵ Middleton, *Radical Martyrdom*, 17.
²⁷⁶ Ibid., 28–9.
²⁷⁷ Ibid., 38.
²⁷⁸ Jesper Hyldahl, 'Gnostic Critique of Martyrdom', in *Contextualizing Early Christian Martyrdom*, ed. Jakob Engberg and Uffe Holmsgaard Petersen (Frankfurt am Main: Peter Lang, 2011), 119–38, at 122–3.
²⁷⁹ Philip L. Tite, 'Voluntary Martyrdom and Gnosticism', *Journal of Early Christian Studies* 23, no. 1 (2015): 27–54, at 53.
²⁸⁰ As Moss, 'Discourse of Voluntary Martyrdom', 544–5 argues, and Middleton, *Radical Martyrdom*, 27, concedes.
²⁸¹ *Strom.* 4.4.17.3 (SC 463:84).
²⁸² *Strom.* 4.1.1.1, 4.3.12.5, 4.4.14.3 (SC 463:56, 74–6, 78).
²⁸³ *Strom.* 4.4.13.1 (SC 463:76) ὁ γνωστικὸς ὑπακούει ῥᾳδίως καὶτῷ τὸ σωμάτιον αἰοῦντι φέρων.
²⁸⁴ *Strom.* 4.4.14.1 (SC 463:78) Οὗτος οὐ φόβῳ τὸ ἀρνεῖσθαι Χριστὸν διὰ τὴν ἐντολὴν ἐκκλινεῖ ... οὐ μὴν οὐδὲ ἐλπίδι δωρεῶν ἡτοιμασμένων πιπράσκων τὴν πίστιν, ἀγάπῃ δὲ πρὸς τὸν κύριον ἀσμενέστατα τοῦδε τοῦ βίου ἀπολυθήσεται.

But some of the heretics who misunderstand the Lord, having an impious and cowardly love of life; say that true martyrdom is the knowledge of the one and only God (which we also confess), and that he is a self-murderer and suicide who confesses by death; and they spread other cowardly fallacies of this kind to the public.[285]

The other extreme is the voluntary martyr:

But we also say, those who have rushed into death – for there are some, not belonging to us, only sharing the name, who hurry to give themselves up, these miserable murderers dying through hatred to the Creator – these, we say, cast out themselves not as martyrs, even though they are punished publicly. For they do not preserve the character of the martyr of faith, not having known the only God, but give themselves up to an empty death, as the Indian Gymnosophists to useless fire.[286]

Clement attributes inappropriate practices to wrong motives, which in turn originate with wrong beliefs. Neither avoiding nor embracing martyrdom are reliable distinguishers of orthodoxy, but what matters is the right-mindedness of the martyr, in other words, the mind of the true gnostic. The heretics who refuse to confess by death are cowards; those who rush on death lack the right understanding of God. The gnostic, in contrast, loves the Lord and responds in obedience.[287] As Middleton explains, Clement describes the volunteers in terms the Valentinians allegedly applied to the orthodox, and describes the avoiders from the alleged perspective of the volunteers.[288] It is, as Tite, Hyldahl and Middleton suggest, a polemical device. Importantly, Clement does not consider it imperative to be martyred; 'for this is not from us'.[289]

Mullins Reaves draws on social identity theory to show that Clement seeks alternative expressions of Christian identity to martyrdom by death, confronting both those who seek martyrdom and those who dismiss its value. Rather than Clement's position being exclusively a response to heretical Christians, he delineates different levels of belief within the Christian community, the highest being the true gnostic.[290] 'Clement promotes a moderate view of martyrdom death – one that affirms its validity

---

[285] *Strom.* 4.4.16.3 (SC 463:82–4) Τινὲς δὲ τῶν αἱρετικῶν τοῦ κυρίου παρακηκοότες ἀσεβῶς ἅμα καὶ δειλῶς φιλοζωοῦσι, μαρτυρίαν λέγοντες ἀληθῆ εἶναι τὴν τοῦ ὄντως ὄντος γνῶσιν Θεοῦ, ὅπερ καὶ ἡμεῖς ὁμολογοῦμεν, φονέα δὲ εἶναι αὐτὸν ἑαυτοῦ καὶ αὐθέντην τὸν διὰ θανάτου ὁμολογήσαντα, καὶ ἄλλα τοιαῦτα δειλίας σοφίσματα εἰς μέσον κομίζουσι.

[286] *Strom.* 4.4.17.1–3 (SC 463:84–6) Λέγομεν δὲ καὶ ἡμεῖς τοὺς ἐπιπηδήσαντας τῷ θανάτῳ· εἰσὶ γάρ τινες οὐχ ἡμέτεροι, μόνου τοῦ ὀνόματος κοινωνοί, οἳ δὴ αὑτοὺς παραδιδόντες σπεύδουσι τῇ πρὸς τὸν δημιουργὸν ἀπεχθείᾳ, οἱ ἄθλιοι θανατοῦντες. Τούτους ἐξάγειν ἑαυτοὺς ἀμαρτύρως λέγομεν, κἂν δημοσίᾳ κολάζωνται. Οὐ γὰρ τὸν χαρακτῆρα σῴζουσι τοῦ μαρτυρίου τοῦ πιστοῦ, τὸν ὄντως Θεὸν μὴ γνωρίσαντες, θανάτῳ δὲ ἑαυτοὺς ἐπιδιδόασι κενῷ, καθάπερ καὶ οἱ τῶν Ἰνδῶν γυμνοσοφισταὶ ματαίῳ πυρί.

[287] van den Hoek, *Stromate* IV, 17; 'Le concept d'amour domine toutes ces considerations de Clement'.

[288] Middleton, *Radical Martyrdom*, 38.

[289] *Strom.* 4.9.74.1 (SC 463:176) οὐ γὰρ καὶ τοῦτο ἐφ' ἡμῖν.

[290] Mullins Reaves, 'Multiple Martyrdoms', 62–3.

under certain conditions but does not promote it as an ideal achievement. More significantly, Clement advances an alternative type of Christian martyrdom – gnostic martyrdom – in which one's disciplined life, rather than death, bears witness to Christ'.[291]

In *Stromateis* IV Clement discusses gnostic martyrdom, consistent with both his concept of the gnostic path toward deification and his views on the origin and purpose of the persecution which provokes it. Martyrdom, for Clement, is one path to perfection, and dependent on God's determination, not ours. Confession is rooted in a Christian's identity 'in' Christ. It is necessary but does not have to be at trial. Hence, both cowardly avoidance and deliberate provocation of martyrdom are inconsistent with a true gnostic. The *telos* of persecution and martyrdom must be aligned with the *telos* of the gnostic life. I find myself disagreeing with Middleton's assessment that 'when not faced by critics of martyrdom, Clement is as enthusiastic about martyrdom as any other early Christian'.[292] Rather, I propose that Clement's position is consistent with his broader diogmology, and in agreement with van den Hoek, that he is 'moderately supportive of the idea of martyrdom but not at all exhortative'.[293]

Avoiding martyrdom

Between the extremes of martyrdom and apostasy lay the option of flight or lying low.[294] Clement's arguments against provoking martyrdom imply an approval of these. The true gnostic is not irrationally brave, nor afraid of a worse fate.[295]

> But the truly manly one, having the danger arising through the zeal of the multitude before him, courageously awaits what comes ... [they] protect themselves in accordance with correct reason, then upon God really calling them, surrender themselves confirming the call ... From love to God they willingly obey the call, with no other aim in view than pleasing God.[296]

Clement probably fled Alexandria during the persecutions of 202–3, but the timing of his justification of flight in *Stromateis* IV is unknown. He cites Matthew 10:23 in support of his contention that Christians must not be the authors or co-authors of evil, neither for themselves nor the persecutor or murderer. Christ gave instruction to flee

---

[291] Ibid., 63–4.
[292] Paul Middleton, 'Early Christian Voluntary Martyrdom: A Statement for the Defence', *Journal of Theological Studies* 64, no. 2 (2013): 556–73, at 563.
[293] van den Hoek, 'Clement of Alexandria on Martyrdom', 340.
[294] Clement, predating Decius does not discuss *libelli*, although Tertullian disparages the equivalent in *Fug.* 12 (CCSL 2:1150–3).
[295] *Strom* 7.11.66.3, 67.1 (SC 428:208, 210).
[296] *Strom* 7.11.66.4–67.1 (SC 428:208, 210) Ὁ δὲ τῷ ὄντι ἀνδρεῖος, προφανῆ τὸν κίνδυνον διὰ τὸν τῶν πολλῶν ζῆλον ἔχων, εὐθαρσῶς πᾶν τὸ προσιὸν ἀναδέχεται ... οἳ δὲ περιστελλόμενοι κατὰ λόγον τὸν ὀρθόν, ἔπειτα τῷ ὄντι καλέσαντος τοῦ θεοῦ προθύμως ἑαυτοὺς ἐπιδιδόντες, καὶ τὴν κλῆσιν ... ἀλλὰ διὰ τὴν πρὸς τὸν θεὸν ἀγάπην ἑκόντες πείθονται τῇ κλήσει, μηδένα ἕτερον σκοπὸν ἑλόμενοι ἢ τὴν πρὸς τὸν θεὸν εὐαρέστησιν.

rather than present oneself before the judgement seat. He bids us take care of ourselves, to avoid confrontation; the one who ignores this warning is audacious and foolhardy.[297] Flight is not considered valid because persecution is 'evil' – presumably he means in outcome, or he has seriously contradicted himself – nor is it valid because death is to be dreaded. It is valid to avoid complicity in the evil actions of the persecutor.

Although Clement is open to strategies for the avoidance of martyrdom, he never advocates apostasy. Those who avoid confession by death are 'impious' and 'cowardly'.[298] Those who have been compelled to deny are not friends of God; they have failed to love.[299] The one who denies cannot be 'in Christ'.[300] Because the Christian's identity is in Christ, he also denies himself.

> Does not he deny himself, who denies the Lord? For does he not rob his master of his authority, who deprives himself of his relation to him? He then, who denies the Saviour, denies life; for 'the light was life'. He does not call those men small in faith, but faithless and hypocrites, who have the name written on them, but deny that they are believers.[301]

Clement stops short of stating that the one who denies loses his salvation. He presents the positive picture of the true gnostic, for whom it is unthinkable that he would not confess. In his envisioned continuity between this life and the next, those who fall into post-baptismal sin are subjected to remedial discipline, although apostasy is not explicitly mentioned. 'Those falling into sins after washing are those who are disciplined; for the previous works are forgiven, and those coming to pass are purged'.[302]

Was Clement a universalist?[303] McClymond concludes, 'Clement may have held out some hope for universal salvation but without the clarity and definiteness that Origen did'.[304] Daley finds Clement cautious on the subject,[305] but as McClymont concludes, 'when a non-retributive and restorative idea of God's punishment has been fully conceptualized, the outcome is likely to be a doctrine of universal salvation'.[306] However,

---

[297] *Strom* 4.10.76.1–2 (SC 463:180) Ἐπὰν δ' ἔμπαλιν εἴπῃ· « Ὅταν διώκωσιν ὑμᾶς ἐν τῇ πόλει ταύτῃ, φεύγετε εἰς τὴν ἄλλην », οὐχ ὡς κακὸν τὸ διώκεσθαι παραινεῖ φεύγειν οὐδ' ὡς θάνατον φοβουμένους διὰ φυγῆς ἐκκλίνειν προστάττει τοῦτον· βούλεται δὲ ἡμᾶς μηδενὶ αἰτίους μηδὲ συναιτίους κακοῦ τινος γίνεσθαι, σφίσιν τε αὐτοῖς πρὸς δὲ καὶ τῷ διώκοντι καὶ τῷ ἀναιροῦντι· τρόπον γάρ τινα παραγγέλλει αὐτὸν περιίστασθαι, ὁ δὲ παρακούων τολμηρὸς καὶ ῥιψοκίνδυνος.
[298] *Strom*. 4.4.16.3 (SC 463:82–4) ἀσεβῶς, δειλῶς.
[299] *Strom*. 4.6.28.4 (SC 463:102).
[300] *Strom*. 4.9.72.3 (SC 463:174).
[301] *Strom*. 4.7.42.3–4 (SC 463:128–30) Οὐχ ἑαυτὸν ἀρνεῖται ὁ ἀρνούμενος τὸν κύριον; Οὐ γὰρ ἀφαιρεῖται τῆς κυρίας τὸν δεσπότην ὅ γε καὶ στερίσκων αὑτὸν τῆς πρὸς ἐκεῖνον οἰκειότητος. Ὁ τοίνυν ἀρνούμενος τὸν σωτῆρα ἀρνεῖται τὴν ζωήν, ὅτι ⟨⟨ ζωὴ ἦν τὸ φῶς ⟩⟩. Ὀλιγοπίστους τούτους οὐ λέγει, ἀλλὰ ἀπίστους καὶ ὑποκριτάς, τὸ μὲν ὄνομα ὑπογεγραμμένους, τὸ δ' εἶναι πιστοὺς ἀρνουμένους.
[302] *Strom*. 4.24.154.3 (SC 463:314) τοὺς μετὰ τὸ λουτρὸν τοῖς ἁμαρτήμασι περιπίπτοντας τούτους εἶναι τοὺς παιδευομένους· τὰ μὲν γὰρ προενεργηθέντα ἀφείθη, τὰ δὲ ἐπιγινόμενα ἐκκαθαίρεται.
[303] For full discussion see McClymond, *Devil's Redemption*, 239–46.
[304] Ibid., 240.
[305] Daley, *Hope of the Early Church*, 87.
[306] McClymond, *Devil's Redemption*, 242.

Clement does not seem to have 'made the conceptual leap from his general doctrine of salvation to a full-blown teaching on universal salvation'; rather, his concept of *apokatastasis* refers to the elect.[307] His ultimate stance on the apostate thus remains indistinct.

A collective response?

Clement's account of persecution and martyrdom is mainly individualistic. I base this claim on his emphasis that God chooses the martyr, and that martyrdom is one path for the gnostic to pursue. In terms of persecution more broadly, Clement acknowledges that the church as a community is persecuted, but he is primarily interested in the individual's confession of Christ.

Clement observes that Christianity was prohibited from its beginning, by rulers at all levels.

> But our teaching, prohibited at its first proclamation by kings, tyrants, particular rulers and their mercenaries, and innumerable men warring against us, endeavouring within their power to exterminate us, flourishes even more; not as human teaching dies or a weak gift withers (but no gift of God is weak) but unhindered, although prophesied to be persecuted to the end.[308]

Clement regarded the ancient, universal Church as a unity, collecting into one faith all those whom God ordained as righteous.[309] These righteous inevitably face persecution, as predicted (but not decreed) by God. Only those *in* Christ can confess *in* him. The church, despite being prohibited and persecuted, has the responsibility of diffusing the only true wisdom, God's wisdom, throughout the world.[310] Ashwin-Siejkowski notes a 'crucial link between the achievement of perfection and membership of the church ... The church is a school of true philosophy established by the divine pedagogue.'[311] Thus the church acts in service to the Παιδαγωγός within and despite a hostile environment. However, Clement does not paint a picture of the church as a community of support for Christian confessors, but as a repository of divine wisdom. Clement provides no known 'Exhortation to Martyrdom', and does not discuss how the church supports confessors or deals with apostates. Perhaps it was outside of his direct experience. Nor does Clement write a defensive apologetic against persecution. If he can be regarded as

---

[307] Ibid., 243.
[308] *Strom.* 6.18.167.4 (SC 446:396) Καὶ τὴν μὲν φιλοσοφίαν τὴν Ἑλληνικὴν ἐὰν ὁ τυχὼν ἄρχων κωλύσῃ, οἴχεται παραχρῆμα, τὴν δὲ ἡμετέραν διδασκαλίαν ἔκτοτε σὺν καὶ τῇ πρώτῃ καταγγελίᾳ κωλύουσιν ὁμοῦ βασιλεῖς καὶ τύραννοι, καὶ οἱ κατὰ μέρος ἄρχοντες, καὶ ἡγεμόνες μετὰ τῶν μισθοφόρων ἁπάντων, πρὸς δὲ καὶ τῶν ἀπείρων ἀνθρώπων, καταστρατευόμενοί τε ἡμῶν, καὶ ὅση δύναμις ἐκκόπτειν πειρώμενοι· ἣ δὲ καὶ μᾶλλον ἀνθεῖ· οὐ γὰρ ὡς ἀνθρωπίνη ἀποθνήσκει διδασκαλία, οὐδ' ὡς ἀσθενὴς μαραίνεται δωρεὰ <οὐδεμία γὰρ ἀσθενὴς δωρεὰ θεοῦ>, μένει δὲ ἀκώλυτος, διωχθήσεσθαι εἰς τέλος προφητευθεῖσα.
[309] *Strom.* 7.17.107.5 (SC 428:318–20).
[310] *Strom.* 6.18.166.4, 167.3 (SC 446:394–6).
[311] Ashwin-Siejkowski, *Christian Perfection*, 13.

an apologist, it is only to demonstrate the superiority and antiquity of the Christian 'philosophy' in the *Protrepticus*.

Ashwin-Siejkowski argues that Clement's ecclesiology, of which he presents a pioneering exposition, is crucial to Clement's project of perfection, contrary to a dominant scholarly tendency to focus on individualism in Clement's theology.[312] He argues that gnostic perfection is only achieved within the Christian κοινωνία, the 'natural habitat' of the gnostic Christian, and never outside it, and there is 'no tension between the individual and the community'.[313] 'It is within the "Great Church" that a Christian matures and becomes a Gnostic.'[314] Ashwin-Siejkowski supports his thesis by discussing Clement's explication of the characteristics of the true church. He allows that Clement's comments are scattered, without 'coherent elaboration' or 'full doctrines'.[315] He concludes that in Clement's ecclesiology, the visible church is composed of Christians at various levels of maturity in the faith, should contain the marks of unity, holiness, apostolicity and universality and is a διδασκαλεῖον or πόλις governed by the Logos.[316]

Whilst Ashwin-Siejkwski's argument does not contradict the diogmology I have set out and is consistent with Clement's theology of perfection overall, it is noteworthy that this author barely mentions persecution, and does not discuss martyrdom. Furthermore, Clement distinguishes the gnostic martyr, not by membership of a community, but individually. The gnostic alone shows true bravery and love for God. While persecution is directed at Christians collectively,[317] *martyrdom* belongs to the individual. Persecution is inevitable for the group, but must be responded to 'gnostically', with martyrdom providing one path to perfection.

As van den Hoek notes, Clement does not emphasize suffering on behalf of others.[318] He does, however, acknowledge some mutual benefit. Calling to make public confession is given to some, in order that by their witness and confession all might be benefitted. Those in the church will be confirmed in faith and heathens seeking salvation will be led to faith and the rest amazed.[319] In *Stromateis* VII Clement presents the gnostic labouring in the Lord's vineyard, freely choosing to do good and in expectation of due reward. Such a gnostic is only tested by God's permission, for the benefit of others, so they may be encouraged and strengthened by his endurance. The apostles, whom Clement regards as proficient in all paths to perfection, were brought to trial and martyrdom for the establishment and confirmation of the churches.[320] The benefits of persecution to the church therefore come through God's choice of individuals.

Mullins Reaves proposes that when greater sacrifice is demanded of group members, individually-oriented Christians such as Clement's gnostic will be less inclined to

---

[312] Ashwin-Siejkowski, *Christian Perfection*, 191–2; e.g. Mullins Reaves, 'Multiple Martyrdoms', 66.
[313] Ashwin-Siejkowski, *Christian Perfection*, 191–2.
[314] Ibid., 191.
[315] Ibid., 193.
[316] Ibid., 193.
[317] *Strom.* 4.11.78.2, 79.3 (SC 463:184, 186).
[318] van den Hoek, 'Clement of Alexandria on Martyrdom', 328, 340. Likewise, Mullins Reaves, 'Multiple Martyrdoms', 68.
[319] *Strom.* 4.9.73.5 (SC 463:176).
[320] *Strom.* 7.12.74.4 (SC 463:230).

perform their Christian social identity for the benefit of the community.[321] I suggest that Clement is not primarily concerned with the communal identity of the gnostic martyr but of the gnostic martyr's identity in Christ, and confession thereof; a subtle but vital difference. The church nurtures the gnostic, but not every gnostic is martyred.

Conclusion

Two principles underpin Clement's diogmology and serve as guard rails which both delineate and restrict the path he follows. Firstly, his perception of what God's goodness means forces the conclusion that God cannot be responsible for persecution, even to the extent of permitting it. Clement can readily blame the Devil and demons for this inevitable ground of conflict, which is inevitable because God predicts it. Clement must nevertheless insist that God is overall in control, and he can and will bring ultimate good out of this cosmic clash. Clement's appreciation of persecution is therefore teleological, its outcomes providential. Despite the potential goodness of outcomes, the evil of the act of persecution is not mitigated and should not be facilitated.

Secondly, Clement frames his theology in terms of the process of perfecting and *teleiosis* which begins in this life and continues into the next. The perfect, gnostic Christian grows in knowledge and love for God, which permits an almost detached experience of persecution in which martyrdom is but one path to perfection. True martyrdom follows the gnostic path, a lifetime of severance from this world that allows one to lose one's life out of love for God. Since God alone chooses those who take this path, it cannot be assumed and should not be actively sought. Whilst apostasy is to be shunned, there are many ways of confessing Christ, by life and by word. This confession is essential because it is intrinsic to the Christian's identity in Christ. For Clement, this confession articulates the fundamental conflict between Christ and the Devil, between a wholly good God and the source of evil in the world. Motive is primary in identifying the true gnostic martyr, as against those who avoid martyrdom from cowardice or who provoke martyrdom. Given that martyrdom is a select path, and given that persecution arises outside of God's will, Clement is comfortable with the avoidance of confession at trial, unless one is certain of one's calling. Even the apostate who does deny his own identity in Christ probably has the opportunity for discipline after death.

Gnosis, not martyrdom *per se*, is Clement's objective, and the Christian gnostic responds to persecution with love, joy, patient endurance, detachment from the world and growth in gnosis. True martyrdom is more than death, and confession without bloody martyrdom is acceptable. Confession is more than martyrdom because it is a way of life in Christ. The true gnostic therefore will not seek out martyrdom, but neither avoid it when it comes, because it is providential. The gnostic does not provoke it, out of love for the persecutor whose sins would be amplified by murder. Therefore,

---

[321] Mullins Reaves, 'Multiple Martyrdoms', 68.

Clement is supportive of the option of hiding and fleeing. Notwithstanding Ashwin-Siejkowski's demonstration of Clement's ecclesiology as the nurturing ground for gnostics, Clement's diogmology is individualistic.

There is thus an internal consistency to Clement's diogmology, and it certainly anchors in Scripture at key points. Nevertheless, questions remain. How is God's providential choice of the martyr and the assurance that God will bring a good *telos* out of persecution consistent with a God who merely declines to prohibit persecution? If confession of Christ is central to the Christian identity, and the locus of resolution of the conflict between God and the Devil, why is God non-permissive of persecution? These questions are not problematic for the other three fathers, because they start with a less constrained concept of God's goodness. Furthermore, they have a greater engagement with the theology of cosmic conflict, as we shall shortly explore.

3

Origen of Alexandria

Purposeful persecution

> *There is reason to call the unique death that is martyrdom, an exaltation.*
> Origen, *Exhortation to Martyrdom*, 50

The theology of Origen (c. 184–254) has a different shape from that of his predecessor Clement. Clement's *teleiosis* suggests broadly linear progress toward perfection; Origen's is circular, a return to the beginning, in what Mark Scott aptly describes as a 'journey back to God'.[1] Origen's diogmology must be understood within this overarching story of the creation, fall, physical life, ultimate perfection and restoration of rational creatures. Both Alexandrians espouse a progressive soteriology and eschatology, but they diverge at key points.

Origen in his context

A life of Origen

Eusebius provides us with most of Origen's biography.[2] Origen was profoundly impacted by persecution.[3] His father was martyred under Septimius Severus; when Origen tried to join him, his mother prevented him by hiding his clothes.[4] When Origen was actively teaching and writing in Alexandria,[5] he wrote of deprivation of Christian property and imprisonment, observing that:

> Our present struggle is against principalities and authorities and the rulers of the darkness of this world ... when losses and dangers, reproaches and accusations are raised up against us, the opposing powers do not do this that we should only suffer these things, but that by means of them we should be aroused either to great anger

---

[1] Mark S. M. Scott, *Journey Back to God: Origen on the Problem of Evil* (Oxford: Oxford University Press, 2012).
[2] Eusebius, *H.E.* Book 6, especially 6.1–3, 14–19, 23–28, 30–36; 7.1 (Loeb 265:8–22, 46–64; 68–78; 82–90, 136).
[3] Scott, *Journey*, 1.
[4] Eusebius, *H.E.* 6.1 (Loeb 265:10); Jean Daniélou, *Origène*, trans. Walter Mitchell (London: Sheed & Ward, 1955), 6–7. Eusebius may be utilizing an established literary 'humility' topos whereby Christians are prevented from specific actions by others, particularly pious mothers.
[5] Eusebius, *H.E.* 6.14 (Loeb 265:50).

or excessive sorrow or to the depths of despair, or ... we should be induced, when wearied and overcome by these nuisances, to make complaints against God.[6]

Eusebius records violence breaking out in Alexandria under Antoninus Caracalla in 215, from which Origen fled to Caesarea.[7] The years between 235 and 284 saw twenty emperors (and even more claimants) in rapid succession,[8] a time of great civil unrest.[9] Although emperors and aspirants would have been preoccupied with power struggles and frontier invasions, exacerbated regional tensions would doubtless have led angry, frightened mobs to readily turn on the local Christians. Nevertheless, Origen's time in Caesarea was remarkably productive in terms of literary output. He produced most of his homilies, most of his treatises, including *On Prayer, On the Pascha* and the *Exhortation to Martyrdom*, commentaries on John, Isaiah, Matthew, Song of Songs, Romans, Psalms, the minor prophets; *Adversus Celsum* and many letters, of which those to Gregory and Julius Africanus are extant.[10] Even Alexander Severus' mother, Julia Mamaea, allegedly discussed theology with Origen.[11]

In 235 Maximinus allegedly persecuted church leaders.[12] Among the confessors were Origen's patron and friend Ambrose, and a Caesarean presbyter, Protoctetus, addressed in Origen's *Exhortation to Martyrdom*.[13] Their imprisonment accords with higher clergy being targeted during this period. Origen, writing in the 240s against Celsus' second-century anti-Christian polemic,[14] notes that many of his contemporaries chose confession and death over denial and liberation.[15] He also acknowledges the discredit attached to Christianity, and predicts, correctly, that the peace currently being experienced by the church (under Philip, 244–9) was soon to end.[16] Eusebius attributes Decius' persecution to hostility toward his predecessor Philip, but this is improbable.[17] Under Decius in 249–50, Origen underwent 'chains and torture for the Word of Christ', his legs stretched in the

---

[6] *Princ.* 3.2.6 (Behr 2:396) aduersum principatus et potestates et mundi huius rectores tenebrarum nobis imminere certamen [Eph 6.12] ... cum damna, cum pericula, cum obprobria, cum criminationes excitantur aduersum nos, non id agentibus aduersariis potestatibus, ut haec tantummodo patiamur, sed ut per haec uel ad iram multam uel ad nimiam tristitiam uel ad desperationem ultimam prouocemur ... conqueri aduersum deum fatigati et uicti taediis compellamur.
[7] Eusebius, *H.E.* 6.19 Loeb 265:62) and see Paul L. Maier, *Eusebius; The Church History: Translation and Commentary* (Grand Rapids: Kregel, 2007), 203 n. 14.
[8] John Boardman, Jasper Griffin and Oswyn Murray, *The Oxford History of the Classical World* (Oxford: Oxford University Press, 1986), 860.
[9] Daniélou, *Origène*, 25.
[10] Eusebius, *H.E.* 6.23–25, 31–32, 36 (Loeb 265:68–78, 82–6, 88–90); Joseph W. Trigg, *Origen*, The Early Church Fathers (London: Routledge, 1998), 45, 53.
[11] Eusebius, *H.E.* 6.21 (Loeb 265:66–8).
[12] Eusebius, *H.E.* 6.28 (Loeb 265:80).
[13] Eusebius *H.E.* 6.23, 28 (Loeb 265:68, 80); Trigg, *Origen*, 43.
[14] For a discussion of Celsus' perspective on Christianity, see Robert L. Wilken, *The Christians As the Romans Saw Them*, 2nd ed. (Newhaven: Yale University Press, 2003), 94–125; Trigg, *Origen*, 52–61.
[15] *Cels.* 2.17 (SC 132:332). Origen attributed persecution to the direct fulfilment of Jesus' Mt. 10:18 prophecy that his followers would be brought before governors and kings, *Cels.* 2.13 (SC 132:318).
[16] *Cels.* 3.15 (SC 136:40).
[17] Eusebius, *H.E.* 6.39 (Loeb 265:92). Eusebius, *H.E.* 6.34 (Loeb 265:88), alleges Philip to have been Christian, but he was probably merely tolerant; Maier, *Eusebius*, 225. Timothy D. Barnes, 'Legislation Against the Christians', *Journal of Roman Studies* 58, nos. 1–2 (1968): 32–50, at 43, notes Dionysius of Alexandria's letter affirming Alexandria experienced a persecution a year *before* Decius' edict.

stocks and enduring threats of fire and torment from his enemies.[18] Origen survived this imprisonment but died soon after.[19] Whereas Clement seems to have been an observer, at arm's length from the lived experience of persecution, this cannot be said of Origen.

Influences on Origen

Origen does not acknowledge succession from Clement;[20] Ashwin-Siejkowski posits that Clement's influence was very early and Origen did not consider himself 'an heir of Clement's theology'.[21] Daley regards Origen's theological method as more explicitly scriptural and ecclesiastical and less concerned with Greek literature and philosophy than Clement's.[22] Origen is certainly more reticent of philosophy's value than Clement.[23] Apart from *Contra Celsum*, Origen rarely quotes or makes direct references to philosophers.[24] He considers philosophy idolatrously introspective and unable to provide saving knowledge of God, because it cannot address sin.[25] Yet he acknowledges the Christian can make good use of philosophy (provided he carefully critiques it)[26] and should be equipped to defend the faith against pagan philosophy.[27] Scott argues that Origen uses philosophy to illuminate theology and keeps opposing positions in tension.[28] Ciner is convinced that Origen consistently distinguished between Christian and Greek tradition, as a Christian theologian well aware of tensions between the two positions, but who was unafraid to confront and respect the truth within differing positions.[29] There is a plethora of scholarly discussion on the relationship of Origen to philosophy, to which only selective treatment can be given in this book.[30]

---

[18] Eusebius, *H.E.* 6.39 (Loeb 265:94).
[19] Maier, *Eusebius*, 213, n.23. Trigg, *Origen*, 61; Danielou, *Origène*, 26.
[20] Despite the inferences of Eusebius, *H.E.*, 6.3, 6.6 (Loeb 265: 16, 26).
[21] Piotr Ashwin-Siejkowski, *Clement of Alexandria: A Project of Christian Perfection* (London: T&T Clark, 2008), 33.
[22] Brian E. Daley, 'Origen's *De Principiis*, A Guide to the Principles of Christian Scriptural Interpretation'. in *Nova and Vereta, Patristic Studies in Honour of Thomas Patrick Hamilton*, ed. John Petruccione (Washington: Catholic University of America Press, 1998), 3–21, at 19–21.
[23] Henri Crouzel, *Origen, The Life and Thought of the First Great Theologian*, trans. A. S. Worrall (San Francisco: Harper & Row, 1989), 156–63.
[24] David I. Rankin, *From Clement to Origen, The Social and Historical Context of the Church Fathers* (Hampshire: Ashgate, 2006), 133–4.
[25] Crouzel, *Origen*, 157–8.
[26] As those who part the hoof but do not chew the cud gain some benefit, *Hom. Lev.* 7.6.4 (SC 286:344–6). In *Ep. Greg.*, (SC 148:186–194) Origen likens the use of philosophy to spoiling the Egyptians (Exod. 11:2, 12:35). See Crouzel, *Origen*, 159–61.
[27] On Origen's employment of philosophical arguments, see Silke-Petra Bergjian, 'Celsus the Epicurean? The Interpretation of an Argument in Origen, *Contra Celsum*', *Harvard Theological Review* 94, no. 2 (2001), 179–204.
[28] Scott, *Journey*, 3–5.
[29] Patricia Ciner, introduction to Orígenes, *Comentario al Evangelio de Juan*/1, Prólogo, F. García Bazán, Introducción, traducción y notas, Patricia, A. Ciner, Biblioteca de Patrística N° 115, Ed. (Ciudad Nueva, Madrid, 2020), 39.
[30] See, for example, Miyako Demura, 'Origen after the Origenist Controversy', in G. D. Dunn and W. Mayer, eds, *Christians Shaping Identity from the Roman Empire to Byzantium: Studies inspired by Pauline Allen*, Supp. *Vigiliae Christianae* 132 (Leiden: Brill, 2015), 117–39; Maren Niehoff, *Jewish Exegesis and Homeric Scholarship in Alexandria* (Cambridge: Cambridge University Press, 2011); George R. Boys-Stones, *Post-Hellenistic Philosophy: A Study of its Development from the Stoics to Origen* (Oxford: Oxford University Press, 2001).

One relevant aspect of recent scholarship is the intensified debate on Origen's indebtedness to Plato,[31] revealing what Scott terms a 'spurious, simplistic and unproductive' dichotomy between 'Origen the Platonist or Origen the Churchman'.[32] Origen certainly appropriates Platonist thought and vocabulary, but he adapts them to Christian theology rather than vice versa and he sees himself as primarily and fundamentally Christian.[33] Mark Edwards has also challenged previous assumptions about Origen as a 'Christian Platonist' who simplistically borrowed from or was dependent on Plato.[34] Origen interacts with Plato, but is 'demonstrably innocent of the copybook Platonism that is foisted on him by ancient and modern critics'.[35] This is certainly the case with Origen's diogmology, which exhibits key differences from Clement's.

Origen insisted that theological and exegetical interpretation must be 'worthy' of the divine and in accord with the rule of faith.[36] De Principiis describes the content of this apostolic teaching, culminating in his method of scriptural exegesis based on these truths.[37] Although Origen emphasized the rule of faith as his hermeneutic principle, he freely speculated on matters that were not explicit in Scripture and the corpus of church writings, and here his engagement with philosophical thought is most evident. It is important to appreciate that we cannot access the entire body of Origen's thought. Most of his massive corpus of works is lost,[38] and more than half of his extant works are in redacted fourth- to fifth-century Latin translations, tainted by perspectives of those who agreed or disagreed with him.[39] Nevertheless, Origen's extant oeuvre does exhibit an internal coherence, albeit with some flexibility, as recognized by Trigg.[40]

Distinctively, Origen taught the pre-existence of intellectual or rational souls[41] in the pre-cosmic realm before their bodily creation.[42] Patricia Ciner considers this pre-

---

[31] A turning point came with Karen Jo Torjesen, *Hermeneutical Procedure and Theological Method in Origen's Exegesis*, Patrische Texte und Studien 28 (Berlin: de Gruyter, 1986), who argued that Origen's exegesis is theologically determined. Pages 1–12 provide a summary of criticisms of Origen's exegetical method with reference to his supposed indebtedness to Greek philosophical method.

[32] Scott, *Journey*, 3.

[33] Ibid., 42.

[34] Mark J. Edwards, *Origen Against Plato* (Aldershot: Ashgate, 2002); Edwards, 'Origen's Platonism, Questions and Caveats', *Zeitschrift für antikes Christentum* 12, no. 1 (2008): 20–38.

[35] Edwards, 'Origen's Platonism', 31.

[36] Shawn W. Keough, 'Eschatology Worthy of God: The Goodness of God and the Groaning of Creation in Origen's *De Principiis*', *StPatr* 46 (2010), 189–94.

[37] Brian E. Daley, 'Incorporeality and "Divine Sensibility": The Importance of *De Principiis* 4.4 for Origen's Theology', *StPatr* 41 (2006): 139–44. This article builds on Daley's 1998 essay, 'Origen's *De Principiis*'.

[38] Ronald E. Heine, 'The Alexandrians', in *The Cambridge History of Early Christian Literature*, ed. Frances Young, Lewis Ayers and Andrew Louth (Cambridge: Cambridge University Press, 2004), 121–7.

[39] For an overview of the textual tradition see Torjesen, *Hermeneutical Procedure*, 14–18.

[40] Joseph W. Trigg, 'Was Origen a Systematic? A reappraisal', *StPatr* 41 (2006), 139–44.

[41] Whilst 'rational creatures' is a common scholarly translation, Ciner prefers to translate νοες as 'intellectual creature', with free-will bestowed by God in the pre-existence, and reserves λογικος for beings endowed with Logos attaining total freedom through spiritual progress, as a better representation of Origen's theology; Patricia Ciner, pers. com. 23/6/21; also Ciner, Introduction to Orígenes, *Comentario al Evangelio de Juan*, 1, 38.

[42] *Princ.* 1.7.1; 2.2.2; 2.9.1; 4.4.8 (Behr 1:120; 1:154; 2:238; 2:578); Scott, *Journey*, 61–3.

existence, which she translates as that which gives origin, to be a fundamental and central pillar of his theology.[43] Although this suggests Platonist influence, Origen distances himself from Plato,[44] situating pre-existence in the eternal being of the Son, whereby God has always been omnipotent.[45] The souls were created good, but fell to different degrees as a consequence of free will, instigated by the Devil.[46] The pre-cosmic fall necessitated the creation of the physical realm, including a place of post-mortem instruction, as a schoolroom or hospital for souls in their divinization or journey back to God.[47] This process, governed by his good providence, extends beyond death, through the aeons.[48] This 'journey of the soul' is central to Origen's exegesis, as well as his theology, as Torjesen demonstrates.[49] Origen organizes his basic themes, such as his trinitarian schema of *De principiis* and the direction and pattern of his exegesis according to this journey, which is the means of redemption, and entails purification (healing) from sin, knowledge of the *Logos* and finally face-to-face knowledge of God.[50]

For Origen, final, total immersion in the divine life will see the end of evil and a return to the primeval cosmic harmony, ἀποκατάστασις.[51] Ciner identifies a correlation or balance between the diversification or divergence of the pre-existent intelligences as a result of their free will, and the subsequent universal and salvific return of each being in unity.[52] Origen taught that all creatures will eventually freely choose subjection to God as a result of teaching, persuasion and educative punishment, which will ultimately cease.[53] The logical corollary of this is universal salvation, including, arguably, of the Devil himself.[54] Controversy arose over these teachings, or at least how they were understood.[55] They were condemned at the Council of Constantinople in 553.[56] Origen's diogmology must be understood within this broader framework; it especially influences his view of the origin of persecution and its *telos*, and hence the appropriate response to it.

[43] Patricia Ciner, introduction to *Comentario al Evangelio de Juan*/1, 37.
[44] Cels. 4.40 (SC 136:290); *Princ.* 3.6.1 (Behr 2:440); Scott, *Journey*, 58–60.
[45] *Princ.* 1.2.10; 1.7.1; 4.3.15 (Behr 1:56–60; 1:120; 2:558) *Hom Gen* 1.1 (PG 12:145) *Com. Jn.* 1.104–5 (SC 120:114–16) Scott, *Journey*, 53–60.
[46] *Princ.* 1.5.3; 1.5.5 *in nobis esse atque in nostris motibus*; 1.8.1; 2.9.6 (Behr 1:96; 102–4; 132–4; 2:244–6) Scott, *Journey*, 62–6.
[47] *Princ.* 2.1.2; 2.9.1, 6; 2.10.6; 2.11.6; 3.6.8 (Behr 1:146; 2:238, 246; 2:262–4; 276–8; 2:452); Scott, *Journey*, 93–100; Daniélou, *Origène*, 277.
[48] *Princ.* 1.6.3; 3.1.13; 3.6.6 (Behr 1:112–4; 2:326–8; 2:448); Daniélou, *Origène*, 285–6; Scott, *Journey*, 98.
[49] Torjesen, *Hermeneutical Procedure*, on Psalm 37 pp. 32–4, 43–8, broadly in Chapter 3, 70–107 and specifically in respect to Song of Songs, 93–6; Numbers, 96–100; Jeremiah, 100–5 and the Gospels, 105–7.
[50] Torjesen, *Hermeneutical Procedure*, 71–87.
[51] *Princ.* 1.6.2; 2.11.6; 3.5.7; 3.6.3 (Behr 1:106–110; 2:276–8; 2:434–6; 2:444); *Cels.* 8.72 (SC 150:340); Daniélou, *Origène*, 287–9; Scott, *Journey*, 150–1.
[52] Ciner, introduction to *Comentario al Evangelio de Juan*/1, 37.
[53] *Princ.* 3.5.8 (Behr 2:436–8).
[54] J. N. D. Kelly, *Early Christian Doctrines*, 5th ed. (London: Continuum, 1977), 473–4. But see later discussion, also Mark J. Edwards, 'The Fate of the Devil in Origen', *Ephemerides Theologicae Lovanienses* 86, no. 1 (2010), 163–70, at 163, and Scott, *Journey*, 151.
[55] Daniélou, *Origène*, 288–9.
[56] For detail see Elizabeth A. Clark, *The Origenist Controversy: The Cultural Construction of an Early Christian* Debate (Princeton: Princeton University Press, 1992). For a defence of Origen's orthodoxy, see Mark J. Edwards, *Catholicity and Heresy in the Early Church* (Surrey: Ashgate, 2009), 79–103 and Crouzel, *Origen*, 169–76.

Origen and Scripture

Origen pioneered the exegetical study of the entirety of Scripture and wrote detailed commentary on whole books. He endeavoured to establish the text accurately, for which he produced the *Hexapla*.[57] Older scholarship, exemplified by Hanson,[58] offers a negative evaluation of Origen's exegesis and assumes a dichotomy between 'Alexandrian' and 'Antiochene' exegesis which is now repudiated.[59] Daniélou offers a more positive appraisal and finds in Origen established trends in Christian exegesis that predate these 'schools'.[60] Simonetti observes that the features of Origen's exegesis, taken individually, can be found in exegetes who preceded him, particularly Clement. Nevertheless, Origen organized and systematized these techniques, expanding and developing them into a 'total synthesis'.[61]

Martens explicates Origen's vision of the ideal scriptural interpreter as one on a spiritual journey culminating in the vision of God.[62] Indeed, as Westerholm observes, Origen regarded the struggle to understand the mysteries of the text as 'one of the divinely appointed means for bringing believers to maturity'.[63] Only Christ's coming makes the full significance of the Old Testament evident, and each text has a link to a spiritual reality, for our edification. Only the mind profoundly shaped by Scripture, in concert with purity of life, is equipped to elucidate it in a manner worthy of God.[64] Kolbet argues that 'Origen's practice of biblical interpretation is better understood as a hermeneutical exercise fostering certain ascetic habits of mind and his experience of deep prayer.'[65] This accords with O'Keefe and Reno's view that the rule of faith was also a rule for life; 'only a person whose vision has been refined by prayer, fasting and self-control could attempt such a passage' to participation in the unspeakable mysteries.[66] Identifying the deeper Christological meaning requires the guidance of the Holy Spirit, and the mind of Christ; 'consequently the spiritual interpretation is only to be understood in a context of contemplation and prayer.'[67] It is often assumed that allegorical interpretation necessarily leads to loss of hermeneutical control. Hall

---

[57] For details see Eugene Ulrich, 'Origen's Old Testament Text: The transmission history of the Septuagint to the third century', in *Origen of Alexandria, his World and his Legacy*, ed. Charles Kannengeisser and William L. Petersen (Indiana: University of Notre Dame, 1988), 3–33.
[58] R. P. C. Hanson, *Allegory and Event* (London: SCM, 1959).
[59] Peter W. Martens, 'Revisiting the allegory/typology distinction: the case of Origen', *Journal of Early Christian Studies* 16, no. 3 (2008), 283–317; also Donald Fairbairn, 'Patristic Exegesis and Theology: The Cart and the Horse', *Westminster Theological Journal* 69, no. 1 (2007), 1–19 and more broadly, Frances Young, *Biblical Exegesis and the Formation of Christian Culture* (Peabody, MS: Hendrickson, 2002), 2.
[60] Daniélou, *Origène*, 161.
[61] Manlio Simonetti, *Biblical Interpretation in the Early Church, A Historical Introduction to Patristic Exegesis* (Edinburgh: T&T Clark, 1994).
[62] Peter W. Martens, *Origen and Scripture: The Contours of the Exegetical Life* Oxford Early Christian Studies (Oxford: Oxford University Press, 2012).
[63] Stephen Westerholm and Martin Westerholm, *Reading Sacred Scripture: Voices from the History of Interpretation* (Grand Rapids: Eerdmans, 2016), 79.
[64] Ibid., 67–101 for the extended argument.
[65] Paul R. Kolbet, 'Rethinking the Rationales for Origen's Use of Allegory', *StPatr* 56 (2013), 41–9.
[66] John J. O'Keefe and Russell R. Reno, *Sanctified Vision: An Introduction to Early Christian Interpretation of the Bible* (Baltimore: Johns Hopkins, 2005), 129; also 132–9.
[67] Crouzel, *Origen*, 73–4. Similarly, Daniélou, *Origène*, 158.

challenges this assumption by emphasizing Origen's Christocentricity. Origen argued that the Holy Spirit produced one unified Scripture with an eschatological fulfilment through Christ in mind throughout.[68]

De principiis 4.1–3 provides Origen's paradigm for scriptural interpretation,[69] but as Daley argues, it is no mere appendix to the work. Rather, the ἀρχαί expounded in Books 1–3 and revisited in 4.4 are both the ontological principles of the world's being and the principles for understanding the content of revelation, and therefore the basis for proper biblical interpretation.[70] Torjesen identifies, in the preface to *De principiis* I, Origen's primary intent to deal with the question of Scripture. The spiritual sense of Scripture provides resolution of the unanswered questions from the apostolic preaching (rule of faith); such truth comes from Christ alone as revealed in his Scriptures.[71] Origen begins by emphasizing the divine inspiration of Scripture, as evidenced by the predicted survival of the persecuted church.[72] He posits three senses of Scripture, corresponding to the three aspects of humanity: body, soul and spirit. The flesh or primary sense of Scripture edifies the simple Christian. The more advanced appreciate its soul and the perfect its spiritual sense.[73] False interpretations of Scripture arise when the bare literal sense is taken without understanding the spiritual sense.[74] The right method must be used, in accordance with the rule of the apostolic church, and this requires the mind of Christ.[75] The key themes, often concealed by the Spirit in narrative form, are the nature of God and his Son, the incarnation, the rational creatures and the origin of wickedness.[76] In order to show spiritual connections to the deeper sense, the Word arranged for certain stumbling blocks, offences and impossibilities to be embedded in Scripture, the mystical meaning of which must be searched out.[77] Origen states, 'and at other times, even impossibilities are legislated for the sake of the more skilful and inquisitive, in order that, giving themselves to the toil of investigating what is written, they may gain a sound conviction concerning the necessity of seeking in such instances a meaning worthy of God'.[78]

Origen's 'answers' to the diogmological questions are sometimes embedded in these deeper spiritual meanings, but not always. Ultimately, his interpretation is rooted in his

---

[68] Christopher A. Hall, 'Origen: Exegete, Theologian, Disciple', in *Sources of the Christian Self: A Cultural History of Christian Identity*, ed. James M. Houston James M. and Jens Zimmerman (Grand Rapids: Eerdmans, 2018), 133–45, esp. 136–41.

[69] Most of the text of *De Principiis* 1–3 and 4.4 is Rufinus' edited Latin version; Behr, Introduction, *On First Principles*, trans. and ed. John Behr (Oxford: Oxford University Press, 2017), lxxxiv–xc; SC 252 and 268. The *Philocalia* ch. 1 contains fragments of the original Greek Περὶ Ἀρχῶν, particularly 4.1–3 (Behr, xcv–xcvi; SC 302). For an introduction, see Behr, *First Principles*, xx–xxiv, xlvi–liv, who agrees with Daley's interpretation of Book IV.

[70] Daley, 'Origen's *De Principiis*', 3–21.

[71] Torjesen, *Hermeneutical Procedure*, 36.

[72] *Princ.* 4.1.1–2 (Behr 2:458–64)

[73] *Princ.* 4.2.4 (Behr 2:496–8)

[74] *Princ.* 4.2.2 (Behr 2:488–92)

[75] *Princ.* 4.2.3 (Behr 2:492–4)

[76] *Princ.* 4.2.7 (Behr 2:508–10)

[77] *Princ.* 4.2.9 (Behr 2:514–16) σκάνδαλα καὶ προσκόμματα καὶ ἀδύνατα.

[78] *Princ.* 4.2.9 (Behr 2:516) Καὶ ἄλλοτε καὶ ἀδύνατα νομοθετεῖται διὰ τοὺς ἐντρεχεστέρους καὶ ζητητικωτέρους, ἵνα τῇ βασάνῳ τῆς ἐξετάσεως τῶν γεγραμμένων ἐπιδιδόντες ἑαυτοὺς πεῖσμα ἀξιόλογον λάβωσι περὶ τοῦ δεῖν τοῦ θεοῦ ἄξιον νοῦν εἰς τὰ τοιαῦτα ζητεῖν.

conviction, held in common with other early fathers, that Christ is the interpretive key for all of Scripture and that he is seen throughout the Old Testament, in types as well as allegories.[79] Types are forms, figures or patterns which illuminate the Christological unity of the text.[80] Allegories are interpretations which claim the deeper rather the surface meaning of the text as the true meaning.[81] Both are 'spiritual' reading strategies that interpret the Scriptures in terms of the divine economy,[82] and both are used extensively by Origen for the same essential purpose. As Torjesen explains, 'his exegesis is thoroughly dominated by his understanding of the Logos', that is, recognition of 'a complex and rich web of relationships between the Logos and Scripture', with whom Scripture originates and in whose presence and teaching the spiritual sense is defined.[83] An awareness of Origen's exegetical strategies is therefore helpful in understanding the Scriptural basis of his theology of persecution.

Persecution: Permitted by God

The first diogmological question concerns the origin or source of persecution, specifically the involvement of God. Origen's starting point, as Clement's, is that there is only one God, that God is good and is not the source of evil. Origen's diogmology is, however, more detailed and coherent than his predecessor's. Not content to merely accept humanity's fall, Origen ventures behind it.

The goodness and providence of God

In *De principiis*, Origen affirms that God is the Creator and providential administrator of the world; nothing came about by chance.[84] God is incomprehensible, and far better than we can perceive him to be; unspeakably and incalculably superior, the purest and the brightest.[85] He is 'a simple intellectual being', containing no greater or lesser parts, but is unity and oneness, 'the intellect and source' from which all intellect originates.[86] Only the Father, Son and Holy Spirit have goodness in their essential being.[87] Being good, God loves everything that exists; he detests nothing he has made and he cares for all things.[88] God could not at any time have ceased to do good, to create and to provide.[89]

---

[79] O'Keefe and Reno, *Sanctified Vision*, 24–5.
[80] Ibid., 69.
[81] Ibid., 89.
[82] Ibid., 90.
[83] Torjensen, *Hermeneutical Procedure*, 108.
[84] *Princ.* 2.1.4. (Behr 1:150).
[85] *Princ.* 1.1.5 (Behr 1:28–30).
[86] *Princ.* 1.1.6 (Behr 1:30) Non ergo corpus aliquod aut in corpore esse putandus est deus, sed intellectualis natura simplex, nihil omnio in se adiunctionis admittens; uti ne maius aliquid et inferius in se habere credatur, sed ut sit ex omni parte μονας, et ut ita dicam ἑνας, et mens ac fons, ex quo initium totius intellectualis naturae uel mentis est.
[87] *Princ.* 1.2.13; 1.5.3; 1.6.2 In hac enim sola trinitate ... bonitas substantialiter inest, 1.8.3 (Behr 1:64; 96; 106; 136).
[88] *Comm. Jo.* 20.17.148 (SC 290:228).
[89] *Princ.* 1.4.3 (Behr 1:84).

Against those who posit a dualistic distinction between a God of goodness and a God of justice, Origen argues that both goodness and justice apply to the one Creator God, for goodness necessarily encompasses justice.[90]

God governs his creation by providence, which is an extension of his goodness. Origen insists that all things are sent by God; nothing happens without his will. He goes further than Clement, in asserting that God permits evil, in a controlled way:

> All those events that happen in the world, which are considered indifferent, whether they be sorrowful or are of any other kind, are brought about neither by God nor yet without him; not only does he not prevent those wicked and opposing powers who wish to wreak such events, but he even permits them to do so, although only on certain occasions and to certain persons ... Therefore, the divine Scripture teaches us to accept all that happens to us as sent by God, knowing that nothing happens without God. That such is the case, that is, that nothing happens without God, how can we doubt, when our Lord and Saviour clearly proclaims and says, *Are not two sparrows sold for a penny, and not one of them shall fall onto the ground without your Father who is in heaven?*[91]

Origen cites Matthew 5:44–45, in which Christ urges imitation of the Father, who treats good and evil people alike with gracious generosity, in defence of God's goodness to all his creation.[92] God's children are not to fear what men can do, because not even sparrows fall to the ground without the Father's permission (Mt.10:28–31). Divine providence completely embraces all things, including persecution and suffering as well as sustenance.[93] The mission of the church and the provision of inspired Scripture are also providential, divinely empowered to bring about God's purposes.[94]

Nevertheless, Origen's view of providence is not deterministic. The world is not subjected to God by necessity or force, 'but by word, by reason, by teaching, by exhortation to better things, by the best instruction, and by threatenings, merited and appropriate'.[95] This involves training, even chastisement, in ways which God alone determines, but which 'always preserves the free will of rational creatures'.[96] In fact,

---

[90] *Princ.* 2.5.1–4 (Behr 2:188–200).

[91] *Princ.* 3.2.7 (Behr 2:398) ... quae fiunt in hoc mundo, qaue media aestimantur, siue illa tristia sint siue quoquomodo sunt, non quidem a deo fiunt nec tamen sine deo, dum malignas et contrarias uirtutes talia uolentes operari non solum non prohibet deus, sed et permittit faecere haec, sed certis quibusque et temporibus et personis ... Propterea docet nos scriptura diuina omnia quae accidunt nobis tamquam a deo illata suscipere, scientes quod sine deo nihil fit. Quod autem haec ita sint, id est, quod nihil sine deo fiat, quomodo possumus dubitare, domino et saluatore euidenter pronuntiante et dicente: Nonne duo passeres asse ueneunt, et unus ex ipsis non cadet super terram sine patre uestro, qui in caelis est?

[92] Origen, *Cels.* 4.28 (SC 136:250) Specifically, Origen refutes Celsus' accusation that the Christian God has abandoned his world to attend to Christians alone.

[93] *Cels.* 8.67; 8.70 (SC 150:330, 336–8).

[94] So argues Peter W. Martens, 'On Providence and Inspiration: A Short Commentary on ΠΕΡΙ ΑΡΧΩΝ 4.1.7'. *StPatr* 41 (2006), 201–6. Similarly, Mark W. Elliott, *Providence Perceived: Divine Action from a Human Point of View* (Berlin: De Gruyter, 2015), 17–18.

[95] *Princ.* 3.5.8 (Behr 2:436) sed uerbo ratione doctrina prouocatione meliorum institutionibus optimis comminationibus quoque dignis et conpetentibus.

[96] *Princ.* 3.5.8 (Behr 2:438) seruata omnius rationabilibus creaturis arbitrii libertate unusquisque debeat dispensari.

Scott interprets Origen's theodicy as a defence of providence. Against the implication that the problem of evil means God does not govern creation equitably, he insists that evil is a theological, not a philosophical problem for Origen.[97] McClymont states that Origen's theology rests on the two axiomatic principles of human freedom and the 'reality, goodness, and justice of divine providence'.[98]

Against both dualism and fatalism, Origen maintains both the goodness and justice of divine providence,[99] which provides, in Scott's words, a 'benevolent response of divine providence to the misuse of freedom'.[100] Scott explains Origen's concept of providence as the outworking of God's solution to the fall of souls.[101] Evil appeared in the world because of the departure of the spirits from God, of their own free will, not by creation of intrinsically evil or hostile natures.[102] The physical creation and souls' embodiment provide a training and healing ground for the souls' 'journey back to God'. Suffering in this world thus serves a remedial purpose.[103]

Origen, like Clement, insists that the foreknowledge of God is not the cause of future events.[104] But unlike Clement, he broadens his view of what God does permit to encompass persecution and suffering. Discussing Paul's calling as an apostle, Origen notes that people may be called to suffer or be martyred for Christ and yet not be chosen to see it through, since they do not endure the tortures and imprisonments to the end.[105] Those whom God foreknew were predestined to conform themselves to Christ by suffering (Rom. 8:29). However, Origen insists that 'foreknowledge should not be considered the cause of predestination', but rather, individual merit comes from what God sees in the future, just as for us it is what is seen in the past.[106] Origen wrote that all things were created equal in the beginning, but the free will of creatures allowed them to diversify into those who would imitate God and those who would fail: 'vessels to honour and dishonour'.[107] Ultimately, both the just and unjust will receive what they deserve, but meanwhile, whatever an individual receives on earth comes from God's providence, according to his judgement of their progress toward imitating and participating in God.[108]

Although Origen calls on scriptural support, his ideas of the primordial fall of souls and their *apokatastasis* are ultimately speculative. However, Dempsey casts too much

---

[97] Scott, *Journey*, 2, 32–3.
[98] Michael McClymond, *The Devil's Redemption: A New History and Interpretation of Christian Universalism*, 2 Vols. (Grand Rapids: Baker, 2018–19), 1:254.
[99] Scott, *Journey*, 35–9.
[100] Ibid., 40.
[101] Ibid., 76.
[102] *Princ.* 3.4.5 (Behr 2:422).
[103] Scott, *Journey*, 99–100.
[104] *Philoc.* 25.2–3 (SC 226:216–26); *Comm. Rom.* 1.5.52.3 (SC 532:168–70) And see Scott, *Journey*, 86–91.
[105] *Comm. Rom.* 1.4.50.2 (SC 532:164).
[106] *Comm. Rom.* 1.5.52.3 (SC 532:170) Praecedit ergo praescientia de eis per quam noscuntur quid in se laboris et uirtutis habituri sint ita praedestinatio sequitur, nec tamen rursum praedestinationis causa putabitur praescientia.
[107] *Princ.* 2.9.6 (Behr 2:246) et alia quidem ad honorem alia autem ad contumeliam, citing Rom. 9:22–23.
[108] *Princ.* 1.8.4; 2.9.8 (Behr 1:138–40; 250); see also Michael T. Dempsey, 'The Politics of Providence in the Early Church: Toward a Contemporary Interpretation', *Didaskalia* 26 (2016), 109–34, at 114.

blame on Origen for what he sees as the eventual corruption of the scriptural concept of providence into 'the unabashed determinism of Calvinism'.[109] Dempsey considers Origen's doctrine of providence to be 'no longer concerned with the material fulfilment of the biblical promise for creation by dethroning the powers of evil, but with resolving the philosophical conflict between the goodness of God and the existence of evil'.[110] This, Dempsey argues, exonerates God from evil, but at the cost of blaming victims for their own suffering because creatures merit their own reward or punishment.[111] Perceiving the powerful as divinely appointed justified the status quo and promoted subsequent Christian imperialization.[112] In this, Dempsey fails to account for the full picture of Origen's theology, in particular the centrality of *apokatastasis*, in which evil will eventually be defeated. Origen may have been so (mis-)appropriated – and granted Dempsey is ultimately more critical of Augustine's role in the 'morphing' of providence – but Origen himself does not see providence overriding free will, but rather wooing and re-educating it. As Elliott demonstrates, Origen is concerned with how God's providence works *with*, rather than *against*, human free will.[113] Souls are directed with their own wills and have the freedom to follow God, without coercion.[114] Ciner notes that the tension between divine providence and human freedom is reconciled by Origen in *apokatastasis*, and that he maintains a synergy between divine grace and human freedom.[115] Origen was ultimately satisfied with the consistency of his schema, even though the discussion has subsequently moved on. Nevertheless, as Scott suggests, 'providence, through its patient, persistent, persuasive power, seems to override freedom in the end'.[116] Origen attempts to mitigate this by allowing indefinite ages for all to freely choose God.

Free will and the opposing powers

If, as Origen argues, evil is not attributable to God, it must originate in a departure from God. Whilst the early fathers agree that the Devil and demons fell by their own free will – and Clement stops here – Origen offers a unique perspective on the origin of demons, and their ultimate fate.[117] Origen posits that God initially created an equal population of intellectual beings. Although constituted good, they had free will, and over time became negligent, or 'colder' in their love for God. The Devil fell first, and others followed him in rebellion.[118] The choices these souls made determined their status as angels, humans or demons and so they were embodied in the created cosmos.[119] Thus,

---

[109] Dempsey, 'Politics of Providence', 121.
[110] Ibid., 113.
[111] Ibid., 114.
[112] Ibid., 115–6, 132.
[113] Elliott, *Providence Perceived*, 14–16, 20–2.
[114] *Princ.* 2.1.2 (Behr, 1:146); *Hom. Gen.* 3.2 (SC 7:114–6) nihil sine prouidentia ... non, sine uoluntate (distinguishing between God's providence and his will).
[115] Ciner, introduction to *Comentario al Evangelio de Juan*/1, 38.
[116] Scott, *Journey*, 163.
[117] See Scott, *Journey*, 51, 63–6, 71–2, 130–51.
[118] *Cels* 4.65 (SC 136:344–8) 6.43 (SC 147:284–6) *Princ.* 1.5.4–5; 1.8.3 (Behr 1:96–104; 134–8).
[119] *Princ.* 1.5.3–4 (Behr 1:92–100).

God did not create the Devil and demons *per se*, but created sinless intellectual beings who *became* these entities.[120] God did not cause evil to subsist in the Devil, but the act of turning away engendered it.[121] Consequently the whole of this mortal life is full of struggles and trials caused by the enmity of those who fell; the Devil and his angels, the 'opposing powers'.[122]

Early Christians considered all demons to be evil, and the objects of pagan worship.[123] Demons, accordingly, are responsible for catastrophes, heresies and persecutions, indeed anything opposed to Christianity. The worst aspects of paganism, including divination, are attributable to them.[124] Demons lead men astray with false doctrines and ideas.[125] The souls of those who betray and condemn Christians are demon-filled.[126] Persecution is attributable to demons' influence on those who condemn and betray Christians and on the opposing powers, or rulers of this world.[127] Demons take advantage of the human inclination to sin; human will must cooperate, however, as demons have no power unless one surrenders to them.[128]

> And since God wanted to sustain the word of Jesus among men, demons have been powerless, although they made every effort to eliminate Christians; for they stirred up against the Word and those believing in him, emperors, senators, all rulers and their people, those not understanding the irrational and evil activities of the demons. But the word of God is mightier than all, and although being hindered, taking the hindrance as nourishment to grow, it advances and has won more souls, for this God willed.[129]

Christians are neither subject to demons, nor hurt directly by them,[130] because Christ has triumphed over the Devil and demons.[131] The martyrs especially demonstrate Christ's victory over evil powers, and are themselves conquerors, by sharing in his suffering.[132]

---

[120] *Com. Jn.* 2.13.97 (SC 120:270); *Cels.* 4.65 (SC 136:348); 7.69 (SC 150:174).
[121] *Com. Jn* 20.22.184 (SC 290:248–50); *Princ.* 1.5.3, 1.8.4 (Behr 1:92–6; 138–42).
[122] *Princ.*1.5.2; 1.6.3 contrariis uirtutibus (Behr: 1:90–92; 112).
[123] *Cels.* 8.39 (SC 150:258) πάντας δαίμονας εἶναι φαύλους. And see Everett Ferguson, 'Origen's Demonology', in *Ministry, Initiation and Worship,* vol. 1 of *The Early Church and Today*, ed. Everett Ferguson (Abilene: Christian University Press, 2012), 193–209.
[124] *Cels.* 2.51 (SC 132:402–6); 5.5 (SC 147:24); 8.31 (SC 150:240–2); *Mart.* 45 (GCS 2:41–2).
[125] *Princ.* 3.3.2–3. (Behr: 402–4) falsa scienta ... sapientiae principum huius muni.
[126] *Cels.* 8.36, 43 (SC 150:252–4, 268).
[127] *Princ.* 3.2.1 (Behr 2:382).
[128] *Princ.* 3.2.2; 3.3.4 (Behr 2:384–6; 406); *Cels.* 8.33 (SC 150:246); they rule those who have subjected themselves to evil rather than to God.
[129] *Cels.* 4.32 (SC 136:264) Καὶ ἐπεὶ ὁ Θεὸς ἐβούλετο κρατῆσαι ἐν τοῖς ἀνθρώποις τὸν τοῦ Ἰησοῦ λόγον, οὐδὲν δεδύνηνται δαίμονες, καίτοι γε πάντα κάλων κινήσαντες, ἵνα μὴ Χριστιανοὶ μηκέτ᾽ ὦσι· τούς τε γὰρ βασιλεύοντας καὶ τὴν σύγκλητον βουλὴν καὶ τοὺς ἄρχοντας πανταχοῦ ἀλλὰ καὶ τοὺς δήμους αὐτούς, οὐκ αἰσθανομένους τῆς ἀλόγου καὶ πονηρᾶς τῶν δαιμόνων ἐνεργαόας, ἐξετάραξαν κατὰ τοῦ λόγου καὶ τῶν πιστευόντων εἰς αὐτόν· ἀλλ᾽ ὁ πάντων δυνατώτερος τοῦ θεοῦ λόγος, καὶ κωλυόμενος ὡσπερεὶ τροφὴν πρὸς τὸ αὔξειν τὸ κωλύεσθαι λαμβάνων, προβαίνων πλείονας ἐνέμετο ψυχάς· θεὸς γὰρ τοῦτ᾽ ἐβούλετο.
[130] *Cels.* 8.34 (SC 150:250).
[131] *Hom. Jer.* 14.11.2 (SC 238:88).
[132] *Cels* 8.44 (SC 150:268) Ferguson, 'Origen's Demonology', 198; As I will show in Chapter 4, Origen and Tertullian agree on this point: Tertullian, *Mart.* 4.3 (CCSL 1:5–6) and *Apol.* 27.7 (CCSL 1:139).

Humans are individually responsible for obeying either God or malignant influences.[133] However, our will alone is insufficient; to choose the good requires divine assistance, to strengthen our weakness.[134] Furthermore, the opposing powers are under divine restraint, something Clement fails to address. Ultimately, demons must serve their Creator's will,[135] and despite persecution the word of God providentially advances.[136]

> But we also are persecuted only when God permits, giving the tempter authority to persecute us; but when God does not will us to suffer, even in the world that hates us, miraculously we go in peace and confidence in the one who says, 'have courage, I have overcome the world'. And truly he has overcome the world, therefore the world is powerful only as far as its overcomer wills.[137]

Persecutors and the Devil are not entirely lost in Origen's schema, however. Scholarly debate on Origen's alleged universalism is considerable, largely because Origen seems to contradict himself, sometimes appearing to affirm and other times deny this doctrine.[138] McClymond identifies Origen's *apokatastasis* as 'a constitutive element within an interconnected and influential set of Christian teachings', emphasizing that subsequent 'Origenists' evinced very different versions of universalism.[139] Origen is most ambivalent with respect to the possibility of 'ultimate impenitence' and the Devil's salvation.[140] Edwards proposes that Origen taught the surrender and submission of the Devil rather than his salvation, because it was the perversity of the Devil's will, not his nature, that caused his damnation.[141] Scott contends that Origen believed that the Devil, as Devil, must be destroyed, but that the rational creature who became the Devil will be purged and restored at the *apokatastasis*.[142] Scott ultimately does consider Origen a universalist, reconciling his apparent contradictory statements in terms of adaptation to the spiritual discernment of his audiences.[143] This seems the most credible explanation. What is most important for Origen's diogmology is that ultimately evil will be annihilated.

---

[133] *Princ.* 3.1.4-6; (Behr 2:290-300).
[134] *Princ.* 3.2.2-3 (Behr 2:384-8).
[135] *Cels.* 8.31 (SC 150:242).
[136] *Cels.* 4.32 (SC 136:264).
[137] Origen, *Cels.* 8.70 (SC 150:336-8) Καὶ ἡμεῖς δέ, ὅτε μὲν ἐπιτρέπει ὁ θεὸς τῷ πειράζοντι δοὺς ἐξουσίαν τῃῆ τοῦ διώκειν ἡμᾶς, διωκόμεθα· ὅτε δ' ὁ θεὸς ⟨οὐ⟩ βούλεται τοῦθ' ἡμᾶς πάσχειν, καὶ ἐν μισοῦντι ἡμᾶς τῷ κόσμῳ παραδόξως εἰρήνην ἄγομεν καὶ θαρροῦμεν ἐπὶ τῷ εἰπόντι· ⟨⟨Θαρσεῖτε, ἐγὼ νενίκηκα τὸν κόσμον.⟩⟩ Καὶ ἀληθῶς νενίκηκε ⟨⟨τὸν κόσμον⟩⟩, διόπερ ⟨ἰσχύει ὁ κόσμος⟩ εἰς ὅσον ⟨ὁ⟩ νικήσας αὐτὸν βούλεται.
[138] *Princ.* 1.6.3, 3.6.5-6 (Behr 1:112-14; 2:446-50); *Comm. Rom.* 5.6.416.6 (SC 539:452) suggests the Devil's destruction (as death); but 5.10.452.15 (SC 539:522) hints that Lucifer may ultimately be bound by chains of love. *Comm. Jo.* 32.3.26-40 (SC 385:198-204) implies that the Devil is included in the 'all things' given into Jesus' hands: H Crouzel, ed. *A Letter from Origen to Friends in Alexandria*, Orientalia Christiana Analecta 195 (Roma: Pont. Inst. Or. Stud, 1973), 135-50.
[139] McClymond, *Devil's Redemption*, vol. 1, 232-4.
[140] Ibid., 261-2.
[141] Edwards, 'Fate of the Devil in Origen', 163-70.
[142] Scott, *Journey*, 139, 146. See also McClymond, *Devil's Redemption*, esp. 231-320 on Origen.
[143] Scott, *Journey*, 149 but see Scott's whole argument 129-60.

Evil, persecution and the will of God

As with Clement, Origen's concept of what God's 'goodness' entails determines God's relationship to evil and consequently to persecution. Origen asserts that God does not cause evil but *permits* it for his purposes. It has been said that Origen did not regard evil as 'real'; Lanzilotta attributes this to the Platonic metaphysical and ontological doctrine of the non-substantiality of evil.[144] Certainly, Origen acknowledges that God can only produce what is good: evil appeared by an act of departure of spirits from God, and God consequently created this world as a place of amendment in which creatures may choose to return to God.[145] Lanzillotta's conclusion that for Origen, 'evil has no real existence', could be misconstrued as a dismissal of the real impact of evil, but this is not what Origen intends. Daniélou explains that Origen rejects both uncreated matter as the source of evil and the Stoic idea that evil is only apparent. Evil is consistent with God's goodness because, in Origen's opinion, 'evil is certainly real, but it can be conducive to good, and it will eventually cease to exist'.[146]

Scott's detailed analysis clarifies the issue; he concludes that Origen considers evil to exist paradoxically, subsisting parasitically and temporarily in creation.[147] Firstly, the ontological 'non-existence' of evil is explained in Origen's commentary on John 1:3, 'all things through him were made, and without him nothing was made'.[148] Origen identifies evil with the 'nothing' that was made 'without' God, because everything that comes from God is good. Evil is opposed to good as 'not being' is opposed to 'being', and all existence comes from God. Therefore, evil is the deficiency of goodness that arises from moving away from God, the supreme good.[149] Secondly, evil is not substantial, because it was not there at the beginning, and it will not last forever; it will be destroyed in the *apokatastasis*.[150]

Origen states that evil is the opposite of good[151] and that evil is a defect of the soul which requires removal.[152] Evil, like good, can be selected or avoided.[153] All creatures are capable of both good and evil, with evil obtained in proportion to one's conduct.[154] Good opposes evil and either both are real or both are unreal.[155] Origen, against Celsus, regards evil as indefinite, sometimes increasing and sometimes decreasing, but not

---

[144] Lautaro Roig Lanzillotta, 'Greek Philosophy and the Problem of Evil in Clement of Alexandria and Origen'. *Estudios griegos e indoeuropeos* 23 (2013), 207–23, at 220. But as Scott notes, Plato, unlike Origen, thought evil would not end; Scott, *Journey Back to God*, 175 n. 8, citing *Theaetetus* 176.
[145] *Princ.* 2.1.2 (Behr 1:146).
[146] Daniélou, *Origène*, 277.
[147] Scott, *Journey*, 24–5.
[148] *Comm. Jo.* 2.13.91–94, 2.13.99 (SC 120:264–8, 270) πάντα δι' αὐτοῦ ἐγένετο, καὶ χωρὶς αὐτοῦ ἐγένετο οὐδὲ ἕν.
[149] *Comm. Jo.* 2.96 (SC 120:268–70); also *Princ.* 2.9.2 (Behr 2:238); Recedere autem a bono non aliud est quam effici in malo. Certum namque est malum esse bono carere.
[150] *Princ.* 3.6.3 (Behr 2:444) non enim iam ultra mali bonique discretio, quia nusquam malum, also *Com. Jn.* 2.13.93 (SC 120:266) ἀνυπόστατον εἶναι τὴν κακίαν.
[151] *Princ.* 2.5.3 (Behr 2:196) bono malum contrarium est.
[152] *Princ.* 2.10.6 (Behr 2:262).
[153] *Princ.* 3.1.3 (Behr 2:288).
[154] *Princ.* 1.8.3-4 (Behr 1:134–42).
[155] *Cels.* 2.51 (SC 132:404).

constituting a fixed number of evils.[156] God is stronger than all evil, and will destroy evil at the consummation of all things, which is when God will be all in all.[157]

Origen can therefore, by implication, view the evil of persecution as part of the temporary state of creation, and something which God can use for good, without denying its hardship and horror, which he himself experienced. Origen recognizes that persecutions come by means of the hostile powers, not for the purpose of suffering as an end, but to provoke anger, sorrow, despair and complaint against God. None of these things happen by chance, for as Jesus said, 'You would have no power over me, unless it were given to you from above'.[158] No occurrences in the world, either good or bad, happen apart from God; he does not merely 'not prevent' those wicked and opposing powers from accomplishing their purposes, but also permits them to do so.[159]

Critically, Origen goes further than Clement, in attributing persecution to the *permission* of God, not simply his lack of *prevention*. Furthermore, although God is not the author of evil, he does at times call corporeal and external evils into existence to convert and correct individuals using sufferings.[160] In his treatise on Psalm 4:7, 'Who will show us the good things?' Origen argues that good and evil come from our own efforts, but also from outside, whilst always under providential control. Experience shows that the righteous are not always blessed and that the wicked sometimes prosper. Therefore, the absolute promises of prosperity and safety given to the godly must be interpreted allegorically. Tribulations cannot be evil, since we are told to boast in them.[161] Job was shown to be righteous through what befell him, and 'all things work together for good' (Rom. 8:28). Origen concludes that the good that is promised refers to eternal reward rather than health and wealth in the present life.

Justice therefore extends beyond the immediate trials of this life. Origen will not allow a false dichotomy between 'justice' and 'goodness'.[162] For Origen, the final restitution of all things renders apparent injustices just, a teleological perspective like Clement's. Everyone will be subject to punishment for his sins at the final judgement, although this punishment is educational. This mortal life is full of struggles and trials, caused by the enmity of the Devil and his angels, but the *telos* of the righteous will be in the renewal of heaven and earth.[163]

Persecution in unity with Christ

If God does permit persecution and other sufferings due to external evils, it follows that he must have a purpose in this. Suffering is not gratuitous or meaningless; one who

---

[156] *Cels.* 4.62–4 (SC 136:338–44).
[157] *Cels.* 8.72 (SC 150:340–4).
[158] *Princ.* 3.2.6 (Behr 2:396–8) non haberes aduersum me potestatem, nisi esset tibi data desuper. Jn 19:11.
[159] *Princ.* 3.2.7 (Behr 2:398) non solem non prohibet deus, sed et permittit facere haec.
[160] *Cels.* 6.56 (SC 147:318–20).
[161] Origen, treatise on Psalm 4:7, *Philocalia* 26 (SC 226:234–66); at 26.5 (SC 226:248) καυχᾶσθαι ἐν ταῖς θλίψεσι. The actual quote from 'the Apostle' is 'Rejoice (χαίροντες) in hope, be patient (ὑπομένοντες) in tribulation, be constant in prayer', Rom. 12:12.
[162] *Princ.* 2.5.3 (Behr 2:194–7).
[163] *Princ.* 1.6.1–3 (Behr 1:104–14).

suffered as Origen did could hardly hold that view. Like Clement, he regards persecution as inevitable; God in his foreknowledge predicted it, even though this foreknowledge was not determinative of events.[164] But Origen goes further, fleshing out a more complete diogmology centred on unity with Christ and confession of the Name. For Origen, persecution is inevitable because it results from a Christian's allegiance to and unity with Christ.

Persecution is inevitable

God predicted persecution because it is inevitable for those who align themselves with Christ. This is the heart of Origen's diogmology, which significantly extends that of Clement. Writing his *Exhortation* to the imprisoned confessors, Origen reminds them that 'affliction upon affliction' is prophesied for mature athletes of Christ.[165] Paul wrote that 'all who desire to live a godly life in Christ Jesus will be persecuted' (2 Tim. 3:12). Origen establishes the reason for this by precedent and careful diogmological argument which elucidates the reason for persecution.

Origen emphasizes the connection with historical precedent more than the other three fathers. God's people, his prophets and apostles, have always been persecuted. This is particularly emphasized in his *Homilies on Jeremiah*. Origen regards Jeremiah as paradigmatic for the sufferings of Christians. Commenting on Jeremiah 1:1–10, he repeats Stephen's accusatory 'Which of the prophets did not your fathers persecute?' (Acts 7:52). As Paul warned in 2 Timothy 3:12, 'of necessity those who wish to live piously in Christ Jesus in every sense will be persecuted'. Origen adds the words 'of necessity', and notes that the persecution comes from 'opposing powers through every kind of means they can find'.[166] Those who are persecuted should not be dismayed on account of this but persevere, praying that they are persecuted unjustly, not justly. That is, not persecuted for any injustice, sin or greed on their part; rather, those who are persecuted for righteousness are blessed.[167] Jeremiah suffered at the hands of those who would not hear the truth and were powerful in this age, but the kingdom of God is from greater places than this age (Jn 18:36). Just like those who gave pain to the prophet, the judge of the martyrs sits in a courtroom and leads a soft life, while the Christian, in whom Christ is judged, is filled up with bitterness, oppressed by the unjust and condemned.[168]

Origen brings New Testament texts into his Old Testament exegesis, in accord with his conviction that the Scripture gives a unified account of Christ and his people. The antecedent persecuted prefigure Christ, whilst persecuted Christians post-figure him.[169] We cannot have the lot of the prophets and apostles without suffering, affirms

---

[164] *Philoc.* 25.3 (SC 226:222–6).
[165] *Mart.* 1–2 (GCS 2:3–4) θλίψις ἐπὶ θλίψει.
[166] *Hom. Jer.* 1.13.2 (SC 232:224) Τίνα τῶν προφητῶν οὐκ ἐδίωξαν οἱ πατέρες ὑμῶν; . . . καὶ ἀναγκαῖόν ἐστι τοὺς θέλοντας ζῆν εὐσεβῶς ἐν Χριστῷ Ἰησοῦ πάντως ὑπὸ δυνάμεων ἀντικειμένων δι' ὧν εὑρίσκουσι σκευῶν διώκεσθαι.
[167] *Hom. Jer.* 1.13.2 (SC 232:224–6) ref. Mt. 5:11–12 and compare 1 Pet. 2:20.
[168] *Hom. Jer.* 14.17 (SC 238:106).
[169] O'Keefe and Reno, *Sanctified Vision*, 81–3.

Origen; we will suffer and be hated as they were, and be given the message for which they were hated. Jeremiah was vilified by those to whom he spoke truth and he prayed for vindication from his persecutors. The prophets were condemned for reproving, blaming and reproaching; we should expect the same.[170] The principalities and powers who rose against Christ are those who rise against his people.[171] Acts 5:41 relates how the apostles, having suffered a beating before the Jewish council, rejoiced to be counted worthy to suffer dishonour for Christ's name.[172]

Citing 2 Corinthians 12:10 and Ephesians 6:24, Origen exhorts Christians to strive for the prophetic and apostolic life, not avoiding what is troublesome, but imitating the athlete who will not receive the crown without contest.[173] The way that leads to life is hard, and just as the Passover feast comes with bitter herbs, so in this life we enjoy nothing sweet.[174] Paschor the priest struck Jeremiah, just as Ananias the priest commanded Paul to be struck.[175] Jesus gave his back to the whips as the word of God is insulted and abused by the unbelieving; those who scheme against Christians despise the teaching and effectively spit on Jesus who upholds it.[176] This is echoed in other works: Celsus scoffed at the Christians' willingness to die for Christ, given that his own disciples denied him. Origen counters that this early fault was followed by many instances of boldness and willingness to die, as Christ himself had predicted; 'rejoicing that they were counted worthy to suffer shame for his name'.[177] This became a precept among Jesus' followers. Origen concludes that those who have deserved to be scourged and chastened by the Lord are those to be received as sons. They, through endurance of trials and tribulations, will not be separated from the love of God. Conversely, those who do not offer themselves to God and prepare their souls for trial are effectively abandoned by God.[178]

Christians have thus been warned of, and specifically prepared for, persecution. In his *Exhortation*, Origen exegetes Isaiah 28:9–11 to remind Ambrose and Protoctetus they are no longer babes in Christ (1 Cor. 3:1; Heb. 5:12) and have been weaned from milk; for such Isaiah promises 'affliction upon affliction'. The one who does not refuse, but welcomes affliction, welcomes 'hope upon hope', in 'yet a little while'.[179] Therefore affliction should be welcomed. As Paul says, the sufferings of the present time are incomparable to the glory to be revealed (Rom. 8:18). This is a light and momentary affliction that is outweighed by the heavier weight of glory being prepared for us (2 Cor. 4:17). We must not look at the present sufferings but at the prizes kept for athletes (2 Tim. 2:5). God multiplies his benefits and gifts to those who have demonstrated they

---

[170] *Hom. Jer.* 14.14.2 (SC 238:96–8); Heb. 11:37–38.
[171] *Hom. Gen.* 9.3 (SC 7:248–50).
[172] *Cels.* 2.45 (SC 132:386–8).
[173] *Hom. Jer.* 14.14.4–5 (SC 238:98–100).
[174] *Hom. Jer.* 14.16.3 (SC 238:104).
[175] *Hom. Jer.* 19.12.2 (SC 238:222) Jer. 20:2; Acts 23:2.
[176] *Hom. Jer.* 19.12.3 (SC 238:222–4).
[177] *Cels.* 2.45 (SC 132:386) ⟨⟨χαιροντες⟩⟩, ⟨⟨ὅτι κατηξιώθησαν ὑπὲρ τοῦ ὀνόματος ἀτιμασθῆωαι⟩⟩ Acts 5:41.
[178] *Princ.* 3.1.12 (Behr 2:322–4) *derelinqui dicuntur a deo* ref. Heb. 12:6, Rom. 8:35–39.
[179] *Mart.* 1 (GCS 2:3) θλίψις ἐπὶ θλίψει … ἐλπίδα ἐπ' ἐλπίδι … ἔτι μικρόν.

love him by despising, as far as they can, their earthen vessel.[180] Anyone who does not understand this, he maintains, has never really thirsted for God.[181]

Persecuted for the sake of Christ

Persecution is inevitable because it arises from the fundamental identity of Christians. They are persecuted for the name of Christ. Origen makes this clear to Ambrose and Protoctetus.

> And so, I pray that throughout all the current trial, remembering the abundant reward stored up in heaven for those persecuted and reviled for righteousness' sake and on account of the Son of man, you rejoice and leap and skip for joy, just as the apostles once rejoiced when they were counted worthy to suffer dishonour for his name.[182]

In undertaking to live the Christian life, Origen reminds them, we made a covenant with God, to take up our cross and follow him, losing our soul for his sake in order to find it.[183] The command to take up the cross is found in all three synoptics, each of which Origen cites in full to prove his point.[184] 'If we wish to save our soul in order to get it back better than a soul, let us lose it by our martyrdom.'[185]

The conflict between disciples and the world is reiterated in Origen's commentaries and homilies on both Old and New Testaments. Origen likens the loving self-offering of the martyr to a whole burnt offering, likewise the one who takes up his cross daily to follow Jesus, crucifying himself to the world.[186] Christ's disciples were not of the world, for Jesus chose them out of the world; Christ came to transfer their citizenship from among the things below to among those above.[187] The world does not know, but hates and persecutes, those who are being transformed into the form of the future world, rather than being conformed to this world.[188] This is a lifelong transformation, according to Origen's interpretation of Romans 8:36: 'For your sake we are being killed all the day long; we are regarded as sheep to be slaughtered.' It is insufficient for someone to be killed or crucified for Christ in one hour, but it should be throughout his life – 'all day long.'[189] Allegorizing the departure of the Israelites from Egypt, Origen likens the

---

[180] *Mart.* 2 (GCS 2:4) Rom. 7:24; 2 Cor. 5:4.
[181] *Mart.* 3 (GCS 2:5) Ps. 42:1–2.
[182] *Mart.* 4 (GCS 2:5) Εὐχόμην οὖν ὑμᾶς παρ' ὅλον τὸν ἐστηκότα ἀγῶνα μεμνημένους τοῦ ἀποκειμένου πολλοῦ ἐν οὐρανοῖς μισθοῦ τοῖς διωχθεῖσι καὶ ὀνειδισθεῖσιν ἕνεκεν δικαιοσύνης, καὶ ἕνεκεν τοῦ υἱοῦ τοῦ ἀνθρώπου, χαίρειν καὶ ἀγαλλιᾶν καὶ σκριτᾶν, ὥσπερ οἱ ἀπίστολοι ἐχάρησαν ποτε καταξιωθέντες ὑπὲρ τοῦ ὀνόματος αὐτοῦ ἀτιμασθῆναι, alluding to Mt. 5:10–12; Lk. 6:23; Acts 5:41. Trans. Wendy Mayer, pers. com.
[183] *Mart.* 12 (GCS 2:11).
[184] Mt. 16:24–27; Mk 8:34–37; Lk. 9:23–25.
[185] *Mart.* 12 (GCS 2:12) Εἰ θέλομεν ἡμῶν σῶσαι τὴν ψυχὴν, ἵνα αὐτὴν ἀπολάβωμεν κρείττονα ψυχῆς, μαρτυρίῳ ἀπολέσωμεν αὐτήν.
[186] *Hom. Lev.* 9.9.4 (SC 287:116) holocaustum me ipsum obtuli ad altarem Dei.
[187] *Comm. Jo.* 19.20.136; (SC 290:128) ref. Jn 15:19.
[188] *Comm. Rom.* 9.1.9 (SC 9.1.6; 555:72) ref. Rom. 12:2.
[189] *Comm. Rom.* 7.11.3 (SC 7.9.2; 543:336–8).

oppression of Pharaoh at the Red Sea to waves of persecution: 'All who wish to live piously in Christ will suffer persecution.'[190] Similarly God's people must always be prepared for the attack of enemies: 'Amalekites'.[191]

Origen links the persecution of believers with that of Jesus. Christ is persecuted in the believer; the betrayer of Jesus' disciples betrays Jesus. Jesus' words to Saul on the Damascus road, 'Why do you persecute me? ... I am Jesus whom you are persecuting', indicate that Christ identifies with his suffering followers.[192] Origen observes that Christ is judged in each of the martyrs, in those who testify to the truth. When they are imprisoned, he is imprisoned; when they thirst, he thirsts. When a Christian is judged or slandered because he is a Christian, Christ is the one judged. He is the one imprisoned and punished, as indicated in the account of the sheep and goats. 'Hence if a Christian is judged not for something else, not for his own sins, but because he is a Christian, Christ is the one judged.'[193] Throughout the world, when everybody speaks against the Christians, it is Jesus who is judged and brought to trial and sentenced. Anyone who rejects what they hear of Christianity has done no less than sentence Jesus as one who is false.[194]

Furthermore, Origen affirms that Christians are also united with Christ in his supernatural conflict and victory. This important theme, only hinted at by Clement, is well developed by the Carthaginians and to a significant extent by Origen. Origen sees Christ's death as a victory over the Devil,[195] a redemptive payment and propitiatory sacrifice.[196] It is a payment in blood to buy back those who had been bought by the Devil through sins committed.[197] Origen taught that the fallen rational beings, the Devil and his angels, continue in a state of enmity with God's people. The whole of mortal life is a struggle against the opposing powers.[198] The destruction of Pharaoh at the exodus is often used as a type of Christ's destruction of the Devil and his hordes.[199] Idolatry is demonic, instigated by Satan and the false gods themselves are demons. To sacrifice is to feed these demons and to bear responsibility for the evils they wreak on earth.[200] The Enemy fails to persuade Christians to commit idolatry and so tries to force us, by empowering those over whom he has authority to take Christians to trial, making them either idolaters or martyrs.[201] For Origen, human prosecution masks a greater conflict:

---

[190] *Hom. Exod.* 5.3 (SC 321:160) Omnes qui uolunt pie uiuere in Christo persecutionem patientur; ref. 2 Tim. 3:12.

[191] *Hom. Lev.* 6.6. (PG 12:474–6) *Hom. Exod.* 11.1 (SC 321:326). Here and elsewhere on 2 Tim. 3:12, Origen merges persecution with temptation.

[192] *Comm. Jo.* 1.71 (SC 120:96); 20:136 (SC 290:224) ref. Acts 9:3–5.

[193] *Hom. Jer.* 14.7 (SC 238:80) Οὐκοῦν κἂν δικάζηται Χριστιανὸς οὐ δι' ἄλλο τι, οὐ διὰ τὰς ἰδίας ἁμαρτίας, ἀλλ' ὅτι Χριστιανός ἐστι, Χριστός ἐστιν ὁ δικαζόμενος. ref. Mt. 25:36.

[194] *Hom. Jer.* 14.8.1 (SC 238:82).

[195] *Comm. Matt.* 13.9 (PG 13:1118); Kelly, *Early Christian Doctrines*, 186.

[196] *Comm. Rom.* 3.5.236.1 (SC 539:122–4) *redemtio, propitio*; *Com. John* 28.19.165 (SC 385:142).

[197] *Hom. Exod.* 6.9 (SC 321:192–4); *Comm. Jo.* 6.53.274 (SC 157:338) ὠνούμενος τῷ ἑαυτοῦ αἵματι ἀπὸ τοῦ ταῖς ἁμαρτίαις ἡμᾶς πιπρασκομένους ἀγοράσαντος.

[198] *Princ* 1.6.3 (Behr 1:112) *omnis haec habet uita mortalium, reluctantibus scilicet et repugnantibus aduersum nos his.*

[199] E.g. *Hom. Exod.* 6.1 (SC 321:172).

[200] *Mart.* 45 (GCS 2:41–2).

[201] *Mart.* 32 (GCS 2:28).

But when the souls of those who die for the Christian faith depart from the body with glory, they purge the power of the demons, and exhaust their schemes against men ... again the souls of the godly, stripped from bodies for the sake of godliness, shall destroy the army of the wicked one. For I think that the demons perceive that those victoriously slain for the sake of religion destroy their domination, but those weakened through toil who deny their religion come under their hand, so they persevere to gain Christians over, their confession being punishment to them and their denial a relief.[202]

Another apt metaphor for this conflict is the arena, since Christians died there for their confession. Origen incorporates this in his *Exhortation*; martyrs welcome affliction as noble athletes, before a theatre filled with human, angelic and demonic spectators watching their contests.[203] Citing Ephesians 6:12, Origen affirms that we wrestle against principalities and powers,[204] but not by exercise of bodily strength and wrestling arts. Rather, these struggles are losses and dangers, calumnies and false accusations, by which the hostile powers hope to drive us to anger, sorrow or despair. They hope to fatigue and overcome Christians, so they complain against God as if he were unjust, consequently weakening faith, disappointing hope and leading to wrong thinking about God.[205]

The foundational elements of Origen's diogmology are now discernible. The evils of idolatry are instigated by the Devil and demons in their rebellion against the good God. Christians, united with Christ, oppose these evil powers and their works and are persecuted, just as Christ was. This is consistent with the world's treatment of God's people in the past, but Christians now join the very battle that Christ wages and fight alongside him in the arena of persecution. God permits this persecution and oversees it providentially for his good ends.

The rewards of persecution

Like Clement, Origen sees present good resulting from persecution, a goodness in continuity with eternity. Whilst Clement is rather vague as to what this looks like, Origen provides a detailed and integrated account. This is nested within his eschatology of a return to creation's original good state in complete assimilation to God. As Scott summarizes:

---

[202] *Cels.* 8.44 (SC 150:268–70) Ἀλλ' ἐπεὶ αἱ ψυχαὶ τῶν διὰ χριστιανισμὸν ἀποθνῃσκόντων δι' εὐσέβειαν μετ' εὐκλείας ἀπαλλαττόμεναι τοῦ σώματος καθήρουν τὴν δύναμιν τῶν δαιμόνων καὶ ἀτονωτέραν αὐτῶν ἐποίουν τὴν κατὰ τῶν ἀνθρώπων ἐπιβουλήν ... καὶ τότε πάλιν αἱ ψυχαὶ τῶν εὐσεβούντων καὶ δι' εὐσέβειαν ἀποδυομένων τὰ σώματα καθελοῦσι τὸ τοῦ πονηροῦ στρατόπεδον. Ἐγὼ δ' οἶμαι ὅτι αἰσθόμενοι οἱ δαίμονες ὅτι οἱ μὲν νικῶντες καὶ δι' εὐσέβεαν ἀποθνῄσκοντες καθαιροῦσιν αὐτῶν τὴν δυναστείαν οἱ δὲ διὰ τοὺς πόνους ἡττώμενοι καὶ τὴν θεοσέβειαν ἀρνούμενοι ὑποχείριοι ἐκείνοις γίνονται, ἔσθ' ὅτε προσφιλονεικοῦσι τοῖς παραδιδομένοις Χρισταινοῖς, ὡς κολαζόμενοι μὲν ὑπὸ τῆς ὁμολογίας αὐτῶν ἀναπαυόμενοι δὲ ἐπὶ τῷ ἀρνήσει αὐτῶν.
[203] *Mart.* 1, 18 (GCS 2:3, 16–17).
[204] *Princ.* 3.2.5 (Behr 2:396) aduersum principatus uel aduersum potestates.
[205] *Princ.* 3.2.6 (Behr 2:396–8).

Origen interlaces the cosmic narrative of the soul's journey back to God with the theological narrative of God's providential care for humanity. God does not leave us to our own devices as we plunge toward annihilation. On the contrary, God intervenes by creating the material world to function as the schoolroom or hospital for our re-education and amelioration.[206]

The four fathers each acknowledged that persecution contributed to the building of a Christ-like character. For the Alexandrians, growing in likeness to Christ begins in this life and continues into the next over a gradual process of progression in virtue and enlightenment.[207] Therefore they see the trials of this life, including persecution, as educational and medicinal. Like Clement, Origen sees salvation as a process of growing in likeness to God. By progressive stages of renewal, the Christian will 'perhaps be able at some time, with difficulty, to behold the holy and the blessed life'.[208] Origen also sees the value of suffering in shaping the Christian, but unlike Clement, makes God the author of these sufferings.

Present good

Origen asserts to Celsus that God calls some external evils, such as suffering, into existence for the purpose of correction and cure, just like fathers, teachers, pedagogues and physicians do.[209] In *De prinicipiis*, Origen teaches that God, our physician, desires to remove the defects of our souls contracted from sins and crimes, by employing 'penalties'.[210] God chastens whom he loves, therefore, according to Hebrews 12:6–8, those who are scourged and chastened by the Lord are those he deems to be sons. Through endurance and trials they are therefore able to claim that nothing can separate them from God's love (Rom. 8:35–39). Conversely, those who do not offer themselves to God are effectively abandoned by God.[211] God, who knows every person's heart, draws out hidden evil by means of external circumstances with the object of purification.[212] This process of healing extends beyond this world,[213] so present suffering should be seen in this broader context.

Origen, like Clement, sees suffering as educational and medicinal. 'Paradise' in the afterlife is a 'school for souls' in which they are retrospectively instructed concerning their life experiences.[214] The world is also a hospital for souls and God is both Teacher and Physician.[215] The divine Physician, the Word of God, uses diverse measures to heal the sick, some of which are necessarily painful.[216] He adapts his therapies to individual

---

[206] Scott, *Journey*, 161.
[207] Ibid., 101–2.
[208] *Princ.* 1.3.8 (Behr 1:80–2) uix si forte aliquando intueri possumus sanctam et beatam uitam.
[209] *Cels.* 6.56 (SC 147:318–20).
[210] *Princ.* 2.10.6 (Behr 2:262) penalibus curis.
[211] *Princ.* 3.1.12 (Behr 2:322–4).
[212] *Princ.* 3.1.13 (Behr 2:326–8).
[213] *Princ.* 3.5.7–8 (Behr 2:434–6).
[214] *Princ.* 2.11.6 (Behr 2:278) schola animarum.
[215] Scott, *Journey*, 93–4.
[216] *Philoc.* 27.9 (SC 226:298–300).

needs; sweet and bitter medications, soothing plasters and cautery.[217] Therefore even the sufferings of persecution can be entrusted to God as his providential work for the healing and training of the soul. In his commentary on John 8:41*ff*, Origen observes that the promise of being sons of the Father, in likeness to God and imitation of him, is linked to loving one's enemies and praying for one's persecutors.[218]

Commenting on Psalm 4:6, 'Who will show us some good?' Origen reasons that tribulations cannot be evil if the Apostle tells us to rejoice in them (Rom. 12:12). 'Many are the afflictions of the righteous' (Ps. 34:19) and the Lord delivers from them, as Job was shown to be righteous by what befell him. All things, says Paul, work together for good (Rom. 8:28).[219]

Good for others

Origen is more focused on the individual Christian's salvific journey than the witness to outsiders, as evident in his *Exhortation to Martyrdom*. The focus of confession is primarily before God, even though the audience of the contest – angels, demons, all humanity – is greater than the immediate observers.[220] When describing the reproach of neighbours, Origen is disinterested in their reaction, focused on 'not only the revealed martyrdom, but also the hidden, perfectly winning the contest';[221] in other words, being martyred genuinely for the sake of God who knows our hearts.

Origen even writes apology reluctantly: Jesus did not make a verbal defence before his accusers, and even now his defence rests in the lives of his genuine disciples, which refute all slanderous accusations.[222] He is worried that his written defence to Celsus will weaken this testimony, which rests on facts and the power of Jesus.[223] Even Celsus approved of those who bear witness to Christianity by their death.[224] But for Origen, the primary value of this witness is that it signifies the truth of Jesus' predictions that his followers would also be persecuted.[225] Origen does not seem to embrace any urgency for conversion of the wicked in this life, probably because of his belief in *apokatastasis*.[226]

Origen does recognize some benefit of the martyrs' witness for other Christians, however. Discussing the faithlessness of Jeremiah's Israel, Origen poses Jesus' question: 'will the Son of Man find faith on the earth at his return?'[227] Origen laments that his community is not faithful, and reminisces of past times of noble martyrdom, when

---

[217] *Hom. Ezeck* 3.8 (PG 13:693–4).
[218] *Comm. Jo.* 20.17.147–8 (SC 290:228); reiterated in 20.33.292, 309 (SC 290:300, 308).
[219] *Philoc.* 24.5 (SC 226:250) Πολλαὶ αἱ θλίψεις τῶν δικαίων.
[220] *Mart.* 18 (GCS 2:16–17).
[221] *Mart.* 21 (GCS 2: 19) Μὴ τὸ ἐν φανερῷ δὲ μόνον μαρτύριον, ἀλλὰ καὶ τὸ ἐν κρυπτῷ τελείως ἀναλαβεῖν ἀγωνισώμεθα.
[222] *Cels.* Pref. 2 (SC 132:68).
[223] *Cels.* Pref. 3 (SC 132:68).
[224] *Cels.* 1.8 (SC 132:94).
[225] *Cels.* 2.13–17 (SC 132:318–32).
[226] This would be the logical conclusion; *Cels.* 8.72 (SC 150:340–4).
[227] *Hom. Jer.* 4.3.2 (SC 232:264) Mt. 24:12–13, 24.

everyone gathered to bury the martyrs and teach the catechumens about faithfulness based on the martyrs' example. The faithful were few but they were truly faithful, whereas now that the church has become larger, there will be fewer elect.[228] Origen asserts to Celsus that God permits a few to endure death for Christ so that others might be prepared to face it and that the doctrine of Christ might fill the world. God providentially ensures that rulers and the populace can only rage against Christians up to a point; 'that those who were of weaker minds might recover [their courage] for the purpose of death'.[229]

Although Origen reminds the prospective martyrs that men 'from God's portion' will be among all men witnessing to their testimony,[230] his *Exhortation to Martyrdom* is primarily concerned with Ambrose's and Protoctetus' own salvation rather than their influence on others. The martyrs of old and the sufferings of Christ are examples for them,[231] but Origen does not mention their subsequent effect on others.

Future good

Origen's eschatology includes some of his most controversial speculations.[232] It fundamentally arises from his theodicy; evil will finally be conquered through *apokatastasis*.[233] Salvation is gradual. The kingdom of God is continuous between the present world and its eschatological τέλος, when all will contemplate God as ultimate truth and beauty, God will be all in all, and evil will cease to exist.[234] Consequently, as Daley observes, Origen allegorizes apocalyptic texts to fit his progressive model.[235] Origen taught the intrinsic immortality of the soul, which is the continuing principle between the fall of rational creatures, the present mortal body and the resurrected spiritual body.[236] Saints depart this life to 'Paradise', a 'school for souls'. Those who are pure, holy and most receptive will ascend from there through various mansions, following Jesus who ascended before them (Jn 14:1–3; Heb. 4:14). There the saints will grow in knowledge until they attain perfection in beholding and understanding God through purity of heart.[237]

Sinners' bodies, in contrast, must endure *corrective* post-mortem punishments.[238] Annihilation or eternal suffering in hell would not be consistent with *apokatastasis*, so

---

[228] *Hom. Jer.* 4.3.2 (SC 232:264) Mt. 20:16.
[229] *Cels.* 3.8 (SC 136:28) πάλιν τε αὖ ἵν' οἱ ἀσθενέστεροι ἀναπνέωσιν ἀπὸ τῆς περὶ τοῦ θανάτου φροντίδος.
[230] *Mart.* 18 (GCS 2:17) πάντες ἄνθρωποι οἵ τε ἀπό τῆς τοῦ Θεοῦ μερίδος.
[231] *Mart.* 33, 37 (GCS 2:28–9, 34–5).
[232] For an overview see David I. Rankin, *The Early Church and the Afterlife: Post-death existence in Athenagoras, Tertullian, Origen and the Letter to Rheginos* (London: Routledge, 2018), and Scott, *Journey*, 101–66.
[233] Scott, *Journey*, xiii.
[234] *Princ.* 1.6.1; 2.11.7 (Behr 1:104–6; 2:278–80) and see Scott, *Journey*, 129–60.
[235] Brian E. Daley, *The Hope of the Early Church: A Handbook of Patristic Eschatology*, (Peabody, MS: Hendrickson, 2003), 48. Likewise Hanson, *Allegory and Event*, 336.
[236] *Cels.* 5.19; 7.32 (SC 147:58–62; 150:84–8) ; *Princ.* 2.8.3–4; 2.10.2–4; 4.4.9 (Behr 2:226–32; 256–60; 578–82).
[237] *Princ.* 2.11.5–7 (Behr 2:274–80).
[238] *Princ.* 2.10.1 (Behr 2:254).

Origen must allegorize the references to fire. Punishment is a self-kindled fire, fuelled by their sins and resulting in tortures of the soul with the objective of ultimate restoration,[239] albeit through initial exclusion from the kingdom of heaven and through the remedial suffering of hell.[240] The logical corollary is that even persecutors and those who deny Christ will ultimately be assimilated back to God of their own free will, after potentially aeons of the patient persuasiveness of God, whose remedial work extends beyond the grave. As I shall show, this stands in marked contrast to the perspective of the Carthaginians.

For Origen, persecution is one of the evils of this world that result from the primordial fall of souls and their separation from God. God providentially uses these experiences for good, along with all the other opportunities of life. Origen is in no doubt that those who faithfully endure persecution will be promptly and tangibly rewarded. Ambrose and Protoctetus must keep their eyes on the prize rather than on present sufferings.[241] In words reminiscent of Clement's, he observes that separation of the soul from the earthly body is easy for those who have already separated from every corporal thing.[242] There is a great reward laid up in heaven for those who are persecuted and reviled for righteousness' sake.[243] The martyr will lose his soul in order to gain it back 'better than a soul', reaping a hundred-fold.[244]

Reward and ranking

Each of the four fathers believed that merit in this life transfers to reward in the next.[245] For the Alexandrians, it determined how far along the journey to perfection one was in the ascent of the soul after death. Origen has a high view of martyrdom in this respect, and encourages Ambrose and Protoctetus toward it. Origen considers that ranking in salvation is established by the difficulties of the contest.[246] Martyrs are given special privileges in the unfolding of eschatological events.[247] Those who share in Christ's sufferings will also share proportionately in the compensatory comfort (2 Cor. 1:5).[248] This suffering encompasses not just martyrdom, but beatings, imprisonment and other afflictions.

Origen encourages Christians to endure afflictions and confess Christ, reminding them of the great reward laid up in heaven for those who are persecuted and reviled for righteousness' sake.[249] Origen proposes to Ambrose that greater suffering under

---

[239] *Princ.* 2.10.4–6 (Behr 2:260–4).
[240] See Lawrence R. Hennessey, 'The Place of Saints and Sinners after Death', in *Origen of Alexandria: His World and His Legacy*, ed. Charles Kannengeisser and William L. Petersen, Christianity and Judaism in Antiquity 1 (University of Notre Dame Press, 1988), 295–312.
[241] *Mart.* 2 (GCS 2:4).
[242] *Mart.* 3 (GCS 2:4).
[243] *Mart.* 4 (GCS 2:5); Mt. 5:10–12.
[244] *Mart.* 12, 14 (GCS 2:11–14).
[245] 'Merit' should not be understood anachronistically in terms of the medieval concept of the treasury of merit, but in terms of individual actions based on free choice.
[246] *Princ.* 2.1.2 (Behr 2:146); *Mart.* 14–15 (GCS 2:96–7).
[247] Hanson, *Allegory and Event*, 346, citing Origen, *Comm. Rev.* frag 34; *Mart.* 42 (GCS 2:39–40).
[248] *Mart.* 42 (GCS 2:39).
[249] *Mart.* 4 (GCS 2:5), citing Mt. 5:10–12, Lk. 6:23.

persecution in this life will be recompensed with greater reward in the next. He bases this on Jesus' promise that those who have left more in this life will receive a hundred-fold and eternal life.[250] He wonders how many will attain to blessing and hopes he might 'become a martyr to God in Christ so that I might receive manifold, or as Mark says, a hundred-fold'.[251]

Origen suggests that martyrs who lose worldly goods and children will be blessed more than those who lose less. Those who are tortured more severely in their bodies should take a higher place than those who are not, so also those who have given up many worldly possessions, fame and family for martyrdom.[252] Martyrdom is an expression of gratitude to God, a reciprocation:

> A saint, being generous, and wishing to respond to benefits bestowed by God, seeks what he can do for the Lord concerning everything he has obtained from him; and he finds that nothing else can be repaid by a man of good intention that will balance these benefits as perfection in martyrdom.[253]

Martyrdom is the greatest gift one can give to God. It was a likely consequence of confession, which carried the promise of being confessed in turn by Christ. It was the ultimate way one takes up the cross to follow Jesus. If we wish to save our soul in order to get it back better than a soul, let us lose it by martyrdom, Origen advises, because the alternative is to attempt to gain the world by forfeiting one's soul.[254] The martyrs exemplify the pure, holy and receptive ones who rapidly transit the various mansions and proceed to perfection, and, washed of every sin, will 'pass our existence with our fellow contestants near the altar in heaven'.[255] The martyrs are exalted beyond the exaltation of those who are righteous but not martyred, hence the cleansing value of their martyrdom for others.[256] Taking this idea further, Bright observes sacramental, even eucharistic influences in Origen's understanding of martyrdom; the martyr offers the cup of salvation in a priestly manner, as an act of worship and expiation.[257]

In his *Dialogue with Heraclides*, Origen expresses his fervent desire to leave his body and be with Christ; death, even by execution, is a means to that end. He is ready to die

---

[250] *Mart.* 14 (GCS 2:14) ref. Mt. 19:27-29.
[251] *Mart.* 14 (GCS 2:14) γενέσθαι μάρτυς ἐν Χριστῷ τῷ θεῷ, ἵωα πολλαπλασίονα λάβω ἤ, ὡς ὁ Μάρκος φησὶν, ἑκατονταπλασίονα ref. Mk 4:8-20 in the parable of the sower.
[252] *Mart.* 15 (GCS 2:15).
[253] *Mart.* 28 (GCS 2:24) Φιλότιμός τις ὁ ἅγιος ὤν, καὶ ἀμείψασθαι θέλων τὰς φθασάσας εἰς αὐτὸν εὐεργεσίας ἀπὸ Θεοῦ, ζητεῖ τί ἂν ποιήσαι τῷ Κυρίῳ περὶ πάντων, ὧν ἀπ' αὐτοῦ εἴληφε· καὶ οὐδὲν ἄλλο εὑρίσκει οἱονεὶ ἰσόρροπον ταῖς εὐεργεσίαις δυνάμενον ἀπὸ ἀνθρώπου εὐπροαιρέτου ἀποδοθῆναι Θεῷ, ὡς τὴν ἐν μαρτυρίῳ τελευτήν.
[254] *Mart.* 12 (GCS 2:12) ref. Mt. 10:37-39.
[255] Mart. 39 (GCS 2:37)...παρὰ τῷ ἐν οὐρανοῖς θυσιαστηρίῳ τὰς διατριβὰς μετὰ τῶν συναγωνισαμένων ποιησώμεθα, alluding to Rev. 6:9.
[256] *Mart.* 30, 50 (GCS 2:27, 46-7) *Comm. Jo.* 6.281-3 (SC 157:342-4); L. Arik Greenberg, '*My Share of God's Reward*': *Exploring the Roles and Formulations of the Afterlife in Early Christian Martyrdom* (New York: Peter Lang, 2009), 145.
[257] Pamela Bright, 'Origenian Understanding of Martyrdom and its Biblical Framework', in *Origen of Alexandria: His World and His Legacy*, ed. Charles Kannengeisser and William L. Petersen. Christianity and Judaism in Antiquity 1 (University of Notre Dame Press, 1988), 180-99.

for the sake of truth, knowing that as soon as the torture is over, he will be at peace with Christ.[258] Nevertheless, Greenberg's assertion that Origen exemplifies 'a martyrological, world-denying fervor', and is 'a zealot for martyrdom and a preacher of defiance against the established authorities',[259] is a step too far. After his youthful desire to die alongside his father, Origen removed himself from the arena of persecution and recommended avoidance of persecution where appropriate.[260] Greenberg has not reconciled his views with Origen's whole diogmology. Origen believes that all rational souls will ultimately be redeemed and that all souls require purification after death. Greer's assessment is more on point: 'Origen's views of martyrdom, prayer, and Scripture merge into one vision of the Christian life as a movement toward perfect knowledge of God and perfect fellowship with Him through Christ.'[261] Nevertheless, in the souls' journeys through the aeons toward perfection, Origen evidently believed that those who endured persecution, confessed Christ and were martyred had a significant head start.

Martyrdom and forgiveness

Origen regards martyrdom as a baptism of blood that brings forgiveness of sins. It is 'the cup of salvation'; the person who drinks it will sit and rule with Christ.[262] It is the second baptism;[263] by it we are 'baptised with our own blood and washed of every sin'.[264] This was an important consideration in the early church, which struggled with the issue of post-baptismal sin. By the third century there was an established public penitential process, culminating in a humiliating *exomologesis*,[265] but some doubted its efficacy for the gravest of sins. Origen identified several ways to obtain remission of sins; baptism, martyrdom, almsgiving, forgiving others and through love. The offering of a calf under the law was a type of baptism, while the offering of a he-goat was a type of martyrdom, whereby the Devil was slain.[266] Likewise, the one who renounces all, takes up the cross and follows Jesus, or who surrenders to martyrdom, has offered himself as a whole burnt offering to God.[267]

Origen acknowledged priestly mediation for certain involuntary or wilful misdeeds, but not for adultery or wilful murder or any other more serious offence.[268] Nevertheless, he wrote that the shedding of the noble martyrs' blood was akin to the sacrifice of

---

[258] *Dial.* 24.10.20 (SC 67:100–102).
[259] Greenberg, *God's Reward*, 134.
[260] *Comm. Matt.* 10:23 (PG 3:897).
[261] Rowan A. Greer, *Origen: An Exhortation to Martyrdom, Prayer and Selected Works*, The Classics of Western Spirituality (London: SPCK, 1979), 17.
[262] *Mart.* 28 (GCS 2:24) οὖν ἐστι τὸ τοῦ σωτηρίου ποτήριον, ref. Mt. 20:21–23; 26:39.
[263] *Mart.* 30 (GCS 2:26).
[264] *Mart.* 39 (GCS 2:37) βαπτισάμενοι τῷ ἑαυτῶν αἵματι καὶ ἀπολουσάμενοι πᾶσαν ἁμαρτίαν …
[265] For a description, see Everett Ferguson, 'Early Church Penance', *Restoration Quarterly* 36, no. 2 (1994), 81–100; J. Patout Burns and Robin M. Jensen, *Christianity in Roman Africa: The Development of its Practices and Beliefs* (Grand Rapids: Eerdmans, 2014), 295–99, 314–18; Sutcliffe, 'Learning Not to Sin: Repentance in Tertullian and Cyprian'. *Colloquium* 53, no. 1 (2021): 73–97.
[266] *Hom. Lev.* 2.4.6 (SC 286:110).
[267] *Hom. Lev.* 9.9.4 (SC 287:116).
[268] Origen, *Or.* 18.8ff (PG 11:530) However, Origen probably did not regard such sinners as irretrievably lost; *Princ.* 1.6.2–3; 2.9.8, 2.10.4, 2.11.6; 3.5.7, 3.6.6 (Behr 1:106–114; 2:250; 260; 276–8; 434–6; 448–50).

Christ.[269] The intercessory power of martyrs was a common belief in the early church. If not actually remitting the sins of others, at least they could efficaciously plead on their behalf at the judgement.

> And perhaps just as we have been redeemed by the precious blood of Jesus, [who] received the name above every name, so by the precious blood of the martyrs some will be redeemed, since they too have been exalted beyond the exaltation of those who were righteous but did not become martyrs. For there is reason to call the unique death that is martyrdom an exaltation.[270]

Origen suggests that the sacrifices of the Law foreshadowed not only the sacrifice of Christ, but the shedding of the blood of the martyrs. Just as the old sacrifices cleansed those for whom they were offered, and as the powers of evil are demolished by the martyrs' deaths in a way analogous to depriving a poisonous animal of its venom, 'we conclude something like this happens in the death of the godliest martyrs, since by an ineffable power many are benefited by their death'.[271] He consequently understands Ambrose's prayer for his 'children' to be more efficacious as a result of his martyr's death.[272]

Victory, justice, vindication

Origen is more specific than Clement about the justice of suffering. At the end of the world, God will bestow on each person what they deserve. One day, all wrongs will be righted; persecutors and those who resist God will receive their just deserts.[273] But, like Clement, Origen views the present life in continuity with the future life. Love will be requited by love; sacrifice and suffering by degrees of reward. The Christian walks, as it were, hand in hand with Christ through present sufferings into a continuity of future glory. God's rule is already a reality in those who obey him, and the consummation of the world will be gradual, as the God-given order is perfected in individuals and eventually in all creation.[274] Therefore, Origen is comfortable allegorizing the apocalyptic aspects of Gospel eschatology in terms of a Christian's growth toward salvation.[275] Although he allows that eternal fire is reserved for the Devil and his angels, he does not frame eternal punishment of the wicked in terms of victorious retribution;

---

[269] *Comm. Jo.* 6.276 (SC 157:338).
[270] *Mart.* 50 (GCS 2:46–7) Τάχα δὲ καὶ ὥσπερ τιμίῳ αἵματι τῷ τοῦ Ἰησοῦ ἠγοράσθημεν, Ἰησοῦ λαβόντος ⟨τὸ ὄνομα τὸ ὑπὲρ πᾶν ὄνομα,⟩ οὕτως τῷ τιμίῳ αἵματι τῶν μαρτύρων ἀγορασθήσονται τινες, καὶ αὐτῶν πλέον ὑψουμένων παρ' ὃ ὑψώθησαν ἂν δίκαιοι μὲν γενόμενοι, μὴ μαρτυρήσαντες δέ· λόγον γὰρ ἔχει τὸ ἰδίως τὸν ἐν μαρτυρίῳ θάνατον ὕψωσιν καλεῖσθαι.
[271] *Comm. Jo.* 6.54.281–3 (SC 342–4) Τοιοῦτόν τι δὴ νοητέον τῷ θανάτῳ τῶν εὐσεβεστάτων μαρτύρων γίνεσθαι, πολλῶν ἀφάτῳ τινὶ δυνάμει ὠφελουμένων ἀπὸ τοῦ θανάτου αὐτῶν.
[272] *Mart.* 38 (GCS 2:35–6). Literally, 'seed', σπέρμα.
[273] *Princ.* 1.6.1 (Behr 1:104) quod meretur expendet.
[274] Daley, *Hope of the Early Church*, 49–50.
[275] E.g. Origen's *Comm.* on Mt. 24 (Series 29–62); Ronald E. Heine, introduction to *The Commentary of Origen on the Gospel of St Matthew*, trans. and intro. Ronald E. Heine (Oxford: Oxford University Press, 2018), vol. 2, 585–652; Daley, *Hope of the Early Church*, 48–9.

he is more concerned to allow their purification and redemption through punishment as the means of Christ's triumph over and final elimination of evil.[276]

Responses to persecution

The right attitude

Origen exhorts the persecuted to persevere, to not be dismayed, but rather hear Jesus' words: 'Blessed are you when men revile you and persecute you and say all kinds of evil against you for my sake. Rejoice and be glad, for your reward is great in heaven, for so they persecuted the prophets before you.'[277] Origen's *Exhortation to Martyrdom* connects the imperative to rejoice with the present and eternal good of persecution, their reward.[278] When the martyr feels his soul drawing back, he must turn to God in his disquietude, praying for God's peace and recalling his sovereignty. Just as the sufferings of Christ abound, so too does his comfort, in which they will share proportionately according to their suffering.[279] They should endure a hard struggle with suffering, joyfully accepting the plundering of their property, knowing that they have far better, eternal possessions.[280]

Origen gives the reason for loving enemies and praying for persecutors, 'that you may become sons of your Father in heaven'.[281] Likeness to God, who loves his creatures, is demonstrated by loving and praying for enemies.[282] In fact, the *only* way to become a son of the Father is to love and pray for one's persecutors.[283] Origen reiterates that vengeance belongs to God; the Christian's role is to do good to persecutors. The extent to which we do good and do not retaliate against our enemies, is the extent that we heap up their punishments by God's judgement.[284] For Origen, patience is the core of Christian witness, the embodiment of the patience of Christ. This enables one to respond to violence with blessing.[285]

Like the second-century apologists, Origen uses Jesus' teachings on non-resistance and prayer for persecutors in defence of the faith, showing their superiority to Plato's teaching.[286] Jesus' teachings are worthy of emulation by all.[287] Christians do not even

---

[276] Daley, *Hope of the Early Church*, 56–8.
[277] *Hom. Jer.* 1.13.2 (SC 232:226) μακάριοί ἐστε ὅταν ὀνειδίζωσιν ὑμᾶς καὶ διώκωσι καὶ εἴπωσι πᾶν πονηρὸν ῥῆμα καθ' ὑμῶν ψευδόμενοι ἕνεκεν ἐμοῦ· χαίρετε καὶ ἀγαλλιᾶσθε, ὅτι ὁ μισθὸς ὑμῶν πολὺς ἐν τοῖς οὐρανοῖς· οὕτως γὰρ ἐδίωξαν τοὺς προφήτας τοὺς πρὸ ὑμῶν, ref. Mt. 5:11–12.
[278] *Mart.* 4 (GCS 2:5) καὶ ἕνεκεν τοῦ υἱοῦ του ἀντηρώπου, χαίρειν καὶ ἀγαλλιᾶν καὶ σκιρτᾶν, ὥσπερ οἱ ἀπόστολοι ἐχάρησάν ποτε, καταξιωθέντες ὑπὲρ τοῦ ὀνόματος αὐτοῦ ἀτιμασθῆναι.
[279] *Mart.* 42 (GCS 2:39–40), citing 2 Cor. 1:5–7.
[280] *Mart.* 44 (GCS 2:41), citing Heb. 10:32–36 (which he attributes to Paul) and 2 Cor. 4:18.
[281] *Comm. Jo.* 20.17.147 (SC 290:228) ὅπως γένησθε υἱοὶ τοῦ πατρὸς ὑμῖν τοῦ ἐν οὐρανοῖς, ref. Mt. 5:44–45.
[282] *Comm. Jo.* 20.148 (SC 290:228).
[283] *Comm. Jo.* 20.292, 309 (SC 290:300, 308).
[284] *Com. Rom.* 9.23.1 (SC 555:154). ref. Rom. 12:19; Lk. 6: 27–29.
[285] *Hom.* 1 on Psalm 38 (PG 12:1394) and see Alan Kreider, *The Patient Ferment of the Early Church: The Improbable Rise of Christianity in the Roman Empire* (Grand Rapids: Baker, 2016), 18–20.
[286] *Cels.* 7.25; 7.61 (SC 150:70–2; 156–8).
[287] Mt. 5:39; *Princ.* 3.1.6 (Behr 2:296) μὴ ἀνωιστῆναι τῷ πονηρῷ *Cels.* 8.35 (SC 150:250–2).

revile the gods, let alone rulers.[288] Followers of Jesus exercise themselves in thinking, saying and doing what is in harmony with his words, blessing when reviled, suffering on and entreating when defamed. Rather than shamefully abusing those who hold different opinions, Christians exhort them to better living. We are careful, he says, not to oppose fair arguments, or be capricious, even in replying to slander.[289]

Confession and martyrdom

Origen values martyrdom and is more explicit as to its benefits than Clement. Martyrdom defeats the powers of evil and brings benefit to others. It is a gift back to God, a sacrifice that cleanses sin, and an exaltation.[290] Nevertheless, whilst desirable, martyrdom should not be provoked. Like Clement, Origen believes voluntary martyrdom makes one complicit in a crime. In an interesting modern perspective, Kolbert notes that Origen's concern for persecutors contrasts with the purpose of torture and persecution as exercises in terror. Torturers must devalue and dehumanize their victims, whereas Origen, following Christ, taught the intentional love of one's enemies.[291] Voluntary martyrs, Origen asserts, act in their own interests (!) being heedless of the blood on their hands and condemning persecutors to greater punishment because of those who out of self-centredness (φιλαυτοῦντες) deliver themselves up unnecessarily. Such will pay a penalty.[292] Even though teenaged Origen allegedly had to be restrained from following his father to martyrdom, the older Origen removed himself before finally submitting when imprisoned. Doubtless these events provided opportunity for him to scrutinize his own motives.

Like Clement, Origen sees the opportunity for martyrdom as wholly providential; 'no one comes to the contest of martyrdom without providence'.[293] He bases this on an exegesis of Matthew 10:28-31, which he terms an 'exhortation to martyrdom'.[294] It is not up to us to 'selfishly' provoke this honour and become complicit in the sin of the persecutor, but when God assigns us to martyrdom, it is our honour and duty to confess and embrace it. Remarking on Jesus' withdrawal to the desert (Jn 11:54) Origen supposes 'the Word wishes to turn us back from hotly and irrationally rushing to struggle unto death on behalf of the truth and to be martyred'.[295]

Those already imprisoned for their confession, such as Ambrose and Protocteus, however, are not voluntary martyrs in the sense of provocation. Other options are past. They have already been called to the contest, by God's providence. They have no option to escape now without recourse to denial, which is anathema. Origen therefore

---

[288] *Cels.* 8.38 (SC 150:256-8) alluding to Rom. 12:14.
[289] *Cels.* 5.63; 7.46 (SC 147:170-2; 150:122-6) citing 1 Cor. 4:12-13.
[290] *Mart.* 4, 28, 30, 50 (GCS 2:4-5, 24-5, 26-7, 46-7).
[291] Paul R. Kolbet, 'Torture and Origen's Hermeneutics of Non-violence', *Journal of the American Academy of Religion* 76, no. 3 (2008), 545-72, at 564.
[292] *Comm. Jo.* 28.23.194-5 (SC 385:156-8).
[293] *Mart.* 34 (GCS 2:30) οὐκ ἄνευ προνοίας ἔρχεταί τις ἐπὶ τὸν τοῦ μαρτυρίου ἀγῶνα.
[294] *Mart.* 34 (GCS 2:30) μαρτύριον προτρεπόμενα.
[295] *Comm. Jo.* 28.23.192 (SC 385:156) βουλομένου τοῦ λόγου ἐπιστρέψειν ἡμᾶς ἀπὸ τοῦ θερμότερον καὶ ἀλογιστότερον ἐπιπηδᾶν τῷ ἕως θανάτου ἀγωνίζεσθαι περὶ τῆς ἀληθείας καὶ μαρτυρεῖν.

encourages them with the prize to be won; their final confession will be a deliverance.[296] This will necessarily be an act of faith; 'For with the heart one believes and is justified, and with the mouth one confesses and is saved' (Rom. 10:10). Their word and heart must have the same believing disposition for their justification and salvation.[297]

Origen is concerned that confession may, problematically, be only partial. Unless the confessor rejects all evil thoughts of denial and doubt inspired by the Devil, says nothing inconsistent with confession, bears all reproach and mockery, is not diverted from his purpose from any other affection, even for the care of his family, and belongs totally to God, he has not *fully* confessed. 'But if we are lacking even one of them, we have not filled up but have defiled the measure of our confession.'[298] Such are building on the foundation with straw (1 Cor. 3:12). Conversely, those who suffer more in torture or in deprivation of worldly goods or loved ones are worthy of greater honour and will reap a hundredfold.[299] The grateful saint will find that there is no better gift to God in recompense for his benefits, as perfection in martyrdom.[300]

Apostasy

Origen, more explicitly than Clement, condemns the apostate: 'How great an abominable currency is the evil word of denial and the evil word of publicly proclaiming another god, and the evil oath by human Fortune, an unfounded matter.'[301] This is the very worst pollution of the soul, akin to an adulterous bride, or a man's consort with a prostitute.[302] The apostate returns to Satan, whom he renounced at baptism: who then will pray for him?[303] Origen envisions a theatre full of spectators witnessing his friends' martyrdom. As they contest victoriously for Christianity, they will be cheered on by watching angels. If they are defeated, the demons cheer and the deniers will join them in hell, taken captive by the Devil and numbered among his. 'He has become like the devil through his denial … For how will he be clean, who is defiled with blood and murder, by the abhorrent lapse of denial, and stained by so great an evil?'[304] Again, 'even if one avoids present punishment by men, he will not escape the hands of the Almighty'.[305]

---

[296] *Mart*. 2–3 (GCS 2:3–5).
[297] *Mart*. 5 (GCS 2:7).
[298] *Mart*. 11 (GCS 2:11) εἰ δὲ, κἂν ἑνί τινι λείποιμεν, οὐκ ἐπληρώσαμεν, ἀλλ᾽ ἐμολύναμεν τὸ τῆς ὁμολογίας μέτρον.
[299] *Mart*. 14–15 (GCS 2:14–15).
[300] *Mart*. 28 (GCS 2:24).
[301] *Mart*. 7 (GCS 2:8) πηλίκον βδέλυγμα νομιστέον εἶναι τὸ πονηρὸν τῆς ἀρνήσεως ῥῆμα, καὶ τὸν πονηρὸν τῆς ἄλλου θεοῦ ἀναγορεύσεως λόγον, καὶ τὸν πονηρὸν κατὰ τύχης ἀνθρώπων, πράγματος ἀνυποστάτου, ὅρκον.
[302] *Mart*. 10 (GCS 2:10).
[303] *Mart*. 17 (GCS 2:16); 1 Sam. 2:25.
[304] *Mart*. 18 (GCS 2:18) τῷ διαβόλῳ διὰ τῆς ἀρνήσεως ὡμοιωμένον … πῶς γὰρ ἔσται καθαρός, αἵματι καὶ φόνῳ, τῷ βδελυκτῷ τῆς ἀρνήσεως πταίσματι μεμιασμένος, καὶ ἐμπεφυρμένος τηλικούτῳ κακῷ.
[305] *Mart*. 22 (GCS 2:20). Citing 2 Macc. 6.

Those who deny Christ, or are ashamed of him, will be denied before the Father, and Christ will be ashamed of them.[306] The one who wishes to drink with Jesus must not prepare a table for demons, must not share the cup of demons.[307] To sacrifice to demons is to feed them, and thus to be liable for prosecution for the evil committed by demons;[308] it is a question of fellowship.

Nevertheless, Origen believes that lost souls, even the apostate, can ultimately be restored during the long process of correction in the next life. As Scott explains,[309] Origen affirms the reality of hell, especially in his homilies, as a dissuasion from sin, whereas for more enlightened audiences he leaves open the possibility of an end to such punishment, consistent with his belief in its remedial value.

> And in those ages to come God will show the riches 'of his grace in kindness', since the worst sinner, who has blasphemed the Holy Spirit and been ruled by sin from beginning to end in the whole of this present age, will afterwards in the age to come be brought into order, I know not how.[310]

It is difficult to interpret this in any other way than as an anticipation of the eventual restoration of apostates.

Avoidance

Between the extremes of provoking one's own martyrdom and overtly denying Christ when pressed to confess, lie several opportunities to avoid the potential for questioning and arrest. One could lie low or even actively withdraw, avoiding a public stand. The ability to lie low would depend on the good will of pagan neighbours and one's prominence as a citizen. It could be argued that this was a genuine reliance on God's providence, or it could be seen as cowardice.

Origen rebutted Celsus' criticism of Jesus' withdrawal by presenting it as a matter of prudence, consistent with his life.[311] Celsus asserted that Jesus lived a miserable life, hiding out of fear, but Origen responds, to the contrary. 'Now, it is not poor management to guard against danger, or withdraw, not through fear of death, but from a desire to benefit others by remaining in life, until the proper time came for the one who assumed human nature to suffer a death that benefits humankind.'[312] Origen uses the example of Jesus, who was clearly in control of his circumstances and foreknew the specific day of his arrest, to introduce a new reason for avoiding provocation: preserving oneself for ongoing work. 'If a Christian ever flees it is not from cowardice, but in obedience to the

---

[306] *Mart.* 37 (GCS 2:34); Mt. 10:33, Lk. 9:26.
[307] *Mart.* 40 (GCS 2:37–38).
[308] *Mart.* 45 (GCS 2:41–2).
[309] Scott, *Journey*, 140–2.
[310] Origen, *PEuch.* 27.15, as cited by Scott, *Journey*, 145.
[311] *Cels.* 1.65 (SC 132:256–8).
[312] *Cels.* 1.61 (SC 132:244) Οὐκ ἔστι δ' ἀγεννὲς τὸ μετ' οἰκονομίας περιιστάμενον τοὺς κινδύνος μὴ ὁμόσε αὐτοῖς χωρεῖν, οὐ διὰ φόβον θανάτου ἀλλ' ὑπὲρ τοῦ χρησίμως αὐτὸν τῷ βίῳ ἐπιδημοῦντα ἑτέρους ὠφελεῖν, ἕως ἐπιστῇ ὁ ἐπιτήδειος καιρὸς τοῦ τὸν ἀνειληφότα ἀνθρωπίνην φύσιν ἀνθρώπου θάνατον ἀποθανεῖν, ἔχοντα τι χρήσιμον τοῖς ἀνηρώποις.

command of his teacher, that so he may preserve himself, and benefit others to salvation.'[313] Perhaps Origen saw himself as providentially preserved by his mother's actions, for service to the church; from his later suffering and imprisonment it is clear he was no coward.

There is also the option of active withdrawal, or flight from persecution. Whilst maintaining that Matthew 10 was primarily directed to the apostles, Origen applies it to later disciples.[314] Specifically, Matthew 10:23 in its literal sense teaches withdrawal from persecution as far as possible. Jesus both taught and exemplified this, as Origen explains in both his commentaries on Matthew 14:13–14[315] and John 11:54.[316] The former describes Jesus' withdrawal to a desolate place when he heard of John's execution, the latter refers to Jesus no longer walking openly among the Jews after Caiaphas predicts his death.

> The literal meaning teaches us to withdraw, so far as possible, from those who persecute us and from situations where we anticipate being plotted against because of the Logos. This would be reasonable, but on the contrary, to come to close quarters with dangerous situations when it is possible to avoid them is rash and reckless. And who would still be doubtful about avoiding such situations when Jesus not only withdrew when it came to the matters related to John, but also teaches and says, 'If they persecute you in this city, flee to the other' (Mt. 10:23). Therefore, when trial comes no thanks to us, we must endure it very nobly and bravely, but it is reckless not to avoid it if this is possible.[317]

> I think that these words and those like them have been recorded because the Word wishes us to turn back from rushing too hastily and irrationally to struggle unto death on behalf of the truth and to suffer martyrdom. For, on the one hand, it is right not to shun the confession nor to hesitate to die for the truth if one has been caught in the struggle about confessing Jesus. But, on the other hand, it is no less right also not to provide an opportunity for such a great trial, but to avoid it by every means, not only because the outcome of such an act is unclear to us, but also so that we may not be responsible for causing those who would not, in actual fact, have become guilty of pouring out blood, to have become more sinful and impious [by doing so], if we act in our own interest and take no thought for those who plot against us unto death. These people will experience greater and more serious

---

[313] *Cels.* 8.44 (SC 150:270) Κἂν φεύγῃ δέ τις Χριστιανός, οὐ διὰ δειλίαν φεύγει, ἀλλὰ τηρῶν ἐντολὴν τοῦ διδασκάλου καὶ ἑαυτὸν φυλάττων καθαρὸν ἑτέρων ὠφεληθησομένων σωτηρίᾳ.
[314] *Mart.* 34–35 (GCS 2:29–33).
[315] *Comm. Matt.* 10.31.23 (SC 162:254).
[316] *Comm. Jo.* 28.23.192–4 (SC 385:156).
[317] *Comm. Matt.* 10.31.23 (SC 162:254) trans. Heine, 2018, 58. Τὸ μὲν ῥητὸν διδάσκει ἡμᾶς ὅσῃ δύναμις ἀπὸ τῶν διωκόντων, καὶ τῆς προσδοκίας τοῦ διὰ τὸν λόγον ἐπιβουλεύεσθαι, ἀναχωρεῖν· τοῦτο μὲν γὰρ κατὰ τὸ εὐλόγιστον γένοιτ' ἄν, τὸ δὲ δυνάμενον ἔξω εἶναι τῶν περιστατικῶν ὁμόσε χωρεῖν αὐτοῖς προπετές ἐστι καὶ θρασύ. Τίς δὲ ἔτι ἀμφιβάλοι ἂν περὶ τοῦ ἐκκλίνειν τὰ τοιαῦτα, τοῦ Ἰησοῦ οὐ μόνον ἐπὶ τοῖς κατὰ τὸν Ἰωάννην ἀναχωρήσαντος, ἀλλὰ καὶ διδάσκοντος, καὶ λέγοντος· «Ἐὰν διώκωσιν ὑμᾶς ἐν τῇ πόλει ταύτῃ, φεύγετε εἰς τὴν ἑτέραν.» Ἐπελθόντα μὲν οὖν οὐ παρ' ἡμᾶς πειρασμὸν ἀναγκαῖον ὑπομένειν εὐγενῶς λίαν καὶ τεθαρρηκότως· παρὸν δὲ ἐκκλίνειν, τοῦτο μὴ ποιεῖν τολμηρόν.

punishment because of us, if we are self-centred and do not consider the things of others (1 Cor. 10:24) and deliver ourselves to be killed when this necessity has not overtaken us.[318]

Origen uses Jesus' withdrawal to introduce a third reason for avoiding provocation, by equating it with humility. Jesus withdrew when his hour had not yet come (Jn 7:30) and Origen states that this was written for our imitation.[319] For this reason, explains Origen, we must heed the words, 'If they persecute you in this city, flee to another' (Mt. 10:23).[320]

> Now, in the same way that he teaches us through such things to withdraw in persecutions and plots against us, so in others you would find him withdrawing also from things the world holds to be good, so that through these examples, too, he might teach us to flee honours and positions of superiority in the world.[321]

This correlates Origen's various concerns; martyrdom is an exaltation, but it must not be a *self*-exaltation. It must be a pure confession, acknowledging that one is brought to martyrdom by God's providence alone. As Rizzi observes, Origen insists that martyrdom is not the result of human effort, but a sign of choosing by the God who knows the secrets of human hearts.[322] This is why seeking out or provoking martyrdom is a sign of self-love, of seeking worldly honours rather than the heavenly reward.

The church's response

Community

Origen's writings display a consciousness that persecuted individuals are part of a persecuted community. However, Origen presents a different picture of the persecuted

---

[318] *Comm. Jo.* 28.23.192-4 (SC 385:156) trans. Heine, 1993, 332-3. Ταῦτα καὶ τὰ τούτοις παραπλήσια ἀναγεγράφθαι νομίζω βουλομένου τοῦ λόγου ἐπιστρέφειν ἡμᾶς ἀπὸ τοῦ θερμότερον καὶ ἀλογιστότερον ἐπιπηδᾶν τῷ ἕως θανάτου ἀγωνίζεσθαι περὶ τῆς ἀληθείας καὶ μαρτυρεῖν. Καλὸν μὲν γὰρ ἐμπεσόντα εἰς τὸν περὶ τοῦ ὁμολογεῖν τὸν Ἰησοῦν ἀγῶνα μὴ ἀναδύεσθαι τὴν ὁμολογίαν, μηδὲ μέλλειν περὶ τὸ ὑπεραποθανεῖν τῆς ἀληθείας. Οὐκ ἔλαττον δὲ τούτου καλὸν καὶ τὸ μὴ διδόναι ἀφορμὴν τῷ τηλικούτῳ πειρασμῷ ἀλλὰ παντὶ τρόπῳ περιίστασθαι αὐτόν, οὐ μόνον διὰ τὸ περὶ τῆς ἐν αὐτῷ ἐκβάσεως ἄδηλον ἡμῖν, ἀλλὰ καί ἵνα μὴ ἡμεῖς πρόφασις γενώμεθα τοῦ ἁμαρτωλοτέροις γενέσθαι καὶ ἀσεβεστέροις τοῖς οὐκ ἄν μὲν τῷ ἔργῳ τοῦ ἡμῶν ἐκκεχύσθαι τὸ αἷμα γενομένοις ἐνόχοις, εἰ τὰ παρ' ἑαυτοὺς ποιοῦντες ἐκκλίνομεν τοὺς μέχρι θανάτου ἡμῖν ἐπιβουλεύοντας, ἐσομένοις δὲ ἐν πλείονι καὶ βαρυτέρᾳ κολάσει παρ' ἡμᾶς εἰ φιλαυτοῦντες καὶ μὴ καὶ τὰ ἐκείνων σκοποῦντες ἐπιδιδῶμεν αὐτοὺς τῷ ἀναιρεῖσθαι, οὐ τῆς ἀνάγκης εἰς τοῦτο καταλαβούσης.
[319] *Comm. Jo.* 28.23.196 (SC 385:158).
[320] *Comm. Jo.* 28.23.198 (SC 385:158) Ἐὰν διώκωσιν ὑμᾶς ἐν τῇ πόλει ταύτῃ, φεύγετε εἰς τὴν ἑτέραν.
[321] *Comm. Jo.* 28.23.209 (SC 385:162) trans Heine, 1993, 335. Ὥσπερ δὲ διὰ τῶν τοιούτων διδάσκει ἡμᾶς ἐν διωγμοῖς καὶ ταῖς καθ' ἡμῶν ἐπιβουλαῖς ἀναχωρεῖν, οὕτως ἐν ἄλλοις εὕροις ἂν καὶ ἀπὸ τῶν νομιζομένων εἶναι ἐν κόσμῳ καλῶν ἀναχωροῦντα, ἵνα καὶ διὰ τούτων διδάξῃ φεύγειν τὰ ἐν κόσμῳ ἀξιώματα καὶ τὰς ἐν αὐτῷ ὑπεροχάς.
[322] Marco Rizzi, 'Origen on Martyrdom: Theology and Social Practices', in *Origeniana Nona: Origen and the Religious Practices of his Time*, Papers of the 9th International Origen Congress 2005, ed. G. Heidl and R. Somos (Leuven: Peeters, 2009), 469-76.

church for external readers than for internal consumption. As Daniélou notes, in *Contra Celsum*, 'he paints an idealized picture of the Christian community and represents Christians as living in detachment from the things of this world', whereas in the commentaries and homilies he 'does not hesitate to reproach the people for their faults'.[323] Origen reminisced about the past days of real faith when there were many martyrs, the church mourned, the catechumens were prepared for martyrdom and there were signs and wonders; fewer believers, but genuine ones.[324] Nevertheless, despite persecution, he recognizes that by God's power, the church was extending throughout the world.[325]

Although Origen directs his *Exhortation* to individuals, the sense of community is evident. Origen writes of strangers holding 'us' in contempt,[326] and uses the first-person plural extensively. Although martyrdom is largely described in individual terms and as an individual response, the great theatre of spectators who will watch the martyrs' contest includes all humanity, both God's people and others.[327] Christian martyrs die in continuity with the prophets and other Jewish heroes, such as the seven brothers of 2 Maccabees, Daniel's three friends and the Lord Jesus himself.[328]

This concept of continuity between God's people in the past, Christ, and Christ's people is an important aspect of typological interpretation of Scripture, as explained by O'Keefe and Reno. Old Testament heroes such as Joshua were types of Christ, prefiguring him and his work. Likewise, Christians post-figure Christ.[329] Origen's employment of this strategy is evident throughout his exegetical writings. With respect to persecution, I described above how he uses Jeremiah as the paradigmatic persecuted prophet, prefiguring Christ, the apostles, and all who suffer for the name in continuity. Similarly, Origen sees the sacrifices of the Law foreshadowing not only Christ's death but that of his martyred followers. So powerful is this image that he proposes their sacrifices may also have atoning power.[330]

Apologetic

Origen's apologetic marks a departure from his predecessors. In the second century, apologists such as Justin, Minucius Felix and Athenagoras presented a public response to persecution, repudiating accusations against Christians and offering a positive defence of the community. Origen's great apologetic work is his *Contra Celsum*, a detailed engagement with Celsus' Λόγος Ἀληθής, which was written around 170-80.[331] The preface makes it clear that Origen's response was not really written as a traditional

---

[323] Daniélou, *Origène*, 40.
[324] *Hom. Jer.* 4.3.2 (SC 232:264).
[325] *Hom. Luc.* 6.9 (PG 13:1816) from Britain to Mauritania, cited by Kreider, *Patient Ferment*, 7.
[326] *Mart.* 2 (GCS 2:3) φαυλίζοιεν ἡμᾶς.
[327] *Mart.* 18 (GCS 2:16-17).
[328] *Mart.* 22-29, 33 (GCS 2:19-26, 28-9). The same exemplars are used by Cyprian.
[329] O'Keefe and Reno, *Sanctified Vision*, 82, and their broader discussion 69-88.
[330] *Comm. Jo.* 6.281-283 (SC 342-4).
[331] Marcel Borret, introduction to *Origène Contre Celse, Introduction, Texte Critique, Traduction et Notes*, 4 vols. Sources Chrétiennes 132 (Paris: Cerf, 1967), Tome I, 73, notes Origen's inversion of Celsus' title, 'en disant qu'il ne voit dans le livre de Celse ni un discours vrai ni un vrai discours'.

apology to outsiders, much less an argument against persecution, but rather directed to those weak in the faith who might be adversely influenced by Celsus' arguments.[332] This is borne out by the heavy use of Scripture, which does not usually characterize apologies directed to pagans. Origen thinks that his written apology will somewhat weaken that defence of Christianity that rests on facts and the manifest power of Jesus. He does not think Celsus' arguments would harm the faith of a true believer and disapproves of believers whose faith can be shaken by Celsus, or who have need of arguments in books in answer to the charges against the Christians in order to confirm their faith.[333] Origen's apology, strikingly, is not an argument against persecution.

Notwithstanding his reservations, Origen tackles the task painstakingly, covering many standard apologetic topics and illuminating Celsus' wrong apprehension of many of the facts behind the accusations, turning them back against Graeco-Roman society, its beliefs and practices. Early apologies had not discussed the prediction of persecution in Scripture, nor its inevitability: that would probably have seemed counterproductive.[334] But Origen cites Jesus' prophecies of persecution of his church, not as an argument against persecution, but to demonstrate the reliability of Jesus' words and the veracity of Christianity.[335] This is an original development. Furthermore, Christians follow Jesus in not resisting their persecutors, and do not avenge themselves on their enemies. God does not permit all Christians to be destroyed, only a few, so those of weaker minds might revive their courage. God interposes his providence so that kings, rulers and populace can only rage against them up to a point.[336] Origen's response to Celsus is therefore not primarily a plea to pagans in authority, but an aid to those struggling with the ideas of Christianity. True Christians do not need apologetics; it is for those on the boundary.

Conclusions

Origen's diogmology is firmly embedded in his overarching and well-developed theology of the soul's fall and return to God. The rebellion of free-willed rational creatures accounts for the enmity between the Devil's world and God's, and the resulting spiritual battle which must be fought. Persecution is an inevitable aspect of this battle. The whole situation and its eventual resolution are under God's providential control, a conviction Origen shares with Clement.

Origen departs from his predecessor at the crucial point of persecution's aetiology: God brings certain evils into play and permits persecution. God is more involved in the process than Clement will allow. Origen is therefore more open to the benefits of persecution, particularly the example the martyrs set for the church community, and God's choice of individuals for the exaltation of martyrdom.

---

[332] *Cels.* 1 Pref. 4 SC 132:70).
[333] *Cels.* 1 Pref. 4 (SC 132:72).
[334] See also Ruth Sutcliffe, 'No Need to Apologise? Tertullian and the Paradox of Polemic Against Persecution'. *StPatr*, 126 no. 123, 267-78.
[335] *Cels.* 2.13 (SC 132:318-24).
[336] *Cels.* 3.8 (SC 136:28).

Origen is much more explicit than Clement that the world is the stage of a cosmic conflict between God and the Devil. Persecution is under God's control, the Devil under God's restraint. Christians share Christ's battle with the Devil. Therefore, Origen acknowledges that God calls some evils into existence for his educative and medicinal purposes and takes a more active role in his people's persecution experience than Clement allows. Persecution directly results from the fundamental identity of Christians, upholding the name of Christ. Christ is persecuted in the believer, united in conflict and victory over the Devil. Martyrdom specifically achieves this so Origen's appraisal is positive. Therefore, he uses more explicit arena and battle metaphors than Clement.

Origen sees martyrdom as an advantage, greater suffering and loss bringing greater reward in the life to come. Further, he sees martyrdom as imparting forgiveness, as sacramental, even potentially providing cleansing for others. He emphasizes the reward, and the likeness to God achieved by the non-vengeful Christian. In fact, so valuable is martyrdom that Origen warns it must not be sought for self-exaltation but remains God's providential prerogative. Its very desirability is a temptation, so Origen specifies three reasons for not provoking it. It would implicate one in the persecutors' sin, it would be self-aggrandisement, and it might be better to preserve oneself for service to God and others. Furthermore, Origen emphasizes that not only is confession essential, but it must also be pure and complete, which is no light undertaking.

Nevertheless, Origen shares Clement's lack of urgency for the conversion of the wicked in this life, because of their similar views of progressive salvation and the opportunity for post-mortem repentance. Origen brings a new flavour to apologetics. He wants the truth and superiority of Christianity to be made known, yet Origen does not produce an argument about the injustice of persecution or plead for its cessation. He understands that persecution is inevitable in this life, until all the evil opposition is removed, and everything brought back to God.

4

Tertullian of Carthage

Pedantic polemicist

> Our battle is that we are summoned before tribunals, there we struggle under mortal danger for the truth. However, it is a victory to obtain that for which we have struggled. This victory has both the glory of pleasing God and the plunder, eternal life.
>
> Tertullian, Apology 50

If this discussion were a drama, Quintus Septimius Florens Tertullianus would be the main protagonist. I say this not on account of his particularly dramatic writing style, although he has that, but because he commands the stage. Of the four fathers, Tertullian has the most consistent and well developed diogmology and makes the greatest contribution to the discussion of Christian identity and apologetics. Introducing him now takes us back a generation to the late second and early third centuries, cotemporaneous with Clement. Tertullian offers a significant contrast with the Alexandrians, a contrast largely but not entirely carried over to Cyprian. Some aspects of their theology of persecution are quite at odds, which makes their common ground more impressive.

Tertullian in context

Tertullian (c. 160–c. 220 CE) was the first theologian of the Latin West.[1] Very little is known of his life, and the date and circumstances of his death are obscure.[2] There is no evidence that he was personally the subject of persecution or trial, that he fled or confessed or was martyred, despite his detailed writing and strong opinions on these topics. Timothy Barnes ironically conjectures that Tertullian may have been a martyr whom the church preferred to forget.[3] Tertullian was no stranger to controversy but

---

[1] For a survey of Tertullian's theology, see Eric Osborn, *Tertullian: First Theologian of the West* (Cambridge: Cambridge University Press, 2003); Geoffrey D. Dunn, *Tertullian* (New York: Routledge, 2004), 35–38. For comparisons with Pauline theology, see David E. Wilhite and Todd D. Still, ed. *Tertullian and Paul*, vol. 1 of Pauline and Patristic Scholars in Debate (New York: T&T Clark, 2013).
[2] For a brief survey of Tertullian's life and works see Dunn, *Tertullian*, 3–11. Jerome, *De Viris Illustribus*, 53, https://la.wikisource.org/wiki/De_viris_illustribus_(Hieronymus)#Caput_LIII provides a short biography, largely debunked by Timothy D. Barnes, *Tertullian: A Historical and Literary Study* (Oxford: Clarendon, 2005) 3–29.
[3] Barnes, *Tertullian*, 59.

did not receive the level of posthumous condemnation that Origen did. Tertullian may have been a presbyter, or at least in a position of influence in the church, given that he was involved in debriefing the 'sister' who received ecstatic visions.[4]

A context of persecution

The most significant exposure to persecution for Tertullian was probably around the time of emperor Septimius Severus' visit to Africa Proconsularis in 203. This seems to have inflamed an emperor-fervour among the populace and prompted the martyrdoms of Perpetua and her companions in Carthage.[5] Tertullian later attested that Severus was well disposed toward Christians,[6] an apparent contradiction attributable to the distinction between persecution *by* Severus and persecution *under* Severus.[7] Christians may have often wondered why the emperor of the day did not do something about persecution. This seems to be the tenor of apologies directed at emperors which, when ignored, gave the impression of imperial hostility. Barnes suggests ill-feeling toward North African Christians would have arisen from suspicion they were unenthusiastic about the native African Severus' ascension, declining to join festivities. Perpetua and her companions may have been selected as victims in games marking Severus' tour. Presumably Tertullian was in Carthage during the 203 executions, and he evidently accessed an early version of the *Passio*,[8] yet he does not state he witnessed it. Tertullian did, however, write *Scorpiace* in 'a time of persecution', taken to be around 203. At this critical time the Gnostics' heretical 'poison' was allegedly deterring Christians from martyrdom.[9]

> Christians have been tried, by fire, others by sword, others by beasts, others meanwhile hunger in prison for the martyrdom they taste by clubs and claws. We are like rabbits, appointed for hunting ... those who oppose martyrdoms, interpreting salvation as destruction, changing sweet to bitter, light to darkness, preferring this miserable life to that blessed one.[10]

Tertullian's later writings, including his more rigorist works, were written in the latter part of Severus' and during Caracalla's reigns, and contain several references to

---

[4] *An.* 9.4 (CCSL 2:792) Post transacta sollemnia dimissa plebe, quo usu solet nobis renuntiare quae uiderit ...
[5] Barnes, *Tertullian*, 88, referencing *Apol.* 35.4.
[6] *Scap.* 4.5–4.6.
[7] As W. H. C. Frend, *Martyrdom and Persecution in the Early Church* (Cambridge: James Clarke, 2008), 121, who notes that 'persecution went on automatically, if sporadically, whoever the emperor might be', with the provincial governor playing the most important role.
[8] *An.* 55.4 (CCSL 2:862–3) cf. *Passio* 4.3 (Rebillard, 308).
[9] Clement, *Strom.* 4.4.16.3 (SC 463:82–4); Tertullian, *Scorp.* 1.5 (CCSL 2:1069); *Praescr.* 4 (CCSL 1:189-9) and see Barnes, *Tertullian*, 55.
[10] *Scorp.* 1.11–13 (CCSL 2:1070–1) Alios ignis, alios gladius, alios bestiae Christianos probauerunt, alii fustibus interim et ungulis insuper degustato martyrio in carcere esuriunt. Nos ipsi ut lepores, destinata uenatio ... martyriis refragantur salutem perditionem interpretantes tam dulce in amarum quam lucem in tenebras reformant atque ita miserrimam hanc uitam illi beatissimae praeuertendo ...

persecutions.¹¹ These were perceived as increasing.¹² Christians, including some clergy, were fleeing persecutions and also seeking to bribe their way out of persecution,¹³ and Christians were being imprisoned and sent to mines.¹⁴ *Ad Scapulam*, written in 212, reminds the proconsul of past repercussions and the example of Severus. Persecution thus permeates Tertullian's entire oeuvre, not just those works for which it is the main topic.

A context of argument

Tertullian's writings encompass apologetics, polemics against Jews, Gnostics, Monarchianism and Marcion, and treatises on theological and practical topics, for which I will largely adhere to the chronology of Barnes.¹⁵ In almost every work there is an awareness of and reference to Christian persecution, and throughout this diversity of genres Tertullian's ideas on persecution remain remarkably consistent, irrespective of his audience. Because each work is a polemic against an opponent, the emphases vary in service to the particular argument and the audience to which it is directed. The overriding style of his work is argument, and he argued to win. As Dunn observes,

> He did not preach (and I use the word loosely) simply to edify or extol a congregation. He did not engage in exegesis simply to unlock the meaning of Scripture. He did not write systematic theology simply to contemplate the mysteries of God. He preached, interpreted Scripture and wrote in order to argue ... In everything he wrote, however, there was some point in dispute, some quarrel to be had and some error to be corrected.¹⁶

Tertullian was a passionate perfectionist and a highly skilled rhetorician.¹⁷ He employed whatever rhetorical strategies were necessary to win his arguments,¹⁸ with the result that his opinions and stance appear to change from one work to another, even to the point of outright contradiction. For example, in *De paenitentia* (c. 198–203) he argues that repentance is to be sought by all, but in *De pudicitia* (c. 210) he denies that forgiveness and reconciliation are available for the worst sins, except through

---

[11] *Marc.* 1.27.5 (CCSL 1:471); *Cor.*1 (CCSL 2:1039–41); *Cast.* 12.3-4 (CCSL 2:1032); *De fuga; Prax.* 13.8 (CCSL 2:1175); *Jej.* 12.2 (CCSL 2:1270–1); *Pud.* 22 (CCSL 2:1328–30); *Ad Scapulam*.

[12] *Fug.* 1.1 (CCSL 2:1135); *Cor.* 1.5 (CCSL 2:1040) records Christians complaining that their 'long and good peace' had been jeopardized by the soldier's actions.

[13] *Fug.* 5.1, 11.1; 12.1 (CCSL 2:1141, 1148, 1149).

[14] Tertullian, *Jej.* 12.2 (CCSL 2:1270).

[15] Barnes, *Tertullian*, 30–56. Barnes revised his chronology in his 1984 edition, 325–9. Dunn, *Tertullian*, 7-9 critiques Barnes' chronology, particularly regarding 'Montanist' influence. Barnes' chronology has also been reviewed by David I. Rankin, *Tertullian and the Church* (Cambridge: Cambridge University Press), 1995, xiv–xvii.

[16] Dunn, *Tertullian*, 9–10.

[17] David E. Wilhite, 'Rhetoric and Theology in Tertullian: What Tertullian learned from Paul', StPatr 65 (2013), 295–312, at 295. See also Robert D. Sider, *Ancient Rhetoric and the Art of Tertullian* (London: Oxford University Press, 1971) and Geoffrey D. Dunn, 'Rhetorical Structure in Tertullian's Ad Scapulam'. *Vigiliae Christianae* 56, no. 1 (2002), 47–55.

[18] Dunn, *Tertullian*, 23.

martyrdom. In *Ad uxorem* (c. 198–203) he seems to allow flight in persecution, whereas in *De fuga* (c. 208) he does not. As I argue elsewhere,[19] these differences largely reflect the different audiences for which he writes, and the purpose of the writing. In general, he does become more 'rigorist' over time, particularly with respect to flight, military service, remarriage and penitence, but we must not overlook the 'rigorism' evident even in his earliest works, which rail against Christian involvement in arena shows and associations with idolatry.

The traditional assumption that a conversion to Montanism around 206 largely accounts for developments in Tertullian's perspectives has been replaced with a consensus that, whilst he was certainly influenced by the New Prophecy, he did not break away from the orthodox church.[20] Different emphases likely reflect a shift in Tertullian's interests and his engagement with new detractors that would drive his arguments in a specific direction.[21] While it may still be appropriate to speak of 'pre-Montanist' versus 'Montanist' works, reflecting this influence and interest, I will refer to the latter as his more 'rigorist' period. It is notable that throughout his writings, Tertullian's diogmology is remarkably consistent. His high view of martyrdom and the need for disciplinary preparation, for instance, is as evident in his early work *Ad martyras* as in his final extant work, *Ad Scapulam*.

Tertullian employs Stoic and dialectic strategies in his arguments,[22] despite expressing reservations about philosophy, not least as the source of heresies.[23] He regularly cites pagan authors and classical learning.[24] Eric Osborn concludes that although Tertullian considers philosophy imperfect and that rational inquiry is to be based on the rule of faith, he utilizes philosophy to convince educated pagans of the truth of the gospel.[25]

Scripture was Tertullian's authoritative primary source, to be interpreted in conformity with the rule of faith, with Christ as the unifying theme of salvation

---

[19] Sutcliffe, 'To Flee or Not to Flee? Matthew 10:23 and Third Century Flight in Persecution', *Scrinium* 14, no. 1 (2018), 133–60.

[20] See Rankin, *Tertullian and the Church*, 41–51; William Tabernee, *Prophets and Gravestones: An imaginative history of Montanists and other early Christians* (Peabody MS: Hendrickson, 2009), 2–3; David E. Wilhite, 'The Spirit of Prophecy: Tertullian's Pauline Pneumatology', in *Tertullian and Paul*, vol. 1 *of Pauline and Patristic Scholars in Debate*, ed. David E. Wilhite and Todd D. Still (New York: T&T Clark 2013), 45–71. Likewise, Moss, 'Justification of the Martyrs', in *Tertullian and Paul*, 104–18, at 106, 118, considers that Tertullian's pre-Montanist views on martyrdom differed little from his later 'Montanist' views.

[21] Tabernee, *Prophets and Gravestones*, conjectures on these influences in his imaginative narratives.

[22] For a discussion of Tertullian's views on philosophy, see François-Régis Doumas, 'L'évolution de Tertullien dans son attitude vis-à-vis de la philosophie', parts 1 and 2, *Théophilyon* 2, no. 1 (1997), 121–47; 2, no. 2 (1997), 497–521 and Eric Osborn, 'Was Tertullian a Philosopher?' *StPatr* 31 (1997), 322–34.

[23] *An*. 2 (CCSL 2:783–5) *Praescr*. 7 (CCSL 1:192–3).

[24] Osborn, *Tertullian*, 33. For an overview of Tertullian's references, citations and allusions to Latin writers, see David I. Rankin, *From Clement to Origen: The Social and Historical Context of the Church Fathers* (Hampshire: Ashgate, 2006), 69–70.

[25] Osborn, *Tertullian*, 31, 39 referencing *Praescr*. 13–14.

history.[26] Tertullian uses Scripture extensively, except in apologetic works designed for pagan readers.[27] He insists that the Scriptures belong to the true church, not to heretics, who have no right to use them.[28] Tertullian is thought to have largely made his own Latin translations from the Greek Scriptures.[29] He was particularly indebted to the Apostle Paul.[30] Tertullian adapts his hermeneutical methods and use of historical context, skilfully modifying his exegesis to his polemical objectives,[31] for example, the extent to which Matthew 10 applies to contemporary Christians.[32] Tertullian uses typology and allegory but also promotes the literal sense of Scripture.[33]

The identification of Tertullian's exegetical 'strategies' is somewhat difficult because he appears inconsistent. Atkinson discovered that 'separation of key texts in order to note a change in their usage is not, in itself, a valid approach. Only by a consideration of such texts in relation to specific theological and practical issues can a development in Tertullian's thought be legitimately and convincingly traced.'[34] Dunn argues that the hermeneutical principles Tertullian presents in *De praescriptione* 'were not part of a systematic and theoretical overview. They were specific to one issue.'[35] Rather, Tertullian adapts his exegetical strategies to the context and the arguments put forward by his opponents.[36] This is particularly evident with his use of Matthew 10:23. Nevertheless, Tomsick identifies six principles of interpretation within Tertullian's writings: use of any available argument, reading a passage in historical context, determining sense by the meaning of words, taking scripture literally, with allegory only used when the literal interpretation is impossible, clear rules are more binding than examples, and unclear passages are to be interpreted by more clear passages.[37] But Tertullian does not always stick to these guidelines. As Litfin notes, Tertullian's overarching hermeneutical device is best understood as his appropriation of the rule of faith, with Christ as the unifying

---

[26] Bryan M. Litfin, 'Tertullian's Use of the *Regula Fidei* as an Interpretive Device in *Adversus Marcionem*'. StPatr 42 (2006), 405-10, at 408-9. For more detailed engagement with Tertullian's exegesis, see T. P. O'Malley, *Tertullian and the Bible: Language, Imagery, Exegesis* (Utrecht: Dekker & Van de Vegt, 1967); Dunn, *Tertullian*, 19-23; Dunn, 'Scriptural Exegesis'; Still and Wilhite, *Tertullian and Paul*, for Tertullian's use of Paul, especially Everett Ferguson, 'Tertullian, Scripture, Rule of Faith and Paul', in *Tertullian and Paul*, vol. 1 of *Pauline and Patristic Scholars in Debate*, ed. David E. Wilhite and Todd D. Still (New York: T&T Clark 2013), 22-33; Osborn, *Tertullian*, 151-2; Sider, *Ancient Rhetoric*, 131; Richard D. Tomsick, 'Structure and Exegesis in Tertullian's *Ad Uxorem* and *De Exortatione Castitatis*'. StPatr 46 (2010), 9-15.
[27] Dunn, *Tertullian*, 19.
[28] Tertullian, *Praescr.* 15-19 (CCSL 1:199-201); Dunn, *Tertullian*, 21; Dunn, 'Scriptural Exegesis', 144-6.
[29] Dunn, *Tertullian*, 21.
[30] Everett Ferguson, 'Tertullian, Scripture, Rule of Faith', 23.
[31] Geoffrey D. Dunn, 'Tertullian's Scriptural Exegesis in *De praescriptione haereticorum*', *Journal of Early Christian Studies* 14, no. 2 (2006), 141-55, esp. 142, 153. See also Sutcliffe, 'To Flee or Not to Flee?', 143-4.
[32] In *Scorpiace* 9 he argues it does, but in *De fuga* he is adamant that verse 23 does not.
[33] Dunn, *Tertullian*, 22-23; Dunn, 'Scriptural Exegesis', 151-5.
[34] Philip C. Atkinson, 'A Study in the Development of Tertullian's Use and Interpretation of Scripture, with Special Reference to his Involvement in the New Prophecy' (PhD thesis, University of Hull, 1976), Pref. iv.
[35] Dunn, 'Scriptural Exegesis', 141.
[36] Ibid., 142.
[37] Richard D. Tomsick, 'Structure and Exegesis in Tertullian's *Ad Uxorem* and *De Exortatione Castitatis*', StPatr, 46, 2010, 9-15.

theme of salvation history.[38] Litfin discounts using scattered exegetical principles from Tertullian's works as keys to his hermeneutical system; Tertullian is much more interested in biblical interpretation with a view to bringing specific doctrinal questions in line with the overall truth of Christian faith.[39] Context, specifically the objective and audience of his argument, will therefore be the most fruitful approach to analysing Tertullian's use of Scripture.

Context is particularly important when investigating Tertullian's theology of persecution, because persecution is discussed or referred to in nearly every one of his extant works. Tertullian's most complete and coherent diogmology occurs in *De fuga in persecutione*, a late work. Nevertheless, these developed ideas are foreshadowed consistently in earlier works, particularly *Ad martyras*, *Ad nationes*, *Apologeticum*, *Scorpiace* and evident in the late work *Ad Scapulam*.

An alternative context?

Daniel-Hughes and Kotrosits present an alternative account of influences on Tertullian. They argue that his writings, rather than being 'windows into already circulating martyrological discourse or real early Christian communities', represent participation in 'a larger set of cultural preoccupations with, and fantasies of, Roman power and juridical scenes'.[40] They conclude that 'Tertullian's own accounts of confrontations with Roman power seem to be literary imaginations'.[41] This work, based on a detailed examination of Graeco-Roman representations of power, inserts Tertullian into a post-colonial framework in which imagination or 'fantasy' enables the inhabitants of Roman colonies to understand their social context. Such 'fantasies' are stimulated by visual representations of Roman power which act as propaganda, and find expression in literature.[42] Juridical scenes and impressions of Roman justice are particularly fruitful subjects, because of the contrast between the physical absence of high-level Roman rulers and their presence by proxy in local bureaucracies.[43] Trials and courtroom scenes in particular provide fuel for imaginative idealizations and elaborations of power which find expression in such genres as Greek novels and philosophical lives, petitions, various inscriptions and Christian literature.[44]

The authors cite a convincing array of examples and secondary opinions to support their contention that 'Roman rhetoric and propaganda on law and justice, combined with the ironies, arbitrariness and/or mystery of ancient juridical processes, and the absence of Roman rulers themselves' prompted the use of fantasy to arbitrate questions of right and wrong, offer a sense of reparation and fairness and 'consolidate and

---

[38] Litfin, 'Tertullian's Use of the *Regula Fidei*', 408–9.
[39] Ibid., 405–10; 405–6.]
[40] Carly Daniel-Hughes and Maia Kotrosits, 'Tertullian of Carthage and the Fantasy Life of Power: On Martyrs, Christians and Other Attachments to Juridical Scenes', *Journal of Early Christian Studies* 28, no. 11 (2020), 1–31, at 29.
[41] Ibid., 29.
[42] Ibid., 8–9.
[43] Ibid., 9.
[44] Ibid., 11, n. 32.

produce a stable identity where there is none'.[45] They rightly detect such influences in apologetic literature, including that of Tertullian. However, their conclusions regarding Tertullian overstep their carefully presented evidence by attributing a degree of dependency which overlooks Tertullian's stated and demonstrated intent.

Daniel-Hughes and Kotrosits assert that Tertullian fabricates his accounts of Christian–Roman confrontations from literary sources using tropes indicative of fantasies of Roman power. They present Tertullian as isolated from reality, producing literary imaginations 'hardly indicative of any Christian concerns at all'.[46] Christians' violent conflicts with Roman officials are deemed to be constructed 'gothic melodramas' reflecting 'the fantasy life of power', and ultimately not a fundamentally Christian discourse or perspective.[47] His portrayal of Christian–Roman conflict is 'drawn up largely, if not exclusively, through his reading of literature',[48] for the authors assert he would have little exposure to or real knowledge of Roman judicial procedure.[49] Further, the authors posit there is little evidence for Carthaginian Christians at all in Tertullian's time. They conclude that Tertullian's accounts 'seem to be literary imaginations', which helped the transition from 'Christian as a slanderous and empty epithet to a positively claimed self-descriptor'.[50]

Certainly, Christian apologies can be viewed as petitions, which the authors identify as 'important venues for articulations of ideology and social relationships', in which trial narratives such as those of Justin's *Apologies* provide a medium for expression of judicial fantasies.[51] The second-century apologies can be considered in this light. However, as I have shown, Tertullian's apologies are not petitions for persecutions to cease.[52] Rather, they are petitions for Christians to not be persecuted from ignorance, which reflect Tertullian's theology of the Christian's identity as a sufferer for the name of Christ. Tertullian's employment of the petition, replete with trial and judiciary tropes, can readily be seen as a demonstration of his literary adaptability.

Whilst Daniel-Hughes and Kotrosits are correct to recognize clear parallels in Tertullian's writings with the fantasy life of Roman power which they describe, they omit any reference to the much more dominant and stated primary literary source used by Tertullian: Scripture. The evidence that Tertullian draws his ideas and frames his arguments fundamentally from sacred literature is not considered. On the contrary, they consider his work to be 'hardly indicative of any specifically Christian concerns at all', and not revelatory of 'a particularly Christian discourse or perspective'.[53] Tertullian, they assert, 'imagines a god who doles out real justice',[54] which hardly does justice to his expositions of the consistency of God's goodness and justice in *Adversus Marcionem*.

---

[45] Ibid., 16.
[46] Ibid., 3.
[47] Ibid., 3.
[48] Ibid., 17.
[49] Ibid., 18.
[50] Ibid., 29.
[51] Ibid., 15, n. 51.
[52] Ruth Sutcliffe, 'No Need to Apologise? Tertullian and the Paradox of Polemic Against Persecution', StPatr 23, 267–78.
[53] Daniel-Hughes and Kotrosits, 'Fantasy Life of Power', 3.
[54] Ibid., 16.

Whilst the authors' objective is not to provide a theological perspective on Tertullian, this surely goes beyond the evidence. His heavy indebtedness to Scripture and his theological concerns are evident throughout his oeuvre and provide a much more coherent and consistent basis for his discussions of persecution than the sources presented by the authors. Tertullian certainly adapts his use of Scripture to his arguments, and he may well be unrepresentative of his community in his rigorous opinions, but that does not demand that we look beyond his stated claims to articulate a Scriptural perspective.

One important basis for the authors' claims is the assertion that Tertullian invented a Christian community in Carthage for which there is essentially no evidence.[55] There is, however, strong evidence for a significant Carthaginian Christian community a few decades later in Cyprian's time, which makes it likely to have been quite well developed in Tertullian's. The detailed survey of early African Christianity by Burns and Jensen acknowledges the value of the early Christian literature in testifying to an established community in the second and third centuries. 'Fortunately, the extensive treatises of Tertullian and the eighty letters associated with Cyprian's episcopate yield as much information on Christian life as can be gathered in any other region of the Roman world in this period.'[56] Furthermore, the fact that Tertullian's descriptions of persecution find parallels in near contemporary writers increases our confidence that his accounts are not fabricated. There is a form of circular reasoning in the dismissal of Tertullian's testimony regarding the nature and experiences of the community due to perceived 'absence of real evidence otherwise suggesting communities of Christians even into the third century'.[57] Tertullian and contemporary writers *provide* such evidence, which is dismissed as unreliable in the absence of 'evidence'. One argument presented for the unreliability of Tertullian's testimony is the different portraits he paints of the Christian community for outsiders compared with insiders,[58] but this is readily attributable to different rhetorical objectives in different works. Origen does the same in his community.

Irrespective of whether Tertullian indeed wrote in frustrated isolation, with few contemporary readers, or if he was an active member of a real community whose concerns he shared, his is not an isolated or incongruent perspective. Both he and Origen present the church differently for outsiders and insiders. Tertullian is aware of, and utilizes, common themes from martyr acts and apologies and addresses heresies that are also the target of his contemporaries. Even Clement, who is cheese to Tertullian's chalk in so many ways, shares similar perspectives and concerns and presents the realities of the persecution experience. Cyprian, a mere generation later, testifies to essentially the same environment, albeit with the imposition of the Decian persecution.

The authors briefly discuss several literary sources which they suggest could form a basis for Tertullian's creative fantasies.[59] Whilst it is likely that Tertullian 'invents' his

---

[55] Ibid., 26–17.
[56] J. Patout Burns and Robin M. Jensen, *Christianity in Roman Africa: The Development of its Practices and Beliefs*. Grand Rapids: Eerdmans, 2014, L.
[57] Daniel-Hughes and Kotrosits, 'Fantasy Life of Power', 30
[58] Ibid., 26–7.
[59] Ibid., 20.

specific opponents,[60] the arguments he opposes, such as dualist heresies and illegitimate avoidance of martyrdom, are also engaged with by his contemporaries. Although Tertullian refers to Perpetua via a written source rather than a personally witnessed event,[61] this does not mean that the event did not occur. Tertullian would only know her vision from a written source, and he cites it as authoritative, which would lack credibility if the event had not occurred in living memory. The Pliny–Trajan correspondence is presented as a source from which Tertullian constructed his perception of contemporary judicial procedures against Christians. Corke-Webster has similar concerns, which I have addressed in Chapter 1.

In response to the assertions of Daniel-Hughes and Kotrosits I contend that Tertullian's presentation of persecution must be interpreted theologically and can be demonstrated to arise predominantly from his interpretation of Scripture. This does not necessitate genuine first-hand experience of a phenomenon which was evidently the common experience and interest of contemporary Christian communities. Tertullian generously employs trial and judiciary language and motifs because cosmic conflict lies at the heart of his theology of persecution. The world which opposes Christians does so at the Devil's instigation. Confession at trial is the pinnacle of the Christian's duty to confess the name of Christ. Tertullian relies on the just and righteous God of Scripture to provide ultimate justice. The identity of 'Christian' which the authors attempt to deconstruct is fundamentally the identity of bearing the name of Christ, and the unity with him which that entails. All these aspects are fundamentally theological, not the product of fantasies of Roman power. The remainder of this chapter will serve as a defence of this contention.

Persecution comes from God

Tertullian articulates the first question of diogmology (which actually prompted me to take the approach presented in this book): 'We ought to first attend to determine the status of persecution itself, whether it comes from God or from the devil.'[62] This marks him as a theologian who will build his practical response to a problem on a systematic foundation. It also flags the first major distinctive of Tertullian's diogmology. Whilst based on the common ground of God's goodness, his providential control of persecution and the role of the Devil and fallen humans in its outworking, Tertullian goes beyond Clement's 'non-prohibition' and Origen's 'permission' to situate the origin of persecution with God himself.

---

[60] For example, David E. Wilhite on Marcionites, 'Marcionites in Africa: What Did Tertullian Know and When Did He Invent It?' *Perspectives in Religious Studies* 4 (2016): 437–52.
[61] Daniel-Hughes and Kotrosits, 'Fantasy Life of Power', 21.
[62] *Fug.* 1.2 (CCSL 2:1135) animaduertentes ante determinari oportere de statu ipsius persecutionis, utrum a Deo ueniat an a diabolo.

Goodness and justice

Writing against Hermogenes' implication that God is unwilling or unable to amend the evil that is intrinsic to matter, Tertullian argues that God is the highest good and is eternal; evil is not eternal, but has a beginning and an end.[63] God's goodness cannot legitimately be defended by forcing a dichotomy between God and 'evil' matter.[64] As Kearsley notes, God's very freedom is the guardian of his goodness.[65] God resists evil imposed from elsewhere and is able to guarantee the good. God's omnipotence marks him as Creator, and his goodness, foreknowledge and rationality condition the exercise of his infinite power.[66]

Tertullian's response to Marcion focuses on God's goodness *in* judgement. Tertullian argues there is only one good and providential God, a description only suited to the Creator.[67] The Creator God, while yet a judge, is good, because a good God must also be just.[68] The weakness of Marcion's 'New Testament' god was in not judging or censuring evil. Marcion allegedly argued, concerning the fall:

> If [the Creator God] is truly good, and so unwilling that such an event [i.e. the fall] should happen, and prescient so as not to be ignorant of the consequence, and powerful enough to avert it, it would never have come ... Since, however, it has come, the contrary is absolutely true, that God must be believed to be neither good, nor prescient, nor powerful.[69]

In reply, Tertullian states that the Creator's works testify to his goodness and his power. In his prescience God granted humans free will, along with clear warnings against its abuse. This free will, to obey or resist, stamps humans as the image of God.[70] This is the appropriate constitution for humanity; God's goodness has purpose, unlike Marcion's god's 'purposeless goodness'.[71] God's prescient warning to humanity is Tertullian's defence against the criticism that, if God foreknew of the fall, why did he not prevent it? For Tertullian, a good God must execute retribution: 'God is not otherwise wholly good than as the rival of evil.'[72] Tertullian regards it as insufficient for Marcion's god to not will evil, and to merely prohibit it; for by not avenging it, he acquits it. By not punishing it, he lets it go free. I imagine he would have had the same objection to Clement's position.

---

[63] *Herm.* 11 (CCSL 1:406). A similar position to Origen, interestingly.
[64] *Herm.* 16 (CCSL 1:410).
[65] Roy Kearsley, *Tertullian's Theology of Divine Power* (Carlisle UK: Paternoster, 1998), 20.
[66] Ibid., 18–19, referencing *Marc.* 2.7
[67] *Marc.* 4.36.1–3 (CCSL 1:643–4).
[68] *Marc.* 2.17.1 (CCSL 1:494) which, according to Adonis Vidu, *Atonement, Law and Justice: The cross in historical and cultural contexts* (Grand Rapids: Baker Academic, 2014), was consistent with developed Graeco-Roman concepts of justice.
[69] *Marc.* 2.5.2 (CCSL 1:479–80) Si enim et bonus, qui euenire tale quid nollet, et praescius, qui euenturum non ignaret, et potens, qui depellere ualeret, nullo modo euenisset ... Quod si euenit, absolutum est e contrario deum neque bonum credendum neque praescium neque potentem.
[70] *Marc.* 2.5.3–7 (CCSL 1:480–1).
[71] *Marc.* 2.6.1–2 (CCSL 1:481) inrationaliter bonum.
[72] *Marc* 1.26.5 (CCSL 1:470) qui non alias plane bonus sit, nisi mali aemulus.

Providence and free will

Kearsey notes that Tertullian's God can do anything he considers appropriate, in order to bring about what he wills.[73] This personal divine freedom of will and power contradicts the Stoic notion of fate.[74] Tertullian, like the other fathers, interprets Matthew 5:44–45 as an explanation of God's impartial providence and rational goodness.[75] Humans have free will and are responsible for their actions, but Tertullian does not subsume providence to this. God the Creator foreordained our glory before the ages, revealing it in the last days.[76] If it is God's will, Christians will suffer persecutions, and if it is not, the heathen will be restrained, for not even sparrows fall without his will.[77] But when trouble does arise, for pagans it is as punishment and for Christians it is a warning; suffering does not really injure Christians because their concern is not for this life.[78] Punishments in this life last a relatively short time, at the most until death. But everlasting punishment is our due unless we fear God; it is better to fear God than the proconsul.[79] According to Tertullian, since the matter is wholly in God's hands, we should leave it to his will; one must not second-guess God's providence but only choose the course that is certainly right.[80]

Tertullian, like the other fathers, places the responsibility for the fall with human free will, rather than directly with the Creator. Nothing sinful can come from God, so the liberty of humans alone is responsible for the fall.[81] Humans are culpable despite the Devil's seduction, because their free will pertains to their image and likeness of God.[82] Therefore, people are responsible for good or bad choices, and God is not responsible for human misuse of free will, even though he foreknew it.[83] So far, there is little to distinguish Tertullian's views on free will from the Alexandrians'.

The adversary

Tertullian identifies various influences on the human soul, including the 'supreme powers', which he defines as 'the Lord God and his adversary the Devil'.[84] God is infinitely good and the Devil, who in his impatience led men into sin, is superlatively evil.[85] The Devil taught greed that he might rival God and be on equal footing – good and evil being extremes of equal magnitude.[86] The Devil corrupts the good things that

---

[73] Kearsey, *Divine Power*, 19.
[74] Ibid., 21.
[75] *Marc.* 1.23.3–4 (CCSL 1:465).
[76] *Marc.* 5.6.1–6 (CCSL 1:678–9).
[77] *Fug.* 3.2 (CCSL 2:1139); Mt. 10:29–31.
[78] *Apol.* 41.5 (CCSL 1:156).
[79] *Apol.* 45.7 (CCSL 1:160), alluding to Mt. 10:28–31.
[80] *Paen.* 6.3–4, 6.17 (CCSL 1:330, 331). *Fug.* 5.2 (CCSL 2:1141).
[81] *Marc.* 2.5–6 (CCSL 1:479–82).
[82] *Marc.* 2.8.2 (CCSL 1:484) sed liber et suae potestatis qui seductus est, sed imago et similitudo dei fortior angelo.
[83] *Marc.* 2.6.1; 2.9.8–9 (CCSL 1:481, 486).
[84] *An.* 20.5 (CCSL 2:812) deus dominus et diabolus aemulus.
[85] *Pat.* 5.3–14, 21 (CCSL 1:303–5).
[86] *Pat.* 16.2–4 (CCSL 1:317).

God has made.[87] The Devil, filling the world with the lie of his divinity, leads human nature astray, having infected it with the seed of sin.[88]

Tertullian affirms there are limitations to the Devil's power and states that the Devil could not possibly prevail against the Son.[89] The Devil's legion had no power over the swine (Mk 5:9–13) whose bristles God counts, together with the hairs of holy men.[90] The Devil nevertheless has his own power over those who do not belong to God; the nations are given him as a free possession.[91] But against the household of God, the Devil can do nothing by his own right, although God may grant the Devil the power to bring Christians to trial and to execute, to punish or to humble them.[92] Tertullian does not see the Devil as a god,[93] merely the chief of demons, a class of fallen spiritual beings whose purpose is the destruction of humanity.[94] Malignant demons are, he asserts, assigned to human souls at birth:[95]

> These exhale obscuring infections of demons and angels which corrupt the mind bringing rage and hideous insanity or furious passions and various errors, of which the most potent is this by which it commends these gods and captures and deceives minds, to obtain for itself proper nourishment of fumes and blood offered to statues and images.[96]

The heathen gods themselves are demons, to whom the pagans sacrifice the blood of Christians.[97] Pagans who try to force Christians to sacrifice, by manipulation and cruelty, are prompted to do so by the Devil, who is jealous of God's favour to Christians. The demons know they are no match for Christians, but from obstinacy and fear they seek to injure, even though the Christians' resistance brings their defeat.[98]

Against Marcion, Tertullian emphasized that even though God created the Devil, the Devil fell of his own free will and departed from his created nature; therefore, God cannot be blamed for the fall. God precondemned him, but deferred the Devil's destruction for the same reason he postponed the restitution of humanity. God thus *allowed for a conflict* whereby humans could crush the enemy with the same freedom of his will as had caused the fall. This would rightly lay blame on the Devil, not God, and recover humanity by a worthy victory. The Devil's punishment will be more bitter by his being vanquished by those he had previously injured, and God's goodness will

---

[87] *Spect.* 2.5–7, 12 (CCSL 1:228–30).
[88] *Marc.* 5.17.9, 10 (CCSL 1:714–5).
[89] *Fug.* 2.5 (CCSL 2:1138).
[90] *Fug.* 2.6 (CCSL 2:1138) alluding to Mt. 10:30.
[91] *Fug.* 2.6 (CCSL 2:1138). Isa. 40:15.
[92] *Fug.* 2.7 (CCSL 2:1138–9).
[93] *Marc.* 5.18.12–13 (CCSL 1:720).
[94] *Apol.* 22.1–4 (CCSL 1:128).
[95] *An.* 39.1, 3 (CCSL 2:842).
[96] *Apol.* 22.6 (CCSL 1:129) Eadem igitur obscuritate contagionis adspiratio daemonum et angelorum mentis quoque corruptelas agit furoribus et amentiis foedis aut saeuis libidinibus et erroribus uariis, quorum iste potissimus, quo deos istos captis et circumscriptis mentibus commendat, ut et sibi pabula propria nidoris et sanguinis curet simulacris et imaginibus.
[97] *Apol.* 23.4–5, 19 (CCSL 1:131, 133).
[98] *Apol.* 27 (CCSL 1:138–9).

be magnified.⁹⁹ This provides the basis for Tertullian's understanding of martyrdom as a God-ordained way of gaining victory over the Devil, as the martyr shares in Christ's suffering and victory. This is central to Tertullian's diogmology. Tertullian, like the Alexandrians, attributes everything which opposes God to the Devil. Tertullian's distinctive contribution, and his point of departure from them, is the way he defines evil and the involvement of God with it. By giving God more of an active role, as it were hosting the conflict, Tertullian provides a foundation for his highly developed cosmic conflict diogmology.

God permits evil and wills persecution

Is persecution 'evil'? Clement blurs the distinction between evils and persecution, using the same argument for each, that God wills neither, but refrains from prohibiting them. Origen distinguishes between persecution and evils generally; God permits both evil and persecution and presides actively over the latter. Tertullian argues that God *causes* some evils and *causes* persecution. Each of them situates their conclusion in their understanding of God's goodness.

Tertullian distinguishes between evils that God causes and those which he does not. Against Marcion, Tertullian argues that nothing 'evil' comes from God and that man sinned by his own free will.¹⁰⁰ Nevertheless, nothing happens against the will of God, and God did not interfere to prevent the occurrence of what he wished not to happen, or it would have removed the free will which God willed for man.¹⁰¹ Tertullian elaborates: in Isaiah 45:7 God proclaims himself the source of evil. Defining the Greek word κακός as meaning troubles and injuries, Tertullian asserts there are two kinds of evil: sinful evils (*mali culpae*) and penal evils (*mali poenae*). The former are morally bad, and they are authored by the Devil. The latter are operations of justice passing sentence against the evils of sin, and God is their author, which is compatible with his justice. Penal evils no doubt seem 'evil' for those enduring them, but they are still intrinsically good, because they are just and defensive of good and are hostile to sin. Therefore they are worthy of God. Evils that belong to justice, such as Old Testament punishments, must not be evil but good.¹⁰² Thus God permits evil, including sin and death and permits (with restraint) the author of sin, the Devil.¹⁰³ Tertullian therefore presumes God not only permits persecution, but is effectively its originator, in the cause of ultimate justice.

Tertullian's apparent self-contradiction, in assigning persecution at times to the Devil and at times to God, is due to different polemical purposes in his writings. In *De idololatria* and *Apologeticum*, Tertullian attributes persecution to the Devil. The Devil instigates idolatry and influences idolaters against God's people. The powers and dignities of the world are God's enemies and punish God's servants.¹⁰⁴ The injustice of

---

[99] *Marc.* 2.10 (CCSL 1:486–8).
[100] *Marc.* 2.6 (CCSL 1:481–2).
[101] *Marc.* 2.7 (CCSL 1:482–3).
[102] *Marc.* 2.14 (CCSL 1:491–2).
[103] *Marc.* 2.28.1 (CCSL 1:507).
[104] E.g. *Idol.* 18.7–9, 21.1–3 (CCSL 2:1120, 1121–2).

persecution ultimately stems from the Devil, who tries to overthrow Christians' conviction through persecutors – Tertullian's very audience in *Apologeticum*. 'Certainly, that spirit of daemonic and angelic nature, which, because of its divergence and enmity out of jealousy of God's favour (to us), wars against us from your minds, regulating and equipping by secret influence to all ... perversity of judgement and unreasonable cruelty.'[105]

Tertullian's concern in *Apologeticum* is the injustice of persecution, which arises from ignorance of Christianity. His stated concern was that Christians should not be condemned without being understood.[106] For this he condemns his pagan audience, who are doing the Devil's work. In *De idolatria*, his chief concern is to deter his readers from any fellowship with the Devil's works.

In *Scorpiace*, Tertullian's objective is to counter those who teach avoidance of martyrdom. Therefore, his argument rests on affirming that martyrdom is good, because it is required by God, by whom idolatry is forbidden: martyrdom strives against and opposes idolatry, and also delivers from it. This is the heart of Tertullian's diogmology: God appointed martyrdoms so we may make trial with our opponent, the Devil. By martyrdom the Devil is trampled – not merely escaped from, but vanquished.[107] Tertullian thus refutes the assertion that God merely permits, but does not ordain, such 'evils'.

In *De fuga*, Tertullian goes further still. 'It is enough to prescribe that nothing happens without the will of God ... Therefore, both evil and sin are from God; nothing from the Devil and nothing from us ourselves.'[108] Because his rhetorical purpose is to deter flight, he carefully distinguishes God-ordained persecution as an 'evil', from the *injustice* of it, which is of the Devil. Persecution, which tests his servants, is especially worthy of God. This is the issue, and why Tertullian is so adamant that Christians should not flee; it is how the Lord will sift his people. Since persecution improves the servants of God, it cannot be imputed to the Devil.[109] Tertullian distinguishes the act itself from both its motivation and outcomes. The Devil's objective is to destroy faith and subvert salvation, an evil outcome, which he tries to obtain by the evil means of injustice. God's objective is to save, and to defeat the Devil, and he ordains persecution for this purpose, albeit with the necessary element of demonic injustice.

Nevertheless, persecution *appears* to proceed from the Devil because it is unjust. The injustice necessary for a trial of faith does not legitimize persecution, but only supplies an agency. So, the will of God is primary, in his testing of faith by persecution. But the instrument of persecution, the injustice of trial, is of the Devil.[110] Injustice

---

[105] *Apol.* 27.4 (CCSL 1:139) ille scilicet spiritus daemonicae et angelicae paraturae, qui, noster ob diuortium aemulus et ob Dei gratiam inuidus, de mentibus uestris aduersus nos proeliatur occulta inspiratione modulatis et subornatis ad omnem ... et iudicandi peruersitatem et saeuiendi iniquitatem

[106] *Apol.* 1.2 (CCSL 1:85) Vnum gestit interdum, ne ignorata damnetur; likewise, *Ad Nat.* 1.1.1–4 (CCSL 1:11).

[107] *Scorp.* 6.1 (CCSL 2:1079).

[108] *Fug.* 1.2 (CCSL 2:1135) Satis est quidem praescribere nihil fieri sine Dei uoluntate ... Ergo et malum a Deo et delictum a Deo, nihil in diabolo, nihil etiam in nobis ipsis.

[109] *Fug.* 1.7 (CCSL 2:1136).

[110] *Fug.* 2.1 (CCSL 2:1136–7).

proportionally attests to the righteousness it opposes, so righteousness is perfected in injustice, as strength is perfected in weakness (1 Cor. 1:27). 'Thus, even injustice is employed, that righteousness may be approved in putting unrighteousness to shame.'[111] In summary, Tertullian asserts: 'Truly the authorisation for persecution comes from God for the trial of faith, however its ministry is truly the injustice of the devil for ordering persecutions – certainly by the devil, but not originating from the devil.'[112]

Nevertheless, Satan can only act against God's servants by God's permission.[113] Here Tertullian applies Isaiah 45:7, which he formerly used to distinguish types of evil, to God's use of persecution: 'I am he who makes peace and creates evil.' God is the author of the outcome of persecution, whether life or death, wounding or healing: 'I will smite and I will heal, I will make alive and put to death.'[114] God is Lord of all, therefore without God's will not even a sparrow falls to the ground.[115] Persecution may seem evil to people, but the fault is in our perception.[116]

Finally, in *Ad Scapulam*, Tertullian admits the tension between the ordaining of Christians to suffer and the culpability of the persecutors. Persecutions do not alarm Christians, he asserts, because they accept what they are getting into. Persecutions stem from ignorance, as he argues in *Apologeticum*.[117] Tertullian's purpose in this treatise is to place Scapula firmly on the Devil's side, not God's. No state shall avoid punishment for shedding innocent blood; the contemporary disasters were a sign of God's impending wrath.[118] To persecute Christians is to fight against God.[119] The individual persecutor is responsible for that sin, and although Christian suffering was ordained, Scapula and even Carthage itself will suffer the consequences.[120] Tertullian attacks pagans for complicity with the Devil, but does not criticize Christians for compliance with the sin of persecutors, because in their persecution and martyrdom, Christians actually oppose the Devil.

Moss identifies an 'important but subtle shift in Tertullian's position', in terms of the roles of God and the Devil. She subsequently clarifies this, concluding that 'Tertullian's view of martyrdom develops, but does not appear to change radically'.[121] Although I prefer the label 'differing emphases' over 'development', beyond semantics we both recognize consistency across Tertullian's oeuvre. Tertullian emphasizes different aspects in different works; in apologies he argues against the injustice and ignorance

---

[111] *Fug.* 2.1 (CCSL 2:1137) Ita et iniquitas adhibetur, ut iustitia probetur confundens iniquitatem. Compare Rom. 5:21–6:1; Osborn, *Tertullian*, 7, observes that Tertullian 'found truth in an unending series of paradoxes'.

[112] *Fug.* 2.2 (CCSL 2:1137) arbitrium enim Domini persecutio propter fidei probationem, ministerium autem iniquitas diaboli propter persecutionis instructionem – ita eam per diabolum, si forte, non a diabolo euenire credimus.

[113] *Fug.* 2.7 (CCSL 2:1138).

[114] *Fug.* 3.1 (CCSL 2:1139) Ego sum, qui facio pacem et condo malum ... Ego percutiam et sanabo, ego uiuificabo et mortificabo; Deut. 32:39.

[115] *Fug.* 3.2 (CCSL 2:1139) ref. Mt. 10:29–31; Lk. 12:6–7.

[116] *Fug.* 4.1 (CCSL 2:1139–40).

[117] *Apol.* 1.4–5 (CCSL 1:85–6) also *Scap.* 1.1 (CCSL 2:1127) ab ignorantibus patimur.

[118] *Scap.* 3 (CCSL 2:1129–30).

[119] *Scap.* 4.1 μη Θεομαχειν (as in Acts 5:39).

[120] *Scap.* 4.8, a primordio mandatum, i.e. of the governors; 5.3 (CCSL 2:1131, 1132).

[121] Moss, 'Justification of the Martyrs', 114, 118.

which prompts persecutors, highlighting their complicity with the Devil's work, and ultimate defeat. In his anti-heretical polemics, he refutes the idea that evil comes from a separate god, or from matter. In *Scorpiace,* he exhorts Christians to be on the side of God, not demons, and accept their destiny to suffer. In *De fuga* he must originate persecution with God, as a good thing from which Christians should not flee.[122] These are ultimately not contradictions, but each is a key part of Tertullian's full understanding of the source of persecution.

Tertullian, in contrast to Clement, finds justice in the injustice of persecution. Whilst he also emphasizes the good results of persecution, he sees the good of persecution itself. This goes beyond the *a priori* assumption that all things God ordains must be good. Although Tertullian's eschatological perspective prioritizes the resurrection and final just outcome,[123] only in the hope of which current injustice can be tolerated,[124] his argument transcends teleology. A good God must *necessarily* punish evil; everything just is good, and nothing is good which is unjust.

Persecution for the name: The cosmic arena

Of the four fathers, Tertullian most clearly identifies persecution as the very battleground between Christ and the Devil. Those who uphold the name of Christ are necessarily persecuted for that name, and as they share in the sufferings of Christ so they will also share in his victory.

For the name

In Matthew 10:22, Christ states explicitly that 'you will be hated by all for my name's sake. But the one who endures to the end will be saved.' Tertullian argues that this passage applies beyond the apostles to all Christians:

> How much more shall we [than the apostles], for whom it is necessary to be delivered up by parents? Thus, by allotting this very betrayal now to the apostles, now to all, he pours out universal destruction upon all on whom the name, along with the hatred you will collect, rests.[125]

Against the Valentinians' alleged denial that confession is not to be made on earth,[126] Tertullian argues that all of Matthew 10 – hatred for the name, betrayal, persecution,

---

[122] Sutcliffe, 'To Flee or Not to Flee?'
[123] *Res.* 21 (CCSL 2:946–7).
[124] *Marc.* 1.27.1–2; 2.11; 2.13.1–4 (CCSL 1:470–1, 488–9, 489–90).
[125] *Scorp.* 9.5 (CCSL 2:1085) Quanto magis nos, quos a parentibus quoque tradi oportet?Ita ipsa hac permixtione nunc ad apostolos, nunc ad omnes disponendo [eundem] in uniuersos nominis exitum effundit, in quibus consederit nomen cum odii sui lege.
[126] *Scorp.* 10.1 (CCSL 2:1087) Tertullian may be referring to the *Testimony of Truth* regarding completeness of confession, or an unknown source. See Philip L. Tite, 'Voluntary Martyrdom and Gnosticism', *Journal of Early Christian Studies* 23, no. 1 (2015), 27–54, at 38–41.

forceful examination, torture and confession or denial – also occur on earth. The implication, supported by the imperative to confess Christ, is that these are inevitable.[127] Against Marcion, Tertullian asserts that persecutions and sufferings were foretold for those associated with his name.[128]

Equating his addressees' situation with that in 1 Peter, Tertullian uses the evidence of present persecutions, as predicted both by Christ and in Zechariah 9:9–16, to prove to Marcion the continuity and consistency of the Old and New Testaments.[129] He sees the inevitability of persecution of Christians as an extension of the consistent animosity toward and persecution of God's people throughout history, culminating in the rejection of the Messiah.[130]

Tertullian cites Matthew 5:10–11, the blessedness of the persecuted, in several different contexts. In *De fuga*, the passage supports his contention that persecution is ordained by God and therefore should not be avoided. 'Happy are they who suffer persecution for my name's sake. Unhappy, therefore, they who, by running away, will not suffer according to the [divine] precept.'[131] In *Scorpiace*, Tertullian argues that martyrdoms have been commanded by God, so he must also have promised a reward, therefore he pronounced blessed those who are persecuted for righteousness' sake. This applies to all Christians, in continuity with the prophets.[132] In *De resurrectione*, the beatitude reminds him that the 'house' which undergoes dissolution through suffering will be restored as a better house after the resurrection.[133] In *De patientia*, Tertullian reminds the reader that the blessing applies to those who patiently endure persecution, turning the other cheek and rejoicing at being worthy of divine chastisement, depriving the enemy of his reward.[134]

In *De fuga*, Tertullian reminds his readers of Christ's imperatives to confess, not deny him;[135] to rejoice[136] and to endure to the end and be saved.[137] Christians are not to fear their persecutors, but to take up the cross and value Christ above one's life.[138] Jesus explicitly stated that his followers would be persecuted on his account, on account of his name, for his sake and for his name's sake.[139] Given that the master/teacher is hated and persecuted, so the servant/disciple should expect to be, in imitating him.[140]

---

[127] *Scorp.* 10.9–17 (CCSL 2:1088–90).
[128] *Marc.* 4.39 (CCSL 1:650–55).
[129] *Marc.* 4.39.8 (CCSL 1:652).
[130] Mt. 5:12; 23:34–35; Lk. 11:49–50; Acts 7:52; Rev. 18:20.
[131] *Fug.* 7.1 (CCSL 2:1144) Felices qui persecutionem passi fuerint causa nominis mei. Infelices ergo qui fugiendo ex precepto non erunt passi.
[132] *Scorp.* 9.1–3 (CCSL 2:1084).
[133] *Res.* 41.2–3 (CCSL 2:975).
[134] *Pat.* 8, 11.9 (CCSL 1:308–9, 312).
[135] Mt. 10:32–33/ Mk 8:38.
[136] Mt. 5:10–12/ Lk. 6:22–23.
[137] Mt. 10:22/ Mk. 13:13 *Fug.* 7.1 (CCSL 2:1144) Qui sustinuerit in finem iste saluabitur; also *Scorp.* 9.5; 10.17 (CCSL 2:1085; 1090) *Praes.* 3.6 (CCSL 1:188).
[138] *Fug.* 7.2 (CCSL 2:1145). See also *Cor.* 11.5 (CCSL 2:1957); *An.* 55.5 (CCSL 2:863); *Scorp* 11.1 (CCSL 2:1090). ref. Mt. 10:26–28 and Mt. 10:38; 16:24–25/ Mk 8:34–35/ Lk. 9:23–24.
[139] Mt. 5:11; Lk. 6:22; Jn 15:21; Mt. 10:18; Mk 13:9; Mt. 10:22; 24:9–10; Mk 13:13; Lk. 21:12, 17 respectively.
[140] Mt. 10:24–25; Jn 15:20. This *super magistrum* is diversely cited by the fathers, usually not in the context of persecution, but more like a general proverb. See Clement, *Strom.* 2:17 (PG 8:1015) re: knowledge; Origen, *Com John* 32.7, 8 (PG 14:766; 773) re: foot washing; Tertullian, *An.* 55.2 (CCSL 2:862); *Praes.* 34.5 (CCSL 1:215); *Val.* 33.1 (CCSL 2:776); *Marc.* 1.14.3; 4.4.5 (CCSL 1:455, 550) re: assorted heretics.

Tertullian uses these passages, quoting extensively from Matthew 10, to refute heretics attempting to dissuade Christians from confession and martyrdom. The *name* is an object of hatred, and persecution attends all possessors of the name, not just the original apostles.[141]

Christians should expect, in taking up the cross, to lose their lives for his sake.[142] Jesus makes no distinction between himself and his name. 'The name' stands for the Christian's association with Christ himself. Jesus explains in John 15:18–25 and 17:14–16 that the world hates Christians because it hates Christ. Tertullian, surprisingly, does not use these Johannine passages, even though he sees a fundamental opposition between Satan's realm and Christ's. Tertullian uses Christ's prediction of hatred for his name to demonstrate that he is the Creator's Christ, 'that very Son of man on whose account our name also is rejected'.[143] Tertullian quotes Paul's words and example extensively in *Scorpiace*, defending the expectation of confession and martyrdom. Suffering is for the kingdom, and is to be gloried in, for we suffer with Christ. Rather than being conquered by suffering, we are more than conquerors. Paul takes pleasure in infirmities 'for Christ's sake'.[144]

Clement, Origen and Tertullian each discern that persecution arises specifically for the name of Christ and only a true Christian – for Clement the one 'in' Christ – will persevere to the end. Tertullian asserts that the person is proved by the faith, not the faith by the person. The things we suffer after the example of Christ show us to be true Christians.[145] But Tertullian takes it further than Clement into an area that Origen also ventures; persecution is the God-ordained battleground with the Devil, in which the persecuted join in Christ's conflict and victory.

United in conflict and victory

The Carthaginians' soteriology includes motifs of recapitulation,[146] ransom/redemption,[147] victory[148] and healing.[149] Middleton demonstrates that, in the martyr acts, martyrdom imparts the benefits of Christ's work, often with explicit parallelism between Christ's and the martyrs' deaths. 'Behind every martyr was the death of Jesus.'[150] The scriptural roots of this are numerous.[151] Christ suffered and foretold that his just ones should suffer equally with him.[152] This should be glory enough for them, to be conformed to his sufferings.[153] Citing Romans 8:17–18, Tertullian equates

---

[141] *Scorp*. 9.1–8 (CCSL 2:1084–5).
[142] Mt. 16:25; Mk 8:35; Lk. 9:24.
[143] *Marc*. 4.14. 17 (CCSL 2:577) ipse erit filius hominis, propter quem et nomen nostrum recusantur.
[144] *Scorp*. 13 (CCSL 2:1094–6).
[145] *Praescr*. 3.6, 12 (CCSL 1:188–9); 1 Jn 2:19 and perhaps alluding to 1 Pet. 4:12.
[146] *An*. 9, 19, 27, 40; *Marc*. 3.9.5; 5.17.1; *recapitulare* (CCSL 1:520, 712).
[147] *Fug*. 12.2–3 (CCSL 2:1149–51); Cyprian, *Eleem* 1, 2 (CCSL 3A:55–6) *Fort*. 6 (CCSL 3:193–4).
[148] *Marc*. 4.20.4–5 (CCSL 1:594–5).
[149] *Scorp*. 5.8–9 (CCSL 2:1078).
[150] Paul Middleton, *Radical Martyrdom and Cosmic Conflict in Early Christianity* (Edinburgh: T&T Clark, 2006), 82–4.
[151] Rom. 8:17; 2 Cor. 1:5; Phil. 3:10, 2 Tim. 2:3; 1 Pet. 4:12–16; Acts 7:54–56.
[152] *Marc*. 3.22.5 (CCSL 1:539).
[153] *Scorp*. 9.6 (CCSL 2:1085).

suffering with Christ with being glorified with him. Just as through the flesh we suffer, so the flesh attains the recompense promised for suffering with Christ.[154]

In this locus of confession, Tertullian boldly portrays Christian suffering as cosmic conflict. In *De fuga* he argues that God so uses the faith of the elect to overthrow Satan, and to expose apostates as Satan's servants.[155] Persecutors of Christians are under secret demonic influence, equipped by the demonic spirits they host to war against Christians with injustice and cruelty. The demons are nevertheless ill-matched against Christians, who resist and attack them back. 'We never triumph over them more than when we are condemned for the persistence of our belief.'[156] Christians desire to suffer in the same way as a soldier suffers war; not out of a desire to suffer *per se*, but because it is necessary to the battle by which victory is achieved.[157]

> Our battle is that we are called before tribunals, to there risk our lives to determine the truth. Victory, however, is to obtain that for which one has contested, the victory and glory, of pleasing God, and the spoil, eternal life. But, you will say, we perish; certainly, when we have taken hold; therefore we conquer, when we are killed.[158]

Tertullian rhetorically utilizes both athletic and military imagery, including oaths of allegiance, in describing the Christian's duty.[159] Christians are directly involved in the battle against the Devil – as participators, not merely imitators.

> But if in the name of contest God plans martyrdoms for us, by which we make trial with our adversary, that [God] may continuously crush him by whom man is willingly crushed, in this God shows great generosity rather than bitterness. Indeed, he wished to make man, pulled out from the Devil's throat by faith, courageously trample him so that he not only escapes but certainly vanquishes the enemy.[160]

God himself appointed the contest of martyrdom; *by this*, humans can trample upon and vanquish their enemy and receive a crown. The same God who offers the reward and crown proclaims the contest and invites the victory.[161] Christ defeated the

---

[154] *Res.* 40.11–12 (CCSL 2:974–5).
[155] *Fug.* 2.2 (CCSL 2:1137).
[156] *Apol.* 27.7 (CCSL 1:139) illos numquam magis detriumphamus quam cum pro fidei obstinatione damnamur.
[157] *Apol.* 50.1 (CCSL 1:169).
[158] *Apol.* 50.2–3 (CCSL 1:169) Proelium est nobis, quod prouocamur ad tribunalia, ut illic sub discrimine capitis pro ueritate certemus. Victoria est autem, pro quo certaueris, obtinere. Ea uictoria habet et gloriam placendi Deo et praedam uiuendi in aeternum. Sed occidimur. – Certe, cum obtinuimus. Ergo uincimus, cum occidimur, denique euadimus, cum obducimur.
[159] *Mart.* 1.2, 3 (CCSL 1:3, 5–6); *Scorp.* 6.1–6 (CCSL 2:1079–80).
[160] *Scorp.* 6.1 (CCSL 2:1079) Sed si certaminis nomine deus nobis martyria proposuisset, per quae cum aduersario experiremur, ut, a quo libenter homo elisus est, eum iam constanter elidat, hic quoque liberalitas magis quam acerbitas dei praeest. Euulsum enim hominem de diaboli gula per fidem iam et per uirtutem inculcatorem eius uoluit efficere, ne solummodo euasisset, uerum etiam euicisset inimicum.
[161] *Fug.* 1.5 (CCSL 2:1136).

Devil; by enduring persecution and confessing Christ, the Christian shares this battle and victory. Tertullian demonstrates this by binding the command to confess Christ to persecution and the prospect of martyrdom.

Here we reach a critical, but nuanced point that separates Tertullian from the other fathers. Is it the confession of the name, or death for the name, that constitutes the victory? Middleton's powerful arguments for martyrdom as participation in cosmic conflict conflate the two. This is not illegitimate, because it is exactly what Tertullian and the martyr acts do, and Middleton's stated focus is on the *Acta*,[162] the worldview of which Tertullian undoubtedly shares. One of Middleton's portraits is that of martyrdom as confession of Christ. The confessional formula is central to the *Acta*, the martyrs suffer for the name. 'The moment of confession or denial is the fulcrum on which everything else depends. It is the moment where the Christian openly affirms his or her relationship with Christ, making oneself a sacrifice to God.'[163] Middleton later states, 'identifying with Jesus through confession, suffering and death resulted in successful martyrdom and faithful struggle'.[164] In terms of participation in Christ's victory, accomplished in his death, Middleton notes, 'in death, they are described as victors and conquerors',[165] and 'in the cosmic war in which they were engaged, the Christians claimed victory by their deaths'.[166] Concluding this section, Middleton states, 'by holding to their confession, they brought life through death', and 'since death was such a potent weapon ... enthusiastic and faithful Christians sought it out, deliberately seeking arrest'.[167]

Tertullian clearly makes little effort to distinguish confession from martyrdom. The other three fathers do; they see alternate ways to legitimately hold to one's confession of Christ without necessarily undergoing martyrdom; the connection is not inevitable. But for Tertullian, martyrdom is essentially the point of confessing. I suggest that this conflation is what *characterizes* Middleton's conception of the 'radical martyr' and what makes Tertullian appear to advocate volunteerism, as I shall discuss below.

Confession unto death

Confession of Christ is, for the fathers, the heart of one's allegiance. In *Scorpiace*, Tertullian steps through Matthew 10 verse by verse to argue that every aspect[168] of the missionary commission applies beyond the disciples to contemporary Christians. This includes the promise to confess those who 'confess in me before men' and to deny those who 'deny me before men'.[169] Regardless of whether Tertullian used an existing Latin scripture or translated the Greek himself, he confirms the contrast between 'in me' and 'me', emphasized by Clement.

---

[162] Middleton, *Radical Martyrdom*, 2.
[163] Ibid., 84–5.
[164] Ibid., 87.
[165] Ibid., 88.
[166] Ibid., 90.
[167] Ibid., 101.
[168] Except the command to flee persecution in verse 23, which is omitted.
[169] *Scorp.* 9.8 (CCSL 2:1085).

> He who confesses himself a Christian, bears witness that he is Christ's and therefore in Christ. If he is in Christ, he certainly confesses in Christ, when he confesses himself a Christian. For he cannot be this without being in Christ. Further, by confessing in Christ he also confesses Christ, since, by being a Christian he is in Christ, while [Christ] himself is also in him.[170]

It should have been enough for Christ to state this, proposes Tertullian, since the reverse would presumably be true, that anyone who denied Christ would deny that he was *in* Christ, and vice versa. However, the Lord expressed it in different terms.[171] He says, 'Who will deny *me*, not *in me*';[172] the one who denies is not in Christ. This is precisely the same argument Clement uses.

Christ foresaw that anyone forced to deny being a Christian would then be compelled to deny Christ himself by blaspheming him.[173] Pliny decided that if someone denied he was a Christian, he would be forced to prove it by cursing or abjuring Christ. Unwittingly, the Romans had identified the crux of the matter: no one could blaspheme Christ if they were truly a Christian (cf. 1 Cor. 12:3). It is therefore futile, asserts Tertullian, to suggest 'though I shall deny that I am a Christian, I shall not be denied by Christ, for I have not denied himself'.[174] By denying he is a Christian, one denies Christ 'in him' and therefore denies Christ himself. Such denial comes from shame, which is why elsewhere Christ states that he will be ashamed of the one who is ashamed of him.[175] It implies one is ashamed of bearing *his* name. Further referencing Matthew 10 in *De fuga*, Tertullian emphasizes the imperative to suffer, not flee, from persecution. Persecutors, who cannot destroy the soul, are not to be feared, nor to be fled; he who values his life more than Christ and fails to take up his cross, cannot be his disciple.[176]

The good of persecution

According to Tertullian, the God-appointed reason for persecution is that it serves as the arena of conflict with the Devil and his minions, by which the Christian triumphs in confessing the name of Christ. Persecuted for the name, Christians suffer along with Christ who was also rejected by the world. Therefore, persecution is intrinsically good, being the means of participating in victory over the Devil. The ultimate good outcome on a cosmic level is the Devil's defeat and Christ's victory, but persecution carries the promise of good outcomes for individuals in this life and the next.

---

[170] *Scorp.* 9.9 (CCSL 2:1085–6) Qui se Christianum confitetur, Christi se esse testatur, qui Christi est, in Christo sit necesse est. Si in Christo est, in Christo utique confitetur, cum se Christianum confitetur. Hoc enim non potest esse, nisi sit in Christo. Porro in Christo confitendo Christum quoque confitetur, qui sit in ipso, dum et ipse in illo est, utpote Christianus.
[171] *Scorp.* 9.10 (CCSL 2:1086).
[172] *Scorp.* 9.11 (CCSL 2:1086) qui me negauerit, non, qui in me.
[173] *Scorp.* 9.12 (CCSL 2:1086).
[174] *Scorp.* 9.12 (CCSL 2:1086) etsi me negauero Christianum, non negabor a Christo, non enim ipsum negaui.
[175] *Scorp.* 9.13 (CCSL 2:1086–7).
[176] *Fug.* 7.2 (CCSL 2:1144–5).

The striking difference between the eschatology of the Carthaginians and Alexandrians is that the former deny post-mortem educative or medicinal punishment. This life is the one chance to attain salvation, for all will face the coming judgement of Christ. This makes patient endurance and confession in this life an imperative, with the critical endpoint of reward or condemnation. This brings an intensity and urgency to Tertullian's consideration of the good of persecution.

This life as discipline

Tertullian consistently interprets suffering, including the suffering of persecution, as disciplinary training, even in his earlier works.[177] He observes that prison, like the desert, is a retreat from the world. Spiritually, the world is the real prison, while those physically imprisoned are kept from idols, sacrifices, arena shows, indecency, temptations and afflictions.[178] Suffering in this life is training. Christians are people ready to die and by deprivation now they make it less difficult to despise life and give it up. Christians should not expect to have pleasure in this life as well as in the next and should expect deprivations, such as loss of livelihood, now.[179] Even the self-denial of women in rejecting fine garments and jewellery will better prepare them for persecution and martyrdom.[180] In his later, more 'rigorist' period, Tertullian promoted fasting and xerophagy as disciplines that would prepare Christians for their inevitable imprisonment. By being physically and mentally prepared for deprivation, sufferings in prison would be a discipline rather than a penalty, and tortures would be better resisted, unlike the well-fed Christian who would merely give the lions a better feed.[181] Opposing remarriage of the widowed, Tertullian emphasizes the advantage of freedom from encumbrances when facing flight, imprisonment and execution.[182]

In *De patientia*, patience operating through mortification of the flesh is a sacrifice acceptable to the Lord. Persecution provides the opportunity; the hardships of flight, the chains, wooden block and bare ground of the prison, the deprivation of worldly comforts; the loss of goods and of loved ones; stripes, fire, cross, beasts or sword.[183] Patience strengthens faith, governs peace, sustains love, instructs humility, awaits repentance, seals the discipline of penance, controls the flesh, preserves the spirit, restrains the tongue, holds back violence, tramples temptations, averts scandal and 'consummates martyrdom'.[184]

In *Scorpiace*, Tertullian reasons that anything which strives against and opposes idolatry must be good. Like the physician's art, suffering causes pain in order to cure. God heals by imitating the malady: destroying death by death, torture by torture, bestowing life by withdrawing it and aiding the flesh by injuring it.[185] Even more

---

[177] *Spect., Idol., Mart., Cult. Fem.* 2, all written around 197 according to Barnes, *Tertullian*, 325.
[178] *Mart.* 2 (CCSL 1:3–5).
[179] *Spect.* 1.5–6, 2.3, 28.3–5 (CCSL 1:227, 228, 250–1); *Idol.* 12 (CCSL 2:1111–2).
[180] *Cult. Fem.* 2.13.4 (CCSL 1:369–70).
[181] *Jej.* 12.2, 17.9 (CCSL 2: 1270–1, 1277).
[182] *Exh. cast.* 12; *Ux.* 1.5 (CCSL 1:378–9).
[183] *Pat.* 13.6–8 (CCSL 1:314).
[184] *Pat.* 15.2 (CCSL 1:316) martyria consummat.
[185] *Scorp.* 5.9 (CCSL 2:1078).

explicitly, in *De fuga*, he asserts that persecution causes the church's faith, love, holiness and discipline to improve, which cannot be imputed to the Devil.[186] Rather, persecution is permitted by God for the trying and refining of faith.[187]

Martyrdom, for Tertullian, is the Christian's chief glory and should be embraced. The Christian is a soldier training for battle, a wrestler training for the arena. Like soldiers, we learn by hardship and toil. Prison hardships should be treated as drills of the mind and body, a preparation for a good contest. Prison is also a wrestling school, in which virtue is built up by hardness and destroyed by softness.[188] Christians glory in tribulations because suffering produces endurance (Rom. 5:3–5). We suffer with Christ and will be glorified with him, and the present sufferings cannot be compared with that future glory (Rom. 8:17–18).[189]

Witness to others

The Carthaginians are motivated by an urgency in this life; now is the time to live up to their calling, to confess Christ, to endure to the end. Confession and martyrdom serve as encouragements to others in the church, and witness to those outside to save themselves while time permits.

Tertullian provides uncompromising exhortation to his fellow Christians. Even when 'encouraging' his readers to martyrdom, he often provides explicit details about their imminent suffering.[190] In his later rigorist period he had no time for weakness: God does not cherish the weak, he rejects them, and the cowardly will face the lake of fire.[191] His encouragements to martyrs are based on their future reward; the present sufferings are a training and preparation for martyrdom.[192] He is less concerned with elevating exemplary martyrs for their exhortational value, as Cyprian does; he is a taskmaster rather than an approver, and prods rather than praises.

In contrast to *Apologeticum* and *Ad Scapulam,* where he displays Christians to outsiders as united in their joyful anticipation of confession, martyrdom and reward, in works such as *De spectaculis* Tertullian presents a harsher view of the church for internal consumption. In his castigations of worldly Christians, he is apt to contrast their slack lifestyle with the rigor required in preparation for martyrdom, rather than with martyr figures as such. 'You are delicate, Christian, if you covet pleasure in this life ... Tell me, can't we live without pleasure, who with pleasure ought to die?'[193] Those who want 'spectacles' should desire the Christian glories of martyrdom: the wrestlings, contests and blood shed for Christ.[194] Tertullian's exemplary martyr is the soldier who

---

[186] *Fug.* 1.6 (CCSL 2:1136).
[187] *Fug.* 3.1 (CCSL 2:1139).
[188] *Mart.* 3 (CCSL 1:5–6).
[189] *Scorp.* 13.2–4 (CCSL 2:1094).
[190] E.g. *Mart.* 4.2 (CCSL 1:6) gladium grauem, et crucem excelsam, et rabiem bestiarum, et summam ignium poenam, et omne carnificis ingenium in tormentis; similarly, *Pat.* 13.6 (CCSL 1:314).
[191] *Fug.* 7.2 (CCSL 2:1144–5).
[192] *Mart.* 3 (CCSL 1: 5–6).
[193] *Spect.* 28.3, 5 (CCSL 1:250–1) Delicatus es, Christiane, si et in saeculo uoluptatem concupiscis ... Dicas uelim: non possumus uiuere sine uoluptate, qui mori cum uoluptate debebimus.
[194] *Spect.* 29 (CCSL 1:251–2).

rejected the military crown, but even he serves mainly as a source of admonishment to his detractors. 'What have you in common with the flower which will die? You have a flower in the shoot of Jesse ... an unspoilt, non-withering, everlasting flower, which the good soldier, in choosing it progresses in heavenly rank. Blush, fellow soldiers of his.'[195] When Tertullian looks to an example of a martyr in a positive, encouraging sense, it is Christ who is his perfect, patient model.[196]

Tertullian was convinced of the value of martyrdom as witness to nonbelievers.[197] He informs Scapula that those who witness the noble patience of Christian martyrs will be provoked to investigate and, learning the truth, will become followers too.[198] Even though his *Apologeticum* systematically refutes anti-Christian arguments and exposes the injustice of their persecution, Tertullian attributes this injustice to ignorance. Christianity must not be persecuted for the wrong reasons; it must be properly known. Yet even then he recognizes that persecution is inevitable, and providential for the bringing about of the defeat of Satan and his idolatries, and for the conversion of those who reflect on the martyrs' powerful witness. The persecutors' cruelty is an attraction to Christianity, provoking an increase in number as if the blood of Christians were 'seed'.[199] For in observing Christians' obstinacy, people ask what there is in Christianity and once they learn, they join them.

The ultimate good

Discipline, patient endurance and witness to others in this life all come to fruition in the next. Without a hope beyond the grave, what would be the point of these struggles? Wysocki concludes that persecution and martyrdom significantly influenced the development of third-century African eschatology.[200] 'The problem of suffering during persecutions entailed questions about the meaning of life, about Christian reference to the world and to the state and about what happens to a man dying in unjust persecutions.'[201] Although persecution through the first three centuries was discontinuous, and the 'increase' in the number of eschatological writings may simply reflect what is extant, Wysocki argues for both quantitative and qualitative eschatological development in third-century Carthage.[202]

Pelikan observes that eschatology was prominent in Tertullian's writings, and influenced other aspects of his theology. Tertullian was convinced that God would

---

[195] *Cor.* 15.2–3 (CCSL 2:1065) Quid tibi cum flore morituro? Habes florem ex uirga Iesse ... florem incorruptum, immarcescibilem, sempiternum. Quem et bonus miles eligendo in caelesti ordinatione profecit. Erubescite, commilitiones eius ...
[196] *Pat.* 3 (CCSL 1:300–2).
[197] *Scorp.* 8.1 (CCSL 2:1082) ex testimonio religionis et proelio confessionis pro iustitia.
[198] *Scap.* 5.4 (CCSL 2:1132) et ipse statim sequitur.
[199] *Apol.* 50.13 (CCSL 1:171) *sperma*.
[200] Marcin R. Wysocki, 'Eschatology of the Time of Persecutions in the Writings of Tertullian and Cyprian', *StPatr* 65 (2013), 379–93.
[201] Ibid., 381.
[202] Ibid., 382.

shortly bring the end of the world, and do so violently and dramatically.[203] As Daley demonstrates, although Tertullian does not explicate this idea at length, it permeates his oeuvre.[204] Tertullian directly applies the Gospel persecution and *parousia* passages to the persecutions and martyrdoms of his time.[205] He affirms that the Christian hope in time of persecution rests on the confidence of future resurrection to final judgement of the righteous and the wicked.[206] His clear perspective on the resurrection of the flesh leads him to elaborate, for the first time, a Christian doctrine of an intermediate state.[207] Here the souls of the dead await their final punishment or reward in two distinct regions in Hades, anticipating their eternal fates, which are realized at the resurrection and final judgement.[208] Tertullian argues that the physical body is the locus of confession and martyrdom as well as eschatological reward.[209] Bodily mutilation is no impediment.[210]

As Pelikan notes, Tertullian's most vivid discussions of eschatology deal with the eternal punishment and hellfire awaiting the unfaithful.[211] These include idolaters and persecutors, who are the Devil's agents. The resurrected righteous will witness the spectacle of their punishment in everlasting fire.[212] The righteous, clothed in perfect, angelic bodies, will live forever in the kingdom of heaven.[213] Thus the present time of persecution and suffering will end in a great reckoning, and Christians experience a tension between longing for an end to suffering and the fear of judgement. In fact, it is the Christians themselves who uphold the present world, which provides the only opportunity for the wicked and persecutors to repent.[214]

Martyrdom and reward

In *De fuga*, Tertullian describes persecution as a contest proclaimed by God, who offers the crown and rewards and calls us to the prize.[215] Tertullian encourages those about to undergo a good contest – superintended by the living God and trained by the Holy

---

[203] *Fug.* 12.9 (CCSL 2:1153); *Apol.* 32.1 (CCSL 1:142-3) and see Jaroslav Pelikan, 'Eschatology of Tertullian', *Church History* 21, no. 2 (1952), 108-22, at 109-10.
[204] Brian E. Daley, *The Hope of the Early Church: A Handbook of Patristic Eschatology* (Peabody, Mass.: Hendrickson, 2003), 34.
[205] Pelikan, 'Eschatology of Tertullian', at 114-15.
[206] *Res.* 21.3-4, 25.1-3 (CCSL 2:946-7, 953) and see Daley, *Hope of the Early Church*, 34-5.
[207] Daley, *Hope of the Early Church*, 36-7. Daley considers this to be developed from Montanism.
[208] *An.* 7.3-4, 55, 58 (CCSL 2:790, 861-3, 867-9) *Marc.* 4.34.14-15 (CCSL 1:638); *Res.* 17 (CCSL 2:941-2).
[209] *Res.* 8.5-6; 21.3-4 (CCSL 2:931-2, 946-7); Wysocki, 'Eschatology of the Time of Persecutions', 383. For analysis of Tertullian's *De resurrectione* see David I. Rankin, *The Early Church and the Afterlife: Post-death Existence in Athenagoras, Tertullian, Origen and the Letter to Rheginos* (London: Routledge, 2018), 89-109.
[210] *Res.* 40.12-15, 56.1 (CCSL 2:974-5, 1003).
[211] Pelikan, 'Eschatology of Tertullian', 112.
[212] *Apol.* 48.13-15 (CCSL 1:168); *Spect.* 30 (CCSL 1:252-3) *Res.* 35.6-7 (CCSL 2:967); *Paen.* 12.1-4 (CCSL 1:339).
[213] *Marc.* 3.24.6; 5.10.14-16 (CCSL 1:542, 694-5); *Res.* 62 (CCSL 2:1010-11) *An.* 56.7 (CCSL 2:864).
[214] *Apol.* 32.1 (CCSL 1:142); *Scap.* 3.3, 3.5, 4.1 (CCSL 2:1129-30) Pelikan, 'Eschatology of Tertullian', 116.
[215] *Fug.* 1.5 (CCSL 2:1136).

Spirit – with the prize of eternity, heavenly citizenship and everlasting glory.[216] Sufferings and loss in this world mean nothing compared with the divine reward.[217] In *Apologeticum* he describes a victory that carries the glory of pleasing God and the spoil, which is eternal life, the instruments of torture being garments decked with palm leaves and a triumphal chariot.[218] In *De corona*, the soldier who refused the military garland was *now* completely equipped in the apostles' armour and crowned more worthily with the white crown of martyrdom.[219] In *Ad Scapulam*, Tertullian is certain that reward will be in proportion to conflict.[220] Just as in gladiatorial combat, where more wounds bring more crowns, glory, privileges, contributions and other worldly memorials, God will provide an eternity of fame. The mansions in the Father's house accord with different deserts; as one star differs from another in glory, so greater gain costs greater effort.[221]

Tertullian supports the idea of a superior reward for martyrs above other faithful Christians. In several places, Tertullian cites Revelation 6:9–10, stating that the martyrs' souls would be preserved 'under the altar' in Paradise.[222] Drawing on a version of the *Passio Perpetuae et Felicitatis*,[223] he queries:

> And how is it that, the region of Paradise revealed to John in the Spirit, set under the altar, displays no other souls within it except of the martyrs? How is it that Perpetua, bravest martyr, on the day of her passion in the revelation of Paradise, only saw martyrs there, unless the sword guarding the entrance permitted none to enter except those who died in Christ, not in Adam?[224]

This has led some scholars to argue that Tertullian believed that only martyrs go straight to heaven,[225] a position contrasted with Cyprian's,[226] or as Gonzalez postulates, a community associated with Perpetua.[227] However, taken in context, those who died 'in Christ, not in Adam' must refer to *all* faithful believers. Furthermore, a few sentences

---

[216] *Mart.* 3.3 (CCSL 1:5).
[217] *Mart.* 4.9 (CCSL 1:7).
[218] *Apol.* 50.2-3 (CCSL 1:169).
[219] *Cor.* 1.3 (CCSL 2:1040).
[220] *Scap.* 4.8 (CCSL 2:1131) Sed maiora certamina maiora sequuntur praemia.
[221] *Scorp.* 6.4, 6.7–8 (CCSL 2:1079-1080), multae mansiones apud patrem, alluding to Jn 14:1–4 and 1 Cor. 15:41.
[222] *An.* 55.4 (CCSL 2:862-3); *Or.* 5.3 (CCSL 1:260); *Res.* 25.1; 38.4, 43.4 (CCSL 2:953, 971, 978-9) subicitur altari.
[223] *Passio.* 13.8 (Rebillard, 318) Tertullian's version attributes Saturus' vision to Perpetua.
[224] *An.* 55.4 (CCSL 2:862-3) Et quomodo Iohanni in spiritu paradisi regio reuelata, quaue subicitur altari, nullus alias animas apud se praeter martyrum ostendit? Quomodo Perpetua, fortissima martyr, sub die passionis in reuelatione paradisi solo illic martyras uidit, nisi quia nullis romphaea paradisi ianitrix cedit nisi qui in Christo decesserint, non in Adam?
[225] Wilhite, 'Tertullian on the Afterlife: 'Only Martyrs are in Heaven' and Other Misunderstandings'. *Zeitschrift für antikes Christentum* 24, no. 3 (2020), 490–508; n. 45 cites a representative sample.
[226] Wysocki, 'Time of Persecutions', 383–4.
[227] Eliezer Gonzalez, 'The Afterlife in the *Passion of Perpetua* and in the works of Tertullian: A clash of traditions', *StPatr* 65 (2013), 225–38. The hypothesis of polemic underlying apparent contradictions between Tertullian and Perpetua has been challenged by David E. Wilhite, 'Perpetua of History: Recent Questions', *Journal of Early Christian Studies* 25, no. 2 (2017), 307–19.

later, Tertullian reminds his readers, 'You have a treatise by us concerning Paradise, in which we have established that every soul is deposited in the lower region until the day of the Lord'.[228]

Wilhite addresses this difficulty, arguing that Tertullian's claim has been recently misunderstood, because of 'a failure to contextualise his remark within his rhetorical strategy' against the Valentinian belief in the soul's ascent through multiple heavens.[229] Wilhite's solution is that Tertullian concedes that true Christians, those disciplined by the Spirit, are those who confess unto death, whether they die publicly or not.[230] Elsewhere in *Apologeticum* Tertullian claims post-mortem bliss for all Christians.[231] Wilhite's insight is that 'Tertullian understands all true Christians as "martyrs": a martyr is a faithful "witness" unto death', retaining the primordial meaning of *martyr* as witness.[232] This would certainly accord with Tertullian's conflation of confession and martyrdom and insistence that those 'in Christ' must confess 'in him'. Wilhite, in consensus with older scholarship,[233] has proven his case: Tertullian does not consign martyrs to *heaven* ahead of other faithful, but he goes a little further than Wilhite suggests, granting martyrs a unique assurance.

Discussing 2 Corinthians 5:6, being at home in the body and absent from the Lord, Tertullian appears to make an exception for martyrs: 'For no one estranged from the body steadfastly abides with the Lord except by the prerogative of martyrdom, lodging in Paradise, not the lower regions.'[234] Paradise is 'under the altar', but not in heaven, for heaven is only opened at the end of the world.[235] Nevertheless, elsewhere Tertullian discerns a priority in the reward of martyrs. He interprets 1 Corinthians 15:35-44, 'not all flesh is the same flesh', as a difference of honour, not nature; of prerogative, not communal substance.[236] Paul uses figures to distinguish the martyrs as the 'flesh of birds' which aspire to ascend, in contrast to the flesh of men (servants of God) of beasts (the heathen) and of fishes (the baptized).[237] Tertullian insists the difference is one of glory, not substance, in the resurrection.[238]

Furthermore, he makes it clear that only martyrs have *assurance* of acceptance at the judgement. Martyrdom causes sufferings that effect cures for eternity.[239] For Tertullian, confession in martyrdom definitely wins salvation, which is the essential meaning of Christ's promise to confess those who confess in him.[240] He considers that

---

[228] *An.* 55.5 (CCSL 2:863) Habes etiam de paradiso a nobis libellum, quo constituimus omnem animam apud inferos sequestrari in diem domini.
[229] Wilhite, 'Tertullian on the Afterlife'.
[230] Ibid., 499.
[231] Ibid., 495, citing *Apol.* 47.13.
[232] Wilhite, 'Tertullian on the Afterlife', 499.
[233] Ibid., 499-503.
[234] *Res.* 43.4 (CCSL 2:978-9) nemo enim peregrinatus a corpore statim immoratur penes dominum, nisi ex martyrii praerogatiua, paradiso scilicet, non inferis, deuersurus.
[235] Wilhite, 'Tertullian on the Afterlife', 498, citing *An.* 55.3.
[236] *Res.* 52.11 (CCSL 2:997) Non omnis caro eadem caro; non ad denegandam substantiae communionem sed praerogatiuae peraeqationem, corpus honoris, non generis, differentiam redigens.
[237] *Res.* 52.11-13 (CCSL 2:997) alia caro uolatilium, id est martyrum, qui ad superiora conantur, alia piscium, id est quibus aqua baptismatis sufficit.
[238] *Res.* 52.15 (CCSL (2:997).
[239] *Scorp.* 5.10 (CCSL 2:1078).
[240] *Marc.* 4.21.8-9 (CCSL 1:599) Mt. 10:32-33.

Jesus' teachings about enduring to the end to be saved, valuing Jesus above one's own life, losing one's life for his sake all refer to martyrdom.[241] In this sense, the martyrs who especially participate in Christ's sacrifice are held in assurance 'under the altar' in 'Paradise', awaiting their vindication. In this sense they have a distinct advantage over other faithful Christians.

Martyrdom and forgiveness

Tertullian regards martyrdom as so meritorious as to be salvific. Because salvation necessitates remission of all sin, martyrdom – the second baptism – must bring forgiveness. Tertullian believes baptism imparts forgiveness of all sin, even the most heinous.[242] Since baptism marked a radical change of life, it required adequate preparation through a long catechumenate.[243] Likewise a return to the fold after excommunication required public penitence, culminating in a humiliating *exomologesis*.[244] Although he allows a once-only 'second repentance' in *De paenitentia*,[245] later in *De pudicitia*, he is adamant that serious post-baptismal sins (murder, adultery or idolatry/apostasy) could not be forgiven through *exomologesis*,[246] but only by God at the final judgement.[247] The only assurance for forgiveness for such sins would be martyrdom, the second baptism.

Whilst all the dead, heathen and Christian, remain in a subterranean Hades until the resurrection,[248] the martyrs alone are *subicitur altari*. This special place of glory

---

[241] *Scorp.* 10.17–11.5 (CCSL 2:1090–1).

[242] Tertullian, *Bapt.* 5.6–7, 20.1 (CCSL 1:281–2, 294); *Pud.* 16.5 (CCSL 2:1312).

[243] For an overview of the third-century catechumenate, see J. Patout Burns and Robin M. Jensen, *Christianity in Roman Africa: The Development of its Practices and Beliefs* (Grand Rapids: Eerdmans, 2014), 168–69; Alan Kreider, *The Change of Conversion and the Origin of Christendom* (Eugene OR: Wipf & Stock, 1999), 21–32; Gerald L. Sittser, 'The Catechumenate and the Rise of Christianity', *Journal of Spiritual Formation and Soul Care* 6 (2013), 179–203; Alistair Stewart-Sykes, 'Catechumenate and Contra-Culture: The Social Process of Catechumenate in Third Century Africa and its Development', *St. Vladimir's Theological Quarterly* 47, no. 3–4 (2003), 289–306; Edwina Murphy, 'Cyprian, Scripture and Socialisation: Forming faith in the catechumenate and beyond', in *The Intellectual World of Christian Late Antiquity: Reshaping Classical Traditions, 100–600 CE*, ed. Lewis Ayres, Matthew R. Crawford and Michael Champion (Cambridge: Cambridge University Press, 2023), 153–65; Megan DeVore, '*Catechumeni*, not "New Converts": Revisiting the *Passio Perpetuae et Felicitatis*', StPatr 91 (2017), 237–48.

[244] See Everett Ferguson, 'Early Church Penance', *Restoration Quarterly* 36, no. 2 (1994), 81–100; Burns and Jensen, *Christianity*, 295–99, 314–18; Sutcliffe, 'Learning Not to Sin: Repentance in Tertullian and Cyprian', *Colloquium* 53, no. 1 (2021), 73–97.

[245] Tertullian, *Paen.* 7.10 (CCSL 1:333) Haec igitur uenena eius prouidens deus clausam licet ignoscentiae ianuam et intinctionis sera obstructam aliquid adhuc permisit patere. He viewed it as an extension of incomplete baptismal repentance and seems to allow forgiveness of all types of sin; *Paen.* 4.1, 7.2 (CCSL 1:326, 332).

[246] Tertullian, *Pud.* 5.5 (CCSL 2:1288) calls them *principalium utique delictorum*: the principal sins, for which there could be no restoration of peace; *Pud.* 12 (CCSL 2:1302–3). These related to the Decalogue and the prohibitions imposed on Gentile Christians in Acts 15:29. *Pud.* 19.26 (CCSL 2:1323) Horum ultra exorator non erit Christus; haec non admittet omnino, qui natus ex Deo fuerit, non futurus Dei filius, si admiserit.

[247] Tertullian, *Pud.* 2.12 (CCSL 2:1285) Alia erunt remissibilia, alia inremissibilia. He now denies that the parables of the lost coin, sheep and son apply to post-baptismal sin; *Pud.* 9.10 (CCSL 2:1297–8). *Pud.* 3 (CCSL 2:1285) *Pud.* 11.2, 12.11 (CCSL 2:1302, 1303).

[248] *An.* 55 (CCSL 2:861–3).

relates to Tertullian's understanding that 'the sole key to unlock Paradise is your own life's blood'.[249] The prayer 'Thy kingdom come' is the asking for the final vindication of these martyrs at the end of the age, after the resurrection and the destruction of the Devil and Antichrist.[250] Tertullian explicitly anticipates forgiveness of sins and guaranteed salvation for martyrs:

> Who, having joined us does not eagerly desire to suffer, that he may purchase the whole favour of God, that he may obtain all pardon from him by the compensation of his own blood? For all sins are remitted by this action ... When condemned by [the Romans] we are acquitted by God.[251]

He presents martyrdom as the only guaranteed solution to post-baptismal sin,[252] and a way of recompensing Christ.[253] In *De pudicitia* he asserts that martyrdom is the only thing which can restore the prodigal son.[254] This baptism of blood was the sole opportunity to renew one's water baptism.[255] Of the four fathers, he is the strongest proponent of absolution through martyrdom, which is consistent with his high view of martyrdom as the peak of Christian confession.

Nevertheless, Tertullian does not believe that martyrs and confessors could unreservedly advocate for others. In *De pudicitia* he argues that sins cannot be remitted through the intervention of the church.[256] Only God, not the clergy, has the right to arbitrate on and remit sin. The so-called power of martyrs to remit sin led to imprisoned confessors being swamped by supplicants, seeking peace from those who were risking their own. But Tertullian argues that a martyr can only purge his or her own sins; only Christ's death was able to redeem the lives of others. Major sins can only be washed away by the martyrdom of the sinner himself, not by another's.[257]

Final vindication

In contrast to the Alexandrians, Tertullian equates vindication of the persecuted with their sharing in Christ's concrete and imminent eschatological victory. The end of the world is imminent and there will be a just reckoning at the final judgement. God will recompense tribulation to those who afflict Christians, when the Lord is revealed from heaven.[258] The martyrs' souls cry out for this vindication.[259] The persecuted will

---

[249] *An.* 55.4 (CCSL 2:862–3), Tota paradisi clauis tuus sanguis est.
[250] *Or.* 5.3 (CCSL 1:260); *Res.* 25.1 (CCSL 2:953).
[251] *Apol.* 50.15–16 (CCSL 1:171) Quis non, ubi requisiuit, accedit, ubi accessit, pati exoptat, ut totam Dei gratiam redimat, ut omnem ueniam ab eo compensatione sanguinis sui expediat? Omnia enim huic operi delicta donantur ... cum damnamur a uobis, a Deo absoluimur.
[252] *Scorp.* 6.9 (CCSL 2:1080).
[253] *Res.* 8.6 (CCSL 2:932).
[254] *Pud.* 9.21 (CCSL 2:1299).
[255] *Pat.* 13.7 (CCSL 1:314) *ad occasionem secundae intinctionis*; *Bapt.* 16 (CCSL 1:290–1).
[256] For the contrast with *De paenitentia*, see Sutcliffe, 'Learning Not to Sin'.
[257] *Pud.* 22.1–5 (CCSL 2:1328–9).
[258] *Marc.* 5.16.1 (CCSL 1:710) 2 Thess. 1:4–8.
[259] *Or.* 5.3 (CCSL 1:260).

participate in judgement of their persecutors, and part of the joy of the blessed redeemed will be the sight of the spectacle of divine retribution as the tables are turned.[260] Think about that prospect, repent and stop persecuting, is the essence of Tertullian's warning to Scapula.[261]

Conclusion: Persecution is good

Although all four fathers acknowledge that God providentially works to make good ultimately come from evil, Tertullian alone describes persecution itself as 'good'.[262] It is 'especially worthy of God',[263] it is good because it is divine.[264]

Tertullian seeks to retain God's complete sovereignty over evil, allowing him to be the cause of penal evils and of persecution, but not of sinful evils, nor of the injustice of persecution. Tertullian's eschatological perspective and high view of martyrdom allow him to attribute persecution to God because it is God's ordained cosmic conflict and in the final judgement all will be set right. The 'goodness' of persecution will be seen not only in its good outcomes, but in relation to the battle against evil itself. This cosmic battle relates to the Christian's fundamental identity in Christ and the imperative to share in Christ's battle and victory in the arena of persecution by confession of the name. Martyrdom brings forgiveness of sins and specific, immediate reward. For this reason, martyrdom should be embraced, arguably even sought, and certainly never resisted. These features of Tertullian's diogmology underpin his adamant and uncompromising stance on the appropriate response of Christians to persecution.

The appropriate response to persecution

Given Tertullian's concept of persecution as the divinely ordained means of joining Christ's victory over the demonic world, it is not surprising that, of the four fathers, he advocates the most positive response to persecution. His is the most focused advocacy of martyrdom, and the most uncompromising rejection of its avoidance. He exhorts to accept and embrace it, both for the good to be received now and for the greater reward that comes from greater suffering.

The right attitude

Tertullian pronounces those who suffer persecution to be happy, whereas those who avoid it by running away in disobedience, to be unhappy.[265] In *Scorpiace* he quotes 1

---

[260] *Spect.* 30 (CCSL 1:252–3).
[261] *Scap.* 3.1, 4.1, 5.3 (CCSL 2:1129–30, 1132).
[262] *Fug.* 4.3 (CCSL 2:1141) bonum persecutio [est].
[263] *Fug.* 1.3 (CCSL 2:1135) Deo dignam esse.
[264] *Fug.* 4.1 (CCSL 2:1140) Si autem statu quidem bonum quod a Deo uenit – nihil enim a Deo non bonum, quia diuinum, quia rationale.
[265] *Fug.* 7.1 (CCSL 2:1144) *felices . . . infelices.*

Peter 4:13–16 on the glory of suffering for Christ.[266] In *Apologeticum* he emphasizes that persecuted Christians rejoice if defamed, and do not defend themselves if prosecuted. If questioned, the Christian confesses and if condemned, he returns thanks.[267] But Tertullian is a rather miserable comforter. Although he claims to write to nourish the spirits of the martyrs,[268] he expounds themes of suffering, endurance of hardship, training, asceticism, bravery, set against a stark litany of the tortures awaiting them. Whilst he can encourage his readers with treatises on patience and angelic rejoicing at the sinner's repentance,[269] he declares that what will truly give him joy is the sight of God's fury being meted on the persecutors of Christians.[270]

Throughout his works, Tertullian emphasizes Christian non-vengeance. He situates this requirement in the character of God, the call to love in imitation of God, and the Christian's confidence that it is God who will avenge. He traces, against Marcion, the continuity of the non-retaliation principle from creation onward, in imitation of the loving God who providentially provides for all.[271] The *lex talionis* promoted restraint; the Creator had always enjoined patience, based on trust that he alone would rightly dispense justice. Christ's injunctions do not oppose this law, but rather further it. In *De patientia* Tertullian advocates patience as a means of disarming an aggressor.[272] Revenge is akin to impatience and, whilst it appears to soothe pain, is actually rendering evil for evil, making both parties equally guilty.[273] In *De anima* Tertullian refutes Carpocrates by showing how we are to love our neighbours and respond to the heathen 'adversary'.[274] He observes to Scapula, 'certainly everyone loves their friends; however it is Christians alone who love their enemies'.[275]

This love, rather than fear of persecution, is Tertullian's stated motivation in warning Scapula to desist from fighting against God's people. Following other apologists, Tertullian emphasizes that Christians do not revile their persecutors, but pray for them; for they are not the emperor's enemies, but his intercessors.[276] 'If we are commanded . . . to love enemies, whom have we to hate? Likewise, if when injured we are forbidden to reciprocate, lest action puts us on a par, whom are we able to injure?'[277] Spirit-filled Christians could never avenge themselves, nor shrink from suffering that by which they are tested.[278] Those who do avenge cruelty are, at least from Tertullian's perspective, no longer regarded as Christian.[279]

---

[266] *Scorp.* 12.2–3 (CCSL 2:1092).
[267] *Apol.* 1.12 (CCSL 1:87).
[268] *Mart.* 1.1 (CCSL 1:3).
[269] *Paen.* 8 esp 8.3 (CCSL 1:334–5) Laetantur caeli et qui illic sunt angeli paenitentia hominis; heus tu peccator, bono animo sis: uides ubi de tuo gaudeatur!
[270] *Spect.* 30.3 (CCSL 1:252) Quid admirer? Quid rideam? Ubi gaudeam, ubi exultem . . . ?
[271] *Marc.* 4.16.1–5 (CCSL 1:581–2).
[272] *Pat.* 8.7–9 (CCSL 1:309).
[273] *Pat.* 10.1–3 (CCSL 1:310).
[274] *An.* 35.2 (CCSL 2:836–7).
[275] *Scap.* 1.3–4 (CCSL 2:1127–8) Amicos enim diligere omnium est, inimicos autem solorum Christianorum.
[276] *Apol.* 30, 31 (CCSL 1:141–2).
[277] *Apol.* 37.1 (CCSL 1:147) Si inimicos, . . . iubemur diligere, quem habemus odisse? Item, si iidem laesi uicem referre prohibemur, ne de facto pares simus, quem possumus laedere?
[278] *Apol.* 37.1–3 (CCSL 1:147–8).
[279] *Apol.* 46.16–17 (CCSL 1:162).

Nevertheless, Tertullian takes delight in the prospect of the ultimate punishment of persecutors. He overtly rejoices at the day of judgement that will consume persecuting governors in fiercer fires than those with which they burned Christ's followers.[280] Is Tertullian hypocritical in delighting in the destruction of those he purports to love? Despite his somewhat distasteful style, he recognizes that evil cannot be brushed over; the good God is also just. The reason the persecuted Christian eschews personal hatred or vengeance is because vengeance belongs to *God*. If there were no ultimate divine justice and recompense in view, no ultimate victory over evil and its perpetrators, then present personal non-retaliation would have no reasonable basis.

The potential for persecution was cause for fear in Tertullian's community. Local flare-ups of mob violence, individual denunciations or false accusations could lead to imprisonment awaiting prosecution at the whim of the governor. Imprisonment involved deprivation and family destitution. The convicted could be exiled or killed. It would be easy to lose sight of God's providential control of the situation, easier to fear rather than to trust, to waver and to focus on the present than on eternity. Tertullian is aware of these risks, and that Jesus anticipated the fear they would inspire (Mt. 10:26–28). However, Tertullian tends to equate fear with weakness, and generally uses Matthew 10:28 for its warning – destruction of soul and body in hell[281] – rather than its exhortation: 'fear not'.

In *Scorpiace* he links God's providence and power to the exhortation 'fear not', in Jesus' missionary discourse. The governors slay the body, but God rules the soul; we shall not fall to the ground in vain if we choose to be killed by men rather than God.[282] In *De fuga* he berates the fearful who flee or hide rather than face persecution; they should act rightly and trust God's providence.[283] Paul bids us to support the weak, he allows, but not when they flee! Rather, fear must be put away; he who fears is deficient in love.[284] Avoidance of God-ordained persecution constitutes being ashamed of Christ. Christ does not cherish the weak but rejects them. He does not teach us to flee our persecutors but to not fear them, who can merely destroy the body and not the soul in hell. For whoever values his life more than Christ is not worthy of him, and the fearful will ultimately be consigned to the lake of fire.[285]

Patient endurance

Patience is demonstrated in endurance.[286] For Tertullian this primarily means endurance to the point of martyrdom. In *Scorpiace*, Tertullian emphasizes the link

---

[280] *Spect.* 30.3 (CCSL 1:252).
[281] For example, *Res.* 35.1–7 (CCSL 2:966–7).
[282] *Scorp.* 9.8 (CCSL 2:1085).
[283] *Fug.* 4.3–5.3 (CCSL 2:1141–2).
[284] *Fug* 9.1–3 (CCSL 2:1146–7); 1 Jn 4:18.
[285] *Fug.* 7 (CCSL 2:1144–5).
[286] Alan Kreider, *The Patient Ferment of the Early Church: The Improbable Rise of Christianity in the Roman Empire* (Grand Rapids: Baker, 2016), 20–5, sees Tertullian's concept of patience as challenging the Graeco-Roman association of patience with the powerless and servile. Kreider has been criticized for ignoring the philosophers' perspective on patience as a philosophical virtue; Brian Litfin, 'Was the Early Church "Patient"?' Oct 2016. https://www.thegospelcoalition.org/reviews/patient-ferment-of-the-early-church/

between endurance and suffering for the name which Matthew 10:22 highlights. Enduring to the end *means* bearing persecution, betrayal and death, as did the Teacher and Master.[287] Confession is required on this earth where family members betray each other and where we endure to the end.[288] The requirement for endurance delegitimizes fleeing persecution.[289] 'Do we prove the faith from persons, or persons from the faith? No one is wise unless faithful, no one is greater unless a Christian, however no one is a Christian except the one who perseveres even to the end.'[290]

For Tertullian, being faithful unto death, the reward of which is the crown of life (Rev. 2:10) *means* confession and martyrdom, not merely keeping the faith throughout life. He applies this passage to the soldier who refused the military crown,[291] and to those who are martyred and whose souls are now kept under the altar.[292] Persecution is a contest worthy of God, who both proclaims the conflict and offers the crown, for the promotion of his glory.[293] In *De patientia*, Tertullian proclaims patience as the highest virtue.[294] The model of patience is God himself, who became incarnate and bore the enmity of his opponents.[295] Patience underpins faith and obedience. Impatience, following the Devil's lead, begets sin.[296] Patience allows us to bear persecution and suffering in this life, knowing that the dead are called to Christ.[297] Patience precludes vengeance and permits rejoicing at inflicted suffering;[298] by patience the Christian endures torture and deprivation.[299]

Confession and martyrdom

Tertullian believes this life is a disciplinary preparation for confession and martyrdom, aided by the Holy Spirit, in the knowledge that the world is about to end in judgement. Therefore, Tertullian can envisage no legitimate alternative to bold confession and fearlessly facing martyrdom. Any alternative that seeks to avoid this destiny is to be rejected as a form of denial. This position contrasts starkly with Clement's, and even Origen's, despite the latter's relatively high view of martyrdom. It is also a position from which Cyprian will depart.

Tertullian expects the Spirit to guide the confessor.[300] He regards the Spirit as a person,[301] the representative or deputy of the Son and third in the *trinitas* of the

---

[287] *Scorp.* 9.6 (CCSL 2:1085).
[288] *Scorp.* 10.17 (CCSL 2:1090).
[289] *Fug.* 7.2 (CCSL 2:1144) Quid ergo me iubens fugere uis in finem sustinere?
[290] *Praescr.* 3.6 (CCSL 1:188) Ex personis probamus fidem, an ex fide personas? Nemo est sapiens nisi fidelis, nemo maior nisi christianus, nemo autem christianus nisi qui ad finem usque perseuerauerit.
[291] *Cor.* 15.1, 3 (CCSL 2:1064–5).
[292] *Scorp.* 12.6–9 (CCSL 2:1093).
[293] *Fug.* 1.5 (CCSL 2:1136).
[294] *Pat.* 1.6–7 (CCSL 1:299–300).
[295] *Pat.* 3 (CCSL 1:300–2).
[296] *Pat.* 5 (CCSL 1:303–6).
[297] *Pat.* 9 (CCSL 1:309–10).
[298] *Pat.* 10–11 (CCSL 1:310–12).
[299] *Pat.* 13 (CCSL 1:313–4).
[300] *Scorp.* 11.3 (CCSL 2:1090); Mt. 10:19–20.
[301] Wilhite, 'Spirit of Prophecy, 46, 63–4. Wilhite concludes that Tertullian's pneumatology is thoroughly Pauline.

Godhead as the fruit derived from the shoot is third from the root.[302] He describes how the Spirit is bestowed at chrismation and the laying of hands, after cleansing by baptism.[303] Even his early works show a conviction that the Spirit's leading produces spiritual discipline and guides the Christian to the ultimate witness in martyrdom. Tertullian reminds confessors that the Holy Spirit has entered the prison with them, will remain with them and lead them to the Lord.[304] The hardships they experience are a discipline and a training for the contest they will undertake.[305] Discipline and martyrdom, both promoted by the Spirit, are connected in Tertullian's thought, as Wilhite explains. Disciplined Christians and martyrs are Spirit-led; discipline enables martyrdom.[306]

Tertullian defends the practices of spiritual discipline; fasting, xerophagia, monogamy, as reins upon the appetite, in opposition to the 'Psychics', whom he accuses of gluttony and opposing the Paraclete.[307] The Paraclete enjoins stations for fasting and prayer, in contrast to the Psychics' attribution of them to the Devil.[308] Fasting and xerophagies accustom Christians to imprisonment and deprivation, inspiring confidence for endurance of the final conflict and providing less fleshly concern for the tortures to work on. In contrast, he alleges that the 'Psychic' martyr Pristinus could not cope with abstinence and had to be intoxicated in order to face trial, dying in the very act of apostasy.[309] Bray suggests that Tertullian's greatest fear for a prospective martyr was for them to succumb to the temptations of the world, hence the need for stringent preparation and Tertullian's emphasis on ascetic discipline.[310] Tertullian saw the Paraclete as an essential helper to enable Christians to embrace martyrdom.

> Therefore, the Paraclete, who leads into all truth, is necessary, and encourages all to endurance. And those who have received him will neither flee from persecution nor learn to buy it off, for they have himself, who is for us, even speaking in [our] interrogation, thus helping [us] in suffering.[311]

Opposing patripassianism, Tertullian asserts that the Spirit of God suffered in the Son, and likewise we can only suffer for God if the Spirit is in us. He speaks through us; not suffering himself but bestowing the power and capacity for suffering.[312]

---

[302] *Prax.* 8.4–7 (CCSL 2:1167–8).
[303] *Bapt.* 6–8 (CCSL 1:282–3).
[304] *Mart.* 1.3 (CCSL 1:3).
[305] *Mart.* 3 (CCSL 1:5–6).
[306] Wilhite, 'Spirit of Prophecy', 66.
[307] *Jej.* 1.1–2 (CCSL 2:1257).
[308] *Jej.* 11.4–6 (CCSL 2:1270).
[309] *Jej.* 12 (CCSL 2:1270–1).
[310] Gerald L. Bray, *Holiness and the Will of God: Perspectives on the Theology of Tertullian* (Atlanta: John Knox, 1979), 47.
[311] *Fug.* 14.3 (CCSL 2:1155) Et ideo Paracletus necessarius, deductor omnium ueritatum, exhortator omnium tolerantiarum. Quem qui receperunt, neque fugere persecutionem neque redimere nouerunt, habentes ipsum, qui pro nobis erit, sicut locuturus in interrogatione, ita iuuaturus in passione.
[312] *Prax.* 29.7 (CCSL 2:1203) and see Wilhite, 'Spirit of Prophecy', 63, on this passage; the Spirit/divine person enables 'our' suffering for Christ ... the Spirit 'in us' (*in nobis*) is the one who 'speaks through us' (*loquitur de nobis*) our 'confession' (*confessionis*).

Furthermore, for Tertullian, the Paraclete directs the Christian toward martyrdom. Concerning the detractors of the crown-refusing soldier, he asserts that as they had rejected the prophecies of the Holy Spirit, they now supported refusing martyrdom.[313] In *Scorpiace*, he argues from Matthew 10 for the necessity of martyrdom; valuing Christ more than life, losing life to find it everlastingly, and being assured that the Holy Spirit will answer by them.[314] Absent from Tertullian's reckoning (in contrast to Cyprian's) is any idea that the Paraclete might direct a Christian to a course of action other than martyrdom, such as flight.

Martyrdom as confession

Tertullian's view of martyrdom is so uniformly positive, and his aversion to denial so comprehensive, that he effectively *conflates* confession and martyrdom. The confessor should expect to be martyred and embrace it as the Christian's calling to which the Holy Spirit leads and empowers them. Any other path is at best tenuous, and ultimately smacks of fear, a weakness he equates with denial.

Ad martyras predates Perpetua's martyrdom, but his addressees had similarly been imprisoned for their 'witness', presumably awaiting the governor's verdict. Later persecutions, particularly under Decius, saw some *confessores* who were released, some who perished before their trials and those who ultimately lost their lives by execution. All were considered confessors by Cyprian. Tertullian, however, sees imprisonment as a training ground in the discipline necessary to face martyrdom.[315] *Scorpiace* is Tertullian's polemic against heretics who would deter weak Christians from martyrdom in a season of persecution.[316] Extensive use of Matthew 10 supports his contention that martyrdom is expected and necessary, conflating confession and martyrdom.[317] Confession is elicited by and inextricably linked to persecution and the suffering of death, by which the confessor saves his life everlastingly.[318]

Tertullian even conveys this diogmology to persecutors in *Apologeticum*, again assuming that confession, a Christian's identification with Christ, will be fatal. Christians are not ashamed of Christ, they rejoice to be reckoned his servants and condemned with him.[319] In reality, the state has no power over Christians, who freely will to be Christians and be condemned rather than apostatize. They suffer as in a war, for the glory and victory of the struggle, and the attaining of eternal life. They conquer when killed.[320] Likewise in *Ad Scapulam*:

> Indeed, we are neither perturbed nor alarmed about that which from ignorance we suffer, coming to this sect, certainly accepting the conditions of this contract, we

---

[313] *Cor.* 1.4 (CCSL 2:1040).
[314] *Scorp.* 11.1–3 (CCSL 2:1090–1).
[315] *Mart.* 3 (CCSL 1:5–6).
[316] *Scorp.* 1.5 (CCSL 2:1069–70) contemporary with Perpetua's martyrdom.
[317] *Scorp.* 9 (CCSL 2:1084–7).
[318] *Scorp.* 10.14 –11.2 (CCSL 2:1089–90).
[319] *Apol.* 21.3 (CCSL 1:123).
[320] *Apol.* 49–50 (CCSL 1:168–71).

join these battles discharging our souls, desiring to obtain that which God has counter-promised, and fearing those sufferings with which he threatens the alternative life. Further, we strive with all your ferocity, breaking forth even further, rejoicing much more in condemnation than absolution.[321]

In Tertullian's mind, confession and martyrdom are one, and since the former is essential, the latter is to be embraced.

Any volunteers?

Tertullian is undoubtedly pro-martyrdom; but does he encourage provocation of it? This discussion is often entangled in the circular argument regarding his alleged Montanism, and whether volunteerism was a hallmark of Montanism.[322] Tertullian does give the impression he applauds volunteerism, but each of his arguments must be taken in their polemical context. In *De pudicitia*, his disgust with the pardoning of adultery prompts promotion of martyrdom as the only means of pardon,[323] rather than relying on an absolution the church cannot give. Tertullian regards the soldier who refused the military crown despite his inevitable fate as 'alone a Christian',[324] because *De corona* serves to rebuke cowardice in the face of the attention resulting from the soldier's provocative confession. In *De spectaculis* he wants to dissuade Christians from participating in the false glory of the very arena in which Christians are killed. Rather, the Christian should 'glory in the palms of martyrdom'.[325]

In *Scorpiace* he decries the heretics ('Gnostics') who oppose martyrdoms, thereby representing salvation to be destruction and making something sweet and light into bitterness and darkness.[326] His response is to elaborate martyrdom's benefits: it produces good, it is necessary. God has commanded it, and we have a duty to suffer it.[327] Martyrdom is good because it opposes and delivers from idolatry; it heals for salvation by suffering that imitates the maladies of torture, punishment and death.[328] Furthermore, the greater one's suffering, the greater the reward.[329] 'Believers', he concludes, 'are obligated to suffer martyrdom.'[330]

Tertullian considers the worst a Christian can do is deny his Lord. His purpose in *De fuga* is to equate flight with denial and dissuade from it. The closest Tertullian

---

[321] *Scap.* 1.1–2 (CCSL 2:1127) Nos quidem neque expauescimus, neque partimescimus ea quae ab ignorantibus patimur, cum ad hanc sectam, utique suscepta condicione eius pacti, uenerimus, ut etiam animas nostras exauctorati in has pugnas accedamus, ea quae Deus repromittit consequi optantes, et ea quae diuersae uitae comminatur pati timentes. Denique cum omni saeuitia uestra concertamus, etiam ultro erumpentes, magisque damnati quam absoluti gaudemus.
[322] Refuted by William Tabbernee, 'Early Montanism and Voluntary Martyrdom'. *Colloquium* 17, no. 2 (1985), 33–44.
[323] *Pud.* 9.21 (CCSL 2:1299); *Scorp.* 6.9 (CCSL 2:1080).
[324] *Cor.* 1.4 (CCSL 2:140) solus Christianus.
[325] *Spect.* 29.1–3 (CCSL 1:251) ad martyrii palmas gloriare.
[326] *Scorp.* 1.13 (CCSL 2:1071).
[327] *Scorp.* 2.1; 8.1 (CCSL 2:1071, 1082).
[328] *Scorp.* 5 (CCSL 2:1076–9).
[329] *Scorp.* 6.7 (CCSL 2:1080).
[330] *Scorp.* 8.8 (CCSL 2:1084) debitricem martyrii fidem.

comes to directly advocating voluntary martyrdom is when confronting Scapula with the inevitability of facing God's wrath if he persecutes God's people.[331] In this context, he suggests that all the Christians just might rush forth to the combat to prove they have no dread of his cruelties, and even invite their affliction. He reminds Scapula of Christians *en masse* presenting themselves to Arrius Antonius in Asia, who allegedly told them if they wished to die there were precipices and halters. What will Scapula then do with so many thousands of Carthaginian Christians whom he will have to slaughter?[332] Given the level of exaggeration involved in this work, such as his excessive enumeration of Christians, it seems most likely that this threat is a rhetorical strategy. Tertullian senses the urgency of compelling pagans to repent in this life. Whereas Clement and Origen are concerned that a voluntary martyr might be drawn into the sin of the persecutors, this is not a consideration for Tertullian, who places the blame directly on the persecutors who share the Devil's sin. They need to desist and repent while they can.

The most significant argument against Tertullian promoting radical martyrdom as a universal goal is that, as far as we know, Tertullian was neither a confessor nor a martyr himself. If this argument from silence is persuasive, Tertullian's motives for his apparent self-contradiction remain conjectural. Possibly he was waiting for an individual call by the Spirit as exemplified in the martyr acts.[333] While Tertullian's contemporary Clement singles out the voluntary martyr for disparagement, as Middleton observes, Tertullian seems to make no real distinction between types or groups of martyrs.[334] Middleton suggests that Tertullian encourages taking control of one's own death, even presenting examples of pagan suicides for Christians to emulate,[335] but he stops short of making him an overt promoter of voluntary martyrdom.[336] As with Origen's *Exhortation*, the addressees of *Ad martyras* were already incarcerated as confessors, so their imminent martyrdom was only 'voluntary' as an alternative to apostatizing, a distinction not always appreciated. Tertullian certainly views martyrdom as an appropriate goal, but even in *De fuga*, he leaves to God the fate of the one who chooses to face, not flee, persecution.[337] Perhaps because of what he witnessed, as well as his conviction of the necessity of confession and the benefits of martyrdom, he regards the two as inevitably linked. Thus, to exhort a Christian to step forward and confess is effectively to exhort them to step forward to death.

Apostasy

Considering these imperatives, in Tertullian's mind the apostate was worse than the pagan. The Christian who apostatizes squanders the substance received from his Father

---

[331] *Scap.* 3.5–4.1 (CCSL 2:1129–30).
[332] *Scap.* 5.1–2 (CCSL 2:1131–2).
[333] Tabbernee, 'Early Montanism', 34 observes this in the *Acta*.
[334] Paul Middleton, 'Early Christian Voluntary Martyrdom: A Statement for the Defence', *Journal of Theological Studies* 64, no. 2 (2013), 556–73, at 565.
[335] *Mart.* 4.4–8 (CCSL 1:6–7); Middleton, *Radical Martyrdom*, 35.
[336] Middleton, *Radical Martyrdom*, 29.
[337] *Fug.* 5.2 (CCSL 2:1141).

in baptism: the Holy Spirit and, in consequence, eternal hope. The apostate cannot make satisfaction to the Father and has wasted his baptism: 'Who will fear to waste what he has the power of afterwards recovering? Who will be careful to preserve to perpetuity what he will not be able to lose to perpetuity? Security in sin is likewise an appetite for it.'[338]

Tertullian was adamant that the episcopal church could not pardon the apostate, only God himself could; at the final judgement.[339] In contrast to the Alexandrian view, there was no post-mortem opportunity for repentance. Tertullian's one concession, although partial, is to recognize that one who apostatizes against his will under the extreme duress of torture has scars that show he yielded unwillingly, unlike the adulterer who yields for pleasure. Their flesh was truly weak, they mourn and repent and seek expiation, for a sin which could be remitted anew, in God's mercy.[340] In this life, however, there was only one sure way in which the apostate could atone for his sin and regain his salvation; the greater baptism, that of blood, in martyrdom.[341]

Stay or flee?

Tertullian was effectively one of the *stantes*, in that he continued his work without being delated, imprisoned, confessing at trial, fleeing or being martyred (as far as we know). His opinion on *stantes* is difficult to ascertain and must be teased out of his arguments concerning flight, to which he was definitely opposed, and from his own implied behaviour. He presents a stark dichotomy between facing martyrdom and running away, without seeming to allow for surreptitiously remaining. Tertullian refuses to legitimize any flight which is based on the assumption that God could providentially return the runaway for judgement. The runaway might think he risks denying if he stayed: in this sense he has effectively denied already. Is denial less likely if he flees and is subsequently captured? Far better, asserts Tertullian, to presume one would confess,[342] for providence works both ways. 'But if all is truly with God, why do we not leave it to his decision, acknowledging his virtue and power in that, just as when we flee he can bring us back to the midst, so when we do not flee; even in the midst of the populace turning around to conceal us?'[343] If God's providence applies to flight, Tertullian reasons, it must also apply to staying put. 'Why do you not rather on this side of constancy and faith in God, say, "what is mine, I do; I don't depart; God, if he wills, protects me!" It is preferable for us to stay according to God's decision than to flee by

---

[338] *Pud.* 9.10 (CCSL 2:1297–8) Quis enim timebit prodigere, quod habebit postea recuperare? Quis curabit perpetuo conseruare, quod non perpetuo poterit amittere? Securitas delicti etiam libido est eius.
[339] *Pud.* 12.4–6 (CCSL 2:1302–3) citing Acts 15:19–20; *Pud.* 18.18; 21.15–17 (CCSL 2:1319, 1327–8).
[340] *Pud.* 22.11–15 (CCSL 2:1329–30).
[341] *Apol.* 50; *Res.* 8.6 (CCSL 2:932); *Scorp.* 6.9 (CCSL 2:1080); *Pud.* 9.21 (CCSL 2:1299).
[342] *Fug.* 5.1 (CCSL 2:1141).
[343] *Fug.* 5.2 (CCSL 2:1141) Si uero in Deo totum est, cur non totum relinquimus arbitrio eius, agnoscentes uirtutem et potestatem, quod possit nos sicut fugientes reducere in medium, ita non fugientes, immo et in medio populo conuersantes obumbrare?

our own.'³⁴⁴ Because persecution ultimately comes from God, he would not want us to avoid it. Do we think to thwart his will with our own?³⁴⁵ Imitating Christ, the Christian should hold position, pray to be spared the cup, yet cede to the will of the Father.³⁴⁶ Tertullian's guidance to the *stantes* is to trust in God's providence, endure to the end and be willing to confess and to suffer.

Nevertheless, Tertullian would not support any attempt to hide or suppress one's Christianity. Although in his *Apologeticum* he is at pains to present Christians as harmless regular people and good citizens, in writing to Christians on issues of lifestyle and discipline he becomes increasingly rigorist. The avoidance of every taint of idolatry would necessarily single Christians out.³⁴⁷ Indeed, Tertullian's anticipation of martyrdom as the ideal and expected outcome of persecution means righteousness will bring one forth into the public gaze and provide the opportunity to die the martyr's death and glorify God, rather than simply dying in bed.³⁴⁸

Tertullian is the outlier among the four, in his opposition to flight. For him it is, at best, a poor choice for a Christian, whose highest calling is martyrdom, and his opposition to it intensifies over time. Early on, Tertullian identifies flight as an occasion for patience, the only time he acknowledges that flight itself may be a form of suffering.³⁴⁹ In *Ad uxorem* flight is the lesser of two evils, not ideal but better than apostasy.³⁵⁰ Defending the actions of the crown-refusing soldier, Tertullian accuses his critics of cowardice with an obvious allusion to Matthew 10:23: 'So they murmur that peace ... is endangered for them. Nor do I doubt that some are already turning their back on the scriptures, readying their luggage, equipped for flight from city to city; for that is all the gospel they care to remember.'³⁵¹

In *De corona* and *De fuga*, Tertullian's argument, and his exegesis, rests on his diogmology: persecution is ordained by God, and is therefore good, so we should not flee it.³⁵² Fearful flight equates to denial.³⁵³ God rejects the weak who flee their persecutors; rather we must not fear them.³⁵⁴ The Holy Spirit encourages us to martyrdom, not to flight. It is better to die at the hands of God than to flee.³⁵⁵

Tertullian's attitude to flight becomes more rigorous over time, even allowing for the different polemical contexts in which he tackles Matthew 10:23.³⁵⁶ Perhaps this

---

[344] *Fug.* 5.3 (CCSL 2:1141–2) Quanto magis ex hac parte constantiae et fiduciae in Deum, si dicis: ego, quod meum est, facio; non discedo; Deus, si uoluerit, ipse me proteget! Hoc potius nostrum est, stare sub Dei arbitrio, quam fugere sub nostro.
[345] *Fug.* 7.1 (CCSL 2:1144).
[346] *Fug.* 8.3 (CCSL 2:1145).
[347] *Spect.* 27:1–2 (CCSL 1:249); sarcastically: nemo te cognoscit Christianum.
[348] *Fug.* 9.4 (CCSL 2:1147).
[349] *Pat.* 13.6 (CCSL 2:1144–45).
[350] *Ux.* 1.3.4–5 (CCSL 1:375–6) non ideo bonum est, quia malum non est.
[351] *Cor.* 1.5 (CCSL 2:1040) Musitant denique tam bonam et longam pacem peri clitari sibi. Nec dubito quosdam, <secundum> scripturas emigrare, sarcinas expedire, fugae accingi de ciuitate in ciuitatem. Nullam enim aliam euangelii memoriam curant.
[352] *Fug.* 1, 2, 4 (CCSL 2.1135–41).
[353] *Fug.* 5.1, 7.2 (CCSL 2:1141, 1144–45).
[354] *Fug.* 7.2 (CCSL 2:1144–45).
[355] *Fug.* 9.4 (CCSL 2:1146–47).
[356] Sutcliffe, 'To Flee or Not to Flee?', 136–44.

intensified response reflects his personal experiences or observations, implied by specific references to persecution in *Scorpiace* and *De fuga*.[357] The opponents with which he engaged may also have changed over time, as his increasingly rigorous stance brought him into new conflicts. This would allow for both thought 'progression' and polemical context. Certainly, Tertullian's consistent exaltation of martyrdom as the Christian's ideal destiny contributed to his increasing opposition to fleeing it, hiding from it, or paying to avoid it.

Money for one's life

Tertullian wrote several decades before Decius, so he does not specifically mention *libelli*. Nevertheless, he is aware of some who pay their way out of persecution, probably under extortion over threatened denunciation. He castigates them in *De fuga,* insisting that such purchased immunity is just another form of flight, and similarly results from cowardice. How unworthy it is to try to ransom with money a person who had been ransomed with Christ's blood! Furthermore, it lays out less for that person than he cost Christ! As the apostles said to Simon, 'Your money be destroyed with you!'[358] Tertullian equates such failure to publicly acknowledge one's Christianity with denying Christ: 'Certainly the refusal of martyrdom is denial.'[359] It is to trust and serve mammon rather than God. No apostle extricated themselves from persecution with money, he contends. Christ laid down his life for us, and we should reciprocate. Likewise, we should die for our brethren, not pay for them.[360] It is not fitting to pay for liberty, because God has ordained our current persecuted situation. Nor is paying for liberty 'rendering to Caesar the things that are Caesar's' (Mt. 22:21) because Caesar regards the Christians as illicit, as criminals; the money goes to the extortionist, not to the government. Consider rather what we owe to God: ourselves, purchased with his Son's blood. We would cheat God by withholding the payment of our lives.[361] Nor is it a legitimate interpretation of 'Give to him who asks' (Mt. 5:42). He who uses intimidation does not 'ask', but threatens and compels. This would be giving out of fear, not out of pity. Such a one takes away a Christian's faith, not his 'extra cloak'.[362]

The church and persecution

Tertullian writes in defence of the church, in *Apologeticum, Ad nationes* and *Ad Scapulam*, presenting it as a misunderstood and unjustly persecuted community which has many fine attributes and of which the dreadful rumours of its practices are untrue. He presents all Christians as having equal conviction, uprightness and willingness to

---

[357] *Scorp.* 1; *Fug.* 1.1 (CCSL 2: 1069–71, 1135).
[358] *Fug.* 12.3–4 (CCSL 2:1150–1) Pecunia tua tecum sit in interitum. Acts 8:20.
[359] *Fug.* 12.5 (CCSL 2:1151) negatio est etiam martyrii recusatio.
[360] *Fug.* 12.6–7 (CCSL 2:1151–2).
[361] *Fug.* 12.9–10 (CCSL 2:1153).
[362] *Fug.* 13.1 (CCSL 1153–4); Mt. 5:40.

die for Christ, in contrast to the vigorous dressing-down the church receives in some of his other works. Tertullian is angered by the difference between the ideal of the church and its actual disposition, but the fault is not with the model or ideal, but with those who do not live up to it. As Rankin explains, where Tertullian emphasizes the church as Christ's body and the Spirit's indwelling, he stresses its perfection, whereas when he views it as a collection of sinful believers, he stresses its sinfulness and the Lordship of Christ.[363]

Rankin's otherwise comprehensive treatise on Tertullian's ecclesiology makes little reference to persecution, other than to the 'authority' of the martyr-confessor within the church.[364] However, Rankin usefully illuminates Tertullian's vision of the church as a church of the Spirit, not constituted solely by an episcopal structure; the church is the context of Christ's saving work, not the source of salvation.[365] The omission of persecution from Rankin's work is surprising, given the attention it receives throughout Tertullian's oeuvre, and the background it provides to the life of his church community.

Like Origen, Tertullian anticipates a beneficial effect of persecution on the church, provided it has the discipline and commitment to embrace it. In *De baptismo*, Tertullian interprets the disciples' experience of the storm on Galilee as a figure of the church, tossed by the sea of the world and its persecutions and temptations; the Lord is roused in its last extremities by the prayers of the saints and calms those storms.[366] Tertullian's insistence that apostates be excommunicated and that the bishop did not have power to reconcile them in this life, is consistent with this picture of the church. The apostate has denied his Christian identity under the Lordship of Christ and forfeited his salvation, effectively leaving the boat. The church must live as a separate community, untainted by the world, in purity and discipline, following the Spirit's leading in preparation for martyrdom.

Confessors and lapsed

Persecution is prominent in the ecclesiology of both Tertullian and Cyprian. I suggest this reflects, in part, the urgency which arises from their expectation of an imminent *parousia*, in contrast to the Alexandrians' anticipation of a still-advancing community that stretches into post-mortem eternity. If this life is the one chance to secure salvation, then the church's response to persecution must be fully engaged to secure that end.

In *Ad martyras*, Tertullian refers to material help given to imprisoned confessors by the church and by individuals, his own contribution being this letter that seeks to nourish them spiritually.[367] The church in Carthage organized the provision of basic food, because of the deprivations there.[368] Perpetua, imprisoned a decade or so later,

---

[363] Rankin, *Tertullian and the Church*, 59.
[364] Ibid., 181–3.
[365] Ibid., 65–7.
[366] *Bapt.* 12.7 (CCSL 1:288).
[367] *Mart.* 1.1 (CCSL 1:3).
[368] *Mart.* 1.1, 2.7 (CCSL 1:3, 4).

describes spiritual and material support from the church.³⁶⁹ This shows a solidarity with the confessors.

Tertullian considers that the church should maintain the discipline that will support and not hinder the Christian's destiny of martyrdom. They should certainly not be disparaging confessors such as the crown-refusing soldier, out of concern for their own comfort and safety.³⁷⁰ Given the seriousness of apostasy, those who denied Christ were removed from communion. The logical corollary was that the lapsed had lost their salvation; they had returned to the Devil's fold.

Persecution and church growth

Tertullian maintained that persecution, rather than being a deterrent, results in more attraction to Christianity and consistent growth in number, like seed.³⁷¹ His famous quote, *semen est sanguis Christianorum*, does not specifically state 'of the church'.³⁷² The immediate context, however, makes it clear that he believes that the more Christians are cut down, the more attractive Christianity becomes, and the more its numbers increase. Here in the closing argument of *Apologeticum*, Tertullian attributes the attraction to Christians' faithful endurance and hope of salvation, in the face of the obvious injustice of the persecution.³⁷³

Tertullian makes the exaggerated claim that Christians constitute almost the majority in every city, although being so unobtrusive they are known more as individuals than as organized communities.³⁷⁴ Although the first significant rise in Christian number coincided with more widespread persecution, as Hopkins argues, this does not prove causation.³⁷⁵ Hopkins concludes that persecution was beneficial for Christian growth, but does not clearly explain why, focusing instead on its appeal to the poor and to women, its exclusivity and literary basis and the dominance of small house-based churches with their greater internal cohesiveness. Lee, disputing a strong correlation between church growth and persecution, suggests a more significant factor for the exponential growth of Christianity in Roman times was the Christians' compassionate acts toward society's neglected.³⁷⁶ This also underlies Tertullian's claim: despite the spillage of blood, Christianity was undeniably attractive.

Persecution showcased the Christians' response in terms of patient continuance in well doing and loyalty to Christ. The distinctive closeness of Christian community and its members' love for one another contrasted with the behaviour of pagans. '"See," they say, 'how they love one another'; for they themselves hate one another; "and how they

---

³⁶⁹ *Passio*. 3.7 (Rebillard, 307)
³⁷⁰ *Cor*. 1.4–5 (CCSL 2:1040).
³⁷¹ *Apol*. 50.13 (CCSL 1:171); also *Scap* 5.4 (CCSL 2:1132).
³⁷² The textual apparatus of *Apologeticum* (CCSL 1:171) supplies no variant textual reading.
³⁷³ *Apol*. 50.12–16 (CCSL 1:171).
³⁷⁴ *Scap*. 2.10 (CCSL 2:1128).
³⁷⁵ Keith Hopkins, 'Christian Number and its Implications'. *Journal of Early Christian Studies* 6, no. 2 (1998), 185–226.
³⁷⁶ Morgan Lee, 'Sorry, Tertullian', *Christianity Today* 58, no. 10 (2014), 18. Lee cites contemporary evidence.

are ready to die for one another"; for they will be more ready to slaughter one another.'[377] As the apostate emperor Julian later noted, the 'impious Galileans' support not only their own poor 'but ours as well'.[378]

Apology: Persecution for the right reason

Written apologies of the second century were a public response from self-styled representatives of the church, presenting a Christian perspective on the antagonism of pagans toward the followers of Christ.[379] Tertullian made a significant and innovative contribution to apologetics, consistent with his comprehensive theology of persecution. *Ad nationes*, *Apologeticum* and *Ad Scapulam* develop many of his predecessors' arguments, however he also displays an integrated apprehension of the providential origin, purpose, benefits and appropriate response to persecution, which they did not. Tertullian determines that Christians must be persecuted. He pleads, not for persecution to cease, but for Christians to be persecuted for the right reasons. It is essential to distinguish between Tertullian's exhortation to individual persecutors to desist for their own sake, and his conviction of the inevitability of persecution, generally.

Whilst Tertullian covers the classic apologetic arguments,[380] he also advances beyond them, in his strategies and in his underlying theology. Strategically, he argues from natural law that persecution merely for the name of Christian was illogical and unjust, harmful to society and condemnatory of the persecutors. The laws that convict Christians are flawed.[381] Tertullian does more than employ more skilful and nuanced arguments than his apologetic predecessors, however; his most important contribution to apologetics is theological. Tertullian uniquely addresses the tension within apology, which he identifies at the climax of his *Apologeticum*:

> Therefore, you say, 'why do you complain that we attack you, if you want to suffer, since you ought to love those by whom you suffer what you wish?' Certainly, we wish it, in the manner of a soldier [suffering] war ... Our battle is that we are summoned before tribunals, there we struggle under mortal danger for the truth. However, it is a victory to obtain that for which we have struggled. This victory has both the glory of pleasing God and the plunder, eternal life. But we perish.

---

[377] *Apol.* 39.7 (CCSL 1:151) Vide, inquiunt, ut inuicem se diligant, ipsi enim inuicem oderunt, et ut pro alterutro mori sint parati, ipsi enim ad occidendum alterutrum paratiores. See also *Scap* 4.7 (CCSL 2:1131) regarding Christians' exemplary lives.

[378] Julian, *Letter to Arsacius.* in *A Few Notes on Julian and a Translation of His Public Letters*, trans. Edward J. Chinnock (London: David Nutt, 1901), 75–8 as quoted in D. Brendan Nagle and Stanley M. Burstein, *The Ancient World: Readings in Social and Cultural History* (Englewood Cliffs NJ; Prentice Hall, 1995), 314–15.

[379] This section draws on Sutcliffe, 'No Need to Apologise?'

[380] As listed in Sutcliffe, 'No Need to Apologise?' n. 33.

[381] *Apol.* 2, 4.4–13; 24, 37, 49, 50 (CCSL 1:87–91, 1:93–4, 1:133–5, 1:147–9, 1:168–9, 1:169–71). *Scap.* 2.2 3.1, 5.3 (CCSL 2:1127, 1129, 1132). For full discussion see Paul Livermore, 'Reasoning with Unbelievers and the Place of the Scriptures in Tertullian's Apology', *Asbury Theological Journal* 56, no. 1 (2001), 61–75; Sutcliffe, 'No Need to Apologise?' 272–3.

Certainly, when we have obtained a place. Therefore, we have conquered, when we are killed, and finally we escape, when covered over.[382]

The question is valid: why complain against persecution, when it is a battle Christians desire, that brings victory? Theologically, Tertullian realizes that persecution for the name was not only inevitable but entirely appropriate, and unlike his predecessors he is not shy of affirming this, even to pagans. '[This sect] pleads for nothing in her case, nor is astonished at her circumstances. She knows she conducts herself as a foreigner on the earth, as an outsider she easily finds enemies, she has her race, abode, hope, favour and honour in heaven.'[383]

Tertullian informs Scapula that Christians are not perturbed by what they suffer from the persecutors' ignorance, because it is their contractual obligation.[384] Christians are not ashamed of Christ, but rejoice to be his servants and to be condemned with him.[385] Tertullian consistently identifies the confession *of* Christ as the defining mark of the Christian, consequently bringing confession *by* him before the Father.[386] This confession only acquires moral force when it faces pressure to deny, which is the opportunity provided by persecution.[387] Tertullian also makes this argument in his apologetics.

The hatred of the heathen toward Christians is unjust because it is based on culpable ignorance.[388] The impetus is demonic,[389] but God allows persecution to occur through such evil instrumentation,[390] because martyrdom strives against and opposes idolatry.[391] Tertullian warns Scapula that to persecute Christians is to fight against God.[392] Persecutors are responsible for this sin, and although persecution is God-ordained, Scapula and even Carthage itself will suffer the consequences.[393] The battle transcends local social conflict; confession of Christ is a victory against Satan, a participation in

---

[382] *Apol.* 50.1–3 (CCSL 1:169) Ergo, inquitis, cur querimini, quod uos insequamur, si pati uultis, cum diligere debeatis, per quos patimini quod uultis? Plane uolumus, uerum eo more, quo et bellum miles … Proelium est nobis, quod prouocamur ad tribunalia, ut illic sub discrimine capitis pro ueritate certemus. Victoria est autem, pro quo certaueris, obtinere. Ea uictoria habet et gloriam placendi Deo et praedam uiuendi in aeternum. Sed occidimur. Certe, cum obtinuimus. Ergo uincimus, cum occidimur, denique euadimus, cum obducimur.

[383] *Apol* 1.2 (CCSL 1:85) Nihil de causa sua deprecatur, quia nec de condicione miratur. Scit se peregrinam in terris agere, inter extraneos facile inimicos inuenire, ceterum genus, sedem, spem, gratiam, dignitatem in caelis habere. He reiterates this idea of Christians as foreigners in *Cor.* 13.4 (CCSL 2:1061).

[384] *Scap.* 1.1–2 (CCSL 2:1127) Nos quidem expauescimus, neque pertimescimus ea quae ab ignorantibus patimur, cum ad hanc sectam, utique suscepta condicione eius pacti …

[385] *Apol.* 21.25–28 (CCSL 1:127), citing the apostles' experience in Acts 5:41.

[386] Mt. 10:32 and Lk. 12:8; ὁμολογεω, confess/profess, ἀρνεομαι, deny; Mk 8:38 and Lk. 9:26; ἐπαισχυνομαι, be ashamed. Tertullian quotes or refers to these words of Jesus regularly: *Idol.* 13.6 (CCSL 2:1113); *Fug.* 7.2 (CCSL 2:1145); *Scorp.* 9.8, 10.4 (CCSL 2:1085, 10.87–8); *Prax.* 26.9 (CCSL 2:1197); *Carn. Chr.* 5.3 (CCSL 2:881); *Cor.* 11.5 (CCSL 2:1957); *Marc.* 4.21.10 (CCSL 1:599).

[387] *Fug.* 1.3, 1.5–6, 3 (CCSL 2:1135, 1136, 1139).

[388] *Nat.* 1.1 (CCSL 1:11).

[389] *Apol.* 27 (CCSL 1:138–9).

[390] *Apol.* 50.12 (CCSL 1:171).

[391] *Scorp.* 6, 11 (CCSL 2:1079–81, 1090–2) Also *Marc.* 2.14 (CCSL 1:491).

[392] *Scap.* 4 (CCSL 2:1130–1).

[393] *Scap.* 5 (CCSL 2:1131–2).

Christ's victory over the adversary. 'We never triumph over [demons] more than when we are condemned for the persistence of our belief.'[394] The persecuted are vindicated when Christ's victory is consummated.[395] Therefore Christians are content to leave vengeance to God. Therefore, they do not resist evil but pray for their persecutors[396] and this is why, if necessary, they will come forward voluntarily.[397]

Tertullian does not engage in apologetic to reject what he regards to be good, and divinely ordained. Persecution is inevitable and appropriate while the world and Christ are at enmity. The key to Tertullian's apologetic is that Christians must be persecuted *for the right reasons*, for righteousness' sake (Mt. 5:10). They must be persecuted for upholding the name of Christ, not for any supposed crimes or immorality.[398] Because they are innocent of those imputed crimes, the laws must be changed. However, the world will inevitably and 'appropriately' persecute Christians, for upholding the name of Christ and opposing the demonic complicity of the world. The objective of Tertullian's *Apologeticum* is that Christianity be known for what it is, and not be persecuted out of ignorance.[399]

Tertullian considers that the willingness of Christians to die for their confession – martyrdom as witness – draws people to Christ.[400] On becoming a Christian they desire the forgiveness that comes through martyrdom, and condemnation by the Romans brings acquittal from God.[401] For this reason, Tertullian anticipates the effects of persecution on the church to be positive. 'Your injustice is proof of our innocence. For that reason, God allows us to suffer these things ... But your cruelty does not profit your investigation, but is an attraction to our sect. Furthermore, we accomplish more as we are reaped by you; the blood of Christians is seed.'[402]

Tertullian also writes apology because he wants pagans to truly understand their position, as Satan's accomplices in a fight they cannot win.[403] Christians are on the offensive, not the defensive; their battle is cosmic, and their apparent defeat is victory. Persecution, intrinsic to the Christian's identity, will only cease when there is no longer a difference between the world and the church, which for Tertullian means the *eschaton*. Tertullian will never allow compromise between the church and the world.[404] As Bowlin asserts, 'a church without spot or wrinkle should be an offense and a threat, not a benign object of tolerance'.[405] Tertullian's apologetic works exhort pagans to disregard

---

[394] *Apol.* 27.7 (CCSL 1:139) illos numquam magis detriumphamus quam cum pro fidei obstinatione damnamur. Also *Paen.* 5 (CCSL 1:327–329).
[395] Based on Rev. 6:9–11, *An.* 55.4–5 (CCSL 2:862–3), *Or.* 5.3; (CCSL 1:260); *Res.* 25.1 (CCSL 2:953).
[396] *Apol.* 31 (CCSL 1:142); *Scap.* 1.3 (CCSL 2:1127).
[397] *Scap.* 1.2, 5.2 (CCSL 2:1127, 1132).
[398] 1 Pet. 2:19–20, 3:17; *Scorp.* 12.2–3 (CCSL 2:1092).
[399] *Apol.* 1 (CCSL 1:85–7).
[400] *Scap.* 5.4 (CCSL 2:1132).
[401] *Apol.* 50.14–16 (CCSL 1:171).
[402] *Apol.* 50.12–13 (CCSL 1:171) probatio est enim innocentiae nostrae iniquitas uestra! Ideo nos haec pati Deus patitur ... Nec quicquam tamen proficit exquisitor quaeque crudelitas uestra: illecebra est magis sectae. Etiam plures efficimur, quotiens metimur a uobis; semen est sanguis Christianorum! Trans. Souter.
[403] *Scap.* 5.2–3 (CCSL 2:1132); *Spect.* 30 (CCSL 1:252–3).
[404] *Cor.* 2.4 (CCSL 2:1042).
[405] John R. Bowlin, 'Tolerance among the Fathers', *Journal of the Society of Christian Ethics* 26, no. 1 (2006), 3–36, at 17.

rumours and to see the truth about Christianity and her God, to abandon idolatry, join those whom they formerly despised, and save themselves from judgement.

Conclusions

Tertullian sees God's indisputable goodness reflected in his justice and judgement, in the opposition to evil. Persecution is wholly under God's providential control. Humans, influenced by the Devil, choose to persecute, and Tertullian has little sympathy for them. The Devil corrupts and leads humans into sin but is under God's restraint. The Devil is responsible for idolatry and for the injustice inherent in persecution. God postponed the Devil's destruction to allow for a conflict whereby humans participate in Christ's defeat of him. Hence persecution is ordained by God, along with other penal evils, as the battleground for participation in Christ's cosmic conflict.

This makes persecution good, because it is the grounds of the battle with the Devil and an act of justice in his defeat. Therefore, Tertullian can attack pagans for complicity with the Devil's sin and does not hold Christians accountable for supposed complicity with persecutors. Persecution is God's ordained means of testing and proving his people as they fight for the name of Christ. Persecution is therefore inevitable while the world and Christ are in conflict. This will occur up to the *parousia*, which will bring the Devil's final defeat and Christians' vindication. This is why Tertullian criticizes Christians for not living disciplined lives consistent with upholding the name, and criticizes pagans for persecuting Christians out of ignorance.

Persecution, being ordained and inevitable, was predicted in Scripture, is a blessing and something for which Christ prepared his followers. Because Christ suffered, we too who bear his name must also suffer, for the world's hatred of Christ is also directed at us. It is the same cosmic conflict. This is the basis for Tertullian's high view of martyrdom, such that he sees confession and martyrdom inextricably linked. This distinctive is paralleled in the martyr acts and makes Tertullian effectively an advocate of 'radical' martyrdom. He cannot see the Holy Spirit as advocating or preparing Christians for any other course. Any alternative is inferior because it equates, in Tertullian's mind, to denial.

Tertullian's exhortations to discipline and consistency of life are especially intense and urgent because he sees the *parousia* as imminent, with no opportunity for post-mortem repentance. Christians must endure to the end. This also explains his concerns for the positive influence of martyrdom on others. Not that a martyr can save anyone other than himself, but is rather an example of endurance and a powerful witness to outsiders. Tertullian urges persecutors to repent and desist for their own salvation: they will not have a second chance. Tertullian's diogmology makes him concerned for the behaviour of the whole church – how it supports confessors and rejects apostates. It underpins his insistence on never flirting with the Devil's world.

Tertullian, like the other fathers, sees the ultimate good of persecution as eschatological, and certainly believes that the martyrs had an advantage. They have assurance of salvation because of the forgiveness wrought by their second baptism. He is fond of the language of reward and victory. Nevertheless, in contrast to Clement, he sees the value of persecution not just in its *telos* but in the battle itself. For these reasons persecution must not be shunned, and martyrdom not avoided. A Christian does not seek vengeance because that will come from God. Evil is not overlooked, nor given opportunity for gradual repentance and *apokatastasis*; endurance to the end implies martyrdom. There are no second chances beyond this life, so we must live disciplined lives as the Spirit intends. Fear is weakness, effectively denial, because it doubts God's providence. Likewise, flight and other strategies for avoiding martyrdom equate to denial in Tertullian's eyes. Even being one of the *stantes* may be a form of denial if one does not positively stand out as a Christian.

Tertullian appreciates that the church will always be persecuted while the world is at enmity with Christ. No compromise is possible. This allows him to reconcile the tension within apologetic, not to argue against persecution *per se*, but its injustice, and to insist to both persecutors and Christians that persecution be for the right reasons: for the name of Christ.

5

Cyprian of Carthage

Pragmatic pastor

But truly if the one observing the Lord's precepts and bravely adhering to Christ stands against Satan, he will necessarily be conquered, because Christ who is confessed is unconquered.

Cyprian, to Fortunatus

Bishop Cyprian

Thascius Caecilianus Cyprianus (c. 200–58 CE) was an educated, respected but relatively recent convert to Christianity when he was ordained bishop of Carthage in 248.[1] He had not long settled into the role when persecution unexpectedly struck following Decius' decree in 249. Sage notes, 'by the year 250, persecution had become the exception, and its absence had seriously affected the ability of North African Christianity to meet it without profound internal upheaval'.[2] Cyprian's episcopate was an exercise in crisis management. He dealt with mass apostasy as overseer in exile, and with the numerous controversies in the aftermath of the huge pastoral challenges of persecution and plague.[3] The primacy of his pastoral concerns,[4] particularly in the context of his ecclesiology, provide much fruit for comparison with his polemical predecessor Tertullian, and his contemporary Origen.

Life and works

Details of Cyprian's post-conversion life are reasonably well known, due to a biography by his deacon Pontius,[5] a corpus of 82 letters, and his treatises. In *Ad Donatum* Cyprian

---

[1] Graeme. W. Clarke, trans. *The Letters of St. Cyprian of Carthage*, vol. 1 Ancient Christian Writers 43 (New York: Newman, 1984), 17.
[2] Michael M. Sage, *Cyprian*, Patristic Monograph Series 1 (Cambridge MA: Philadelphia Patrstic Foundation, 1975), 29.
[3] J. Patout Burns, *Cyprian the Bishop*, *Cyprian the Bishop* (London: Routledge, 2002), 1–11 summarizes these controversies.
[4] As discussed extensively by Geoffrey D. Dunn, e.g. 'Infected Sheep and Diseased Cattle, or the Pure and Holy Flock: Cyprian's Pastoral Care of Virgins', *Journal of Early Christian Studies* 11, no. 1 (2003), 1–20; 'Cyprian and Women in a Time of Persecution', *Journal of Ecclesiastical History* 57, no. 2 (2006): 205–25.
[5] Pontius, *Vita Cypriani*. For a review, see Sage, *Cyprian*, Appendix IV, 385–94. For detailed discussion of Cyprian's early life, see Sage, *Cyprian*, 95–164.

gives his own account of his conversion. This relative wealth of information underpins Burns' detailed study of Cyprian's episcopate from a social and cultural anthropological perspective,[6] and Brent's discussion of Cyprian in the context of Roman Carthage.[7] Following Bobertz,[8] a number of scholars interpret Cyprian's episcopal role in terms of patronage toward his flock as clients.[9] Whilst this perspective has some merit, it should not be overstated, nor extrapolated to become the foundation for the role of the bishop in North Africa more broadly. Cyprian himself was an *honestiore*, but Dunn convincingly demonstrates that a patronage role was not his foremost model for his episcopacy.[10] Indeed, as Wiles and Clarke argue, Cyprian seems to have consciously rejected his former intellectual heritage.[11] This provides one of several contrasts with Tertullian, despite other evidence of his dependency.

Jerome's brief biography of Tertullian contains an interesting third-hand account of Cyprian's apparent indebtedness to his predecessor: 'Cyprian would never let a day pass without reading Tertullian, and that he often said to him, "Give me my master".'[12] Despite refuting other aspects of Jerome's testimony, Barnes seems convinced that Cyprian's indebtedness to Tertullian's writings was a reliable oral tradition and that Cyprian was inspired by his 'powerful example'.[13]

This may be too generalized a conclusion. Cyprian's *De bono patientiae, De dominica oratione* and *De habitu virginum* reflect to some extent Tertullian's *De patientia, De oratione* and *De virginibus velandis* and *De cultu feminarum*.[14] However, Cyprian's ecclesiology and practical diogmology depart from Tertullian in several respects, as I shall show. Despite living in the same city only a generation apart, and covering some common ground in their writings, their experiences were very different. Cyprian shares much of his foundational theology of persecution with his predecessor Tertullian, but he is without doubt his own man, largely because he had to deal with diogmology in practice, on a scale not experienced by Tertullian.

---

[6] Burns, *Cyprian the Bishop*.
[7] Allen Brent, *Cyprian and Roman Carthage* (Cambridge: Cambridge University Press, 2010).
[8] Charles Arnold Bobertz, 'Cyprian of Carthage as Patron: A Social Historical Study of the Role of Bishop in the Ancient Christian Community of North Africa' (PhD diss., Yale University, 1988).
[9] For example, Hugo Montgomery, 'The Bishop Who Fled: Responsibility and Honour in Saint Cyprian', *StPatr* 21 (1989), 264–67; Alistair Stewart-Sykes, 'Ordination Rites and Patronage Systems in Third-Century Africa', *Vigiliae Christianae* 56, no. 2 (2002), 115–30; David I. Rankin, 'Class Distinction as a Way of Doing Church: The Early Fathers and the Christian Plebs', *Vigiliae Christianae* 58, no. 3 (2004), 298–315.
[10] Geoffrey D. Dunn, 'The White Crown of Works: Cyprian's Early Pastoral Ministry of Almsgiving in Carthage', *Church History* 73, no. 4 (2004), 719–26. Edwina Murphy, *The Bishop and the Apostle: Cyprian's Pastoral Exegesis of Paul* (Berlin: de Gruyter, 2018), 12–13, cautions against reliance on Roman ideals above theological and pastoral motives when interpreting Cyprian.
[11] Maurice F. Wiles, 'Theological Legacy of St Cyprian', *Journal of Ecclesiastical History* 14, no. 2 (1963), 139–49, at 141, 143–5, 147–8; Graeme W. Clarke, trans. *The Letters of St. Cyprian of Carthage*, vol. 1 Ancient Christian Writers 43 (New York: Newman, 1984), 17.
[12] Jerome, *De Viris Illustribus,* cited in Timothy D. Barnes, *Tertullian: A Historical and Literary Study* (Oxford: Clarendon, 2005), 3.
[13] Barnes, *Tertullian*, 5, 194.
[14] Jerome, *De Viris Illustribus* 53, cited in Barnes, *Tertullian*, 3. Murphy, *Bishop, 5,* also suggests Tertullian's *De Pudicitia,* but I believe Cyprian's position is closer to the sentiments of the earlier *De Paenitentia.*

Although Cyprian was not a systematic theologian, his views were subsequently, albeit selectively, influential.[15] Cyprian's writings are occasional; his theologizing on topics such as persecution and martyrdom, the nature and government of the church, baptism, repentance and Christian living are set in the context of the events and controversies of his episcopate. As Clarke reflects, he was 'not a theologian but a pastoralist who had to deal, by force of circumstances, with theological problems embedded in the practical decisions of his administration'.[16] While Cyprian's ecclesiology is well known, Wiles posits that a less overt theology, founded on a literal application of Old Testament texts, informed his doctrines of the priesthood and eucharist with resulting far-reaching but often unrecognized effects.[17]

In terms of additional influences, Cyprian seems to have had little interest in philosophy, with Spanneut describing him as 'a serious theologian ... but the bishop is not a philosopher ... not even a moralist ... The bishop of Carthage is essentially a spiritual.'[18] Like his predecessor, Cyprian was sympathetic to additional revelations through dreams, and expected his readers to accept them as authoritative.[19] Clarke observes that such inspiration was accepted as normal in Carthaginian society, particularly for one in an exalted position.[20]

Cyprian's concern for the balance of unity and purity in the church influenced his diogmology, as did the personal impact of persecution. He finds his ultimate solution to the problem of apostasy in the role of the church. It is the church that is persecuted because of its own failings; it is within the church's discipline that the apostate must demonstrate penitence, and only within the church can martyrdom be validated. As Burns demonstrates, confession of the church became a way of confessing Christ.[21]

Cyprian and Scripture

Cyprian applies Scripture liberally in support of his pastoral concerns in the context of persecution. Fahey provides a useful foundational survey of Cyprian's scriptural usage. Edwina Murphy, building on Fahey's work,[22] provides detailed insights into Cyprian's exegesis, particularly his use of Paul. She identifies a number of reading strategies which Cyprian applies in his use of Paul to achieve his pastoral objectives.[23] Cyprian uses Scripture as the control for the faith and practice of the church, and 'given that the rule of faith is not in dispute, it is unity which provides the distinctive framework for

---

[15] Sage, *Cyprian*, 355–63; Burns, *Cyprian the Bishop*, 10–11; Michael L. White, 'Transactionalism in the Penitential Thought of Gregory the Great', *Restoration Quarterly* 21, no. 1 (1978), 33–51.
[16] Clarke, *Letters*, 1:19.
[17] Wiles, 'Theological Legacy', 143–5, 147–8.
[18] Michel Spanneut, *Tertullien et les premiers moralistes africains* (Gembloux: Duculot, 1969), 65–6. 'Un théologien sérieux ... Mais l'évêque n'est pas un philosophe, ni même un moraliste ... L'évêque de Carthage est essentiellement un spirituel'.
[19] *Epp.* 16.4.1; 20.1.2 (CCSL 3B:94; 106).
[20] Clarke, *Letters*, vol. 1:287–90, nn. 27, 30.
[21] J. Patout Burns Jr., 'Confessing the Church: Cyprian on Penance', *StPatr* 36 (2001), 338–48.
[22] Michael A. Fahey, *Cyprian and the Bible: A Study in 3rd Century Exegesis*. Beiträge zur Geschichte der biblischen Hermeneutik 9 (Tübingen: JCB Mohr, 1971).
[23] Murphy, *Bishop*, 2, 31–2.

his interpretation of Scripture'.[24] Although Cyprian does not explicitly set forth his hermeneutical principles, and wrote no commentaries, Murphy discerns that he considers the Bible a unified work, with 'a declared, but not necessarily employed, priority of the New Testament over the Old'.[25] Cyprian recognizes both literal and typological/spiritual senses as useful to salvation, as the Holy Spirit speaks through the Scriptures.[26]

Murphy concludes that Cyprian's work must be read in the light of his pastoral concerns and the context of his writings as a corpus.[27] Persecution is an essential aspect of that context. Vos makes detailed analysis of Cyprian's use of Scripture in Epistle 58,[28] in which he prepares the Thibarii for imminent persecution. Vos identifies a 'liberal and varied' use of Scripture, with an overall paraenetic focus.[29] Vos, surprisingly, omits any discussion of 58.4, wherein Cyprian affirms that the one who flees persecution is equally a soldier, a martyr and recipient of a crown.[30] Wilhite demonstrates that Cyprian uses two basic strategies: bare citations for a scripturally literate audience, and explanatory exegesis for those he considers subversive.[31] 'Cyprian uses Scripture as a boundary marker of identity, and Cyprian's social identity correspondingly regulates his use of Scripture.'[32]

Context of persecution: Disaster under Decius

Local, sporadic persecution had occurred in Africa until Decius.[33] The couple of decades preceding Decius provided peace and prosperity for the church. Cyprian judged that 'a long peace had corrupted the discipline that had been divinely delivered to us'. Faith had given way and was virtually slumbering, and Christians had been caught up in the pursuit of riches and property.[34] The decree of Decius changed that. Extant evidence for the persecution comprises the Cyprianic corpus, extracts of letters of Dionysius of Alexandria preserved in Eusebius *H.E.* 6–7, the *Passion of Pionios* and the forty-five extant *libelli* from Egypt.[35] Rives' seminal paper presents Decius' decree as

---

[24] Ibid., 170.
[25] Ibid., 171–6.
[26] Ibid., 20.
[27] Ibid., 194.
[28] Nienke Vos, 'A Universe of Meaning: Cyprian's Use of Scripture in Letter 58', in *Cyprian of Carthage: Studies in his Life, Language and Thought,* ed. Henk Bakker, Paul van Geest, and Hans van Loon (Leuven: Peeters, 2010), 65–93.
[29] Vos, 'Universe of Meaning', 90–1.
[30] *Ep.* 58.4 (CCSL 3C:324–5). It warrants merely an entry in a table, Vos, 'Universe of Meaning', 93.
[31] David E. Wilhite, 'Cyprian's Scriptural Hermeneutic of Identity: The Laxist "Heresy"', *Horizons in Biblical Theology* 32, no. 1 (2010): 58–98.
[32] Ibid., 95.
[33] *Ep.* 39.1.1–3.3 (CCSL 3B:186–9) mentions the confessor Celerinus and his family.
[34] Cyprian, *Laps.* 5 (CCSL 3:223). quia traditam nobis diuinitus disciplinam pax longa corrupterat. The church's prosperity is indicated in *Laps.* 5–7, 11–12 and *Ep.* 11.1.2 (CCSL 3B:56–7).
[35] See J. Patout Burns and Robin M. Jensen, *Christianity in Roman Africa: The Development of its Practices and Beliefs* (Grand Rapids: Eerdmans, 2014), 12–19; W. H. C. Frend, *Martyrdom and Persecution in the Early Church* (Cambridge: James Clarke, 2008), 389–439; J. B. Rives, 'The Decree of Decius and the Religion of Empire', *Journal of Roman Studies* 89 (1999), 135–54 and Clarke, *Letters,* 1:22–39.

an innovative restructuring of a religious organization that emphasized cultic performance rather than personal belief.[36] The universal pagan cult was to now be universal in organization, employing established bureaucratic procedures from taxation and censuses.[37] Also novel was the requirement for active individual participation, facilitated by Caracalla's prior bestowal of universal citizenship.[38] Decius' edict was not specifically an anti-Christian measure; extant *libelli* represent a cross-section of society, including pagan clerics.[39] Although Decius would doubtless have anticipated its impact on Christians, and church leaders were early targets, church property was spared and Christian meetings continued. Christians simply had no 'valid' reason to be excused from the objective of universal sacrifice.[40] Even if the Decian edict were viewed by Graeco-Romans solely in socio-political terms, Christians such as Cyprian necessarily perceived it as theological because of their worldview, which differed from that of the pagans. As Tertullian's and Cyprian's apologetics insist, members of the world act in opposition to Christ, whether they realize it or not.

Although the crisis was triggered by imperial decree, this does not preclude the nature of the actual 'persecution' being 'bottom-up'. If 'conspicuous refusal to observe a civic festival would no doubt have drawn the unfavourable attention of neighbours and provoked suspicions of disloyalty and misanthropy',[41] how much more refusal to obey a direct edict? As Clarke notes, local authorities would have been aware of the potentially non-compliant Christians in their community, especially prominent leaders. Once so identified, on refusal to sacrifice they could be imprisoned awaiting trial by the governor under established precedent.[42] With no clear penalties prescribed, local authorities had to defer to the governor to sentence the non-compliant.[43] Rives' more recent work explores the role of animal sacrifice in the persecution of Christians.[44] He suggests that Decius' edict invested animal sacrifice, previously of little concern, with a new cultural significance. Prior to Decius, animal sacrifice seems to have played little if any role in the trials of Christians,[45] whereas Decius' edict mandated participation in it for all citizens. Rives postulates that animal sacrifice served as a proxy focus of concern, reflective of a changing cultural and socio-political significance of the practice as a marker of Roman imperial identity and individual obligation to the imperial government.[46] By this stage, animal sacrifice had, for Christians, become associated with demon worship, and become incompatible with Christian identity.[47]

---

[36] Rives, 'Decius'.
[37] Ibid., 150.
[38] Ibid., 152.
[39] Ibid., 140.
[40] Ibid., 141–2.
[41] Ibid., 147.
[42] Clarke, *Letters*, 1:24, 35.
[43] Rives, 'Decius', 37.
[44] James B. Rives, 'Animal Sacrifice and the Roman Persecution of Christians (Second to Third Century)' in Jitse Dijkstra and Christian Raschle, eds, *Religious Violence in the Ancient World: From Classical Athens to Late Antiquity* (Cambridge: Cambridge University Press, 2020), 177–202.
[45] Rives, 'Animal Sacrifice', 185.
[46] Ibid., 189.
[47] Ibid., 198–9.

It is not the case, as de Ste. Croix asserts, that the populace were uninvolved in the Decian persecution, with 'little or no sign of persecuting zeal among the masses'.[48] Cyprian withdrew, worried about the mob's attacks on Christians being exacerbated by his presence in, and premature return to, Carthage.[49] The old prejudices would doubtless have resurfaced – Cyprian later refers to the stock complaints against Christians in *Ad Demetrianum* – due to heightened resentment against those who did not have the empire's interests at heart in disobeying the emperor's edict. What better opportunity for *delatores* to come forth?[50] Governors would have discretion as to the punishments inflicted, but the mood of the populace could still be determinative.[51] This complex interaction of local determinants makes Moss's assertion that Christians were 'prosecuted not persecuted'[52] overly simplistic.

Men, women and children were required to attend publicly and taste sacrificial meat, pour a libation and offer incense.[53] Consequently, they would obtain a *libellus* signifying their compliance. Prominent Christians such as the bishops were singled out; Eusebius records the confession and imprisonment of bishops Alexander of Jerusalem and Babylas of Antioch, with Dionysius barely escaping from Alexandria.[54] Cyprian seems to attribute Fabian of Rome's death to persecution.[55] Bishops were compelled to lead their congregations in compliance, which some did.[56] Cyprian predicts that a leader's collapse leads to his followers' downfall.[57] Many Christians in Carthage voluntarily stepped forward to comply with the edict, pre-empting its consequences.[58] Some sacrificed on behalf of their households and clients, ostensibly to protect them.[59]

Panels of local commissioners were established and deadlines for compliance were set. Latecomers, defectors and defaulters could be denounced and rounded up. Initially, the non-compliant were imprisoned, awaiting trial at the governor's next visit. This imprisonment was not itself the definitive punishment, but a holding state, with a potential secondary agenda of inducing recantation.[60] Imprisoned confessors

---

[48] G. E. M. de Ste. Croix, 'Why Were the Early Christians Persecuted?' in *Christian Persecution, Martyrdom and Orthodoxy*, ed. Michael Whitby and Joseph Streeter (Oxford: Oxford University Press, 2006), 105–52, at 137.
[49] *Epp.* 7.1; 20.1.2, 43.4.2 (CCSL 3B:38, 106–7, 204–5) and see Clarke, *Letters*, 1:197, n. 32.
[50] Clarke, *Letters*, 1:34 and Cyprian's caution in *Ep.* 5.2.1 (CCSL 3B:27–8).
[51] J. Patout Burns and Robin M. Jensen, *Christianity in Roman Africa: The Development of its Practices and Beliefs* (Grand Rapids: Eerdmans, 2014), 14, 18. Numidicus and his family seem to have been the victims of mob attack; Cyprian, *Ep.* 40. See also Graeme W. Clarke, trans. *The Letters of St. Cyprian of Carthage*, vol. 2, Ancient Christian Writers 44 (New York: Newman 1984), 197.
[52] Candida Moss, *The Myth of Persecution: How the Early Christians Invented a Story of Martyrdom* (New York: HarperOne, 2013), 14.
[53] As stated in extant Egyptian *libelli*. See also Cyprian, *Laps.* 8–9 (CCSL 3:225).
[54] Eusebius, *H.E.* 6.39–40 (Loeb 265:92–98); Cyprian, *Ep.* 55.9.1 (CCSL 3B:266) eo tempore cum tyrannus infestus sacerdotibus dei . . . comminaretur; Burns and Jensen, *Christianity*, 13.
[55] Clarke, *Letters*, 1:221, n. 4 (*Ep.* 9.1.2).
[56] Cyprian, *Ep.* 67.1.1 (CCSL 3C:447).
[57] Cyprian, *Ep.* 9.1.2 (CCSL 3B:44–5).
[58] *Laps.* 7–9 (CCSL 3:224–5).
[59] Cyprian, *Ep.* 55.13.2–14.2 (CCSL 3B:270–2).
[60] Clarke, *Letters*, 2:134, n. 4 (*Ep.* 31.1). See also *Ep.* 37.1.3 (CCSL 3B:178) and Clarke, *Letters*, 2:173, n. 9.

experienced increasing deprivation as time went on, which could encourage recantation.[61] Some died under these circumstances, and Cyprian regarded these as martyrs.[62] More died and more lapsed when torture was introduced later in the persecution.[63] Clarke identifies the sequence from the Cyprianic correspondence: in early 250 there were as yet no privations, tortures or deaths.[64] By mid-April of 250, tortures had been introduced for recalcitrant confessors.[65] By mid to late summer of 250 some were dead.[66] Convicted confessors could be executed, but the main punishment seems to have been exile and confiscation of property.[67]

Some Christians took the option of pre-emptively leaving the cities, enduring hardship and loss of property.[68] Among these were some bishops, including Cyprian,[69] many of whom were sheltered by other Christians.[70] Cyprian consistently identifies his own action as 'withdrawal' (*secedo, recedo*), not 'flight' (*fuga*) and provides his justification in Epistle 20.[71] Some Christians purchased *libelli* through an agent or by bribery,[72] but the poorer masses lacked resources to either flee or pay. Cyprian's emphasis subtly changes from supporting all the poor to supporting the meritorious poor; Clarke suggests they were in need because they remained steadfast.[73] These formed the mass of *stantes*, those who stayed, neither coming forward to sacrifice nor departing.[74] Dionysius of Alexandria's description of the persecution describes a similar situation to that in Carthage.[75] After about twelve months from the set date, prisoners were gradually released and exiles allowed to return.[76] The issues surrounding the large number of *sacrificati* and *libellatici* were subsequently faced in both Carthage and Alexandria. The Cyprianic corpus is therefore a treasure trove, providing detailed insight into the different reactions to persecution and the bishop's theological response to each.

---

[61] *Laps.* 2 (CCSL 3:221–2) *Ep.* 22.2 (CCSL 3B:117–8) provides some insight into prison conditions; Clarke, *Letters*, 1:330–1, 338, n. 22.
[62] *Ep.* 12.1.2 (CCSL 3B:68).
[63] Cyprian, *Laps.* 13 (CCSL 3:227–8).
[64] Clarke, *Letters*, 1:187, n. 12 referring to *Ep.* 5 and 190, ref. to *Ep.* 6.
[65] *Ep.* 10.1 (CCSL 3B:46–8).
[66] *Epp.* 28.1.2; 37.3.1 (CCSL 3B:133, 180).
[67] *Epp.* 10.1.1, 24.1.1 (CCSL 3B:46–7, 121–2) and Clarke, *Letters*, 1:230, n. 5.
[68] *Ep.* 41.1.2 (CCSL 3B:196–7) refers to tradesmen who presumably had to abandon their tools; Clarke, *Letters*, 2:205, n. 6. Cyprian commends them: *Ep.* 12.2.2 (CCSL 3B:68–9) and Clarke, *Letters*, 1:253–4, nn. 18, 19.
[69] *Ep.* 20 (CCSL 3B:106–10) provides his justification.
[70] Cyprian, *Ep.* 30.8 (CCSL 3B:149); Clarke, *Letters*, 2:131, n. 47; also Clarke, *Letters*, 1:182, n. 2.
[71] *Ep.* 20 (CCSL 3B:106–10); Clarke, *Letters*, 1:207–8.
[72] Cyprian, *Ep.* 30.3.1 (CCSL 3B:141–2). cf. Tertullian, *Fug.* 12–13 (CCSL 2:1148–53).
[73] Clarke, *Letters*, 1:185.
[74] *Epp.* 5.2.1; 14.2.1–2. (CCSL 3B:27–8, 80–2); *Ep.* 34.4.1 (CCSL 3B:169); Clarke, *Letters*, 1:293, n. 1.
[75] Eusebius, *H.E.* 6.41–42 (Loeb 265:98–112); C. Wilfred Griggs, *Early Egyptian Christianity: From its Origins to 451 CE* (Leiden: Brill, 1990), 68.
[76] Clarke, *Letters*, 2:4–19.

Aftermath

Cyprian subsequently faced significant controversies; on the restoration of the lapsed, on rebaptism of heretics or schismatics, and the Novatian schism.[77] The sheer number of *sacrificiati* and *libellatici* and the different circumstances surrounding their individual lapses, made the problem no theoretical abstraction. Simplistic or generalized solutions such as permanent excommunication or unfiltered reconciliation would not work. Therefore, Cyprian resolved to wait until he and the community could come together in a time of peace to consider each individual case. Until then, only penitents on their deathbed could be readmitted.[78] His chief concern throughout was to achieve a balance between the condemnation of sin and the enabling of repentance and reconciliation.[79]

When the Decian persecution subsided, Cyprian returned to Carthage to face additional crises. Convinced of the world's senescence and imminent end,[80] he remarked on the more frequent wars, famines and pestilences that were raging, including the North African plague from 251.[81] In 252 Cyprian referred to renewed popular outcry for a bishop to be thrown to the lion. This was probably another local outburst due to the plague, potentially accompanied by a local edict requiring expiatory sacrifices.[82] Cyprian's correspondence becomes coloured by anticipation of renewed persecution, no longer for discipline of the church, but as the prelude to the end of the world.[83] Nevertheless, scholarly consensus refutes previous ascriptions of persecution to Decius' successor Gallus.[84]

Valerian and Gallienus' joint principate followed the upheaval of ten emperors in five years, major military confrontations, foreign invasions, and an ongoing plague.[85] Meanwhile Christians, busy with the Novatian schism and baptismal controversies,[86] were largely ignored. Valerian was initially friendly toward Christians,[87] but in 257 the emperors mandated compliance with traditional rites, singling out Christian leaders.[88] In August 257, Cyprian was exiled to Curubis for a year, during which he wrote Epistle 76 to his fellow clergy and Christians exiled to the Numidian mines, to encourage

---

[77] On reconciliation of the lapsed, see Burns, *Cyprian the Bishop*, 25–50; Maurice Bévenot, 'The Sacrament of Penance and St. Cyprian's *De lapsis*', *Theological Studies* 16, no. 2 (1955), 175–213; Dionysius' letter to Fabian, *H.E.* 6.42 (Loeb 265:110–12). Eusebius in *H.E.* 6.43 (Loeb 265:112--24) describes the Novatianist schism, mentioning Cyprianic correspondence. For Dionysius' policy on the lapsed see *H.E.* 6.44 (Loeb 265:124–6) and for the eastern churches Clarke, *Letters*, vol. 2, 11–13.
[78] *Ep.* 55.4.3–55.5 (CCSL 3B:260–1).
[79] *Ep.* 68.1.2 (CCSL 3C:463–4).
[80] *Dem.* 3–5 (CCSL 3A:36–7).
[81] *Mort.* 2; *Dem.* 2, 5 (CCSL 3A:17–18; 35–36, 37).
[82] *Ep.* 59.6.1 (CCSL 3C:346–7). Burns and Jensen, *Christianity*, 21; Graeme W. (trans) *The Letters of St. Cyprian of Carthage*, vol. 3, Ancient Christian Writers 46, (New York: Newman, 1986), 245–7, n. 31.
[83] E.g. *Fort.* Pref. 1. Letters of 253 anticipating persecution are 56, 57, 58, 60, Clarke, *Letters*, 3:29.
[84] E.g. W. H. C. Frend, *Martyrdom and Persecution in the Early Church* (Oxford: Blackwell, 1965), 414. For a detailed analysis, see Clarke, *Letters*, 3:4–17; Burns and Jensen, *Christianity*, 22.
[85] See Graeme W. Clarke (trans.), *The Letters of St. Cyprian of Carthage*, vol. 4, Ancient Christian Writers 47 (New York: Newman, 1989, 1–14; Burns and Jensen, *Christianity*, 22–6.
[86] Burns, *Cyprian the Bishop*, 141–65.
[87] Eusebius, *H.E.* 7.10.
[88] Eusebius, *H.E.* 7.11; Cyprian, *Ep.* 80.1.2 (CCSL 3C:626–7); Clarke, *Letters*, 4:9–12.

them, even as he anticipated his own martyrdom. Epistles 77, 78 and 79 are the exiles' encouraging replies. Cyprian was subsequently executed in Carthage.[89]

In terms of diogmology, Cyprian appears as the most pragmatic of the four fathers. As a pastor dealing with the lived experience of persecution, with little opportunity to theologize more broadly, his distinctive thought applies mainly to questions regarding response to persecution. He certainly has answers for the foundational questions: the origin, reason and *telos* of persecution, in which his coherence with, and probable indebtedness to, Tertullian is evident. But even here his pastoral concerns provide the framework.

The good God is in control

Cyprian's thoughts on the origin of persecution must be gleaned from his occasional writings. He was no dualist, nor Stoic fatalist, but evidently shared Tertullian's perspective, recognizing God's active role in the outworking of persecution.

The providence of a good and patient God

Cyprian does not theologize on the nature of God or the problem of evil. His theology is, as Wiles concludes, 'the common stock of Christian tradition'.[90] Cyprian takes it for granted that God is one; *unus Deus*, the unity of God being the basis of the unity of the church.[91] The first and most fundamental commandment of God forbids idolatry; worship is due to the one true God alone.[92] In him alone we trust and in him we must glory.[93] In describing God as merciful, patient, just, showing gentleness and loving kindness, and yet displaying anger against those who reject him, Cyprian assumes the righteousness of God without questioning God's right to bring evil and suffering as punishment.[94] Patience is fundamental to the character of the good God, and intrinsic to God's providential care and his ultimate justice.[95] Cyprian exhorts his readers to imitate the patient and impartial goodness of God, rather than the impatience of the Devil.[96]

Cyprian's view of God's pervasive providence is seen in a variety of contexts. Writing to Cornelius about divine appointment of bishops, Cyprian cites Matthew 10:28–31. Since 'not even the least events take place without the will of God, would anyone suppose that events of the highest and greatest importance can take place in the Church of God without God's knowledge and permission?'[97] All things are governed by his will

---

[89] *Epp.* 80, 81 (CCSL 3C:626-30); *Act. procon. Cyp.* 4, cited in Clarke, *Letters*, 4:13.
[90] Wiles, 'Theological Legacy', 148.
[91] *Unit.* 4 (CCSL 3:252) Eph. 4:4.
[92] *Fort.* 2 (CCSL 3:188-9); *Dem.* 6 (CCSL 3A:37-8).
[93] *Test.* 3.10 (CCSL 3:97-9).
[94] For example, the just deserts of apostasy; *Laps.* 7 (CCSL 3:224-5).
[95] *Pat.* 4-5 (CCSL 3A:119-21).
[96] *Pat.* 5 (CCSL 3A:120). See also Edwina Murphy, 'Imitating the Devil: Cyprian on Jealousy and Envy', *Scrinium* 14, no. 1 (2018), 75-91, at 90-1.
[97] *Ep.* 59.5.2. (CCSL 3C:345) Cum ille nec minima fieri sine uoluntate dei dicat, existimat aliquis summa et magna aut non sciente aut non permittente deo in ecclesia dei fieri.

and sovereign judgement.[98] God is prescient of the future and 'deliberates for the true salvation of his own [people]'.[99] The patient God providentially provides for good and evil alike.[100] God brought the Decian persecution for his good reasons, and likewise he brought reprieve. Nevertheless, Cyprian believes it appropriate for those suffering persecution to pray for its termination,[101] and regularly referred to the restoration of peace as from the Lord.[102]

Cyprian's view of providence was doubtless reinforced by his experiences of persecution and plague and the pastoral response required of him as bishop. Suffering had a purpose; when weakness and destruction seize Christians, their strength is made perfect.[103] Everyone dies, but not identically; 'the righteous are called to their place of refreshing, the unrighteous are snatched away to punishment'.[104] Martyrdom is not in anyone's power but is, in the condescension of God, visited on those whom God deems deserving.[105]

Free will and sin

Murphy observes that Cyprian 'does not theologise on the "freedom of the will"' and does not oppose it to the sovereignty of God. He emphasizes calling people to respond with faith, to persevere and to pray for the salvation of their persecutors.[106] Like his contemporaries, Cyprian considers the freedom to believe or disbelieve to lie in the human will. As Murphy notes, in *Epistle* 59 he cites John and Paul to emphasize that we are free to choose to follow Christ or not.[107] Murphy identifies Cyprian's 'sense of prevenient grace' in God's intervention to save, although people can choose whether to respond or not.[108] Cyprian exhorts Christians to renounce jealousy and impatience,[109] in imitation of Christ rather than the Devil, insisting that indwelling or possession still entails choice for good or evil.[110] Whilst appreciating that different degrees of temptation and suffering might underlie an apostate's lapse, Cyprian ultimately held the lapsed responsible for their choices to deny Christ.[111]

Although convinced that God had sent persecution for good cause and good outcomes, Cyprian does not deny the individual responsibility of persecutors. Echoing Tertullian, he condemns Demetrianus[112] for the injustice of persecuting Christians,

---

[98] *Ep.* 59.5.3. (CCSL 3C:345) *arbitrio regi et gubernari*.
[99] Mort. 19 (CCSL 3A:27) *suis consulat ad uerum salutem*.
[100] *Pat.* 4–5 (CCSL 3A:119–21), ref. Mt. 5:45.
[101] *Laps.* 1 (CCSL 3:221).
[102] For example, *Ep.* 26.1.2 (CCSL 3B:126) *pace nobis a domino reddita*.
[103] *Mort.* 13 (CCSL 3A:23–4).
[104] *Mort.* 15 (CCSL 3A:24) *Ad refrigerium iusti uocantur, ad supplicium rapiuntur iniusti* …
[105] *Mort.* 17 (CCSL 3A:26).
[106] Murphy, *Bishop*, 183–6.
[107] Ep. 59.7.2–4 (CCSL 3C:348–49) citing Jn 6:68–70, 1 Jn 2:19 and Rom. 3:3–4; Murphy, *Bishop*, 184.
[108] Murphy, *Bishop*, 185.
[109] *Zel. liv.* 3,17; *Pat.* 3, 13 (CCSL 3A:76, 85; 119, 125–6).
[110] As Murphy, *Bishop*, 183 notes, Cyprian's context and pastoral priorities did not involve Judaizers, Pelagians or other stimuli to unpack free will and grace further.
[111] *Laps.* 8, 10, 13 (CCSL 3:225, 226, 227–8).
[112] Demetrianus is otherwise unknown; for an appraisal of their interaction see Sage, *Cyprian*, 275–80.

whom Demetrianus blamed for the evils befalling Carthage. 'For these things happen not ... because your gods are not honoured by us, but because God is not honoured by you.'[113] Just as Tertullian warned Scapula not to fight against God, so Cyprian warns Demetrianus.[114] Importantly, being controlled by the indwelling of Christ or by diabolic possession does not override free will, but as Murphy observes, is linked with a person's choice to imitate one or the other.[115] God's just use of persecutors' injustice did not exonerate them, nor was it outside of their free will. Persecutors could and should recognize their injustice and repent; it was not yet too late. The Carthaginians' response to persecutors' sole accountability contrasts with that of the Alexandrians. Clement and Origen are concerned that a would-be martyr not become complicit in the persecutors' sins, but this aspect seems not to trouble Cyprian or Tertullian.

Devil on a leash

Cyprian associates the Devil with the world, as the foe to be resisted. The Devil is the one to whom pagan sacrifice was actually offered.[116] Daily life in the world is a battle against the Devil.[117] Christians suffer more than others in the world because they must also struggle with the attacks of the Devil.[118] The Devil, with his 'darts and weapons', has perfected all kinds of 'temptation and arts and snares' for humanity's overthrow, since his first attack in Eden.[119] The more courageous a person is, the more savagely the Devil attacks him,[120] 'seeking to cast down those whom he sees to be still standing'.[121] He seeks to exploit weaknesses, utilizing a variety of temptations, 'and when he is unable to secretly deceive, he threatens freely and openly, holding out the terror of turbulent persecution, to conquer God's servants; always restless, and always hostile, crafty in peace, violent in persecution'.[122] Cyprian thus broadens the cosmic conflict to embrace all of Christian life, not just the trial of martyrdom. This is a major point of difference from Tertullian.

Murphy discerns that 'the Devil was the source of the jealousy and envy that caused his own downfall and that of humanity'.[123] The Devil's fall was a result of his jealousy of humans made in God's image, despite his own initial acceptance and love by God.[124] The Devil destroyed himself first, then subsequently destroyed others. Cyprian presents

---

[113] *Dem.* 5 (CCSL 3A:37) Non enim ... quod di uestri a nobis non colantur, sed quod a uobis non colatur Deus.
[114] *Dem.* 10, 23 (CCSL 3A:40–1, 48–9).
[115] *Ep.* 59.7.2–3 (CCSL 3C:348) and *Ep.* 69.15.1–16.1 (CCSL 3C:493–5). Murphy, 'Imitating the Devil', 78.
[116] *Laps.* 8 (CCSL 3:225).
[117] *Mort.* 4 (CCSL 3A:18–19).
[118] *Mort.* 9 (CCSL 3A:21).
[119] *Fort.* Pref. 2 (CCSL 3:183) tela et iacula ... omnia genera temptandi et artes adque incidias.
[120] *Ep.* 14.3.1 (CCSL 3B:82).
[121] *Ep.* 61.3.2 (CCSL 3C:383) Eos quaerit deicere quos uidet stare.
[122] *Zel. liv.* 2 (CCSL 3A: 76) et cum latenter non potest fallere, exerte adque aperte minatur, terrorem turbidae persecutionis intentans, ad debellandos seruos Dei inquietus semper et semper infestus, in pace subdolus, inpersecutione uiolentus.
[123] Murphy, 'Imitating the Devil', 75.
[124] *Zel. liv.* 4 (CCSL 3A:76).

Cain the persecutor as a model of imitating the Devil, while Abel, the first martyr, patiently imitated Christ.[125] When Cyprian reminds Fortunatus that Christian persecution is inevitable, he uses the same exemplars, including Cain and Abel, as he uses in *De zelo et livore* and *De bono patientiae*.[126] Cyprian, following Tertullian, thus situates the basis of persecution in the jealousy and impatience of those persecutors in the world who imitate the Devil. Nevertheless, the army of the Devil is not to be feared. Cyprian confidently proclaimed, 'greater is the Lord to protect than the Devil to assail ... Greater is he who is in you than he that is in the world.'[127]

Cyprian recognizes that God allows the Devil to cause evil within the limits of God's purposes. He places the 'evils' of persecution and plague under God's providence, accepting that these things come from God. Adversities are a sign of the last days, attended by persecution, plague and other suffering,[128] signs of the senescence of the world, as divinely predicted.[129] He accepts that this life is affected by evil, but what matters are the different purpose and outcomes for Christian and non-Christian.[130] He teaches Quirinus that men are tried by God for the purpose of being proved, and that the Devil has no power against man unless God allows it.[131] In addition to a general 'necessity' for persecution, Cyprian also sees contingent circumstances in which God acts. God brought on the Decian persecution for warning and chastisement of the church. The long peace had corrupted their discipline, and a heavenly rebuke was required to arouse their faith. They deserved even more, because God's law had been forsaken.[132] There had been compromise with the enemy – the world – as foretold by apostles and prophets.[133] God's policy, explicit in Deuteronomy 13:3, is to prove his people, to test the completeness of their love for him.[134] There cannot be a victory without a battle.[135] Cyprian evidently believes that God ordains and supervises persecution, along with other trials of life, and permits the Devil's instrumentation.

Persecution with purpose

Cyprian's perception of the reason for persecution is aligned with Tertullian's. Persecution is inevitable, provoked by the world's hatred of Christ and of those who bear his name.

---

[125] Murphy, 'Imitating the Devil', 83.
[126] *Fort.* 11 (CCSL 3:201–11).
[127] *Fort.* 10 (CCSL 3:198) maior est Dominus ad protegendum quam diabolus ad inpugnandum ... Maior est qui in uobis est quam qui in isto mundo; 1 Jn 4:4.
[128] *Fort.* Pref. 1 (CCSL 3.183); *Ep.* 58.1.2 (CCSL 3C:320).
[129] *Mort.* 2 (CCSL 3A:17–18); *Ep.* 58.2.2 (CCSL 3C:321).
[130] *Mort.* 15 (CCSL 3A: 24–5).
[131] *Test.* 15, 80 (CCSL 3:106–7; 162–3).
[132] *Laps.* 5–6 (CCSL 3:223–4).
[133] *Laps.* 7 (CCSL 3:224–5); *Ep.* 11.1.2, 3 (CCSL 3B:56–7).
[134] *Mort.* 11 (CCSL 3A: 22–3).
[135] *Mort.* 12 (CCSL 3A:23) Nisi praecesserit pugna, non potest esse uictoria.

Inevitable and purposeful

Cyprian reminds Fortunatus that persecutions should not surprise the Christian, since it was foretold that the world would hate us. God promised that we will be recompensed and rewarded, outweighing what we suffer here.[136] From the beginning of the world, the righteous have been oppressed by the unrighteous. God's people have always advanced through afflictions and wrongs, in following the narrow path. The world hates Christians because it first hated Christ.[137] Cyprian cites the Olivet discourse in full, which he consistently applies to the time of persecution, as the sign of the end of the world. He also cites examples of Abel, Jacob, Joseph, David, Elijah and Zacharias, the three friends in the furnace, Tobias and the seven brothers in Maccabees, emphasizing this continuity.[138] Matthew 10:22 and parallel accounts of Jesus' prediction of hatred by all for his name's sake are referenced repeatedly by Cyprian and his correspondents.[139] In *Ad Quirinum* the passage serves as a proof text that hatred of the name was predicted.[140] Together with Deuteronomy 6:3, these passages from Matthew are also proofs 'that nothing is to be preferred to the love of God and Christ'.[141] To the Thibarii, Cyprian cites 1 Peter 4:12–14, that they should not be surprised by trials, 'since the Lord has already foretold that these things would be so in the very last days'.[142]

In *De mortalitate*, Cyprian reminds Christians that God predicted wars, famines, pestilences and earthquakes should arise, with adversity increasing in the end times.[143] In his treatise on patience, Cyprian cites John 16:33, the Lord's prediction that in the world they would have tribulation.

> We who are greatly shaken by the attack of the devil, longstanding in the battlefield, are wearied with the conflict with an inveterate and skilful enemy; beyond the various and asiduous battles of temptations, must also in the contest of persecutions forsake our patrimonies, undergo imprisonment, bear chains, expend our souls, endure sword, beasts, fires, crosses, and finally all kinds of tortures and punishments, endured in the faith and courage of patience.[144]

Cyprian, like Tertullian, but unlike second-century apologists, presents the inevitability of persecution even to persecutors. Rather than weakening his argument, he uses it to confront Demetrianus with the prediction of God's wrath against

---

[136] *Fort.* Pref. 4.11 (CCSL 3:186).
[137] *Fort.* 11 (CCSL 3:201–11) ref. Jn 15:18–21; 16:2–4.
[138] *Fort.* 11 (CCSL 3:201–11).
[139] E.g. to his clerical brethren *Epp.* 14.2.2 (CCSL 3B:88; 155) qui tolerauerit usque ad finem, hic saluabitur; and from confessors 31.4.1 qui perseuerauerit usque ad finem, hic saluus erit.
[140] *Test.* 3.29 (CCSL 3:123–4) De odio nominis ante praedictum.
[141] *Test.* 3.18 (CCSL 3:112) Dilectioni Dei et Christi nihil praeponendum.
[142] *Ep.* 58.2.2 (CCSL 3C: 321) quando haec futura in nouissimis temporibus dominus ante praedixerit.
[143] *Mort.* 2 (CCSL 3A:17–18).
[144] *Pat.* 12 (CCSL 3A:125) qui diabolo impugnante plus quatimur. qui in acie cotidie stantes inueterati et exercitati hostis colluctationibus fatigamur, quibus praeter uarias et asiduas temptationum pugnas in persecutionum quoque certamine patrimonia relinquenda sunt, subeundus carcer, portandae catenae, animae impendendae, gladius, bestiae, ignes, cruces, omnia denique tormentorum ac poenarum genera fide et uirtute patientiae perferenda.

persecutors.[145] The same providence which ensures persecution will vindicate Christians and result in punishment of the persecutors.

Cyprian reminds Fortunatus that the inevitability of persecution is reinforced by Christ's imperatives as to how to respond to it.[146] There is no excuse to not suffer for Christ; Christians must confess, not deny him.[147] Christians must rejoice,[148] and not fear those who can only destroy the body but not the soul.[149] Whoever loves his life shall lose it, whoever hates his life in the world will keep it eternally. Christians must prefer nothing to Christ – not even family – and must take up the cross and follow him,[150] enduring to the end.[151] In this, nothing shall separate them from the love of Christ, even though they are slaughtered like sheep for his sake.[152] The same sentiments occur in *De lapsis*; those who lapsed had not heeded Christ's exhortations.[153]

Furthermore, to be persecuted is to be blessed. *Testimonia* 3.16 describes the benefits of martyrdom to Quirinus, using proof texts which include the persecution beatitude.[154] Cyprian also recounts to Fortunatus the blessedness of those who are persecuted for righteousness' sake.[155] 'We receive more wages in suffering than what we sustain in the suffering itself.'[156] The same encouragement is exchanged with Moyses and his fellow confessors.[157] Cyprian's consistent message is that persecution is expected and it is purposeful, because it is part of the greater, 'cosmic' conflict between Christ and his adversary.

Participation in conflict

Cyprian recognizes that Christians are engaged in conflict with the Devil, and must stand bravely, in order to conquer.[158] Martyrs contend not merely with men or wild beasts, but with Satan himself; the Devil is the real adversary; persecutors and executioners are merely his helpers or tools. Christian hope paradoxically consists in the war itself, because by that very conflict the righteous obtain their reward: 'our hope consists in this great war'.[159] Therefore, when persecution challenges a well-prepared soldier of God, he will not be overcome; his faith is prepared for martyrdom and through that very warfare he will be crowned.[160]

---

[145] *Dem.* 21 (CCSL 3A:47).
[146] *Fort.* 5–6 (CCSL 3:191–5).
[147] Mt. 10:32–33/ Mk 8:38.
[148] Mt. 5:10–12/ Lk. 6:22–23.
[149] Mt. 10:26–28.
[150] Mt. 10:38; 16:24–25/ Mk 8:34–35/ Lk. 9:23–24.
[151] Mt. 10:22/ Mk 13:13.
[152] Rom. 8:35–37.
[153] *Laps.* 12 (CCSL 3:227).
[154] *Test.* 3.16 (CCSL 3:107–111).
[155] *Fort.* 12 (CCSL 3:211–14).
[156] *Fort.* 13 (CCSL 3:214) Plus nos accipere in passionis mercede quam quod hic sustinemus in ipsa passione.
[157] *Epp.* 28.1.1; 31.4.1 (CCSL 3B:133; 154–5).
[158] *Test.* 3.117 (CCSL 3:177), citing Eph. 6:10–17.
[159] *Fort.* 10 (CCSL 3:198–9) in ipsis magis bello spem nostram consistere.
[160] *Fort.* 13 (CCSL 3:215–16).

To face martyrdom is to conduct celestial warfare, necessitating spiritual discipline.[161] As the pastor, Cyprian must prepare the divine army entrusted to him. As a soldier going into battle must be trained and prepared, so much more when the enemy is the ancient adversary who has been waging war since the fall and has every kind of snare and temptation at his disposal.[162] Hummel observes that the 'almost exaggerated stress which Cyprian lays on the necessity of a suitable training for the Christian forces and on fitting equipment for the battle of martyrdom' rests on 'his realization of the immense power and sagacity of the enemy challenging the Christian Army'.[163] Nevertheless, the Christian soldier has the upper hand, by having Christ on his side.

> If [Satan] finds Christ's soldier unprepared, if unskilled, if not roused and watchful with his whole heart, he surrounds the ignorant, leads astray the careless and deceives the inexperienced. But truly if the one observing the Lord's precepts and bravely adhering to Christ stands against him, he will necessarily be conquered, because Christ who is confessed is unconquered.[164]

Cyprian reflects on the outcome of such a battle in *De lapsis*. Christ's soldiers, the faithful confessors, returned victorious from the battle in triumphant procession.[165] Others were conquered even before the battlefront.[166] Some who were overcome in the first encounter, subsequently became stronger and 'in that in which they had been conquered were conquerors'.[167] If the vanquished repent and entreat God to rearm them, they can seek the contest anew and this time gain victory.[168]

Distinctively, Cyprian expands the theatre of the cosmic conflict to include the everyday battles of the Christian. The encamped soldier must also be prepared to do battle with 'avarice, with immodesty, with anger, with ambition; our continual and burdensome wrestle with carnal vices, with enticements of the world'.[169] Christians, even during plague, must struggle daily with the attacks of the Devil.[170] Such afflictions are part of the battle, and without a battle there cannot be a victory; the skilled helmsman is recognized in the tempest and in warfare the soldier is proved.[171] One of the Devil's everyday strategies is the temptation to jealousy and envy. When he cannot

---

[161] *Don.* 15 (CCSL 3A:12) The context is death as a gateway to immortality.
[162] *Fort.* Pref. 2 (CCSL 3:183).
[163] Edelhard L. Hummel, *The Concept of Martyrdom according to St Cyprian of Carthage*, Catholic University of America Studies in Christian Antiquity 9 (Washington: Catholic University of America Press, 1946), 73.
[164] *Fort.* Pref. 2 (CCSL 3:183) Si inparatum inuenerit Christi militem, si rudem, si non sollicito ac toto corde uigilantem, circumuenit nescium, fallit incautum, decipit inperitum. Si uero quis dominica praecepta custodiens et fortiter Christo adhaerens contra eum steterit, uincatur necesse est, quia Christus quem confitemur inuictus est.
[165] *Laps.* 2 (CCSL 3:221–2).
[166] *Laps.* 8 (CCSL 3:225) Ante aciem multi uicti.
[167] *Laps.* 13 (CCSL 3:228). et unde superati essent inde superarent.
[168] *Laps.* 36 (CCSL 3:241–2).
[169] *Mort.* 4 (CCSL 3A:18–19) cum auaritia nobis, cum inpudicitia, cum ira, cum ambitione congressio est, cum carnalibus uitiis, cum inlecebris saecularibus adsidua et molesta luctatio est.
[170] *Mort.* 9 (CCSL 3A:21).
[171] *Mort.* 12 (CCSL 3A:23).

subtly deceive, he threatens openly with the fear of persecution to vanquish God's servants – he is always hostile, crafty and fierce.[172] Therefore the Christian must always be armed, against both insidious deceptions and open threats of the Devil, as ready to repel as the foe is always ready to attack.[173] This is a subtle but noteworthy shift from Tertullian, for whom the everyday battles were a discipline in preparation *for* the final battle.

Confessing Christ

Cyprian considers true confession to be in accordance with the Gospel, but necessarily within the church. 'He is unable to have God for his Father, who does not have the Church as mother.'[174] No one can stand and live if they withdraw from the church, just as the house was protected from the angel of death at Passover. The church is designated by the Holy Spirit as the house of God.[175] Therefore, loyalty to the church by catechumens and penitents was a demonstration of loyalty to Christ, against the position of the laxist schismatics. In contrast to heretics and schismatics, the martyred catechumens and genuine penitents, whilst not in eucharistic communion, are somehow embraced within the church.[176]

Burns explains that Cyprian's initial opposition to the reconciliation of the lapsed was based upon 'an understanding of the divine intention in allowing the persecution itself'.[177] While God was still using the persecution to cleanse the church, admission of those who had not undergone the church's penitence would oppose this divine discipline. When persecution ceased, the opportunity to reverse denial by confession was removed, so a different confession was required; submission to the church's penitential discipline.[178] With impending renewal of persecution came a new opportunity for confession and those who had proven their loyalty in penitence should be further supported by readmission.[179] This is clearly set out in Cyprian's *Epistle* 55, in which he explains and defends his decision making.[180]

Cyprian, like the other fathers, believes that Christ suffers in the martyr.[181] Not only does the martyr attribute his victory exclusively to Christ's assistance, but as Hummel states, 'all the merit found in the martyr and all the reward given him is attributed to Christ, because Christ himself dwells in him. Christ struggles and conquers in the martyr and to him belongs the victory crown.'[182] Christ is with the martyr in prison, in flight and in abuse. Hummel argues that Cyprian discerns a real and actual union with

---

[172] *Zel. liv.* 2 (CCSL 3A:75–6).
[173] *Zel. liv.* 3 (CCSL 3A:76).
[174] *Unit.* 6 (CCSL 3:253) Habere iam non potest Deum patrem qui ecclesiam non habet matrem.
[175] *Unit.* 8 (CCSL 3:255).
[176] *Epp.* 18, 19.1, 20.3.2 (CCSL 3B:100–3, 109–10); Burns, 'Confessing the Church', 341.
[177] Burns, 'Confessing the Church', 340–1.
[178] Ibid., 343.
[179] Ibid., 344–5.
[180] Cf. *Ep.* 55.4.1–2 and 55.17 (CCSL 3B:259, 275–6).
[181] Hummel, *Concept of Martyrdom*. 6.
[182] Ibid., 92; ref. *Laps.* 20; *Or.* 26; *Ep.* 10.3.

Christ, established by reception of the eucharist. Furthermore, 'the abiding presence of Christ in the martyr not only frees him from all doubt as to the outcome of the struggle but also gives him a boundless confidence in his eventual triumph'.[183]

Jesus promised that the Holy Spirit would give specific help to the confessor, providing the very words of the confession (Mt. 10:19–20). Cyprian cites this passage to encourage both Fortunatus and those in the mines.[184] He understands that divine help is promised to God's persecuted servants, which means that the victory belongs to Christ, because it is in his contest that the confessor shares.

> [Christ] rejoiced to fight to victory in their midst ... He was present at His own contest; to the warriors and champions of His name He gave spirit, strength and support. And He who for us was once victorious over death, is now in us over it victorious. As He said: *When they deliver you up, give no thought as to what you are to say; for it shall be granted to you at that hour what you are to say. It is not you who speak but it is the spirit of your Father who speaks within you.*[185]

However, only those armed for battle by the church, fortified by the Eucharist, can receive the Spirit's help. The Spirit is available only to those in the church, who received him by the laying on of the bishop's hands. The Spirit of the Father is 'the one who gives strength to His servants and who Himself speaks and confesses within us'.[186] Christ himself helps the martyr because the Holy Spirit is *his* spirit.[187]

Cyprian directly links Matthew 10:32, the acknowledgement of Christ and consequently by Christ, to the blessings of martyrdom as a confession of Christ.[188] Those confessors who died in prison are martyrs, for they have confessed Christ before men and will be confessed by him before the Father; they have endured to the end and will be saved.[189] He reminds Fortunatus of the evils of idolatry, and that there is no excuse not to suffer for Christ, who suffered for us. In this context Christ will confess before his Father those who confess him before men, and deny those who deny him.[190] He adds Paul's reassurance that if we suffer and die with Christ we shall also live and reign with him, but if we deny him, he will deny us,[191] and John's warning that whoever denies the Son 'has not' the Father, but he that acknowledges the Son 'has' both the Son and the Father.[192]

---

[183] Hummel, *Concept of Martyrdom*, 94; ref. *Ep.* 10.1; *Fort.* Praef. 2, 5.10; *Fort.* 10.

[184] *Fort.* 10 (CCSL 3:200), *Ep.* 76.5.1 (CCSL 3C:613–4), citing Mt. 10:19–20 and Lk. 21:14–15.

[185] *Ep.* 10.3 (CCSL 3B:50) Quam laetus illic Christus fuit, quam libens in talibus seruis et pugnauit et uicit ... Certamini suo adfuit, proeliatores atque adsertores sui nominis erexit, corroborauit, animauit. Et qui pro nobis mortem semel uicit semper uincit in nobis. Cum uos, inquit, tradiderint, nolite cogitare quid loquamini. Dabitur enim uobis in illa hora quid loquamini. Non enim uos estis qui loquimini, sed spiritus patris uestri qui loquitur in uobis.

[186] *Ep.* 57.4.2 (CCSL 3B:305–6) qui corroborans seruos suos ipse loquitur et confitetur in nobis.

[187] Hummell, *Concept of Martyrdom*, 94–5; Cyprian, *Ep.* 76.5 (CCSL 3C:613–4).

[188] *Test.* 3.16 (CCSL 3:107–11).

[189] *Ep.* 12.1.3 (CCSL 3B:68–9).

[190] *Fort.* 5 (CCSL 3:191–3).

[191] 2 Tim. 2:11–12; ἀρνεομαι.

[192] 1 Jn 2:23; ἀρνεομαι, ὁμολογεω.

Just as the one who confesses Christ will be confessed by him, so the one who denies Christ will be denied by him. Arguing against the premature readmission of *sacrificiati* and *libellatici*, Cyprian reminded the church that God alone can forgive sins committed against himself, for Christ has said that he will deny the one that denies him, for he alone has authority from the Father to judge.[193] Christ could not have contradicted himself; if he does not deny those who deny, then neither will he confess those who confess. Not even bishops or martyrs can override this and offer reconciliation without penance, for to do so would break the very gospel which establishes them.[194] The deniers have blasphemed against the Holy Spirit, partaking of the cup of demons and are now taking the Lord's cup unworthily, imperilling their salvation.[195] 'Do you consider that the Lord is able to be appeased, whom with treacherous words you dismissed, before whom you preferred your patrimony, whose temple you violated with a profane contact? Do you think he will easily pity you whom you said was not your [God]?'[196]

Hummel asserts that Cyprian does not primarily base his concept of martyrdom on its relationship to Christ, but on the duty of confessing the true God who forbids idolatry. He further states that 'the broader obligation of loyalty to God is completed in the more specific obligation of confessing Christ'.[197] Hummel has identified a critical point; the centrality of confession of Christ (not necessarily in martyrdom) underlines that it is Christ who ultimately defeats idolatry and its demonic facilitators. In confessing Christ, Christians not only secured their identity in Christ but their salvation. They would be confessed before the Father, which meant salvation was effected. But confession could be reversed by subsequent lapse; in *De unitate*, Cyprian warns that confession is only the beginning of glory, one must endure to the end to be saved.[198] Burns tracks the development of Cyprian's thought with respect to the meaning and context of such confession. In times of persecution for the purposes of church discipline, public confession could reverse prior denial.[199] Under the persecution presaging the end of the world, the demonstrably penitent should be strengthened for confession by reconciliation with the church.[200] In the former situation, with the edict operational, confession would likely result in imprisonment and potentially death. In the latter, the confession provided reconciliation which enabled subsequent martyrdom to be authentic.

The good of persecution: The end in sight

For Cyprian, as for Tertullian, persecution is the God-ordained context for a heightened battle between Christ and those who confess him on one side, and the Devil who

---

[193] *Laps.* 17 (CCSL 3:230).
[194] *Laps.* 20 (CCSL 3:232–3).
[195] *Epp.* 16.2.2; 59.12.2. (CCSL 3B:93–4; 3C:356–7).
[196] *Laps.* 35 (CCSL 3:240) Putasne tu Deum cito posse placari quem uerbis perfidis abnuisti, cui patrimonium praeponere maluisti, cuius templum sacrilega contagione uiolati? Putas facile eum misereri tui quem tuum non esse dixisti?
[197] Hummel, *Concept of Martyrdom*, 37–8.
[198] *Unit.* 21 (CCSL 3:264).
[199] Burns, 'Confessing the Church', 341, citing *Epp.* 19.2.3; 25.1.2; 55.4.1–2.
[200] Burns, 'Confessing the Church', 344–5.

administers persecution through his agents on the other. Whilst this battle occurs daily, it reaches its climax in the act of confession, in which the Christian shares Christ's victory. Cyprian's answer to the question of the good of persecution thus rests predominantly, but not entirely, in his eschatology.

Discipline for patience

Cyprian believes that present suffering, including persecution, is both disciplinary and productive of patience. This discipline is not part of the aeons-long medicinal and educational perfecting envisioned by Clement and Origen, nor is it exclusively the harsh training for inevitable martyrdom promoted by Tertullian. Cyprian was convinced that the Decian persecution chastened a complacent church which had become too invested in the present life. It aroused many to faith, exposed the nominal adherents and brought punishment where it was due.[201] The post-Decian plague, which ravaged North Africa, was likewise a discipline and testing for the church.[202] Cyprian recognized that suffering increased faith and he reminded Christians of their daily battles with the Devil, warning that their delight was not to lie with the present world.[203] 'The distinction between us and others who don't know God, is that in adversity they complain and murmur, while adversity does not call us away from the truth of virtue and faith, but proves us by suffering.'[204]

Urging Fortunatus to embrace martyrdom, Cyprian stated that 'the purpose of afflictions and persecutions is that we may be proved'.[205] Persecutions should not surprise us, rather, we should recognize that God helps his people in their persecution and wants us to consider the help he affords and to strengthen our faith.[206] Since Christians can only benefit from persecution if they are within the church, Cyprian's priority is to retain and return as many as possible to the church, without compromising its gospel foundation.[207]

Patience is critical for the endurance of suffering and for perseverance to the end. *De bono patientiae* is an exhortation to the imitation of the patient God. Patience is needed for loving one's enemies and praying for one's persecutors.[208] Citing 1 Peter 2:21-23, Cyprian exhorts his readers to follow Christ's example of patient suffering under persecution.[209] The patience of the Old Testament martyrs in sorrow and suffering permitted the crown to be received.[210] Patience allows Christians to bear not

---

[201] *Laps.* 2 cf. 5 (CCSL 3:221-2, 223).
[202] *Mort.* 13 (CCSL 3A:23-4) Likewise Eusebius, *H.E.* 7.22 (Loeb 265: 182-8).
[203] *Mort.* 4-5 (CCSL 3A:18-19) also evident in *Ad Donatum*.
[204] *Mort.* 13 (CCSL 3A:24) Hoc denique inter nos et ceteros interest qui Deum nesciunt, quod illi in aduersis queruntur et murmurant, nos aduersa non auocant a uirtutis et fidei ueritate, sed conprobant in dolore.
[205] *Fort.* 9 (CCSL 3:197-8) Ad hoc praessuras et persecutiones fieri ut probemur.
[206] *Fort.* 10 (CCSL 3:198-201).
[207] Burns, 'Confessing the Church', 347.
[208] *Pat.* 5 (CCSL 3A:120-1).
[209] *Pat.* 9 (CCSL 3A:123).
[210] *Pat.* 10 (CCSL 3A:123-4).

only the continual battle with temptation but the deprivation, suffering and torment of persecution, with faith and courage; they can be confident in these worldly tribulations because the Lord has overcome the world.[211] The Christian's duty is to patiently await the day of the Lord's vengeance.[212]

Good for others

Because of Cyprian's pastoral emphasis, and his real experience of persecution, the encouragement provided by the exemplary steadfastness of confessors and martyrs is much more prominent in Cyprian's writings than in those of the other fathers. The faith and fortitude of imprisoned and exiled confessors was a source of pride for the church. When the confessors faced the additional trial of torture, some having already died, 'the throng of bystanders watched in wonderment this heavenly, this spiritual contest of God, this battle of Christ'.[213]

Cyprian reminds confessors that they are an example to the rest of the church, and must persevere in conduct befitting that example.[214] Post-persecution, Cyprian wrote of the glorious spectacle of Christ's white-robed soldiers who resisted the world and who serve as an example to their brethren and sisters who would follow them.[215] When he faced his own martyrdom, Cyprian believed it fitting that a bishop confess his faith before his own flock, and that he should bring glory upon all his people by making his confession in their midst.[216]

Cyprian sees the benefits of confession and martyrdom in terms of the individual's salvation and the encouragement to the church, rather than specifically as witness to unbelievers. This impression is undoubtedly skewed, given that most of his extant writings are addressed to Christians, rather than to pagans. Nevertheless, in a similar vein to Tertullian, Cyprian condemns Demetrianus for his assaults on Christians, warning that pagan persecutors face the wrath of God.[217] Despite this, Christians 'pour forth our prayers for your peace and salvation and, propitiating and appeasing God, day and night we entreat constantly and urgently'.[218] Cyprian concludes with a plea to Demetrianus to repent of idolatry and embrace Christ, thereby avoiding his punitive destiny, but unlike Tertullian, he does not presume that it is the martyrs' example that will be convincing.

---

[211] *Pat.* 12 (CCSL 3A:125) citing Jn 16:33.
[212] *Pat.* 21 (CCSL 3A:130–1).
[213] *Ep.* 10.2.2 (CCSL 3B:48–9) Videt admirans praesentium multitudo caeleste certamen dei et spiritale, proelium Christi . . .
[214] *Ep.* 13.3.1 (CCSL 3B:73).
[215] *Laps.* 2 (CCSL 3:221–2).
[216] *Ep.* 81.1 (CCSL 3C:629) congruat episcopum in ea ciuitate in qua ecclesiae dominicae praeest illic dominum confiteri et plebum uniuersam praepositi praesentis confessione clarificare. That this was an exemplary and encouraging stance rather than a reinforcement of patron-client relationship seems most consistent, contra Montgomery, 'The Bishop who Fled'.
[217] *Dem.* 21 (CCSL 3A:47).
[218] *Dem.* 20 (CCSL 3A:47) preces fundimus et pro pace ac salute uestra propitiantes et placantes Deum diebus ac noctibus iugitur adque instanter oramus.

Future reward and vindication

The immediate perils of persecution and plague, attributed by Cyprian to the aging and imminent end of the world, the *senectus mundi*,[219] permeate his writings and inform his eschatology. In this critical time, with judgement perceived to be approaching, he stresses the reward for the faithful, the consolation of being reunited with loved ones and the inevitable damnation of persecutors.[220]

Cyprian's belief in immediate reward for all faithful Christians[221] is central to his encouragement for them to not fear death, and as Bévenot argues, to the legitimacy of reconciliation of the lapsed, who must be reconciled to the church to have any hope.[222] Bévenot correctly concludes that Cyprian believed that ordinary Christians, not just the martyrs, would be rewarded immediately after death.[223] Bévenot argues that Cyprian telescopes the particular and general judgements as, non-specifically, 'when we come to be judged'.[224] Christ 'comes' as each person dies, and at his physical return to his church he will judge those inside her, including the reconciled lapsed.[225] Therefore one's destiny is sealed at one's death (by whatever means) or the *parousia*, whichever occurs first.

The martyrs' pleading for the lapsed will only take place at the final judgement, because the martyrs themselves, although waiting under the altar, are not yet vindicated.[226] Wysocki suggests that Cyprian's view of the immediate reward of all those who die in faith, set in the context of the plagues and persecutions of the dying world, was 'hereto unique'.[227] This presupposes that Tertullian, particularly, taught that only martyrs go straight to heaven, a position Wilhite has successfully refuted.[228] Rather than Cyprian being the innovator, I propose that Tertullian's portrait of the intermediate state was an ingenious answer to heretical notions of the soul and resurrection.[229] Cyprian evidently rejects any delay in the Christian's reward, whether this constitutes a conscious rejection of Tertullian's dual regions of Hades or not. An emphasis on

---

[219] *Dem.* 3–4 (CCSL 3A:36–7); *Mort.* 2, 25 (CCSL 3A: 17–18, 30–31; 36–9) *Fort.* praef. 1 (CCSL 3:183); *Epp.* 58.2, 67.7 (CCSL 3C:321–2; 458); Brian E. Daley, *The Hope of the Early Church: A Handbook of Patristic Eschatology* (Peabody MS: Hendrickson, 2003), 41.

[220] *Mort.* 26 (CCSL 3A:31–2); *Ep.* 58.10 (CCSL 3C:333–4).

[221] *Epp.* 31.3, 58.3.2 (CCSL 3B:153–4; 3C:323–4) *Mort.* 20, 24, 26 (CCSL 3A:27–8, 30, 31–2) but also *Fort.* 12–13 (CCSL 3:211–16) in persecutione militia, in pace conscientia coronatur.

[222] Bévenot, 'Sacrament of Penance', 191–8.

[223] Ibid., 192, drawing on *Laps.* 17, *Mort.* 26, *Fort.* 12–13.

[224] Bévenot, 'Sacrament of Penance', 192–3.

[225] Ibid., 194–5.

[226] Ibid., 196–7 citing Cyprian, *Laps.* 17–18 ref. Rev. 6:9–11.

[227] Marcin R. Wysocki, 'Eschatology of the Time of Persecutions in the Writings of Tertullian and Cyprian', StPatr 65 (2013), 379–93, at 383–4; Cyprian, *Mort.* 16, 26 (CCSL 3A:25, 31–32). However, Origen, Cyprian's contemporary, is confident that at death he will leave his body and be at peace with Christ; *Dialogue with Heracleides* as cited in Robert J Daly, trans. and ann., *Origen: Treatise on the Passover and Dialogue of Origen with Heraclides and his fellow bishops on the Father, the Son, and the soul*, Ancient Christian Writers: The Works of the Fathers in Translation 54 (New York: Paulist, 1992).

[228] Wilhite, 'Tertullian on the Afterlife: 'Only Martyrs are in Heaven' and Other Misunderstandings'. *Zeitschrift für antikes Christentum* 24, no. 3 (2020), 490–508.

[229] But not bereft of Scriptural support; *An.* 55–56 (CCSL 2:861–5) based on 1 Cor. 15:3–4 and Lk. 16:19–31. Also *Res.* 17 (CCSL 2:941–2).

delayed reward or the pre-emptive salvation of martyrs would have been less suited to Cyprian's pastoral concerns.

Cyprian unequivocally points his flock to the afterlife for their hope and consolation in the midst of significant present suffering, but acknowledges that in this life they obtain a foretaste.[230] In contrast, he warns that sinners will experience everlasting fiery punishment, with no scope for repentance or making satisfaction after death.[231] This denial of post-mortem educative or purgative punishment for the wicked, in contrast to the Alexandrians' perspective, largely explains the urgency of the Carthaginians' diogmology. The deadline for shaping one's life aright could be mere days or hours away.

Reward features strongly in Cyprian's exhortations to steadfastness. Cyprian exhorts Fortunatus to persevere to martyrdom, the second baptism, as a goal to be embraced, desired, and requested.[232] He enumerates the hope and rewards for the righteous and martyrs,[233] emphasizing that the reward of our suffering is greater than what is endured in the suffering itself.[234] Christ has saved the church; to be saved one must be in the church, which is why Cyprian can be confident that *all* faithful Christians will be reunited at death. Although Cyprian recognizes the special worthiness of the martyrs, they are not distinguished by receiving their reward immediately,[235] nor is their right to a 'crown' exclusive. Crowns may also be awarded for good works.[236] Although Cyprian, like Tertullian, anticipates an imminent, dreadful end to the world, the hope is more immediate, whether one dies as a martyr or through the plague. 'For it is for him to fear death who is not willing to go to Christ. It is for him to be unwilling to go to Christ who does not believe that he is about to reign with Christ.'[237]

Although Christians look beyond this world of suffering for their security in salvation, Cyprian exhorts virgins in their restraint, 'that which you shall be, you have already begun to be. You possess already in this world the glory of the resurrection'.[238] He reminds imprisoned confessors, 'the life you are now living is not of the present world, it is the life of the world to come'.[239] Given that the present reality of diverse suffering makes daily life in this world a battle with the Devil, Cyprian proposes that Christians should wish to speedily depart rather than remain here. That departure to reward does not necessitate martyrdom, being just as applicable to the one who succumbs to plague. To these he writes: 'God promises you, on your withdrawal from this world, immortality and eternity, and do you doubt?'[240]

---

[230] *Ep.* 37.2 (CCSL 3B:178–80).
[231] *Dem.* 24–25 (CCSL 3A: 49–51); *Ep.* 58.10 (CCSL 3C:333–4).
[232] *Fort.* Pref. 4 (CCSL 3:184–5) Amplectenda res et optanda.
[233] *Fort.* 12 (CCSL 3:211–14).
[234] *Fort.* 13 (CCSL 3:214–16).
[235] *Mort.* 2–3 cf 26 (CCSL 3A:17–8, 31–32).
[236] *Ep.* 10.5.2 (CCSL 3B:55) and see Dunn, 'White Crown of Works'.
[237] *Mort.* 2 (CCSL 3A:18) Eius est enim mortem timere qui ad Christum nolit ire. Eius est ad Christum nolle ire qui se non credat cum Christo incipere regnare.
[238] *Virg.* 22 (CCSL 3F:316) Quod futuri sumus, iam uos esse coepistis. Vos resurrectionis gloriam in isto saeculo iam tenetis.
[239] *Ep.* 37.3.2 (CCSL 3B:181) uita iam uiuitur non praesentis saeculi sed futuri.
[240] *Mort.* 6 (CCSL 3A:20) Deus de hoc mundo recedenti inmortalitatem adque aeternitatem pollicetur, et dubitas?

Martyrdom nevertheless confers special benefit.[241] The patience of the martyrs is to be the role model for persecuted Christians.[242] Martyrdom is a second baptism, 'a baptism greater in grace, loftier in power, more precious in honour'. It is a baptism 'wherein angels baptise, in which God and his Christ exult'.[243] After this baptism no one sins any more. It completes the increase of our faith and associates us with God as soon as we withdraw from the world. Baptism in water brings remission of sins, but baptism in blood brings the crown of virtues; it is to be embraced, desired and requested – provided one is martyred in communion with the church.[244]

Like Tertullian, Cyprian often uses evocative military language, but for Cyprian the endurance itself is the battle which brings victory; our strength is made perfect in weakness (2 Cor. 12:7–9). While others complain, Christians are strengthened by suffering. By treading this narrow way that Christ trod, we receive the reward of his life and faith.[245] Those who stand firm in present sufferings (from whatever cause) are rewarded along with those who are martyred. 'He says all will live and reign with Christ, not only the slain, but whoever standing firm in his faith and in the fear of God, have not worshipped the image of the beast, nor consented to his deadly and sacrilegious edicts.'[246]

Present sufferings are not worthy to be compared with future glory, but rather, 'we receive more as the reward of our suffering than what we endure here in the suffering itself'.[247] Nevertheless, his treatise to Demetrianus adds a Tertullianesque threat of retribution: 'the short enjoyment of those cruel eyes in the persecutions made for us will afterward be compensated by a perpetual spectacle'.[248]

The reason we see the victory/justice/vindication motif stronger in the Carthaginians than in the Alexandrians is because of the Carthaginians' view that God would eschatologically intervene at a point in time, and everything would change. Victory and recompense were concrete because they was perceived as imminent, whether the *parousia* or one's death came first. Reward was tangible and an incentive to confession and martyrdom. The Alexandrians' progressive, continuous view of salvation de-emphasized the eschatological intervention of God as a future-historical event, so the victory-reward aspect, although present, is less sharp. Confession was required of a Christian, suffering was inevitable, and there will be proportionate recompense along the journey to perfection in the afterlife. When faced with death, however, as we see in each *Exhortation to Martyrdom*, the prospect of an end to suffering and a commensurate

---

[241] *Test.* 3.16 (CCSL 3:107–11); Rev. 6:9–11.

[242] *Pat.* 21 (CCSL 3A:130–1); *Laps.* 18 (CCSL 3:230–1).

[243] *Fort.* pref. 4 (CCSL 3:185) hoc esse baptisma in gratia maius, in potestate sublimius, in honore praetiosius, baptisma in quo angeli baptizant, baptisma in quo Deus et Christus eius exultant.

[244] *Unit.* 14 (CCSL 3:259–60) Occidi talis potest, coronari non potest.

[245] *Mort.* 13–14 (CCSL 3A:23–4).

[246] *Fort.* 12 (CCSL 3:214) Viuere omnes dicit et regnare cum Christo, non tantum qui occisi fuerint, sed quique in fidei suae firmitate et Dei timore perstantes imaginem bestiae non adorauerint neque ad funesta eius et sacrilega edicta consenserint.

[247] *Fort.* 13 (CCSL 3:214) Plus nos accipere in passionis mercede quam quod hic sustinemus in ipsa passione. Ref. Rom. 8:18.

[248] *Dem.* 24 (CCSL 3A:49) et in persecutionibus factis oculorum crudelium breuis fructus perpetua uisione pensabitur secundum.

reward would have been as motivational for Origen's addressees as it was for those of Tertullian and Cyprian.

Cyprian believes that the martyrs' merits and the works of the righteous *will* influence the Judge; but on the day of judgement at the end of this world.[249] This does not mean that the martyrs and confessors have *carte blanche* now to restore the lapsed without due penitence; that would harm the lapsed. The martyrs are bidden to wait under the altar; how can anyone think he can avail for others before he himself is vindicated?[250] Furthermore, the gospel is consistent that those who deny will be denied and those who confess will be confessed; the martyrs can do nothing in opposition to the very Gospel which makes them martyrs. No one can be more merciful than God, or undo what God decrees, or suggest that God cannot preserve and protect his church.[251]

Pragmatic responses

Given the similarities between Cyprian's and Tertullian's foundational diogmologies, one might anticipate similar congruence on the Christian response. Indeed, both stress patient endurance, love for one's enemies, fearlessness and joy, although Cyprian personally models these in his writings to a greater extent than his predecessor. Both emphasize the necessity for confession, and both exalt martyrdom, although Cyprian is less focused on martyrdom as the unparalleled pinnacle of confession than Tertullian. Both excoriate apostates, but while Tertullian becomes more uncompromising as to the fate of the lapsed, Cyprian adapts his approach to eventually allow their reconciliation. Tertullian equates any compromise with denial, but Cyprian, like Clement and Origen, considers flight and avoidance valid alternatives to provoking martyrdom. I propose that the differing circumstances and experiences of the two Carthaginians provoked Cyprian to reflect on and revise the practical applications of a common foundational diogmology, rather than to follow his 'master' unquestioningly.

The right attitude

Cyprian emphasizes fearlessness, joy and patience as framing the Christian's appropriate attitude toward persecution. Given the reward which awaits the steadfast, despite the inevitability of their suffering and ultimate death, Cyprian discourages fear. Christ exhorts us to hold death in contempt and not to fear those who can only kill the body and not the soul (Mt. 10:28).[252] 'It is fitting', Cyprian concludes, 'that we endure all manner of tribulation and persecution.'[253] The Thibarii should not panic from fear of approaching persecution and the Antichrist; rather they must fear the one who can

---

[249] *Laps.* 17 (CCSL 3:230).
[250] *Laps.* 18 (CCSL 3:230–1).
[251] *Laps.* 20 (CCSL 3:232–3).
[252] *Fort.* 5 (CCSL 3:193).
[253] *Ep.* 6.2.1 (CCSL 3B:33) pressuras omnes et persecutiones tolerare nos conuenit.

destroy body and soul in hell, and who will punish the worshippers of the beast with fire and brimstone.[254] Cyprian exhorts Fortunatus not to fear persecution, because the Lord's ability to protect is greater than that of the Devil to assault.[255] God will provide help through his Holy Spirit; affliction will serve to promote rather than destroy the faith. Therefore, the persecuted should not think about the danger the Devil brings, but the help which God brings, which is greater than he imagines.[256]

The Christian is in a blessed situation. Cyprian includes Matthew 5:10–12, Jesus' exhortation to rejoice in persecution, as a proof verse for 'the benefits of martyrdom',[257] and an encouragement to Fortunatus.[258] More than the other fathers, Cyprian models joy by expressing it over the encouragement and steadfastness of the martyrs.

> [What] could give me greater joy nor satisfy more my longing than at this moment to be embracing you, clasped by those hands of yours which have preserved their faith in the Lord with purity and innocence, and have scornfully rejected the sacrilegious acts of compliance? [What] could give me greater pleasure or more noble delight than at this moment to be kissing those lips of yours which have confessed the Lord with words of glory and actually to be looked upon by those eyes of yours which have looked down in scorn on this world and have shown themselves worthy of looking upon God?[259]

For Cyprian, joy is both an active choice and a tangible feeling. Cyprian expresses joy for the steadfastness of confessors[260] and the encouragement of others, based on his confidence in what awaits those who rejoice in present sufferings. Given the prospect of reigning with the Lord, confessors must 'inevitably rejoice', and spurn the present tortures, out of joy at what is to be, because it was ordained that righteousness should so struggle.[261] He writes of his overwhelming joy in their faith and fortitude, that Christ rejoices to fight in their midst, and that the martyrs' joy will dry the church's tears.[262] The glory of their confession redounds on the church and its bishop, prompting communal rejoicing.[263] Cyprian can therefore face his own execution with confidence.[264]

Joy, not fear, will sustain the patient Christian. Cyprian emphasizes not just *patientia* but *De bono patientiae*. Christians must imitate Christ's example of patience in their

---

[254] *Ep.* 58.7 (CCSL 3C:329–30).
[255] *Fort.* 10 (CCSL 3:198–201).
[256] *Fort.* 10 (CCSL 3:198–201).
[257] *Test.* 3.16 (CCSL 3:107–11).
[258] *Fort.* 12 (CCSL 3:213).
[259] *Ep.* 6.1.1 (CCSL 3B:29–30) Quid enim mihi optatius et laetius posset accidere quam nunc uobis inhaerere, ut conplecteremini me manibus illis quae purae et innocentes et dominicam fidem seruantes sacrilega obsequia respuerunt? Quid iucundius et sublimius quam osculari nunc ora uestra quae gloriosa uoce dominum confessa sunt, conspici etiam praesentem ab oculis uestris qui despecto saeculo conspiciendo deo digni extiterunt?
[260] *Laps.* 2 (CCSL 3:221–2).
[261] *Ep.* 6.2.1 (CCSL 3B:32) exultetis necesse.
[262] *Ep.* 10.1.1 Exulto laetus at gratulor; 10.3; 10.4.4 (CCSL 3B:46, 50, 53).
[263] *Ep.* 13.1 (CCSL 3B:71–2).
[264] *Epp.* 80.1.3, 81 (CCSL 3C:627–30), Pontius, *Vita*.

lives, deeds and words.[265] Cyprian exhorts Fortunatus to press on and persevere in faith and virtue, citing Matthew 10:22, John 8:31–32 and Luke 12:35–37. The same passages appear in *De bono patientiae*; perseverance and endurance are central to the Christian hope; hope and faith can only attain to their result through patience for we seek future glory.[266] The confessors who die in prison are worthy of special honour, because of their endurance.[267]

Doing good: The other crown

Cyprian placed almsgiving on a level with confession and martyrdom in *De opere et eleemosynis*. Almsgiving secures salvation by cleansing from post-baptismal sin.[268] It appeases God[269] and renders petitionary prayer efficacious.[270] God will reward our merits with a white crown for our labours in peace, and a purple crown for our martyrdom in persecution.[271] Cyprian assures confessors that if they fail to attain martyrdom, their good works would equally confer glory.[272] Murphy observes that just as Cyprian argues that love of wealth had prompted apostasy, he teaches the redemptive value of almsgiving in the context of love of money causing the sin.[273]

The first letter of Peter exhorts Christians to do good. Enduring suffering for doing good is a gracious thing in God's sight; it is better to suffer for doing good than for doing evil.[274] In contrast to Tertullian's emphasis on disciplined endurance, as a pastor Cyprian emphasizes the active pursuit of good works. In *De mortalitate*, Cyprian reminds believers that the plague 'searches out the righteousness of each one ... to see whether they who are in health tend the sick'.[275] Confident of their salvation, Christians could do the work which others feared to do. Writing to confessors, Cyprian cites 1 Peter 3:12 as encouragement to persevere in right behaviour, having been made examples to the rest of the community.

Confessors and martyrs

Cyprian's writings reveal a much more complex relationship between confessors and martyrs than those of the other fathers, probably due to the scale and variety of circumstances in which he participated. Cyprian, like Clement and Origen, believed that consigning a confessor or other Christian to martyrdom was solely the decision of

---

[265] *Pat.* 9, 10, 12 (CCSL 3A:123–5).
[266] *Pat.* 13 (CCSL 3A:125–6).
[267] *Epp.* 12.1.2–3, 14.2.2 (CCSL 3B:68–9; 80–81) citing Mt. 10:22 and Rev. 2:10.
[268] *Eleem.* 1–2 (CCSL 3A:55–6).
[269] *Eleem.* 4 (CCSL 3A:57) solis eleemosynis Deum posse placari.
[270] *Eleem.* 5 (CCSL 3A:57–8).
[271] *Eleem.* 26 (CCSL 3A:72) in pace uincentibus coronam candidam pro operibus dabit, in persecutione purpuream pro passione geminabit.
[272] *Ep.* 10.5.2 (CCSL 3B:54–5). See Dunn, 'White Crown of Works', 715–16, 740.
[273] Edwina Murphy, 'Sin No More: Healing, Wholeness and the Absent Adulteress in Cyprian's Use of John', *Revue des études augustiniennes et patristiques* 64, no. 1 (2018), 1–15, at 8.
[274] 1 Pet. 2:15, 20; 3:17.
[275] *Mort.* 16 (CCSL 3A:25) explorat iustitiam singulorum ... an infirmis seruiant sani.

God. A Christian must refuse the call to sacrifice or be held to deny his Lord. The imperative here is confession, with the understanding that it *could* lead to martyrdom. Cyprian encourages confessors to endure to the end, reminding them of the Holy Spirit's presence with them in prison. The assumption, indeed, the hope is that they will be martyred after their final testimony. 'In our unceasing prayers we beg that the Lord will perfect you, and that as a result of you taking your first steps toward the lofty heights, he makes those whom he has made confessors also into the crowned.'[276]

Cyprian prays that confessors remain steadfast under torture, winning together their heavenly crowns.[277] This has clear parallels to Origen's *Exhortation to Martyrdom*. However, Cyprian encourages his addressees to not feel disappointed or in any way inferior to the martyrs if peace comes before their opportunity to die. This does not seem to have been an option for Origen's friends. 'Either course, therefore, my dearly beloved brothers, equally confers nobility and glory. By the one, the surer way, you hasten to the Lord by the completion of your victory; by the other, the more joyful way, after gaining your glory you obtain a reprieve and flourish in the praises of the church.'[278]

Significantly, those imprisoned confessors who died from deprivation and torture must also be considered true martyrs.

> You should pay special care and solicitude also to the bodies of all those who, without being tortured, nevertheless die in prison, departing this life in glory. They are inferior neither in valour nor in honour, so that they, too, should be added to the company of the blessed martyrs. They have endured, in so far as they were able, whatever they were prepared and ready to endure. A man who, under the eyes of God, has offered himself to torture and to death, has in fact suffered whatever he was willing to suffer. He did not fail the tortures; they failed him.[279]

Similarly, when Christians were later dying of the plague, and regretting not being martyred, Cyprian reminds them that martyrdom is not actually within their power. God knows every heart, their intention to confess, their willingness to be martyred; 'God does not ask for our blood but for our faith.'[280] Likewise, those who die whilst fleeing persecution, by assault, starvation or exposure, are equally dying for the honour

---

[276] *Ep.* 6.4 (CCSL 3B:37) Quod ut consummetur in uobis adsiduis orationibus dominum deprecamur, ut initiis ad summa pergentibus quos confiteri fecit faciat et coronari.

[277] *Ep.* 10.1–4 (CCSL 3B:46–54).

[278] *Ep.* 10.5.2 (CCSL 3B:75) Ergo ultraque res, fratres carissimi, sublimis pariter et inlustris: illa securior ad dominum uictoriae consummatione properare, haec laetior accepto post gloriam commeatu in ecclesiae laude florere.

[279] *Ep.* 12.1. (CCSL 3B:68–9) Corporibus etiam omnium, qui etsi torti non sunt, in carcere tamen glorioso exitu mortis excedunt, inpertiatur et uigilantia et cura propensior. Neque enim uirtus eorum aut honor minor est quominus ipsi quoque inter beatos martyras adgregentur. Quod in illis est tolerauerunt quidquid tolerare parati et prompti fuerunt. Qui se tormentis et morti sub oculis dei obtulit passus est quidquid pati uoluit. Non enim ipse tormentis, sed tormenta ipsi defuerunt... This is perseverance unto death, this is confession of Christ, insists Cyprian, citing Mt. 10:22, 32.

[280] *Mort.* 17 (CCSL 3A:25–6) Nec enim sanguinem Deus nostrum sed fidem quaerit. Likewise in *Ep.* 61 (CCSL 3C:380–4).

of Christ's name. Christ is there with them and the glory of such a martyrdom is no less than one publicly witnessed.[281]

Despite this encouragement, Cyprian was not a proponent of voluntary martyrdom. He withdrew at the outset of the persecution, to reduce attention to and violence against his flock. When the time came, his attitude to his own impending martyrdom was one of acceptance rather than provocation.[282] His refusal to die in Utica was to enable his martyrdom to take place, as he deemed appropriate, in the presence of his own congregation.[283] Whilst this was a manipulation of circumstances, it was neither an avoidance nor a deliberate precipitation of his already assigned fate. Most tellingly, he warns his people:

> Let no one among you stir up trouble for the brethren or offer himself up to the pagans of his own volition. But if a man has been apprehended and delivered up, then he has a duty to speak out, in as much as God who dwells within us speaks at that hour: he has shown that his will is that we should do more than profess our faith; we are to confess it.[284]

The possible exception to Cyprian's anti-volunteerist stance was his initial encouragement of the penitent lapsed to take a renewed opportunity to confess and thus win absolution by their baptism of blood.[285] This was Tertullian's view and if it was an endorsement of volunteerism, Cyprian revised his recommendation as circumstances changed. Burns explains Cyprian's evolving perspective as due to two factors: pressure from his congregation, clergy and colleagues under changing circumstances, and the different character and purposes of the 'persecutions' confronted.[286] The Decian persecution was a discipline of the church, and denial could only be countered by confession, not compromise.[287] The push to prematurely reconcile the lapsed was 'another persecution', to be resisted by a confession that consisted of submitting to the church's discipline.[288] Under these circumstances, the recommendation to reverse previous denial with confession and anticipated martyrdom would seem appropriate.

Cyprian does not consider the living confessor to have attained his or her reward unconditionally; he or she must endure to the end (however one dies) and, furthermore, must live consistently with a confessor's ideals. As the imprisoned confessors' standing led to them being solicited by the lapsed for absolution,[289] Cyprian warned them

---

[281] *Ep.* 58.4.2 (CCSL 3C:324–5).
[282] *Ep.* 80.1.3 (CCSL 3C:627).
[283] *Ep.* 81.1.1–3 (CCSL 3C:629–30). Montgomery's thesis, 'The Bishop Who Fled', 264–7, that this was an act of patronage is better explained by diogmology.
[284] *Ep.* 81.1.4 (CCSL 3C:630) nec quisquam uestrum aliquem tumultum fratribus moueat aut ultro se gentilibus offerat. Apprehensus enim et traditus loqui debet, siquidem deus in nobis positus illa hora loquatur, qui nos confiteri magis uoluit quam profiteri.
[285] *Epp.* 19.2.3; 25.1.2; 55.4.1–2.
[286] Burns, 'Confessing the Church', 347.
[287] Burns, 'Confessing the Church', 340–1.
[288] Ibid., 342; *Laps.* 16 (CCSL 3:230) Persecutio est haec alia.
[289] *Ep.* 20.2.2 (CCSL 3B:107–8).

against undermining the very laws of God which they were supposedly suffering to uphold. This would be using God's grace as a weapon against him; such confessors would lose their crowns.[290] 'It is not martyrs who make the gospel, but that martyrs are made through the gospel'.[291] Cyprian believed that the martyrs' merits would be of great avail – but on the day of judgement.[292] He now asserts that confession is the beginning of glory, but not the full deservedness of the crown; only he who endures *to the end* will be saved (Mt. 10:22). The same passage which Tertullian used to link confession and martyrdom is used by Cyprian to separate them. The confessor, now at risk of greater demonic provocation, will only remain a confessor of Christ so long as he does not blaspheme Christ's dignity and majesty.[293]

Brent offers an alternative explanation of Cyprian's expanded definition of confessor.[294] Dismissing Cyprian's stated concerns, Brent argues that Cyprian knowingly overrode established church tradition that confessors and martyrs could authoritatively reinstate apostates through administration of the eucharist. He presents Cyprian as an innovator with the hidden agenda of 'the establishment of his episcopal authority at the expense of that of the martyrs'.[295] Desiring to suppress a potential replacement for ordination as for baptism, Cyprian allegedly shifted the image-bearing of Christ's suffering from martyr to priest.[296] Brent argues that this is why Cyprian broadened the definition of confessor to not require suffering unto death.[297] Brent presumes this motive underpins Cyprian's significant change of course toward reconciliation of the lapsed. Although Cyprian's diogmology is undoubtedly influenced by his 'innovative' ecclesiology, I consider his consistent diogmology to be a better explanation of his embrace of a wider definition of 'confessor' and 'martyr'. Both Clement and Origen (whose sacramental view of martyrdom Brent effectively opposes to Cyprian's) also broaden the concept of confession and do not, as Tertullian does, conflate it necessarily with martyrdom. I propose that, whilst it evidently suited his developing views of the episcopate, Cyprian primarily sought to encourage those patiently enduring persecution – which he sees as one crown-worthy aspect of the life-long conflict with Satan – in line with his evident pastoral objectives.

Cyprian ultimately determines that a true martyr must be in communion with the church, neither a lapsed nor a heretic, otherwise their martyrdom is void.[298] The baptism of blood is insufficient without peace from the bishop,[299] but restored confessors may anticipate a martyr's crown.[300] To Cyprian, the expected final wave of

---

[290] *Epp.* 28.2.3; 36.2.1 (CCSL 3B:135, 174).
[291] *Ep.* 27.3.3 (CCSL 3B:131) non martyres euangelium faciant, sed per euangelium martyres fiant.
[292] *Laps.* 17 (CCSL 3:230).
[293] *Unit.* 21 (CCSL 3:264–5).
[294] Alan Brent, 'Cyprian's Reconstruction of the Martyr Tradition', *Journal of Ecclesiastical History* 53, no. 2 (2002), 241–68.
[295] Ibid., 255.
[296] Ibid., 259.
[297] Ibid., 261.
[298] *Unit.* 6, 14 (CCSL 3: 253–4; 259–60); *Ep.* 57.1 (CCSL 3B:301–2).
[299] *Ep.* 57.4.1–4.2 (CCSL 3B:305–6).
[300] *Ep.* 60.2.5 (CCSL 3C:377).

persecution marked the end of the world and would be immediately followed by judgement. It was therefore the last chance for confession of Christ and the truly penitent should not be denied strengthening for that.[301]

Immolated salvation

Cyprian, appalled by the mass apostasy of the Decian persecution, was uncompromising in his condemnation. 'Immediately at the first words of the threatening foe the greatest number of brothers betrayed their faith, indeed not cast down by the onset of persecutions but casting themselves down by voluntary lapse ... Didn't he previously appoint both eternal punishment to the deniers and beneficial rewards to the confessors?'[302]

Many sacrificed voluntarily without waiting to be apprehended or interrogated; 'conquered before the battle'. There was no apparent unwillingness, no violence done to plead as an excuse; people forcefully brought about their own ruin.[303] Cyprian is incredulous that one who had previously renounced the Devil and the world could rush to the pagan altar and renounce Christ.

> Wasn't that altar, to which he approached to die, to be his funeral pile? Ought he not to shudder at and flee from the devil's altar, which indeed he had seen to emit a hideous stench, smoke enveloped as the funeral and crematorium of his life? Why bring a sacrifice with you, wretch, why lay out a sacrificial victim? You yourself have come as an offering to the altar, yourself a victim, you have immolated your salvation, your hope, cremated your faith in those deadly fires.[304]

Furthermore, many urged others, or brought children, to follow suit.[305] Cyprian views their actions as an unconscionable apostasy by those who should have known better. Rather than fleeing and leaving their possessions behind, they were held back by worldly wealth and clung to their possessions.[306] Cyprian will have no excuses made. Like Tertullian, Cyprian has some sympathy with one who broke under genuine torture,[307] but the tortures did not come until after the first wave of imprisonments. The voluntary apostates had no wounds to show. It was not, for most, a case of faith failing in the terrifying encounter, but prematurely, 'faithlessness anticipating the struggle'.[308]

---

[301] Burns, 'Confessing the Church', 346.
[302] *Laps*. 7 (CCSL 3:224) Ad prima statim uerba minantis inimici maximus fratrum numerus fidem suam prodidit, nec prostratus est persecutionis inpetu, sed uoluntario lapsu se ipse prostrauit ... Nonne et negantibus aeterna supplicia et salutaria confitentibus praemia ante constituit?
[303] *Laps*. 8 (CCSL 3:225) Ante aciem multi uicti.
[304] *Laps*. 8 (CCSL 3:225) Non ara illa, quo moriturus accessit, rogus illi fuit? Non diaboli altare, quod faetore taetro fumare ac redolere conspexerat, uelut funus et bustum uitae suae horrere ac fugere debebat? Quid hostiam tecum, miser, quid uictimam supplicaturus inponis? Ipse ad aras hostia, uictima ipse uenisti; inmolasti illic salutem tuam, spem tuam, fidem tuam funestis illic ignibus concremasti.
[305] *Laps*. 9 (CCSL 3:225).
[306] *Laps*. 10–12 (CCSL 3:226–7).
[307] *Laps*. 13 (CCSL 3:227–8).
[308] *Laps*. 14 (CCSL 3:228) congressionem perfidia praeuenit.

Cyprian could not countenance these lapsed being readmitted without them demonstrating appropriate remorse through penance. Sharing the Lord's table with devils would make them guilty of the body and blood of the Lord (1 Cor. 10:21; 11:27). Disguised as mercy, it deprived these fatally ill and wounded of the necessary cure for their mortal spiritual wounds by simply covering them over.[309] This is no kindness, but injury, warns Cyprian. It is another persecution, another temptation by which the Devil further assaults the lapsed.[310] Only God can have mercy, he alone can pardon sins against himself, who said that he will deny the one who denies him.[311] Whereas Origen allowed an indefinite time for post-mortem healing and instruction, for Cyprian this ministration had to be applied urgently, in this life. To deny and sacrifice was to immolate one's salvation. Forgiveness for such a heinous act required a response of equivalent gravity: the baptism of blood or a long and arduous penance. A repentant apostate could not be allowed to face death, even as a martyr, without reconciliation. The church's penitential discipline was divinely ordained and medicinal, under the bishop as healer.[312]

Avoidance

Cyprian's position on legitimate options for avoidance of capture and trial situates him closer to Origen than to Tertullian. Perhaps this partly reflects the common contemporary experience of their communities, and their personal acquaintance with actual confessors and martyrs. From Dionysius of Alexandria's comparable account, it seems reasonable to assume that the situation was similar everywhere, including Origen's Caesarea. Cyprian provides the most detail on the various options of obtaining *libelli*, lying low and fleeing, because of his direct dealings with them in his community.

Some Christians seem to have approached officials to pay for the *libellus* without sacrificing, either directly or through a third party.[313] Cyprian's position on these *libellatici* was initially harsh, as was Tertullian's, reminding them that God searches the

---

[309] *Laps.* 15 (CCSL 3:228-9). For a different perspective on Cyprian's medical metaphors, see Gilvan Ventura da Silva and Carolline da Silva Soares 'Protegendo a 'corpo' da igreja: a representaçãi dos lapsi e judaizantes como enfermos por Cipriano e João Crisóstomo', *Revista Jesushistórico*: Revista de Estudios sobre o Jesus Histórico e sua Recepção 10 (2013), 44–61. Against the contention of these authors that Cyprian's representation of the lapsed as contagious sick who threatened the purity of the church, in keeping with a broader rhetoric of discrediting religious opponents and bolstering the bishop's authority, I suggest the authors have not given due weight to the wider context of Cyprian's concern for the lapsed. Above all, Cyprian regarded the premature readmission of the lapsed as harmful *to themselves*; it will worsen their disease. Cyprian wants to heal them through penitence, not close the door on them. Cyprian is not concerned about readmitting remorseful lapsed seeking penance, but only the intransigent who deny they need it (*Epp.* 16.2; 17.1: CCSL 3B:91-3, 96-7). He is not worried about the former polluting the church and uses the argument that readmission of adulterers has not done so, as an argument against Novatian's rigorism, insisting that no one is polluted by another's sin (*Ep.* 55.27.2-3: CCSL 3B:290-1).
[310] *Laps.* 16 (CCSL 3:229-30).
[311] *Laps.* 17-20 (CCSL 3:230-3).
[312] *Laps.* 35 (CCSL 3:240-1); *Epp.* 8.2.1 (CCSL 3B:41); 15.2.1 (CCSL 3B:87); 36.2.1 (CCSL 3B:174); 55.16.2.3, 23.3 (CCSL 274-5, 284); 57.4.3 (CCSL 3B:306-7).
[313] *Ep.* 30.3.1 (CCSL 3B:141-2).

heart and judges words and thoughts as well as deeds. Although they have not polluted their hands with sacrifices, they have polluted their consciences:

> The denier's profession is the testimony of a Christian who disowns what he had been; he says he has done what another has actually committed. Although it is written, 'It is not possible to serve two masters' he has served a secular master, complying with his edict, more obedient to a human authority than to God.[314]

Cyprian therefore initially refused to allow the readmission of *libellatici* to communion without appropriate penitence. Later, he allowed that *libellatici* were not equated with *sacrificati*, and had diverse and sometimes understandable motives.[315] One man specified he was Christian when purchasing to avoid the sacrifice;[316] his repentance should be accepted, as a wounded sheep of Christ's flock, lest he turn to heresy and schism.[317] Individual penitent *libellatici* were subsequently readmitted to communion,[318] as were repentant adulterers.[319]

Cyprian was concerned for the protection of the vulnerable left in Carthage, that they be supported and not subjected to violence.[320] These *stantes* did not step up and sacrifice, nor obtain *libelli*, but they did not draw attention to their defiance of the decree either. Contrary to Tertullian, who assumes the one who withdraws is biased toward denial, Cyprian is confident that if apprehended these would have confessed, and ultimately did so.

> It is the first title to victory to confess the Lord under the violence of the hands of the Gentiles. It is the second step to glory to be withdrawn by a cautious retirement, and to be reserved for the Lord. The former is a public, the latter is a private confession. The former overcomes the judge of this world; the latter, content with God as its judge, keeps a pure conscience in integrity of heart.[321]

Honestiores could not keep a low profile, and were probably specifically targeted for exile and confiscation of property, so many withdrew. Wealthier Christians had the means to maintain themselves in voluntary exile; the poor did not.[322] Cyprian rebuked

---

[314] *Laps.* 27 (CCSL 3:236) Et illa professio est denegantis, contestatio est christiani quod fuerat abnuentis: fecisse se dixit quidquid alius faciendo commisit. Cumque scriptum sit: 'Non potestis duobus dominis seruire', seruiuit saeculari domino, obtemperauit eius edicto, magis obaudiuit humano imperio quam Deo, citing Mt. 6:24.
[315] *Ep.* 55.13.2–15.1 (CCSL 3B:270–3).
[316] *Ep.* 55.14.1 (CCSL 3B:271–2) and Clarke, *Letters*, 3:187, nn. 61, 63.
[317] *Ep.* 55. 15.1 (CCSL 3B:272–3).
[318] *Ep.* 55.17.3 (CCSL 3B:276).
[319] *Ep.* 55.26.1 (CCSL 3B:288–9). See Murphy, 'Sin No More', 6–7.
[320] *Ep.* 7 (CCSL 3B:38–39).
[321] *Laps.* 3 (CCSL 3:222) Primus est uictoriae titulus gentilium manibus adprehensum Dominum confiteri; secundus ad gloriam gradus est cauta secessione subtractum Domino reseruari. Illa publica, haec priuata confessio est; ille iudicem saeculi uincit, hic contentus Deo suo iudice conscientiam puram cordis integritate custodit.
[322] Burns, *Cyprian the Bishop*, 18.

those who sacrificed because of their unwillingness to depart and leave their property.[323] Poorer Christians, the *humiliores*, including many of the lower clergy, had more hope of escaping attention if they remained, and Cyprian disapproved of clerical absence.[324] However, by lying low, some Christians such as tradespeople or merchants may have lost their livelihoods. Specifically, clergy were to provide for these steadfast poor, and minister to the needs of the confessors in prison.[325] However, they should avoid drawing undue attention to their ministry.[326]

Nevertheless, Cyprian warns the *stantes* to consider their deepest motives. If some repented for even considering purchasing *libelli*, how much more should those who did sin and yet deny wrongdoing recognize their guilt.

> Again, how much greater in faith and better in fear are those who, although bound by no crime of sacrifice or *libellus*, because they even thought of these things, confess to the priests of God with grief and simplicity, conscientiously perform penance, cast off the weight from their souls, seeking the healing remedy for even small and moderate wounds, knowing that it is written, 'God is not mocked'.[327]

God cannot be deceived, he knows the hearts of all, and the one who is privately ashamed of Christ is not a true Christian, even if his crime is not openly committed. To such Cyprian exhorts repentance.

Flight

Cyprian was criticized for his withdrawal at the onset of the Decian persecution. The Roman clergy, perhaps following Tertullian,[328] unsubtly reminded the Carthaginian clergy to be 'good shepherds' rather than hirelings, and noted that 'we do not abandon our brothers'.[329] Clarke notes the Roman clergy's use of the pointed terms *relinquere, fugere, desesere* and *relictio*; their own church was now bishop-less.[330] Cyprian, presumably because of his social prominence,[331] justified his withdrawal as a deescalation of violence.[332] Moreover, Cyprian effectively argues that his duty as a shepherd to care for his flock *required* his withdrawal, so he could continue his ministry and yet another community should not lose its bishop.[333] Although he is supportive of

---

[323] *Laps.* 10 (CCSL 3:226).
[324] *Epp.* 14.2.1; 34.4.1 (CCSL 3B:80, 169) and see Clarke, *Letters*, 2:160.
[325] *Epp.* 7.2; 12.2.2 (CCSL 3B:39, 70).
[326] *Ep.* 5.2 (CCSL 3B:27–8).
[327] Cyprian, *Laps.* 28 (CCSL 3:236–7) Denique quanto et fide maiore et timore meliore sunt qui, quamuis nullo sacrificii aut libelli facinore constricti, quoniam tamen de hoc uel cogitauerunt, hoc ipsum apud sacerdotes Dei dolenter et simpliciter confitentes exomologesin consientiae faciunt, animi sui pondus exponunt, salutarem medellam paruis licet et modicus uulneribus exquirunt, scientes scriptum esse: Deus non derideatur; citing Gal. 6:7.
[328] *Fug.* 11 (CCSL 2:1148–9).
[329] *Ep.* 8.1.1–2.2 (CCSL 3B:40–2) bonos pastores ... non deserentes fraternitatem ...
[330] Clarke, *Letters*, 1:208, n. 4.
[331] *Ep.* 8.1.1 (CCSL 3B:40) persona insignis and see Clarke, *Letters*, 1:208–9, n. 5.
[332] *Epp.* 7.1; *Ep.* 20.1.2; 43.4.2. (CCSL 3B:38; 106–7; 204).
[333] There is some evidence that bishops, as prominent Christians, were targeted early on; Fabian of Rome was dying in prison and Dionysius of Alexandria was being hunted.

flight,[334] he characteristically refers to his action as 'withdrawal'.[335] This might be a sign of defensiveness, or because *honestiores* typically accepted voluntary exile.

In defending his decision, Cyprian states he 'followed the directives and instructions of the Lord'.[336] and acknowledges 'the Lord who bade me withdraw',[337] determining that he would return if the Lord provided a sign.[338] Clarke, against Fahey, suggests 'directives and instructions' refers to Matthew 10:23,[339] although the connection seems tenuous. The link to Christ's directive seems much stronger in *De lapsis*: 'and the Lord himself commanded to withdraw and to flee in persecution and both taught that it should be done and did it'.[340] It seems, however, that Cyprian believed that the Lord had specifically directed his withdrawal through a dream or vision. This cognizance of a specific directive rather than a blanket mandate is supported by Cyprian's behaviour in the subsequent persecution, which Cyprian viewed as part of the tribulations of the end of the world rather than God's corrective discipline. Withdrawal was no longer appropriate: the bishop's duty was now to stay with his flock.[341]

Cyprian advises that those who are driven to flight should not fear this, with Christ as their companion.[342] To die in such a situation is to be martyred, but it should not be presumed. Reprieve and persecution are both providential, as is death due to plague.[343] There is no advocacy of flight in *De mortalitate*, because Cyprian did not regard it as legitimate to flee from suffering, *per se*, even for those who could afford to. For those already imprisoned, Cyprian presents martyrdom as something to be embraced and actually requested, and bishops must prepare their people for it.[344] God certainly helps his people in this situation, but not by allowing them escape; God helps them by his presence *with* them in persecution, as the Holy Spirit gives them what to speak.[345] This concords with Tertullian's conviction that the Spirit helps the confessor toward martyrdom, but Cyprian also assumes Christ's presence with the one forced to flee.

Adapting to context

Cyprian accounts for his evolving perspective in *Epistle* 55. From the beginning, he held that apostates must be removed from communion and not reconciled without evidence of repentance. It became more nuanced as he considered mitigating factors and the level of penitential commitment shown, as well as an increasing conviction of the approaching final judgement. Burns recognizes the tension which Cyprian

---

[334] *Ep.* 58.4 (CCSL 3C:324–5).
[335] *Secedo, recedo*; Clarke, *Letters*, 1:207.
[336] *Ep.* 20.1.2 (CCSL 3B:106) sicut Domini mandata instruunt.
[337] *Ep.* 16.4.1 (CCSL 3B:94) dominus, qui ut secederem iussit.
[338] *Ep.* 7.1 (CCSL 3B:38) dominus ostendere.
[339] Clarke, *Letters*, 1:307; Fahey, *Cyprian and the Bible*, 297.
[340] *Laps.* 10 (CCSL 3:226) Et ideo Dominus in persecutione secedere et fugere mandauit adque ut id fierit et docuit et fecit.
[341] *Ep.* 58:1–2 (CCSL 3C:319–23).
[342] *Ep.* 58.4 (CCSL 3C:324–5).
[343] *Laps*. 1 (CCSL 3:221), *Mort*. 17–19 (CCSL 3A:25–7).
[344] *Fort*. praef. 4 (CCSL 3:184–5).
[345] *Fort*. 10 (CCSL 3:198–201).

eventually resolved by situating true confession within the church and its adherents, including penitents and catechumens. 'Cyprian's identification of loyalty to the church as a necessary and effective form of fidelity to Christ helped him to solve the problem of the reconciliation of the lapsed without claiming the power to forgive a sin which had been committed against God or lowering the standard of membership in the church.'[346]

If Cyprian was influenced by Tertullian, it is not surprising that he starts off with an uncompromising approach to those who had sacrificed or purchased *libelli*, or that he recommended martyrdom as an immediate solution. But differences emerge early on. Cyprian was doubtless aware of Tertullian's criticism of clergy withdrawing, but he withdrew for a perceived legitimate and overriding reason. Also, Cyprian was insistent on the importance of formal penance in dealing with the lapsed, a position much more congruent with *De paenitentia* than *De pudicitia*. Tertullian's disgust with reconciliation of adulterers prompted him to write the latter treatise, whereas Cyprian uses the reconciliation of adulterers as a precedent for readmission of the lapsed. Fundamentally, the difference between the two attitudes relates to their different perceptions of the role of the church, specifically the bishop, in granting absolution. Cyprian never wavers from the requirement to confess Christ, or that confession reverses denial, but it is his concept of what that confession means that expands and develops in the context of confession within the church. He is always concerned with motive.

Cyprian's more nuanced response to *stantes, lapsi, libellatici* and voluntary exiles, I suggest, also reflects pragmatism. Cyprian experienced persecution and its range of responses to a greater degree than Tertullian and felt personally responsible for his flock. Tertullian writes as if from a distance; persecution in his time was likely more sporadic than he infers, except perhaps under Severus. Cyprian was in the middle of the greatest apostasy in the history of the church. To employ a rigorist, uncompromising approach would have resulted in the church being decimated. Cyprian's ecclesiology provides the justification for his pragmatic solution; by reconciling the lapsed to the church upon evidence of their penitence, they return to a condition in which they *may* be saved.

The persecuted church

Clement, Origen and Tertullian write as individuals, but Cyprian writes as bishop on behalf of his church. The church is central to Cyprian's theology; the church is the people of God and he, as bishop, is the conduit between God and his people.[347] Cyprian held that to reject the bishop's authority is to reject the laws and the gospel of God – not social mores or responsibilities. The affliction of the church, rather than being an assault on a patron's honour, was the wounding of a shepherd along with his flock, a clear biblical metaphor.[348] For this reason Cyprian takes the responsibility of steering his flock through the persecution crisis very seriously.

---

[346] Burns, 'Confessing the Church', 347.
[347] Burns, *Cyprian the Bishop*, chs 2, 5.
[348] *Laps.* 4 (CCSL 3:222–3).

Who belongs in the ark?

Cyprian's view of the church's constituency develops through the persecution period as he struggles with the tension between unity and purity. In *De lapsis,* the church bears collective responsibility for the tragedy,[349] while individual responses bringing glory or shame on Christ's body.[350] Cyprian subsequently moves to embrace committed catechumens and penitents into an ecclesial penumbra; peace could be granted on their deathbeds, because of their demonstrated commitment to a church to which they were adherent.[351]

Carthaginian Christians contributed to a common fund for the support of clergy, the poor, widows, the ransoming of captives and the care of confessors in prison.[352] Confessors and the 'meritorious poor', indigent because of their stand for Christ, were to be particularly supported.[353] The penitents' contribution to this fund demonstrated their commitment to Christ and the church.[354] The church also sheltered bishops and other fugitives of persecution. Some of the *sacrificiati* did this,[355] and as Burns notes, this carried weight in the decision to readmit such penitent lapsed.[356] Persecution thus upended the social fabric and unity of the church; the poorer *stantes* and the *confessores* exhibited the right response to persecution, while many of the more prominent members who should have been the pillars of the church were now outside it.

Strict insistence on the purity of the church, as Tertullian would have it, would result in permanent excommunication of all lapsed.[357] Without hope of eventual reconciliation, Cyprian feared the lapsed would turn to heresy or abandon Christ altogether. For Cyprian, heresy and schism were an even greater threat to the church than persecution. Persecution brought needed discipline to the church, whereas heresy subverts the faith, corrupts the church and divides its unity.[358] Premature reconciliation of the lapsed was effectively heresy, a further persecution, even more harmful than the first, because it threatened both the unity and purity of the church.[359] Attaining an appropriate balance was the genius of his episcopate.

> We must remain mindful of the mercies of God as we so balance the scales of justice in our government of the Church that to sinners, we do indeed exhibit the full censure of our condemnation but without at the same time depriving them of the medicine of God's compassion and clemency, which enables the wounded to be cured and the fallen to get back up again on their feet.[360]

---

[349] *Laps.* 5 (CCSL 3:223).
[350] *Laps.* 2 (CCSL 3:221–2).
[351] *Ep.* 20.3.2; Burns, 'Confessing the Church', 341 n. 21.
[352] *Epp.* 5.1.2, 77.3.2, 78.3.1, 79.1.1 (CCSL 3B:27; 3C:620, 623, 624).
[353] Clarke, *Letters,* 1:185–6 n. 8.
[354] *Epp.* 21.2.2, 4.1; 33.2.1 (CCSL 3B:112–4; 165) *Laps.* 35 (CCSL 3:241).
[355] *Epp.* 21.2.2; 55.13.2 (CCSL 3B:112–3; 270–1).
[356] J. Patout Burns, 'The Role of Social Structures in Cyprian's Response to the Decian Persecution', *StPatr* 31 (1997), 260–272, at 265.
[357] *Pud.* 5; 9.10; 19.25–26; 21 (2:1287–89; 1297–8; 1323; 1326–28).
[358] *Unit.* 1, 3 (CCSL 3:249–51).
[359] *Laps.* 16 (CCSL 3:229–30).
[360] *Ep.* 68.1.2 (CCSL 3C:464) qui diuinam clementiam cogitantes et gubernandae ecclesiae libram tenentes sic censuram uigoris peccatoribus exhibemus, ut tamen lapsis erigendis et curandis uulneratis bonitatis et misericordiae diuinae medicinam non denegemus.

Cyprian held that penance, correctly performed in and through the church, *was* efficacious in restoring the sinner.[361] Forgiveness was like healing, which the bishop, as healer, must minister to the penitent Christian.[362] Distinctively, it was not the penitence itself which provided the restoration, but the bishop's readmission of the penitent following suitable demonstration of repentance, just as the catechumen was baptized after demonstration of repentance and a changed life. Cyprian held that only the bishop's hands could bestow the Spirit. To put on Christ was to receive the Spirit, which could only happen within the true church, as vested in the episcopate.[363] The purpose of restoration was to bring the sinner back to the ark of the church, within which forgiveness and salvation was once again possible.

Without restoration to the church, the sinner had no hope of forgiveness at the final judgement.[364] Just as God forgave sins through the church-mediated ritual of baptism, so also the sinner could receive forgiveness again through the church-mediated ritual of penance, by demonstration of fidelity to Christ in a new way.[365] The penitent lapsed had proven their fidelity to Christ by persevering in fidelity to his church.[366] Although ultimately, only God could forgive sin, read the heart and judge true penitence, the bishop and clergy could act, in consultation with the laity and confessors, to make a careful judgement on externals in order to grant the peace of the church.[367]

Acceptance back into the church means being 'kept for the Lord', who will come and judge those whom he finds within the church.[368] Burns argues that Cyprian believed loyalty to the church could win forgiveness for apostates.[369] More so, for Cyprian, loyalty to the church was loyalty *to Christ*. As Bévenot argues, this places the reconciled penitent on the same level as other Christians; the forgiveness is real and it is present, not deferred until the judgement, any more than is the case for the rest of the members of the church.[370] I agree with Bévenot that Cyprian believed episcopal forgiveness was truly efficacious,[371] otherwise Cyprian's arguments and actions make little sense. Bévenot's argument turns on the grammar of the citation of Matthew 16:19 as Cyprian's way of expressing the future; their sins should, i.e. *will* be loosed, *solvi autem possent*.[372]

---

[361] *Epp.* 55.26.2; 59.13–14 (CCSL 3B:289; 3C:357–63); Murphy, 'Sin No More', 6.

[362] *Ep.* 17.1.1; *Ep.* 43.2.2; *Ep.* 68.1.2, 4.2; (CCSL 3B:96, 3B:202, 3C:463–4, 467) The priest may employ painful remedies, *Laps.* 14 (CCSL 3:228) Failure to repent properly is to reject healing and to bring harm; Laps. 15 (CCSL 3:228–9). Almsgiving can bring healing, *Laps.* 35–36 (CCSL 3:240–2) *Eleem.* 3 (CCSL 3A:56).

[363] *Epp.* 69.2 (CCSL 3C:471–3), 75.7 (CCSL 3C:587–9) and see Mk 10:16; Acts 8:18; 9:17; 1 Tim. 5:22; 2 Tim. 1:6; Heb. 6:1–2; *Unit.* 6 (CCSL 3:253–4).

[364] *Ep.* 57.1.1, 3.3, 4.3–5.2 (CCSL 3B:301, 305, 306–10), but see Burns, *Cyprian the Bishop*, 40, 70–1.

[365] Burns, 'Confessing the Church', 347; Sutcliffe, 'Learning Not to Sin'.

[366] Burns, 'Confessing the Church', 345.

[367] *Ep.* 55.20.3 (CCSL 3B:279–80).

[368] *Ep.* 55.29.2 (CCSL 3B:294) in ipsa domino reseruari,.

[369] Burns, 'Confessing the Church', 338; Bévenot, 'Sacrament of Penance', 193–4 esp. nn. 70, 212.

[370] Bévenot, 'Sacrament of Penance', 202–4.

[371] *Ep.* 57.1.1. (CCSL 3B:301) Bévenot, 'Sacrament of Penance', 210–11. To be clear, this only applies to those who have adequately demonstrated their repentance.

[372] Bévenot, 'Sacrament of Penance', 210–11. Clarke, *Letters,* 3:218 n. 8, agrees.

In *De lapsis*, Cyprian affirms, 'He <u>is able to</u> grant indulgence, he <u>is able to</u> turn aside his sentence, he <u>is able to</u> gently pardon the penitent, the worker, the beseecher ...'[373]

Tertullian was content to leave apostates outside the church in the knowledge that God would ultimately and fairly judge. Cyprian held that Christ comes to judge the church, and both the catechumenate and *exomologesis* are about being in the church.[374]

Cyprian and apology

Cyprian wrote one extant 'apology': *Ad Demetrianum*. Demetrianus contended that the wars, famine, pestilence currently plaguing the world must be imputed to the Christians, because they did not worship the gods.[375] But he is ignorant of the imminent day of judgement as the censure of an indignant God. 'For these things happen not, as your false complaining and ignorant inexperience of the truth asserts and repeats, because your gods are not worshipped by us, but because God is not worshipped by you.'[376]

Cyprian raises the classic apologists' challenge:[377] either to be a Christian is a crime, or it is not. If it is a crime, one ought to be tortured for denying it, but Christians are tortured when they confess.[378] Cyprian wants Demetrianus to realize the trouble he is in, because reality is different from his perception. Not only are Christians strengthened rather than defeated in persecution, but they submit to it because their avenging will come from God, no less.[379]

> This is why none of us, when apprehended, resists, nor avenges himself against your unjust violence ... the innocent yield to the guilty, the harmless yield to punishments and tortures, sure and confident that whatsoever we suffer will not remain unavenged and that as great as the injustice of the persecution so will be the justice and the weightiness of the vengeance ...[380]

Cyprian understands that persecution and martyrdoms, which are inevitable, occur in continuity with God's people through the ages.[381] But he turns the question of

---

[373] *Laps.* 36 (CCSL 3:241) *Potest* ille indulgentiam dare, sententiam suam potest ille deflectare. Paenitenti, operanti, roganti potest clementer ignoscere ... (my emphases).

[374] For parallels between the catechumenate and penance see Ruth Sutcliffe, 'Learning Not to Sin: Repentance in Tertullian and Cyprian', *Colloquium* 53, no. 1 (2021), 73–97.

[375] See also Tertullian, *Nat.* 1.9; *Apol.* 40–41 (CCSL 1:22–4; 153–6). Absent from earlier apologists, given the prosperous and peaceful Antonine age.

[376] *Dem.* 5 (CCSL 3A:37) Non enim, sicut tua falsa querimonia et inperitia ueritatis ignara iactat et clamitat, ista accidunt, quod dii uestri a nobis non colantur, sed quod a uobis non colatur Deus.

[377] Athenagoras, *Embassy* 1–2 (PG 6:889–96); Theophilus, *To Autolycus* 1.1 (PG 6:1023–5); Justin 1 *Apol.* 4, 7 (PG 6:332–6, 357) *Octavius* 28 (CSEL 2:40–42).

[378] *Dem.* 13 (CCSL 3A:42–43).

[379] *Dem.* 16 (CCSL 3A:44) Laedere seruos Dei et Christi persecutionibus tuis desine quos laesos ultio diuina defendit.

[380] *Dem.* 17 (CCSL 3A:44–5) Inde est enim quod et nemo nostrum quando adprehenditur reluctatur nec se aduersus iniustam uiolentiam uestram ... Innocentes nocentibus cedunt, insontes poenis et cruciatibus acquiescunt certi et fidentes quod inultum non remaneat quodcumque perpetimur quantoque maior fuerit persecutionis iniuria tanto et iustior fiat et grauior pro persecutione uindicta.

[381] *Fort.* 11 (CCSL 3:210–11) martyrum populum non posse numerari.

superiority and dominance around; it is not the Christians who drag the world down, but the world itself is decaying and dying, and will ultimately perish while Christianity endures. Christians are not prostrated by adversity, but rather proved and strengthened; this Cyprian attributed directly to their patience.[382]

Presenting this precis of his diogmology to a pagan persecutor would have seemed a counterintuitive strategy in the second century, and even beyond. In fact, Sage, following Lactantius' assessment, considers Cyprian's use of 'Christian content and meaning' in his apology as 'a weakness', suggesting it was directed at Christians rather than pagans.[383] Lactantius believes that Demetrianus should have been refuted by citing philosophers and historians, rather than by Scripture.[384] But, as Murphy has shown, Cyprian uses fulfilment of Old Testament prophecy to demonstrate the veracity of Scripture.[385] Like Tertullian, Cyprian's focus is on appealing to individual persecutors to look to true salvation while there is still time.[386] While he uses the standard apologetic arguments, Cyprian's goal is not so much to stop persecution as to vindicate Christians of the charges against them and to save Demetrianus and other persecutors. In this he is more the protégé of Tertullian than an imitator of the second-century apologists. Cyprian does not think that persecution will cease before the *parousia*; how can it, while the world opposes the church, which it will always do? Cyprian wants Demetrianus to desist from his persecution because Demetrianus is doomed unless he ceases to fight against God's inevitable victory. Thus, Cyprian's diogmology allows him to accept the inevitability and necessity of persecution, its end in God's own timing, in tension with an appeal to persecutors to consider their own standing before God and change sides in the cosmic conflict.

Conclusions

Cyprian's diogmology is practical, pastoral, and reflects the bidirectional influence of his ecclesiology. His appreciation of the origin, reason, and *telos* of persecution largely mirror Tertullian's, his distinctive contribution being to the individual and corporate response to persecution, based on his wider definition of confession.

Cyprian accepts that God is good and providentially in control, bringing persecution and other trials for his good purposes. Cyprian sees the whole of life as a battle with the Devil, however; the cosmic conflict is not entirely focused on verbal confession and martyrdom. Therefore, one who confesses Christ and endures to the end need not meet that end as a martyr, but as one who perishes in prison, or remains faithful in flight, or as one of the *stantes,* or one who dies of plague while ministering to others. Crowns also await those who persevere in good works. The Devil attacks Christians in all aspects of life but is under God's restraint; we freely choose whom we will follow. This

---

[382] *Dem.* 18–19 (CCSL 3A:45–6).
[383] Sage, *Cyprian*, 279, 359, ref. Lactantius, *Inst.* 5.1 (CSEL 19:402–3).
[384] Lactantius, *Inst.* 5.4 (CSEL 19:412).
[385] Murphy, *Bishop*, 59–60; as did Origen.
[386] *Dem.* 23, 25 (CCSL 3A:48–51).

is a cosmic conflict, playing out against those who bear Christ's name, whom the world hates as it did Christ himself. Persecution is an inevitable aspect of this. It is expected, purposeful, and will increase as the world's end approaches, a fact that Cyprian is unafraid to convey to persecutors themselves. The Christian hope entails this conflict, in which they participate with Christ and share his victory. It is this fight, in all its everyday and final manifestations, for which Cyprian as bishop prepares his Christian soldiers.

Cyprian perceives a real union of the Christian with Christ, through the church, in all aspects of the struggle. This is why it is necessary to be within the ark of the church, sustained by the eucharist and empowered by the Holy Spirit, equipping that only the true church can provide. Within this sphere, endurance to the end can take many forms, as can confession. Although martyrdom is desirable, as a second baptism and means of obtaining a sure crown, the one who is not martyred must not feel disappointed. There are many ways to win a crown, with imminent reward awaiting all faithful Christians.

Cyprian therefore exhorts his flock to imitate Christ's patient endurance in all of life, not just as a disciplinary means to martyrdom. Whether they die in prison, suffer deprivation as a *stantes* or in flight, or die from plague, all are under God's good providence. Therefore, Cyprian can consider ways of avoiding martyrdom as valid, but not quite for the same reasons as the Alexandrians, with their *telos* of *theosis*. Like Tertullian, Cyprian perceives this life alone as the chance to secure salvation. There must be no compromise with the Devil's world, and Cyprian is very concerned with motive, whilst appreciating the diversity of circumstances in which confession may be secured.

6

Summa diogmologica

Everyone therefore who shall confess me before men, I will also confess him before my Father who is in heaven. But whoever shall deny me before men, I will also deny him before my Father who is in heaven.

Jesus, Matthew 10:32–33

The preceding chapters examine how Clement, Origen, Tertullian and Cyprian each understood, theologically, the experience of suffering for the faith. In this final chapter, I compare their ideas in relation to each other, identifying and explaining the common framework across their diverse writings, noting where they diverge and why, and examining their reception of Scripture. The benchmark passages identified in Chapter 1 will provide a framework for this comparative analysis. Subsequently, I will discuss this project's contribution to some supplementary questions. Firstly, I will demonstrate that a diogmological framework can bring together seemingly disparate perspectives: that of a church engaged in cosmic conflict versus a church undergoing patient growth. Secondly, I will offer a diogmological perspective on early Christian social identity. In revisiting the question of the fathers' alleged fabrication of the persecution experience I will argue that their theologies of persecution were intended to be formative of Christian identity. Thirdly, I will revisit the issue of 'voluntary martyrdom' through a diogmological lens.

From the examination of their individual theologies of persecution, it is evident that these third-century fathers held to a broadly consistent theology of persecution across their diverse writings. This common diogmology has the following elements:

1. The one good God is in providential control of persecution, or at least its outcomes.
2. The Devil opposes God and draws humans away into idolatry, with humans freely choosing to follow God or the Devil. Persecutors and apostate Christians have succumbed to the Devil's influence.
3. Persecution is the locus of cosmic conflict between God and the Devil, in which those who confess Christ's name inevitably suffer with him, but also share his victory.
4. God uses persecution to shape character and endurance in this life, with the promise of reward in the next.
5. Therefore, Christians must stand fast and confess the name they bear.

This consistency of thought is significant in light of the four fathers' different intellectual and social backgrounds and their diverse theological perspectives. The fathers are broadly consistent, but they are not uniform. Their differences can be attributed primarily to differences in foundational theology, two aspects in particular. Firstly, they vary in their understanding of the relationship between God's goodness and his providence in persecution. Secondly, they vary in their views of eschatology and with respect to the *telos* of persecution.

The congruence and divergence of their persecution theologies is correlated to their use of Scripture, a conclusion I will expand on below. Where their conclusions agree, they are informed by congruent use of Scripture. Where they are most divergent in their diogmology, they use different Scriptures, and they interpret common passages differently. This observation is interesting within the wider discussion of the relationship between patristic exegesis and theology.

The fathers' theologies of persecution interact with their broader theological constructions and their lived experiences. The relationship is clearly bidirectional. Holding to a theology of one good God in providential control of creation precludes a dualistic explanation of evil and persecution. Persecution, in turn, challenges simplistic ideas of how such a God works for 'good'. Persecution is an experience that demands meaning if it is to be endured; what is its reason? What is its *telos*? Christology, soteriology and eschatology must answer these questions in order for Christian faith to be sustained in the face of this challenge. Persecution is no mere theoretical problem, but a lived experience to which individuals and the church as a community must respond appropriately. The challenge of this experience demands answers from theology, and theology in turn informs praxis.

Five diogmological questions

The method employed in this study utilizes a theological framework provided by five questions to facilitate exploring the diogmology of the four fathers. It has the advantage of allowing a comprehensive summary of the position of each father, and highlights both their commonalities and distinctives.

The origin of persecution

The first question, concerning the provenance of persecution, raises questions of divine goodness and providence and the restraint which God exerts over evils. All four fathers reject dualism; there is no dichotomy within the Christian God, nor is the Devil a deity, but is firmly under God's restraint. If, then, there is one God, and if he is regarded as in control of his creation, and if he is good, the question arises: where does persecution come from? How does it relate to his providence? This is the most fundamental diogmological consideration because it influences all other aspects. There are three non-negotiable principles on which each of the fathers agree (see Figure 6.1).

1. The one God is indeed good, and he is in control; nothing happens apart from him.
2. The Devil, who fell by his own free will, opposes God and seeks to draw humans away from God into idolatry.
3. Humans freely choose whether to follow God or the Devil; they take one of two sides in the conflict.

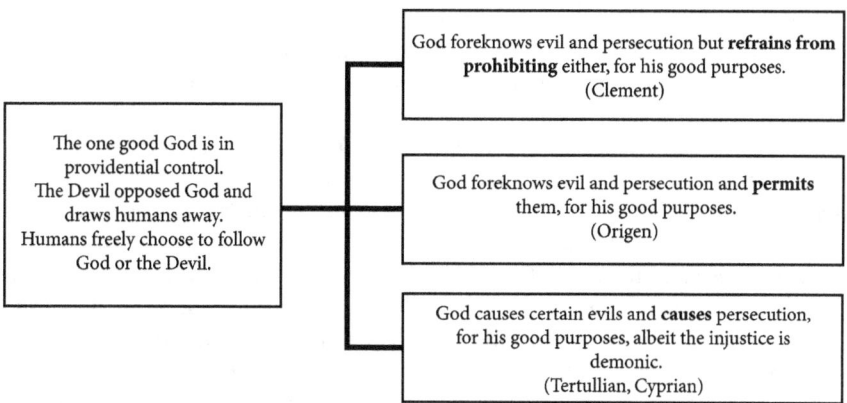

Figure 6.1 Diogmology question 1

Both Alexandrians, perhaps due to Platonist influence, or at least using Platonist vocabulary, understand God's 'goodness' ontologically. He *is* goodness and can only do 'good'. There is some ambiguity as to whether Clement's negative view of persecution drives his view of God's non-permission of it, or vice versa. Clement denies that God wills persecution, or actively brings it about. He only declines to prohibit it. God's providence works *around* persecution to bring good ends. Clement attempts no explanation for how providence can be so detached from an experience which it nevertheless uses for good. His focus is in on outcomes. This ambiguity undoubtedly helps Clement, in his schema of gnostic progress, to see martyrdom as only one path to perfection. It is one outcome and expression of confession, and an individual path. Being chosen for it is God's providential determination for the relative few.

Origen also begins with God's intrinsic goodness, but sees evil as a parasite, a result of departure from good, a negative element that will ultimately be removed from creation. Yet it does not happen 'apart from' God, who created this world of embodiment as the best arena for dealing with it. Origen's concept of God's goodness is permissive of persecution. God foreknows evil and persecution and permits them for his purposes. This means that Origen sees more of God's direct hand in persecution than Clement and is more open to the benefits of martyrdom. For Origen, God's providence works *with* persecution.

Tertullian and Cyprian attribute persecution to the ordination and will of God, for good purposes and good outcomes. Cyprian looks for meaning in persecution and suffering, concluding God uses it for the chastisement and testing of the church and as prelude to the world's end. Tertullian is explicit; persecution is good, because God has ordained it as the arena for cosmic conflict, the means of battle with and victory over the Devil. Tertullian's concept of the goodness of the one God requires it: 'God is not otherwise wholly good than as the rival of evil'.[1] God ordained persecution as the means of conflict with, and destruction of, the Devil, so it must be good. Certainly, the injustice of persecution is demonic, and necessary to the conflict, trial, and ultimate victory, yet even that is under God's restraint. Tertullian is convinced that God's providence works *in and through* persecution. For this reason, he sees persecution as inevitable, it being the grounds of confession, and its climax as martyrdom. God's providence, through the Holy Spirit, directs Christians toward martyrdom and its rewards.

This is the first major area of diogmological divergence among the four, which is significant for two reasons. Firstly, they each approach the question of God's aetiological relationship to persecution from the standpoint of their broader theological frameworks, their understanding of what God's goodness means in the present economy. Secondly, the four fathers each use Scripture differently in addressing this issue. They certainly refer to Scripture in their discussions of God's goodness and providence, the Devil's work, and the basis of persecution, but their arguments are not derived from exegesis. Rather, I propose that they interpret Scripture from the perspective of their existing theological frameworks. There are only two 'benchmark' passages, Matthew 5:44–45 and Matthew 10:28–31, which they consistently cite with respect to providence, and they are not always applied in the context of persecution.

In Matthew 5:44–45, Jesus mandates love for one's enemies and prayer for one's persecutors, in imitation of the God who providentially provides sun and rain for good and evil alike. Clement quotes 'love your enemies' in the context of the inevitability of persecution,[2] but also in describing the qualities of the gnostic.[3] Origen, likewise, uses the passage to emphasize imitation of God in his love for all his creatures.[4] Tertullian also uses it to demonstrate God's impartial goodness,[5] Cyprian to exhort his readers to patiently imitate it.[6]

In Matthew 10:28–31, Jesus assures his disciples of God's oversight, given his knowledge of falling sparrows and the hairs on one's head. Clement does not utilize this passage, but Origen uses it to prove that all things, good and evil, come under God's providence, including persecution.[7] For Tertullian, it provides a basis for asserting that it is God's will whether Christians suffer persecution or not in a given situation,[8]

---

[1] *Marc.* 1.26.5 (CCSL 1:470) qui non alias plane bonus sit, nisi mali aemulus.
[2] *Strom.* 4.14.95 (SC 463:214–16).
[3] *Strom.* 7.14.84.5 (SC 428:260) εὔχεσθαι ὑπὲρ τῶν ἐχθρῶν παραγγείλαντα is a paraphrase.
[4] *Comm. Jo.* 20.17.147–8; 20.33.292; 20.34.309 (SC 290:228, 300, 308).
[5] *Marc.* 1.23.3–4; 4.36.1–3 (CCSL 1:465, 643–4).
[6] *Pat.* 4–5 (CCSL 3A:119–21).
[7] *Princ.* 3.2.7 (SC 268:180–2) *Cels.* 8.70 (SC 150:336–8).
[8] *Fug.* 3.2 (CCSL 2:1139).

and how the Devil is permitted or restrained accordingly.[9] Cyprian insists that no event, of small or great significance, occurs without God's providence.[10]

On what basis then, do the fathers frame their answers to the first question, if not from direct scriptural exegesis? Clement's arguments for the goodness of God in *Paedagogos* 1.8 are largely based on his own thoughts, interwoven with a mixture of Old Testament texts, Sirach and Plato, although he does invoke Matthew 5:44-45 and the gospel of John. He sets out what to him is a logical explanation of how a good God *necessarily* acts, bolstering his argument from Scripture. Clement never really wrestles with the problem of how God's providence can inevitably achieve good ends from something he merely abstains from preventing; he simply accepts that this is so. Origen's discussion of God's nature in *De principiis* 1.1 assumes the readers' familiarity with Scripture as the basis for his arguments but provides few citations. His direct use of Scripture (including Matt 5:44-45) is more extensive in his discussion of God the Creator being the same as the Father, in 2.4. When he takes up the subject of God's goodness in 2.5 it is as a polemic against a dualistic distinction between Old and New Testament 'versions' of God, and he draws on a broad scriptural platform. His conclusion to Book 2, nevertheless, is that he has demonstrated from Scripture that God, the Creator of all things, is good, and just, and all-powerful.[11]

Tertullian's use of Scripture depends on his audience, their scriptural literacy, and his polemical objectives. His case for the goodness and justice of the one Creator God, against the views of the biblically literate Marcion, is saturated with biblical references.[12] In his polemic against Hermogenes, Tertullian argues primarily through logic that good and evil must both be ascribed to God,[13] turning Hermogenes' arguments against him, but with little reference to Scripture. Cyprian has no real occasion to justify what he appears to take for granted, that God is good. This assumption underpins his arguments for God's providential control and his right to direct evil and persecution as he sees fit.

The fathers exhibit a consistent understanding of the role of the Devil and his demons, in fostering idolatry and the persecution that defends it. Their demonology is common to early Christian tradition.[14] It may be supported by scriptural quotations in some contexts,[15] but is also often referred to pagan traditions.[16] Their audience is largely, but not solely, determinative of the details of their discussion of the demonic.

There is thus no well-developed, common exegetical basis for the fathers' answers to the first diogmological question. They use Scripture diversely, and not necessarily to derive their individual arguments. The fathers needed, above all, to absolve God from

---

[9] *Fug.* 2.6 (CCSL 2:1138).
[10] *Ep.* 59.5.2 (CCSL 3C:345).
[11] *Princ.* 2.9.6 (SC 252:364).
[12] E.g. nine in *Marc.* 4.36 (CCSL 1:643-4).
[13] *Herm.* 16 (CCSL 1:410).
[14] Everett Ferguson, 'Demonology of the Early Christian World', in *Lectures presented at the University of Mississippi Feb 1980*, Symposium series vol. 12 (Lewiston NY: Edwin Mellen, 1984), 109-15.
[15] E.g. Origen, *De Principiis* 3.2 (Behr 2:380-98); Tertullian, *Marc.* 5.17-18 (CCSL 1:714-720) and *De fuga*; Cyprian, *Zel. liv.*
[16] Origen, *Cels.* 7.69; 8.33, 8.60-63 (SC 150:174-6; 246; 310-18). Clement, *Protr.* 4 (SC 2:106-127).

the generation of sin, whilst preserving his providential rule. For the Alexandrians, the ultimate solution to evil lies in a gradual, progressive return to the good. In its articulation, they employ vocabulary and concepts from philosophy to articulate a 'deeper' meaning of Scripture. They also rely on much typological and allegorical interpretation, especially of passages concerning the *parousia*, judgement, and hell. In contrast, the Carthaginians foresee a decisive intervention of God at a future point in time, bringing final justice and recompense,[17] a position more readily supported by direct scriptural citations. I propose that in this area of divergence, the fathers' theology is driving their exegesis and their respective views on God's role in persecution follow logically from each theological position.

The reason for persecution

The second diogmological question addresses the purposefulness of and basis for persecution, its *raison d'être*. Regardless of whether God's providence works around, within or through persecution, it cannot be random; it must be purposeful at least in outcome. This purpose must relate to Scripture's testimony that persecution is inevitable. Each of the fathers asserts that God foreknew that persecution would occur and prepared his people for it. Each affirms that persecution is the lot of those who confess the name of Christ. This confluence from their disparate positions on God's causal relationship with persecution, into the common ground of the reason for it, is noteworthy (see Figure 6.2). Significantly, their convergence on this point is marked by a conjunction of consistent exegesis and interpretation of a common body of Scripture.

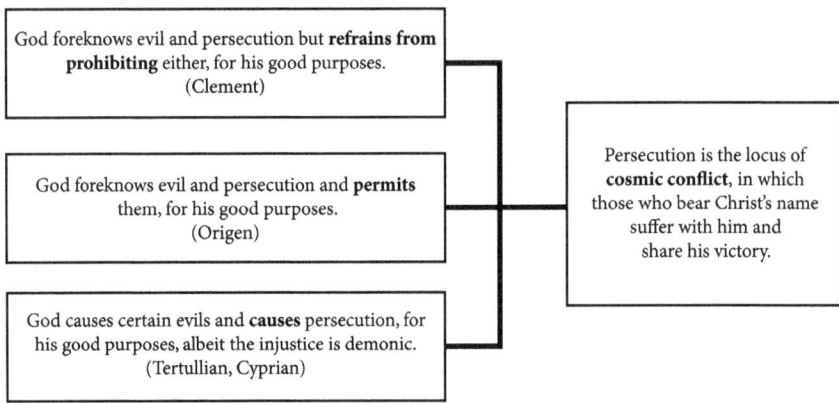

Figure 6.2 Diogmology question 2

The fathers' conviction of the inevitability of persecution is based on four lines of evidence, each derived from the Scriptures:

---

[17] Lautaro Roig Lanzillotta, 'Greek Philosophy and the Problem of Evil in Clement of Alexandria and Origen', *Estudios griegos e indoeuropeos* 23 (2013), 207–23, at 214, 216, 223.

1. Persecution was predicted by God, who is omniscient and never lies.
2. Christians, as God's people, are persecuted in continuity with the prophets and apostles.
3. Jesus pronounces the persecuted to be blessed.
4. Jesus prepared his followers for persecution.

The four fathers are comparable in their use of 'benchmark' passages concerning persecution's inevitability. These passages, predominantly from Matthew (and/or cognates in Mark and Luke), are also used to inform the appropriate Christian response to persecution. All four draw extensively on Matthew 5:10-12 regarding the blessedness of those persecuted for righteousness' sake, on Christ's account – for so the prophets were persecuted before them. Christ's missionary discourse in Matthew 10 is a benchmark pericope for persecution's inevitability, its Christocentricity and Jesus' preparation of his followers for it. Origen, Tertullian and Cyprian repeatedly cite and allude to its passages on opposition from authorities, the Holy Spirit's aid, family betrayal, the servant following the master, the need to fear God not men, God's providential care, the necessity of confessing and not denying Christ, of preferring nothing in this life to him, taking up the cross to follow him, and the anticipation of reward.

Clement's use of Matthew 10, in contrast, is sparse. The exception is his detailed exegesis of verses 32-33, reciprocal acknowledgement and denial of Christ, which for Clement is central to his idea of being 'in' Christ.[18] He also cites verse 23, Christ's instruction to flee persecution, in support of his contention that flight is preferable to abetting the persecutors' sin.[19] Like the others, Clement considers persecution unavoidable, but he situates this inevitability in God's foreknowledge, which he insists does not equate to causality.[20]

Origen often cites or alludes to Matthew 10, sometimes departing from what could be considered the most straightforward reading of the text. His most extensive use of the discourse is in the *Exhortation to Martyrdom*, which also draws on a wide range of Old and New Testament and Apocryphal texts. Origen additionally emphasizes the inevitability of persecution, especially in his *Exhortation*, and stresses the continuity of experience with persecuted prophets and apostles. Origen links the persecution of Christians with that of Christ; Christ is persecuted in the believer and Christians are united with Christ in his suffering and vindication.[21]

---

[18] Strom. 4.9.72–75 (SC 463:174–180).
[19] Strom. 4.10.76.1–2 (SC 463:180).
[20] Strom. 4.11.78.1–2 (SC 463:184).
[21] This mirrors the conclusions of Wesley Thomas Davey, 'Sight in the Tempest: Suffering as Participation with Christ in the Pauline Corpus', (PhD diss., SE Baptist Theological Seminary, 2016), who determines that Paul identifies suffering as derivative from union with Christ and hence a sharing in Christ's own suffering, culminating eschatologically. Because Christ suffered for his people, they in turn suffer with him, following his example. It also accords with the identification of the theme of imitation of Christ in early exhortations to martyrdom, by Candida R. Moss, *The Other Christs: Imitating Jesus in Ancient Christian Ideologies of Martyrdom* (Oxford: University Press, 2010). See also Paul Hartog, 'Themes and Intertextualities in Pre-Nicene Exhortations to Martyrdom', in *The Wiley Blackwell Companion to Christian Martyrdom*, ed. Paul Middleton (West Sussex UK: John Wiley & Sons, 2020), 102–119, at 104 and Jane D. McLarty, 'Early Christian Theologies of Martyrdom', in the same volume, 120–34, at 126–7.

Tertullian regularly applies the Matthew 10 missionary discourse throughout his corpus and offers a systematic exegesis in *Scorpiace*.[22] Of the four fathers, Tertullian most clearly and specifically identifies persecution as the battleground between Christ and the Devil. Tertullian binds the command to confess Christ to an expectation of persecution and martyrdom. By this, the one 'in Christ' participates in the Devil's defeat.[23] In one of his infrequent concurrences with Clement, Tertullian affirms the contrast between confessing 'in' Christ but denying him; the one who denies is not 'in' Christ.[24] Cyprian diverges from Tertullian in recognizing that the cosmic conflict applies equally in all life's difficulties and suffering, in which the Christian patiently endures to the end. Crowns are available for many forms of demonstrating allegiance to Christ, within the context of his church. Thus, Cyprian's distinctive perspective is entwined with his ecclesiology; true confession and martyrdom are only possible within the church, which is Cyprian's equivalent to confession 'in Christ'. Christ suffers in the martyr, even as the martyr is 'in Christ', sustained by eucharistic communion and aided by the Holy Spirit bestowed at baptism.

Overall, despite having different emphases, the fathers largely exegete the same body of Scripture in similar ways. They each recognize a fundamental conflict between the people of Christ and the people of the Devil. Conflict on earth reflects a greater cosmic battle. This agreement is noteworthy, because it occurs despite their differing views on whether persecution is ordained by God. They agree that the basis for persecution is that Christians bear and confess the name of Christ. The name represents their very identity; it is no mere superficial allegiance. All four fathers repeatedly draw on the reciprocal confession/denial passages: Matthew 10:32–33; Mark 8:38; Luke 9:26 and Luke 12:8–9. The one who bears the name of Christ must take up his cross and follow him and must lay down his life.

Additional 'benchmark' passages from 1 Peter are cited extensively and consistently by the fathers in their insistence on being persecuted for the name, not for any misdeeds. The primary responsibility of a Christian is to witness to Christ by confession, identifying with him, and consequently attracting the hatred of the world which opposed him. This required consistency of life, so as not to shame the name, in turn informs their considerations of the appropriate response to persecution.

The good *telos* of persecution

Each of the fathers see a present, positive benefit of trials, for development of Christian character and personal discipline. However, they do not look to this life for the ultimate answers to evil, suffering and persecution; they know their vindication will be in the next life. Such good as may be associated with persecution must relate to its *telos*. The fathers also looked to the eschatological *telos* for a reconciliation of the injustice of persecution with the ultimate justice of God. By identifying the *telos* of persecution and suffering for Christ, we see both the good which results from persecution, and

---

[22] *Scorp*. 9–11 (CCSL 2:1084–92).
[23] *Scorp*. 6.1 (CCSL 2:1079).
[24] *Scorp*. 9.9–11 (CCSL 2:1085–6).

beyond that to the potential good of persecution itself. At the most fundamental level they agree that there is special blessing and vindication of the persecuted in the next life.

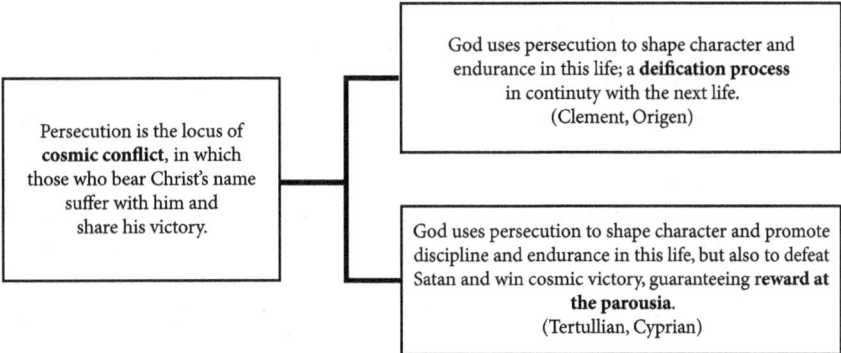

Figure 6.3 Diogmology question 3

The nature of the next life and its continuity with the present is understood very differently by the Alexandrians and Carthaginians. This is the second major area of theological divergence, and it causes variance in their respective understandings of the eschatological good end of persecution (see Figure 6.3). There is a lesser, but still discernible, effect on their perception of good in this life, particularly the extent to which confession and martyrdom may benefit others. Once again, we see dissimilarity in their use of Scripture. Their choices of passages and their interpretation of them are strongly influenced by their eschatology.

The Carthaginians take the most literal meaning of the biblical texts relating to the *parousia* and judgement. They anticipate God's imminent eschatological intervention, bringing final judgement and retribution against unbelievers and persecutors and vindication of the bearers of Christ's name. This is how all wrongs will be righted and evil eliminated and how God's goodness and justice will prevail. Therefore, this life is the one chance to choose a side in the cosmic conflict; one is either with the Devil or with Christ. Hence the urgency of confession and witness in their writings, and the imperatives to stand firm and endure to the end.

As a result of this emphasis, the Carthaginians accentuate the victory/justice/vindication eschatological motifs rather than growth-in-likeness-to-God motifs. Victory and recompense were considered imminent, whether the *parousia* or one's death came first. Battle and arena imagery are emphasized, along with a sense that Christians participate as a united army of God. The church supports confessors and honours martyrs, who serve as worthy examples of victory and encouragement to others still in the conflict. They do not shy away from acknowledging the inevitability of persecution before pagans, but rather emphasize the inevitability of the consequent judgement. Neither Tertullian nor Cyprian are concerned about 'enabling' the persecutors' sins, but rather with provoking their repentance.

Tertullian and Cyprian nevertheless diverge somewhat in their understanding of the nature and scope of the present conflict, which affects their definition of the confessors' victory. Tertullian, in keeping with the martyr acts, situates the victory in the physical death of the confessor.[25] Therefore, the hardships of the persecution experience are disciplines which prepare the confessor for that goal. The nature of endurance is to yield to the Holy Spirit's discipline and seek that goal and the reward which it brings. Cyprian broadens the concept of confessor to include all who uphold the name of Christ throughout every trial of life. The battle encompasses the daily assaults of the Devil. Victory consists in overcoming jealousy, envy and other temptations, in giving of oneself through alms and acts of compassion toward those dying of plague, in maintaining loyalty to the name as *stantes* and in flight, and even in faithfully undergoing penance in submission to the church. All these are forms of conflict, of endurance to the end, and each can win a crown. Cyprian therefore situates the victory in the patient endurance of the confessor to the end of life, by whatever means death comes. Tertullian, focused on martyrdom as a goal, favours passages emphasizing endurance and reward.[26] Cyprian, expanding confession to embrace all the trials of life, often uses medicinal metaphors, exhorting to patient suffering and continuance in good works (1 Pet. 2:21–23).

Because the Alexandrians had a progressive, continuous view of salvation that de-emphasized the eschatological intervention of God as a future-historical event, the suffering–reward reciprocity is less immediate, although it is present. It is a proportionate recompense along the journey to perfection in the afterlife: a greater mansion, a higher position in the School for Souls. They are less concerned with the confessors' interaction with the wider church. Origen makes some reference to the example of the martyrs, and postulates a sacramental, salvific effect of their sacrifice. Yet even this is embedded in their individual relationships with Christ. Both Origen and Clement are concerned to avoid implication in the crimes of their persecutors, but they do not evince the urgency to communicate the prospect of judgement directly to those persecutors. The pathway of martyrdom is for an elect few, by God's providence, and only a minority progress toward perfection in this way. For the remainder, their confession of Christ is worked out in a variety of ways and the τελείωσις continues into the next life. Even the apostates and unbelievers, the persecutors and those otherwise in the Devil's service, will have the opportunity for post-mortem correction. Their punishment, although severe, will be educational and medicinal, as are the trials of the present life. This explains the Alexandrians' favouring of passages which emphasize the value of trials.[27]

These divergent understandings of salvation and eschatology contribute substantially to the fathers' different perspectives on the specific value of martyrdom. The idea of forgiveness through martyrdom, the second baptism, is strongest for Tertullian. For him it is the only guaranteed path to salvation and the peak of Christian

---

[25] Consistent with the description of the 'radical martyr' in Paul Middleton, *Radical Martyrdom and Cosmic Conflict in Early Christianity* (Edinburgh: T&T Clark, 2006), 90.
[26] E.g. Rom. 5:3–5, 8:17–8; Jn 14:2; 1 Cor. 15:41–42.
[27] E.g. Gal. 6:14; 1 Pet. 4:13–16; Heb. 12:6–8; Rom. 8:28.

confession.[28] Cyprian's priority is to ensure that martyrdom occurs within the church's communion, fortified by union with Christ. Christ comes to judge the church. All who remain faithful within her, through various means of holding fast and confessing, can expect a favourable judgement. Clement makes vague reference to martyrdom cleansing sin, but post-mortem educative discipline is his overall solution to post-baptismal transgression. Origen acknowledges forgiveness through martyrdom, but not all attain to complete confession in this way. Origen trusts that God's persistent, non-coercive educational interventions will, over the aeons, ensure that all souls return to him.

All four fathers anticipate that greater faithful suffering for Christ in this life will increase one's reward in the next, but they understand the process differently. Clement interprets Jesus' hundredfold recompense in Matthew 19:29-30 as the gnostic martyrdom by which a person conducts themself out of love for God, disregarding worldly life to live a life free from passion.[29] Clement's hierarchical view of heavenly reward is based on attainment of *gnosis*, not the degree of suffering or on physical martyrdom.[30] Origen draws on this passage in his *Exhortation* to show that the more loss and suffering the martyr undergoes, the higher his place in the next life.[31] Tertullian mainly utilizes the motifs of arena and battlefield to support the idea of greater reward for greater suffering. Cyprian seems much less concerned with degrees of reward compared with different paths to obtaining a crown. When faced with death, however, as we see in the various exhortations to martyrdom, the prospect of an end to suffering and a commensurate reward would have been as motivational for Origen's addressees as it was for those of Tertullian and Cyprian.

One of the most interesting 'benchmark' passages is Revelation 6:9-11, in which the martyrs' souls under the altar are given white robes and told to rest a little longer before their final vindication. The fathers use the same passage in very different ways. Clement is the outlier; he does not derive any eschatological perspectives from it. Rather, he uses the passage to argue against dying clothes, since Christ and the martyrs are clothed only in white.[32] Origen focuses on the altar in his exegesis. He presents the martyrs' location as evidence that their deaths are in some way sacrificial.[33] Tertullian's numerous references to the passage[34] are best understood as providing assurance of the martyrs' reward. The martyrs are thereby signified to have an advantage over other Christians, in keeping with his high view of martyrdom. Cyprian employs the passage variously as a proof-text for the blessedness of the martyrs,[35] to emphasize the necessity of patient endurance of persecution and suffering,[36] and to assert that martyrs' advocacy for the lapsed will only be efficacious at the final judgement.[37] This is a clear example of the

---

[28] *Apol* 50.15-16 (CCSL 1:171); *Scorp.* 6.9; *Pud.* 9.21 (CCSL 2:1080; 1299).
[29] *Strom.* 4.4.15.4 (SC 463:80-2).
[30] *Strom.* 6.13 (CCSL 446:270-74).
[31] *Mart.* 14-15 (GCS 2:14-15).
[32] *Paed.* 2.11 (PG 8:527).
[33] *Comm. Jo.* 6.54.276 (SC 157:338).
[34] *An.* 55.4; *Or.* 5.3; *Res.* 25.1, 38.4, 43.4 (CCSL 2:978-3; 1:260; 2:953, 971, 978-9).
[35] *Test.* 3.16 (CCSL 3:107-11).
[36] *Pat.* 21 (CCSL 3A:130-1).
[37] *Laps.* 18 (CCSL 3:230-1).

fathers' respective eschatological perspectives and emphases driving their exegesis of a passage in different contexts.

Whilst agreeing that persecution brings good in a teleological sense, the fathers differ as to whether persecution itself is in some way 'good'. The first and third questions both have a bearing on this. Clement sees an incidental good which God somehow brings out of persecution, but he does not consider persecution itself to be 'good'. Clement potentially exhibits circular reasoning here. Because he will not consider persecution to be God's will, therefore it cannot be good in an ontological sense. But he also argues that because persecution is not good, it cannot be God's will. He is, I suspect, driven primarily by the conclusions he wishes to reach.

Origen, although denying that God can be the source of 'evil', attributes persecution to the permission of God, not simply to his lack of prevention. It is God's will, and it provides an opportunity for suffering and for confession, which have value in the perfecting of Christians. Origen should therefore be interpreted as distinguishing between evil and persecution, for he acknowledges God permits the latter. Origen stops short of Tertullian's position, however. Tertullian attributes persecution directly to God, as the battleground against idolatry, and therefore explicitly concludes that persecution is intrinsically good. Although Cyprian never pronounces persecution 'good' in so many words, he is satisfied that God is good, and that God sends persecution for his good purposes.

Each father's perception of the 'goodness' attributable to persecution seems related to the emphasis they place on persecution as cosmic conflict, and martyrdom as its pinnacle. Tertullian identifies martyrdom as the apex of the battle, and definitively pronounces persecution, which facilitates it, as good.[38] So good, in fact, that one should not entertain avoiding it. Cyprian's and Origen's more complex considerations of types and degrees of suffering and endurance, and what it means to truly confess, distance them from Tertullian's black-and-white stance. They do not pronounce 'persecution' as 'good', as such, but recognize God's direct working within it for his good ends, through the metaphor of battle. The *conflict* is a good and worthy one, and persecution is its arena. The distinction is subtle, but important. Clement, for whom persecution equates to evil, expresses only a hint of battle rhetoric.

Nevertheless, for each father, the eschatological end does ultimately justify the means, even for Clement, which is how he reconciles God's 'non-prohibition'. They each recognize that confession is of greater value when it comes through testing. This is as true of Clement's gnostic as it is of Tertullian's warrior-athlete. Certainly, for Origen, Tertullian and Cyprian, the battle proves the soldier and the contest the athlete. Hence, in a way, the means also justify the end: the reward allotted in proportion to the suffering. Those who confess Christ and endure persecution patiently will be rewarded. Justice will be done. Despite their varying eschatologies, this is a common conclusion of the four.

---

[38] *Fug.* 1.3, 4.1, 4.3 (CCSL 2:1135, 1140–41).

The relationship of questions 1–3 with questions 4 and 5

The fathers' reflections on the first three diogmological questions, as shown in Figure 6.4, provide the theological foundation for their consideration of the final two – the individual and collective response to persecution.

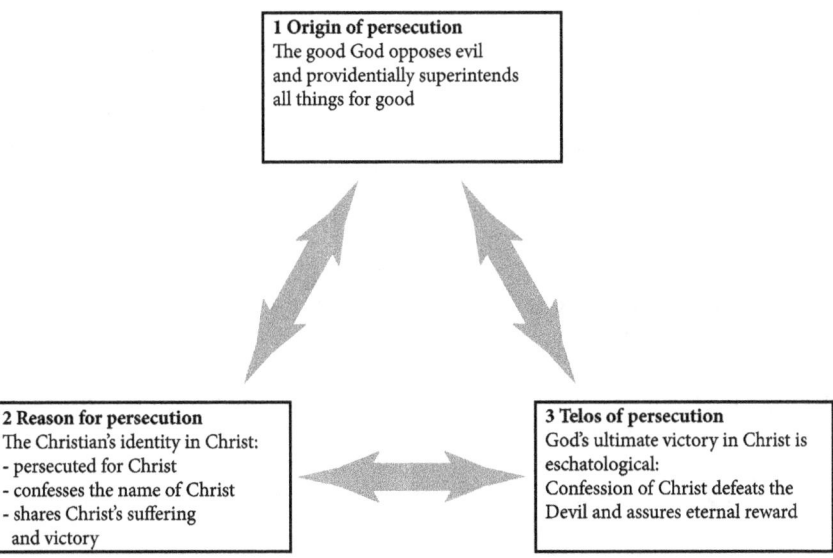

Figure 6.4 Foundational diogmology

The Christian's appropriate response to persecution depends on its origin, reason and endpoint. If persecution was not from God, or was outside his control, or if it did not speak to the Christian's fundamental identity or provide the arena of a conflict of eschatological consequence, then it could rightly be avoided, perhaps at any cost. If, however, persecution is part of God's providential plan, wholly under his control and used by him for the good purpose of the ultimate defeat of evil, then it makes sense for it to be accepted, embraced, rejoiced in, and perhaps even sought.

The individual response

The four fathers' concepts of the appropriate response of the Christian to persecution follow consistently from their foundational theologies of persecution. Where they are in theological agreement, their practical responses concur. With respect to the right attitude of mind and development of character, and the prohibition of denial, they draw on the same body of Scriptures and interpret them congruently. Where their diogmologies diverge, particularly with respect to what constitutes appropriate means of confession, their practical responses vary, and their selection and interpretation of supporting passages differs.

Joy, love, patience, fear

The four share a common perspective on the appropriate mindset and attitudes of Christians in this life. They urge responses such as rejoicing in tribulation and loving one's persecutors. Yet these mindsets are counterintuitive; they can only make sense in the light of a sound and coherent theology of persecution. The goodness and providence of God means that the Christian can trust God's oversight of the persecution, however the details of that oversight are understood. God is the focus of the Christian's response: joy, love, patience and fear. Because God is trustworthy in his goodness and providence, when he decrees persecution to be inevitable it must also be reasonable and purposeful. Because the Christian's identity is in Christ, they join Christ's battle and will share his victory. Therefore, Christians can rejoice to share this battle, knowing that they share his name and his reward. They confess his name, 'in him', and will be confessed by him.

In contrast, if persecution was perceived as the work of an unrestrained evil or capricious deity, if it were outside the good God's control, or if he were indifferent to it, such a god would be objectionable, weak, untrustworthy. Such a god would doubtless invite resistance and rejection by scared and angry humans, who would have to rely on their own strength and cunning to overcome their perils. Submission to this form of oppression would be difficult to characterize as 'blessedness'. If persecution was a merely human conflict, with no vision of a higher goal, resistance might seem futile or unrewarding. The prospect of eternal consequences, a reward of righteousness, a future of confession by Christ, enables suffering to be endured in this life. Because God is good and powerfully in control, persecution has an eternal context and meaning, and this is why the persecuted are blessed.

The fathers draw directly and consistently on Scriptures exhorting to rejoice in persecution,[39] to love one's enemies and pray for one's persecutors,[40] to not resist evil,[41] and to patiently endure to the end.[42] Here, exegesis drives their practical theology. Such responses do not require a pretence of feelings or a denial of reality. On the contrary, their ability to 'fear not' their persecutors derives from their greater fear of God (Mt. 10:28–31). They trust that the Christ whose name they confess will in turn confess them. They fight in unity with him in assurance of sharing his victory. They do not despair at injustice, because they are certain of ultimate vindication. They can love and pray for their persecutors because the just God will exact vengeance.

Practical responses

The four fathers commend the same virtues to Christians in the face of suffering, yet they are not uniform in their practical recommendations for active response. Potential responses, between actively avoiding and actively seeking martyrdom, are informed by the fathers' different diogmologies. Specifically, each father's concept of the role God's

---

[39] Mt. 10:12; Acts 5:41; Jas 1:2–4; 1 Pet. 1:6–7; 4:13–14.
[40] Mt. 5:44; Lk. 6:27–28; Rom. 12:14; 1 Cor. 4:12–13.
[41] Mt. 5:39; Rom. 12:17–21; 1 Pet. 2:23.
[42] Mk 13:13; Lk. 21:19.

providence plays in persecution, and the relationship of martyrdom to the father's teleological perspective, determine which responses they favour. They differ as to whether martyrdom is one option among several appropriate strategies for victory in the cosmic battle, or the definitive one. They agree that persecution presents an unparalleled opportunity for confession of Christian identity; where they differ is in the specifics of what exactly that confession entails (see Figure 6.5). Furthermore, it is likely that the fathers' personal experiences played a role in what was approved or disapproved, although this must remain conjectural.

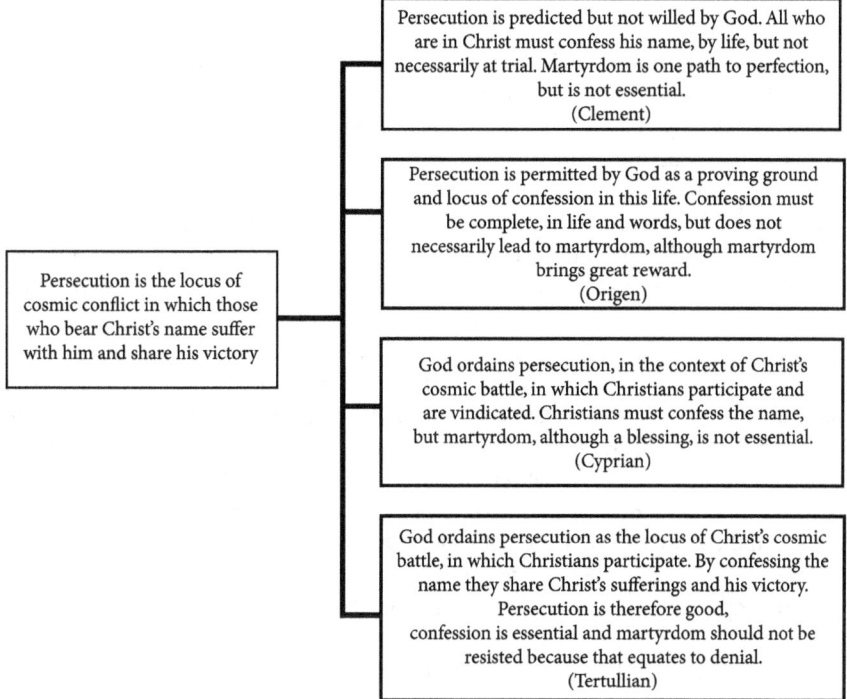

Figure 6.5 Diogmology question 4

Of the four fathers, Clement is the least enthusiastic about martyrdom, because he denies that the 'good' God permits suffering and persecution. God's providence operates by offering choices and opportunities to the would-be confessor, providing multiple paths to gnostic perfection. Clement is focused on the individual's growth through *gnosis*. This can certainly be facilitated by suffering, which has medicinal and educational value. The gnostic accepts death when it comes, having divested self of negative emotions; rejoicing in persecution, loving one's enemies and patiently enduring, knowing that greater rewards await in the next life. Motive is critical: one should not reject martyrdom from cowardice, lacking this gnostic love or understanding. Only the one in Christ can confess in him; confession is essential, but not necessarily at trial. Gnostic martyrdom is giving one's whole life to God out of love.

Therefore, bloody martyrdom, being only one path to perfection, should not be actively sought. Christ must not be denied, but rushing forward to martyrdom usurps God's providence. Furthermore, it makes the martyr complicit in the sin of the persecutors and embroils them in greater judgement. Therefore, Clement is open to ways of avoiding martyrdom which do not compromise confession. Removing oneself, either by lying low or by fleeing, as he himself did, are valid options. It is possible that his reasoning is circular, as Moss proposes; in seeking to legitimate flight he downplays martyrdom as the most desirable option.[43] But even the apostate is probably not lost in Clement's schema, because of his view of the afterlife.

Origen sees this life as part of the soul's journey back to God, a journey of instruction and sanctification in which suffering plays a medicinal and educative role. Origen is more explicit than Clement about the spiritual conflict underpinning persecution and particularly emphasizes the continuity of God's persecuted people under both covenants. Perhaps because of his own experiences, Origen seems to have a more personal appreciation of suffering and martyrdom than Clement. His more detailed theological framework gives God more direct responsibility for persecution and leaves the reader with a more concrete sense of God's direct control and ultimate vindication of the persecuted. Origen believes that confession is not only essential, but must be complete if it is to be valid. It must be completely genuine, the total giving over of self to God; mere loss of life does not suffice.

Origen's position in this respect resembles Clement's gnostic martyrdom, but it also reflects a concern for consistency in Christian life that he shares with Tertullian. Both lament the hypocrisy of split Christian identity; an outward life that conforms to the world when one bears the name of Christ. Although martyrdom is desirable for Origen, he takes the long view of salvation from this life through eternity. The apostate will certainly be punished, but with a view to restoration. Confession and martyrdom are salvific in the sense that they promote one in the rankings of the school of souls. They may also, he speculates, have sacramental value. Nevertheless, Origen does not disparage options other than martyrdom, provided confession is complete and apostasy avoided. Like Clement, he considers volunteerism as complicity in the persecutor's sin. He considers it not dishonourable to avoid danger, but suggests preserving oneself for further service to God, as did Cyprian. Interestingly, Origen's relatively high and exclusive view of martyrdom leads him to warn against seeking it for personal aggrandisement, a perspective unique amongst the four.

Tertullian views persecution as intrinsically good, because it is the God-ordained conflict with idolatry in which the martyr participates. This life is the locus of the battle with the Devil and in which salvation is won or lost. This, for Tertullian, is the meaning of Christian life. Christians should use this life to train as athletes and soldiers, a discipline in preparation for the trials to come. The Holy Spirit prepares and encourages us to martyrdom, in which we have forgiveness of sins and certain salvation; it is the greatest *telos*. This framework results in Tertullian's conviction that the imperative for Christians is to confess, with the expectation of martyrdom and all its benefits. Flight

---

[43] Candida Moss, *Ancient Christian Martyrdom: Diverse Practices, Theologies and Traditions* (New Haven: Yale University Press, 2012), 155.

or withdrawal are therefore, at best, a poor alternative and at worst they equate to apostasy, which is anathema. Tertullian's pro-martyrdom rigorism, albeit adapted to his various polemical objectives, is thoroughly and consistently founded in his diogmology. Tertullian's position requires urgency: confess now, be martyred and received into glory, for this alone will guarantee salvation.

Cyprian, like Tertullian, anticipates the cosmic battle intensifying in the last days, with judgement imminent. Nevertheless, Cyprian does not see martyrdom as inevitably connected to confession. He is more flexible in how one remains faithful to Christ. All of life is a battle with the Devil, and diverse victories provide crowns. God has his reasons for allowing persecution; it may be as a discipline for the church or as a sign of the end. Cyprian's concerns are fundamentally pastoral, and his diogmology is shaped by the real experience of persecution and its aftermath, which Tertullian did not witness on such a scale. Cyprian clearly shares aspects of Tertullian's persecution theology, but it appears tempered by a pastoral pragmatism alien to Tertullian. Therefore, Cyprian's response is to encourage and equip the church for persecution, for patient endurance to the end. Those inside the church are strengthened for the battle by the Holy Spirit through the sacraments; martyrdom within the church wins a crown, but so do confession and good works. There is no excuse for apostasy, for God approves of those who lie low and who abandon their possessions in flight to avoid denial. At all times he is concerned that his flock be strengthened to patiently endure whatever God providentially sends and remain faithful. Confession is essential, but a Christian denied martyrdom should not feel second-class. All who faithfully endure to the end within the ark of the church, whether they live or die (by whatever means) will be saved.

The diversity of the fathers' conclusions is seen most strikingly in the actions they condemned and condoned. All four condemn apostasy, although the Alexandrians' progressive model of salvation permits post-mortem repentance. Faced with an imminent day of judgement, the Carthaginians are urgent in their condemnation of denial. The only one of the four who approaches advocating voluntary martyrdom is Tertullian, and this is because of his conviction that it is God's will as the ultimate desirable outcome of confession. Any lesser goal, and any form of avoidance, equates to denial. Clement, Origen and Cyprian value martyrdom to different extents and in different contexts, each in their own way determining it to be under the providence of God. They each find it valid to withdraw in times of persecution, because of their consciousness that not all are called to this end, beneficial as it might be. Their respective positions are dictated largely by their broader diogmologies, particularly the role which God directly or indirectly has in persecution.

These diogmologies, whilst not removed from Scripture, nevertheless powerfully direct the exegesis of key scriptures regarding the appropriate response of Christians to persecution. This is seen most obviously in their differing exegesis of two 'benchmark' passages, to be discussed shortly.

The communal response

Each of the fathers regarded the target of persecution to be the Christian community, the church, as the earthly representatives of Christ. Tertullian railed against the ignorance that underpinned the injustice of persecution based on unproven abominable activities. Individual Christians were identified and targeted as members of a group, the *Christianoi*. Despite the obscurity of the Christians' legal situation, there is evidence that the pagan community was negatively predisposed to them.

The response of the church as a community encompassed the actions of individuals: non-retaliation, perseverance, hope, willing confession and martyrdom, laying low, flight, dealing with apostasy. The church supported the displaced, the orphans and widows, ministered to imprisoned confessors and commemorated martyrs. These practices reflect the value that the marginalized and persecuted – those who suffered for their identity in Christ – had for the church. This was obvious enough to be an attraction to the sect, according to Tertullian, and to prompt a pagan's observation as to how much the Christians loved one another.[44]

The testimony of the four fathers to the church's response is uneven. This reflects their wider priorities and theology. Notwithstanding Ashwin-Siejkowski's coherent presentation of Clement's ecclesiology as the setting of his 'project of Christian perfection',[45] Clement's response to persecution is almost wholly individualistic. We search in vain for a personal connection to the experiences and collective responses of the persecuted church in Clement's oeuvre. Perhaps this partly reflects his role as a teacher relatively independent of church superintendence.[46] He did not seem compelled to stay when persecution arose in his environment. Clement is focused on the gnostic's development, and he brings persecution into the discussion only when he considers it relevant.

Origen, Tertullian and Cyprian engage more directly and pragmatically with the persecution experience than Clement, both for individuals and collectively. These three each perceive a direct involvement in persecution by God, that engages the church and its members. Each of them wrote 'exhortations to martyrdom' – treatises rich with scriptural passages presenting martyrdom in a positive light and as inevitable and appropriate. Origen and Cyprian have common ground not shared with their immediate predecessors; they were in the thick of persecution. They knew people who were suffering and who were being killed. This likely contributes to the sense of compassionate solidarity evident in Origen's *Exhortation* and to Cyprian's anguish over the lapsed that transcends Tertullian's arms-length, rather uncompromising judgement.

Tertullian and Cyprian testify to the church community's practical engagement with confessors and martyrs over two generations. Their respective affirmations of the church's responsibility reflect their evaluations of the various individual responses to persecution – martyrdom, confession, flight, apostasy – in turn shaped by their diogmologies and experiences. Both Carthaginians demonstrate an interaction between ecclesiology and diogmology. Tertullian distinguished between the 'church of the bishops', or church of the ψυχικοί and the 'church of the Spirit'.[47] The latter embraced

---

[44] *Apol.* 39.7 (CCSL 1:151).
[45] Piotr Ashwin-Siejkowski, *Clement of Alexandria: A Project of Christian Perfection* (London: T&T Clark, 2008), 224.
[46] Wendy Mayer (pers. com. 2021) suggests: 'Most likely Clement's "individualism" lies within his role as a teacher of philosophy (gnosis) modelled on the philosophical schools of the time, where pupils were instructed by a master, and where the concern of the master was with the path of each individual pupil towards philosophical/spiritual happiness/perfection.'
[47] *Jej.* 1.1–2; *Pud.* 21 (CCSL 2:1257, 1326–8).

the Spirit's discipline which prepared it for persecution and martyrdom; the former shunned hardship and confession unto death. Throughout his oeuvre, Tertullian castigates those in the church who compromise with the world. This could involve going to arena shows because no one would suspect their Christianity, or flirting with idolatry. The church of the bishops could not grant reconciliation, only the church of the Spirit could, which meant the only guaranteed absolution in this life comes through martyrdom. Tertullian is not interested in ecclesiastical support of those who flee persecution; they are effectively apostates. He cannot endorse a lifestyle that does not wholly embrace the call to deny oneself and take up the cross of Christ. Arguably, Tertullian is most concerned with the apostates' threat to the *purity* of the church.

Cyprian's foundational theology of persecution certainly reflects Tertullian's in many respects. Their answers to the first three questions are essentially the same, they draw on the same scriptures.[48] Yet Cyprian's ecclesiology is quite different from his predecessor's, and this affects his 'applied' diogmology. Because Cyprian believes that the church of the bishop is indeed the church of Christ and the Holy Spirit,[49] his priority is to retain and return as many as possible to this ark before the end of the world arrives. Many activities within the church or its penumbra (embracing catechumens and penitents) can contribute to the cosmic conflict against the Devil and can win crowns for faithful perseverance. This allows for Cyprian's broader concept of confession, not downplaying martyrdom, but elevating other hardships suffered and good works performed for the name alongside it.

Furthermore, it is likely that the sheer scale of apostasy under Decius created a pastoral challenge that required a more nuanced response from Cyprian than rigid adherence to Tertullian's diogmology. The bishop, as conduit of the Spirit, wielded authority on behalf of Christ to restore the penitent to the fold, outside of which was no salvation. He includes among the faithful both *stantes* and those who fled. He used his authority as bishop to promote mutual support: the church supported fugitives, the *stantes* ministered to imprisoned confessors. Through flight, clerics were preserved to continue God's work. This reflects his understanding that there are multiple ways to confess, within the embrace of the church. It also upended the social structure of the church, as the lower classes now often supported or substituted for the higher, many of the latter having apostatized as they (presumably) perceived they had more to lose. Cyprian is particularly concerned with the *unity* of the church.

Diogmology and the fathers' use of Scripture

Fairbairn established that, predominantly, the respective theological perspectives of the Antiochenes and Alexandrians drove their exegesis.[50] Similar instances are evident in the theology of persecution of the Alexandrines and Carthaginians.

---

[48] Particularly the providence of God in Mt. 5:45, the missionary discourse in Mt. 10; Lk. 6:22–26; 9:23–26; Rom. 12:14–21; 1 Pet. 2:21–23; 4:12–16; Rev. 2:9–13; 6:9–11.
[49] *Ep.* 69.2 (CCSL 3C:471–3).
[50] Donald Fairbairn, 'Patristic Exegesis and Theology: The Cart and the Horse', *Westminster Theological Journal* 69, no. 1 (2007), 1–19.

The two-way street

By attention to 'benchmark' persecution passages, I have discovered that where the fathers' diogmologies converge, they tend to draw on essentially the same body of Scriptures, and interpret them consistently, if not identically. Their exegesis directly informs their theology, notably with respect to the necessity of confession and suffering for the name. Where their diogmologies diverge, they primarily construct a theological argument, drawing on a more diverse array of Scriptures with inconsistent exegetical conclusions. A summary is shown in Figure 6.6.

I submit that the common aspects of their diogmologies are common primarily because they are rooted in common appropriation of Scripture, especially the benchmark passages in Matthew 5 and 10 and in 1 Peter. The points of theological agreement are derived from exegetical agreement, the consistent interpretation of the same body of passages. In these cases, exegesis drives theology (see Figure 6.7). The best example is their consistent use of the reciprocal confession/denial passages (Mt. 10:32–33; Mk 8:38; Lk. 9:26 and 12:8–9). Not only do they all determine the centrality of confession of the name from these passages but they build similar arguments about being 'in Christ'.

Different exegetical strategies such as allegory versus 'plain reading' do not seem to impact these core interpretations. Origen certainly employs allegory and typology when he interprets Old Testament passages in the context of the Christian's cosmic conflict, but he derives the principle of that conflict between the world and Christ's people from the same passages as the other fathers. Tertullian may employ some creative exegetical strategies to the historical context of Matthew 10 to serve different rhetorical purposes, but his broad interpretation of this discourse is consistent with that of the others. Christians can expect persecution: Christ said it would be for his name, and he prepared them for it.

At key points, however, certain distinctives and even outright contradictions occur between the four. At these points, their theology can be seen to drive their exegesis (see Figure 6.8). Differences at the level of the first question, God's involvement in the origin of persecution, are not based on a common exegetical thread. The Alexandrians are particularly driven by their broader theological agendas at this point. Clement's concept of what God's goodness entails requires a rejection of any aetiological role for God in persecution. Origen is committed to his theology of the fall and return of souls, which forms the context for all forms of suffering. The Carthaginians seem to work back from God's objectives to identify his initiating role in persecution. Likewise, the significantly different eschatological frameworks of the Alexandrians and Carthaginians lead them to read Scripture differently at the level of the third question, the *telos* of persecution.

The cumulative effects of these convergences and divergences accounts for the ways in which they advocate appropriate responses to persecution. They find common exegetical ground in the appropriate attitudes of Christians: love of enemies, not fearing but rejoicing, and so on. Here again they draw on the same body of Scripture and interpret it consistently. But their conclusions about the positive steps Christians should take, in terms of hiding, fleeing or seeking martyrdom come from their

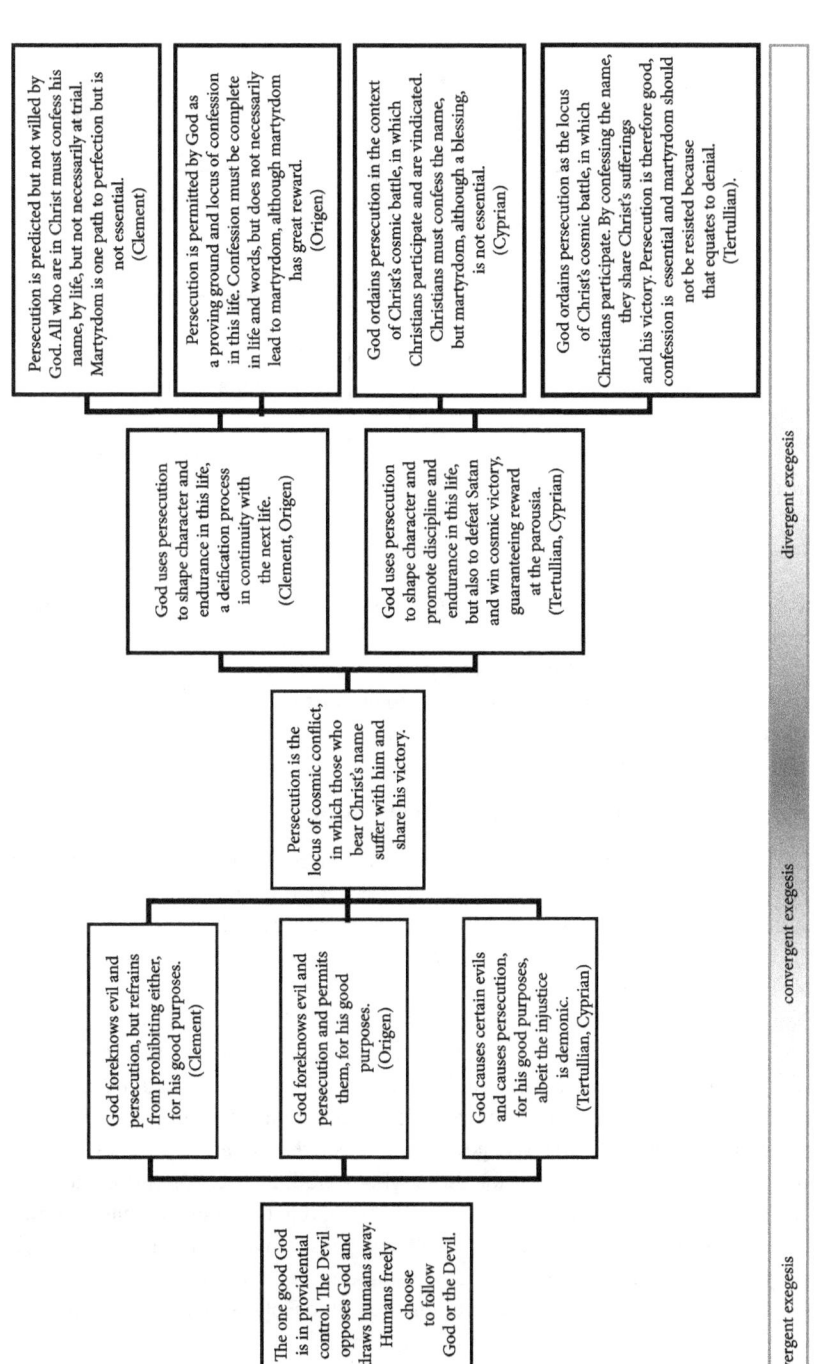

Figure 6.6 Comparative diogmologies

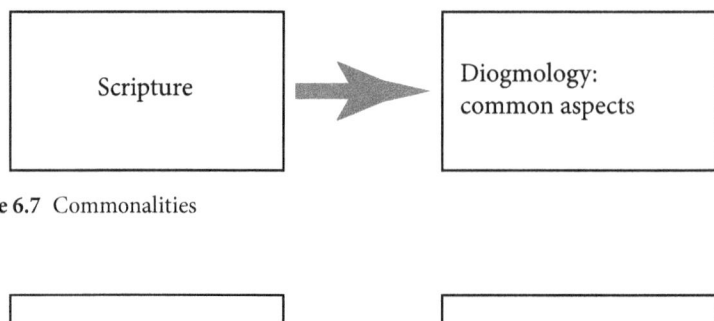

Figure 6.7 Commonalities

Figure 6.8 Divergences

foundational diogmologies and, to some extent, the impact of their particular experiences. In this practical application they do not necessarily consult different Scriptures, but their exegesis of the same passages supports different conclusions. To illustrate this, I will examine the fathers' treatment of two benchmark passages, both from Jesus' missionary discourse in Matthew 10.

Divergent exegesis: The Holy Spirit and confession

In Matthew 10:19–20, Jesus promises that when his disciples are brought to trial, they will have no need to be anxious about what to say, for the Spirit of their Father will speak through them. In Mark 13:11 it is the Holy Spirit who will speak through them and in Luke 21:15 Jesus himself will give them words which their adversaries will be unable to withstand.

Clement understands this to apply to those who are given the task of public, vocal confession, whereby the Holy Spirit imparts what should be said. Nevertheless, such verbal confession is not required of all, and the Spirit's more universal role is to regenerate and disciple the gnostic, such that he or she overcomes fear and trusts in God.[51] Similarly, Origen, citing all three synoptic passages in full in his *Exhortation*, emphasizes that this promise of the Spirit's aid is only for those whom God chooses for this confession, initially the Twelve and now those providentially brought to the contest of martyrdom.[52] Ambrose and Protoctetus are now in this privileged position and can expect the Spirit's help. Both Clement and Origen restrict confession unto martyrdom to those chosen by God's providence, and it is to these select individuals the Holy Spirit supplies words.

---

[51] *Strom.* 4.9 (SC 463:170–80).
[52] *Mart.* 34 (GCS 2:30).

Tertullian and Cyprian assure their readers of the Spirit's presence with confessors in prison,⁵³ a role extending beyond giving them the words to speak. Cyprian, like Origen, places the call to martyrdom with God alone, but Cyprian also believes the Holy Spirit may guide a potential confessor to a destiny other than martyrdom, and support them on that path. The Holy Spirit, he explains, reminds Fortunatus that when the Devil's army comes against us, our hope is in the very war itself, the conflict by which the righteous obtain their reward.⁵⁴ Cyprian stresses the Spirit as the author of the words of Scripture which encourage the confessor.⁵⁵ The Spirit promises in the Gospel that specific words will be given. In fact, Cyprian does not limit the circumstances nor the type of help the Spirit will afford; the only limitation is the confessor's faith.⁵⁶ Cyprian believed that Christ was present with the one who fled, just as much as the one imprisoned.⁵⁷ The presence of the Spirit is the presence of Christ. Christ himself fights in the confessor's fight of martyrdom, giving special support. This goes beyond giving the words to speak; it is Christ's very presence with the confessor. He is the one crowned in us; the victory we gain belongs to him.⁵⁸ Indeed, one who has not received the Spirit (i.e. in the true church) cannot truly confess.⁵⁹ Nevertheless, the Spirit did not intend martyrdom under all circumstances; Cyprian believed that he had a special directive from God's Spirit to withdraw for the sake of his church.⁶⁰

Withdrawal was unthinkable for Tertullian, who held that a bishop must never desert his flock in the face of persecution.⁶¹ Tertullian cannot envisage a situation where the Holy Spirit would not direct and support an individual specifically toward martyrdom. That was the task of the Spirit's presence with them in prison. The promise of the Spirit's speaking was part of Christ's consistent expectation of his disciples taking up the cross in martyrdom. In fact, Tertullian regarded the Spirit's presence in a person to be specifically directed toward the narrow path of confession and martyrdom.

> And therefore, the Comforter is requisite, who guides into all truth, and animates to all endurance. And they who have received him will neither stoop to flee from persecution nor to buy it off, for they have the Lord himself, one who will stand by us to aid us in suffering, as well as to be our mouth when we are put to the question.⁶²

Thus, the same passage is used diversely by the four to encourage the elect minority to confess and be martyred, to exemplify the many ways and contexts in which the

---

⁵³ *Mart.* 1 (CCSL 1:3); *Fort.* 9–10 (CCSL 3:197–201).
⁵⁴ *Fort.* 10 (CCSL 3:198–201).
⁵⁵ specifically, in 1 Jn 4:4; Ps. 27:3–4, 118:6; Exod. 1:12, 6:11–12; Rev. 2:10; Isa. 43:1–3.
⁵⁶ *Fort.* 10 (CCSL 3:198–201).
⁵⁷ *Ep.* 58.4 (CCSL 3C:324–5).
⁵⁸ *Epp.* 10.3; 58.5.2; 76.5.1 (CCSL 3B:50; 3C:326–7; 612).
⁵⁹ *Ep.* 57.4.2 (CCSL 3B:305–6).
⁶⁰ *Epp.*16.4.1; 20.1.2 (CCSL 3B:94, 106).
⁶¹ *Fug.* 11 (CCSL 2:1148–9).
⁶² *Fug.* 14.3 (CCSL 2:1155) Et ideo Paracletus necessarius, deductor omnium ueritatum, exhortator omnium tolerantiarum. Quem qui recuperunt, neque fugere persecutionem neque redimere nouerunt, habentes ipsum, qui pro nobis erit, sicut locuturus in interrogatione, ita iuuaturus in passione.

Spirit represents the presence of Christ with the persecuted, and to argue for martyrdom as the Spirit's primary objective for the Christian. In each case, the interpretation stems from the individual father's broader diogmology, as applied *to* the passage.

Divergent exegesis: The legitimacy of flight

In the context of diogmology, Matthew 10:23 is the example, *par excellence*, of theology directing exegesis. All four fathers cite Jesus' directive, 'when they persecute you in one town, flee to the next', each in the context of persecution, but to justify quite different responses.[63]

Clement insisted that, when Jesus told the disciples in Matthew 10:23 to flee to another city, it was because he wants us to avoid aiding and abetting evil, which would be the case if we did not resist capture and potential murder.[64] Tertullian and Cyprian were also concerned about the punishment persecutors faced by enemies of Christ, but put the onus on the persecutors, who will not escape the day of judgement.[65] But Clement maintained that Jesus bids us take care of ourselves. He who presents himself for capture and judgement becomes guilty of his own death.

Origen also believed that provoking martyrdom implicated oneself in the crime. Martyrdom was God's will for some but should not be sought. Furthermore, Jesus specifically taught and modelled that withdrawal is prudent.[66] Flight to escape punishment is not an act of cowardice, but of obedience, for preservation so one can continue to work for the benefit of others.[67] Although not explicit, Origen's concern for the completeness of confession probably also influences his reticence for all and sundry to embrace the high calling of martyrdom. 'The Word wishes to turn us back from rushing too hastily and too irrationally to struggle unto death on behalf of the truth and to suffer martyrdom.'[68] Thirdly, Origen considers it self-centred and inconsiderate to act this way, in contrast to Tertullian and Cyprian's onus on the persecutor. Just as Jesus taught us to withdraw in persecution, he also taught us to flee honours and positions of superiority in the world,[69] which he considers martyrdom to offer.

Tertullian was convinced that flight in persecution was due to weakness, fear and cowardice.[70] The one who flees from fear of apostatizing has already denied Christ.[71] Ultimately, Tertullian saw the Paraclete and his disciplinary work as enabling

---

[63] Ruth Sutcliffe, 'To Flee or Not to Flee? Matthew 10:23 and Third Century Flight in Persecution'. *Scrinium* 14, no. 1 (2018), 133–60.
[64] *Strom.* 4.10.76.1–77.1 (SC 463:180–2).
[65] *Scap.* 3.1, 3.5 (CCSL 2:1129–30); *Dem.* 24 (CCSL 3A:49–50).
[66] *Comm. Matt.* 10.23 on Mt. 14:1–15 (SC 162:254).
[67] *Cels.* 8.44 (SC 150:270).
[68] *Comm. Jo.* 28.23.192 (SC 385:156) ταῦτα καὶ τὰ τούτοις παραπλήσια ἀναγεγράφθαι νομίζω, βουλομένου τοῦ Λόγου ἐπιστρέφειν ἡμᾶς ἀπὸ τοῦ θερμότερον καὶ ἀλογιστότερον ἐπιπηδᾶν τῷ ἕως τοῦ θανάτου ἀγωνίζεσθαι περὶ τῆς ἀληθείας, καὶ μαρτυρεῖν.
[69] *Comm. Jo.* 28.23.209 (SC 385:162).
[70] Tertullian, *Scorp.* 1.5 (CCSL 2:1069–70). *Scorp.* 12 (CCSL 2:1092–94), *Fug.* 9.3 (CCSL 2:1146).
[71] *Fug.* 5.1 (CCSL 2:1141) certus es te negaturum, si non fugeris, an incertus? Si enim certus, iam negasti.

martyrdom.[72] Tertullian is resistant to the possibility that the Spirit might also direct a Christian to flee, as Cyprian asserted. When Tertullian carefully exegetes Matthew 10 in *Scorpiace* 9–11, he repeatedly insists that the whole discourse applies beyond the Twelve to the Christians of his day, because he is arguing against those who resist martyrdom. Without comment, he simply omits verse 23, the passage advocating flight, from his otherwise complete discussion. In *De fuga*, when his purpose is to argue against flight, he cannot avoid Matthew 10:23, so to prevent it undermining his argument he reverses his position from *Scorpiace*. The missionary discourse, he argues, was restricted to the original mission of the Twelve and does not apply today.[73]

Cyprian embraces the idea of withdrawal for self-preservation, to continue critical work for God. Cyprian felt he could best serve his flock by withdrawal, because his primary responsibility as shepherd was to protect his flock, and he feared that his presence would provoke violence.[74] He based this on direct communication from the Holy Spirit bidding him to withdraw,[75] specifically to not aggravate the violent situation in Carthage.[76] By *sicut Domini mandata instruunt* I believe Cyprian refers to a personal visionary directive, rather than to Matthew 10:23.[77] Cyprian does allude to Matthew 10:23 in *De lapsis*, maintaining it would have been better for apostates to flee, rather than remain to deny the faith. Where Tertullian assumes the one who withdraws is predisposed to deny,[78] Cyprian takes the opposite view; the fugitive 'would certainly confess if he too had been apprehended'.[79] Better to flee than to cling to material goods;[80] flight is a means of avoiding apostasy, 'therefore the Lord commanded us in the persecution to depart and flee; and both taught that this should be done, and himself did it'.[81]

The four fathers undoubtedly turned to Scripture to make sense of the persecution experience. It cannot be explained otherwise than in the context of Christ, and the Bible is Christ's story from beginning to end. They explain persecution theologically in the context of their understanding of this overarching 'story' centred in the work of Christ. The Alexandrians are more inclined to look beneath the surface of the text for

---

[72] *Fug* 14.3 (CCSL 2:1155). So Candida Moss, 'Justification of the Martyrs', in *Tertullian and Paul*, vol. 1 of Pauline and Patristic Scholars in Debate, ed. David E. Wilhite and Todd D. Still (New York: T&T Clark 2013), 104–18, at 106.

[73] Fug. 6.1–2 (CCSL 2:1142).

[74] *Ep*. 7.1 (CCSL 3B:38).

[75] *Ep*. 16.4.1 (CCSL 3B:94).

[76] *Ep*. 20.1.2 (CCSL 3B: 106–7). I believe this is too individual a claim to be an allusion to Mt. 10:23.

[77] Against Graeme.W. Clarke, trans. *The Letters of St. Cyprian of Carthage*, vol. 1, Ancient Christian Writers 43 (New York: Newman, 1984), 307; but in agreement with Michael A. Fahey, *Cyprian and the Bible: A Study in 3rd Century Exegesis*, Beiträge zur Geschichte der biblischen Hermeneutik 9 (Tübingen: JCB Mohr, 1971), 297. Fahey, however, denies that Cyprian directly cites Mt. 10:23a. The connection in *Ep*. 20.1.2 is tenuous, but much stronger in *Laps*. 10, which I consider to be Cyprian's only actual citation of this passage.

[78] *Fug*. 5.1 (CCSL 2:1141).

[79] *Laps*. 3 (CCSL 3:222) *confiteretur utique si fuisset et ipse detentus*.

[80] Cyprian, *Laps*. 10 (CCSL 3:226). Clarke, *Letters*, 1:307–8, commenting on *Ep*. 20, notes the connection between allusions to Christ's withdrawals in Mt. 4:12 and Jn 11:54, the use of Isa. 52:11 and Rev. 18:4, in conjunction with Mt. 10:23 in *Laps*. 10.

[81] *Laps*. 10 (CCSL 3:226) Et ideo Dominus in persecutione secedere et fugere mandauit, adque, ut id fierit, et docuit et fecet.

a deeper meaning, an overall narrative which depends to some extent on speculation. This narrative expresses a progressive soteriology foreign to that of the Carthaginians, and it dominates their exegesis at times. The Carthaginians also contextualize their use of Scripture; Tertullian particularly adapts his exegesis to his polemical objectives. These tendencies have been well described elsewhere. My contribution is the elucidation of the bidirectional influence of theological assumptions and exegesis in the context of the hitherto largely unexplored area of their theology of persecution.

Making diogmological sense of different perspectives

This study achieves several secondary objectives. I have demonstrated a bidirectional influence between persecution and the fathers' theology which has been underrepresented in the literature. Through the lens of benchmark 'persecution' passages, I have provided a diogmological perspective on the fathers' use of Scripture. It remains to bring a theology of persecution to bear on some other conversations. Diogmology can offer a fresh vantage point over familiar terrain.

'Cosmic conflict' or 'patient ferment'?

Paul Middleton argues that early Christians believed they were engaged in a holy war with Satan, not just as participants, but as contributors to the final outcome.[82] Alan Kreider proposes a model of 'patient ferment' to explain the survival and growth of a persecuted church.[83] These 'models' may initially seem at odds, particularly if 'cosmic conflict' is misunderstood as some sort of theology of violence.[84] Understood correctly, however, diogmology reconciles them.

The idea of cosmic conflict is evident in the theology of the four fathers examined here. Although Middleton makes some reference to Clement, Origen, Tertullian and Cyprian,[85] the main sources for his argument are the martyr acts.[86] These are the sources he draws on for his contention that 'the Christians were God's foot soldiers on the front line, and they experienced the skirmishes of war through persecution. Satan and his legions were, therefore, directly responsible for the persecution of Christians.'[87]

This statement requires nuancing if it is to be applied to the four fathers. Certainly, the direct instrument of persecution was considered demonic, but were it left there, excluding God's providential control, their diogmology would be incomplete. Tertullian

---

[82] Middleton, *Radical Martyrdom*, 6. This theme is also identified by McLarty, 'Early Christian Theologies', 129.
[83] Alan Kreider, *The Patient Ferment of the Early Church: The Improbable Rise of Christianity in the Roman Empire*. Grand Rapids: Baker, 2016, 12.
[84] Which Candida Moss, *The Myth of Persecution: How the Early Christians Invented a Story of Martyrdom* (New York: HarperOne, 2013), 9–13, interprets as a dangerous legacy of Christianity's martyrdom narrative.
[85] Middleton, *Radical Martyrdom*, 18–25; 28–39.
[86] Ibid., 2, nn. 71, 81.
[87] Ibid., 81.

recognizes this most clearly when he attributes persecution to God, it being the ordained battleground with the Devil, whilst attributing its injustice to the Devil.[88] The others understand this also. Even Clement (with some ambiguity) determines that persecution, although not God's will and not originated by him, is nevertheless not outside his providential control. This point is key to the fathers' diogmology, because even though they wrestle with, and ultimately disagree as to the extent of God's direct involvement, for none of them does the battle reflect a dualistic conflict between good and evil deities. The Devil is not purely offensive and Christ defensive; God is in control; the Devil is restrained, and his defeat is assured. Persecution is the instrument of destruction of the Devil, not of Christians.

Middleton certainly recognizes this,[89] but I suggest that the martyr acts and apologies that are his primary focus do not exhibit as comprehensive a diogmology as the four fathers, particularly Tertullian.[90] Tertullian's apologetic genius lies in reconciling the necessity of conflict and the 'good' of God-appointed persecution, identifying that the purpose of apology is that Christianity be known and hence persecuted for the right reasons. Middleton's picture of the 'radical martyr' situates the victory in the cosmic battle with confession leading to death. 'In death, they are described as victors and conquerors.'[91] He describes 'an important triad of themes in the death of martyrs: confession; participation in the suffering of Christ; and winning the victory over Satan'.[92] 'Satan's kingdom crumbled with each martyr's death.'[93] He concludes: 'Since death was such a potent weapon in the fight against evil, and since it brought a martyr's reward, enthusiastic and faithful Christians sought it out, deliberately seeking arrest, or wilfully bringing themselves to the authorities' attention ... these radical martyrs.'[94]

The martyr acts, by definition, are the account of deaths for the confession of Christ. They climax, often in the arena, with the proclamation, Χριστιανός εἰμί, *Christianus sum*. In this situation, as with the recipients of the Exhortations to Martyrdom, this was the point of no return: confess or deny. This ultimate, fatal confession was *itself* the point of Satan's defeat. Confession and martyrdom are necessarily conflated in this situation. This, I suggest, is the crux of 'radical' martyrdom, and why Tertullian appears the greatest exponent of it among the four fathers. Tertullian, like the martyr acts, conflates confession and martyrdom: for him that is the climax of the Christian's disciplined life. Not for him the quiet slip into death on a sickbed.[95] If Middleton's thesis about the prevalence of volunteerism is correct, Tertullian had plenty of like-minded company.

But the other three fathers are less black-and-white, less 'radical'. Clement, who I submit is much less 'enthusiastic about Christian death' than Middleton proposes,[96]

---

[88] *Fug.* 1–2 (CCSL 2:1135–9).
[89] Middleton, *Radical Martyrdom*, 90.
[90] This proposition is explored in depth in Ruth Sutcliffe, 'No Need to Apologise? Tertullian and the Paradox of Polemic Against Persecution', StPatr, 23, 267–78.
[91] Middleton, *Radical Martyrdom*, 88, citing Origen and Tertullian as well as martyr acts.
[92] Ibid., 89.
[93] Ibid., 90.
[94] Middleton, *Radical Martyrdom*, 101–2.
[95] *An.* 55.5 (CCSL 2:863).
[96] Middleton, *Radical Martyrdom*, 19.

sees martyrdom as only one path to perfection. Gnostic 'martyrdom' is a whole-of-life progression, which may or may not culminate in verbal confession at trial. Origen, who sees a more permissive role for God in persecution, confines martyrdom to a providentially selected few whose confession must be 'complete'. Like Origen, Cyprian sees several valid alternatives to martyrdom, and most clearly articulates the variety of dimensions of confession apart from execution. These three fathers – particularly the two who endured the Decian persecution – have a cosmic conflict diogmology, but they are not 'radical' martyrs. Furthermore, their non-radical martyrology cannot be simply credited to Clement's alleged *via media* influence, because their diogmologies differ from his at the key points I have highlighted.

With this rider, illuminated by the more 'advanced' persecution theology of the third century over the second, I agree with Middleton's conclusions. The cosmic conflict, centred in confession of the name of Christ, was the *raison d'être* of persecution. From a socio-political perspective, Christians were persecuted for being 'Christian', and theologically, this was true also, and entirely appropriate. Nevertheless, the cosmic conflict should not be restricted to radical martyrdom, if the fathers' complete diogmology is to be respected. Persecuted Christians participate in Christ's conflict with the Devil and ultimately in his victory, whether in agonal confession, in hiding or exile, or in patient, faithful endurance to the end of life. This broader appreciation of the cosmic conflict, which does not necessarily conflate confession and martyrdom, was most fully articulated by Cyprian. This marks a departure from his predecessor Tertullian, but is congruent with the Alexandrians, and consistent with Kreider's 'patient ferment' thesis.

The 'cosmic conflict' theology, so evident in the martyr acts, has been misunderstood and misapplied. Moss argues that the idea of cosmic conflict has been misappropriated in contemporary Christian political discourse,[97] and she is undoubtedly correct. Nevertheless, her conclusion rests on conflation of the original 'cosmic conflict' concept with how it has been distorted, underrepresenting the breadth of the fathers' theological discourse on persecution in her selective citations.[98] Koscheski identifies a 'cosmic war complex' in early martyr accounts, but oversteps the evidence in conflating it with later Christian militia and modern religious suicide bombers.[99] The early Christians did not battle their human opponents: they battled the Devil, deferring all judgement to the good God who is ultimately in control. They attributed the final victory to Christ, in whose victory the martyrs participate. The early Christians fought their cosmic battle by *dying with* Christ, not *killing for* him. This is a fundamental point made by the fathers; Christians love their enemies and leave vengeance to God.

An appreciation of the fathers' complete diogmology necessitates a revision of Koscheski's hypothesis. It is because the true battle had been fought and won by Christ, that the Christian confessor-martyrs share his victory. They were not fighting

---

[97] Moss, *Myth of Persecution*, 13.
[98] Ibid., 192–5 and see Brian W. Shelton, review of *The Myth of Persecution* (by Candida Moss) *Journal of the Evangelical Theological Society* 57, no. 1 (2014), 210–14, at 214.
[99] Jonathan Koscheski, 'The Earliest Christian War: Second- and Third-Century Martyrdom and the Creation of Cosmic Warriors', *Journal of Religious Ethics* 39, no. 1 (2011), 100–24.

autonomously, nor even alongside Christ, but within his same conflict. The victory in which they shared was Christ's own victory. This is because they confess his name and confess it 'in him'. The Christian's weapons are love, submission and patient endurance, not swords, guns or bombs. Christians love and pray for their persecutors because vengeance is God's, not theirs.

This broader understanding of the cosmic conflict model is compatible with a model of patient growth. The fathers emphasize patient endurance as the appropriate response to their adverse environment, which lies at the heart of Kreider's thesis.[100] Alan Krieder argues that the church grew by a patient, slow, progressive 'fermenting' type of growth as empowered by the distinctive habitus or behaviour of Christians.[101] This was a consistent enactment of their message that was also embodied in their catechesis and worship. Kreider suggests that patient persistence in doing good was the primary factor in the growth of Christianity – patience not only in enduring persecution but in living exemplary lives of good works – and identifies exhortation to this 'patient ferment' in the writings of each of our four theologians,[102] as well as in Justin and Lactantius. These brief expositions on the fathers' teaching regarding patient endurance resonate with the diogmology of the four fathers, and are aptly summarized by his citation from Cyprian: '[We] are philosophers not in words but in deeds; we exhibit our wisdom not by our dress, but by truth; we know virtues by their practice rather than through boasting of them; we do not speak great things but we live them.'[103]

Litfin criticizes Kreider for projecting his Mennonite anti-violence perspective onto the early church, overlooking 'counterbalancing statements in which an aggressive or hostile tone can be found', ultimately providing 'an exercise in proving the point'.[104] Shelton suggests Kreider's 'Anabaptist predispositions' influence his judgements on the insufficiently patient Augustine and Constantine and that the patient ferment 'sometimes feels like a separationist lifestyle', with insufficient articulation of the role of patience in 'volatile resistance'.[105] Hartog finds Kreider 'overly optimistic, as if early Christian hearers consistently followed their leaders' exhortations to patience and distinctive lifestyles'[106] – which we understand, particularly from Tertullian, that they did not.

In response, I offer three observations. Firstly, the early church was not perfect, and the general Christian populace did not always live up to the high standards Clement expected of 'gnostics', nor Origen of those who 'confess fully', nor Tertullian of those truly in step with the Spirit's discipline nor even Cyprian's expectations from his flock. There was not always consistency between the ideal of Christian identity and its

---

[100] Kreider, *Patient Ferment*, 14–15.
[101] Ibid., 96–120.
[102] Ibid., 17–31.
[103] Ibid., 13, citing Cyprian, *Pat.* 3.
[104] Bryan M. Litfin, 'Was the Early Church "Patient"?' (Oct 2016) https://www.thegospelcoalition.org/reviews/patient-ferment-of-the-early-church/
[105] W. Brian Shelton, Review of *The Patient Ferment of the Early Church* (by Alan Kreider) *Journal of Theological Studies* 68, no. 2 (2017), 772–4.
[106] Paul Hartog, review of *The Patient Ferment of the Early Church* (by Alan Kreider) *Trinity Journal* 38, no. 2 (2017), 255–8.

'activation' in all circumstances, a point I will discuss further below. But this does not undermine the ideal, nor does it serve as an alternative explanation of Christianity's ultimate acceptance and legitimization. Kreider argues that the early Christians did exhibit patient habitus in their lives; he does not highlight their inconsistency. But even with inconsistency, the fact that the apologists, including Tertullian, could reasonably present the Christians as wholesome people who lived exemplary lives suggests that Krieder does not make an illicit assumption about the general non-violent stance of the early Christians.

Secondly, despite the uncompromising anti-pagan rhetoric of Tertullian and others,[107] the fathers do not advocate conquering this world by violent activity this side of the *parousia*. When they speak of judgement and vindication, it is God's work, not theirs. Therefore, they can love their persecutors and acquiesce with the treatment they receive. When Tertullian focuses his threatening rhetoric on Scapula, and when Cyprian unleashes invective on Demetrianus, they do so with the conviction that the persecutors' days are numbered. They do not threaten Christian insurrection against their persecutors,[108] but rather emphasize God's vengeance on those who harass and slaughter his flock. They appeal to their persecutors to accept the inevitable and change sides, for time is running out. Although Clement and Origen do not express the same urgency because of their eschatological framework, they do not anticipate any change in the Christians' situation brought about by any activity independent of God. In God's good time the world will be reconciled to him.

Thirdly, the question of the fathers' advocacy of patient endurance under persecution can only be fully understood in the context of the fathers' whole diogmology, which Kreider unfortunately does not address. I have demonstrated that the fathers' response to persecution in terms of attitude and action was consistent with, and informed by, their perspective on the origin and inevitability of, reason for and ultimate good resulting from persecution. In this context, patient endurance, as advocated in the Scriptures they exegete, makes perfect sense. The fathers attribute the growth of the church to the power and plan of God, under whom the martyrs and those who suffer play their role. They join with Christ, and it is his victory they will share.

Does 'patient ferment' primarily account for the growth of the church, as Kreider suggests? As a socio-historical hypothesis the question remains open. Theologically, it is certainly compatible with the four fathers' perspectives, because they view the church's persistence and ultimate victory as a work of God, not a matter of human effort. Whether this is because pagans will reflect on the resolution of the martyrs, as Tertullian supposes, or whether it is because they see the Christians' good works, it is subsumed to God's providence. God will cause his church to grow and ultimately to prevail. God predicted and permitted the persecution of his people; it is their destiny to suffer for Christ and with him and share also in his ultimate victory. God will vindicate his people, so vengeance can be left to him.

---

[107] Perhaps Tertullian, like Paul, is an example of thriving with conflict and the dangerous consequences of his preaching, which Shelton suggests Kreider downplays; Shelton, review of *Patient Ferment* (by Alan Kreider), 774.

[108] Note Tertullian threatens Scapula with *Christian* self-sacrifice: *Scap.* 5.2 (CCSL 2:1132).

What the fathers do not at all anticipate is an end to persecution before the *parousia*; the victory will come then, not by human efforts. This is how non-violent patience and the hope of vindication by a just God through participation in cosmic conflict are held in tension. The fathers do not anticipate a church-world alliance, but an overcoming of the world by a God who works for the eternal good of his church. What can be concluded is that a narrative of 'patient ferment' is not necessarily incompatible with one of 'cosmic conflict'.

The fathers' theology is informed by their experiences and is, for them, normative and aspirational, with the objective of shaping Christian identity. Kreider's socio-historical analysis is descriptive, but rooted in a theological idea which resonates with his own tradition. The two perspectives are not inherently contradictory. Furthermore, together they integrate with some insights of social identity theory, as I will subsequently discuss.

Christian social identity

The Christian's identification with Christ in his battle and victory, as expressed in the confession of the name even to death, offers an important theological perspective for discussions of early Christian identity. Social identity theory examines how people view themselves as 'in' one group and view others as 'outsiders', as defined by various boundaries.[109] The present study has identified the association with and confession of the name of Christ as a defining 'boundary' for both Christian self-identification and pagan antagonism. This, rather than a proven and consistent set of behavioural markers, was the reason for Christian condemnation and this, argue the fathers, is what truly sets Christians apart and to which their lives should testify. Behaviour does not define identity; even heretics are martyred. Rather, behaviour should *reflect* identity. One should only suffer for the name of Christian, never as an evil doer. Tertullian is particularly concerned that hypocritical behaviour, such as attending 'spectacles', will belie or obscure that identity.

The declaration *christianus sum* was, from the external perspective, the confession of participation in an illegitimate superstition which undermined societal norms and was potentially treasonous. From the fathers' perspective it was the essential expression of loyalty to one's Lord and God and the prerequisite for being confessed by Christ before the Father. Nevertheless, Clement, Origen, Tertullian and Cyprian differ somewhat as to what 'confession' actually entailed, and the importance of bloody martyrdom.

Tertullian and Cyprian regard both *libellatici and sacrificiati* as having denied the name of Christ. From this perspective, to use Rebillard's expression, they compromised or set aside their Christian identity.[110] Whether this is how the lapsed themselves viewed their actions is impossible to determine; people can move seamlessly from one

---

[109] Philip A. Harland, *Dynamics of Identity in the World of the Early Christians* (New York: T&T Clark, 2009), 6.
[110] Éric Rebillard, *Christians and their Many Identities in Late Antiquity, North Africa 200-450 CE* (Ithaca: Cornell University Press, 2012), 46.

social identity to another, depending on context. Tertullian and Cyprian frame this as an oppositional choice, but this does not require them to be setting up rules that define insider identity as a measure of insider 'loyalty'. They consider these identifying choices as framed by Christ's mandates, the supreme authority outside and above the social 'group'.

Cyprian attributes fear for life and attachment to property as motives of those who obeyed the Decian edict to sacrifice, although Rebillard suggests that some apostates might actually have sympathized with the edict, effectively identifying more with their fellow Graeco-Romans' worldview than that of the church. In the face of conflicting identities (citizen of the empire vs. Christian) the lapsed 'did not activate their Christian membership in the context of their participation in this civic ceremony'.[111] That so many expected to be readily received back into communion without penalty supports this idea. It also coheres with Cyprian's concerns that the church had become indistinct from the world, failing to distinguish between the realm of Satan and that of Christ.[112] Hence Cyprian's insistence on reinforcing that transition back through the formal process of penitence. Referring to the martyr acts and to Tertullian, Lieu states, '"Christian" represents an ultimate, a non-negotiable, identity that even redefines familial and other social roles'.[113] Examples of this include the role reversal of *honestiores* and *humiliores* in the time of Cyprian. Many of the former fled or apostatized, leaving the impoverished *stantes* to care for imprisoned confessors and fugitives.

Rebillard concludes that many Christians did not regard their religious adherence as more significant than other memberships or identities which were shared with non-Christians.[114] Tertullian's chastisement of those who attended shows or were otherwise associated with idolatrous practice, and Cyprian's condemnation of those who clung to worldly possessions confirms that their convictions were not universally shared or 'activated'. Rebillard proposes that the differences between Christians and pagans was a mere 'discursive construct', with 'confessional identities less important than contemporary sources state',[115] which could be a valid sociological observation of the situation in Carthage.

But from a theological perspective, the difference between the ideal Christian identity and the reality for the masses was a crisis that imperilled salvation. One either identifies with Christ and confesses the name, accepting the world's enmity, or one denies Christ, returning to the Devil. Even though the universal achievement of behaviour consistent with identity was unlikely, as Rebillard suggests, this does not negate the fathers' efforts to so influence their communities. Lack of consistent demonstration of loyalty to Christ by appropriate behaviour is indeed a major driver for some of the fathers' writings, with the intention of shaping identity. As Kreider effectively asserts, something must have worked, because Christianity grew, against what could be considered significant odds.

---

[111] Ibid., 51.
[112] Cyprian, *Laps.* 8–12, 15–18 (CCSL 3: 225–7, 228–31).
[113] Judith M. Lieu, *Christian Identity in the Jewish and Graeco-Roman World* (Oxford: Oxford University Press, 2004), 254.
[114] Rebillard, *Many Identities*, 60.
[115] Ibid., 1.

The present study brings a theological perspective to the discussion of Christian social identity. The four fathers sought to define Christian identity in terms of confession of the name, and to shape behaviour accordingly. They derived this identity from Scripture and held it to be true, even though it may not have been representative of wider practice, or as formative of behaviour as they desired. Whilst confession of the name is the ultimate boundary within which true Christian identity is defined, the four differ in the variety of ways 'confession' may ultimately be understood and what behaviours may contradict it. Jensen notes that the New Testament testimony to Christian discipleship necessarily entails suffering and rejection. As I have shown, this was articulated by the four fathers. Jensen concludes that 'Martyrdom is the possibility latent in the Christian identity, for all Christians are called to the "witness" or "testimony" (μαρτύριον) that might result in bloody (or "red") martyrdom'.[116]

Leiu recognizes the Christocentricity of early identity formation,[117] but finds it difficult to identify the accompanying social and behavioural markers.[118] I suggest that this is because her study largely focuses on the second century. The third-century fathers had a more developed diogmology and more comprehensively articulated their understanding of the Christian's identity in Christ. This concurs with Kreider's thesis that early Christianity *was* distinguished by behavioural markers, what he terms the patient habitus of the community. Although Lieu believes the early texts are 'both idealistic and prescriptive', but not 'descriptive',[119] she also recognizes that 'the image of a common life, and of a set of values predicated on mutual support, must surely be an inalienable element in the shared symbols that shaped early Christian identity'.[120]

Returning to Matthew Recla's concern that 'martyrdom' as an act is an inadequate identity marker for Christians, because identity as an analytical tool is insufficiently distinguished from identity as practiced, we are in a position to revisit his concept of 'willingness to suffer'.[121] Recla proposes that 'we intentionally isolate the theological justifications that support "willingness to suffer," which are broadly inculcated in Christian self-understanding, from the act of martyrdom itself'.[122] The individual (a small minority of whom were actually martyred) cannot identify with martyrdom itself, but with this perceived willingness, which will only come to fruition if God wills it.[123] From the theological perspective of the four fathers, this 'willingness to suffer' could equate to the imperative to confess one's identity in Christ. This confession may or may not result in martyrdom.

Recla notes the difficulty of establishing an essential link between martyrdom and individual Christian identity when the vast majority of Christians who have ever lived

---

[116] Michael P. Jensen, *Martyrdom and Identity: The Self on Trial* (London: T&T Clark, 2010), 6.
[117] Lieu, *Christian Identity*, 131.
[118] Ibid., 146.
[119] Ibid., 168.
[120] Ibid., 169.
[121] Matthew Recla, 'Martyrdom and the Creation of Christian Identity', in *The Wiley Blackwell Companion to Christian Martyrdom,* ed. Paul Middleton (West Sussex UK: John Wiley & Sons, 2020), 199–214, at 199.
[122] Ibid., 199.
[123] Ibid., 203–5.

have not been martyred; a mischaracterization of the martyr's role as paradigmatic has led to the overestimation and misappropriation that Moss condemns.[124] But if the identifying paradigm is the imperative to *confess* (equivalent to Recla's 'willingness to suffer', but not necessarily requiring martyrdom) the problem is resolved. All Christians are called to confess, and to never deny, their identity 'in Christ'. This has a theological and a scriptural basis which not all the various 'constructions' of martyrdom necessarily share. Tertullian and the martyr acts sustain the conflation of confession and martyrdom, which has potentially fuelled the problematic version of 'martyrdom identity' whereas the other fathers do not. Our conclusions largely depend on whom we read.

The theological perspective of the fathers, presented in this study, helps to clarify the tension between identity formation and its expression in behaviour. If the name of Christ is central to Christian identity, it must be expressed in behaviour. That behaviour reflects a whole of life confession. This applies variously to Clement's gnostic, for whom (a particular type of) martyrdom is one route to perfection, to Origen's 'complete confession', to Tertullian's narrow view of a disciplined life preparing for confession in death, and to Cyprian's broad spectrum of worthiness for a crown. The fathers' diogmology asserts, 'be this; do this'. Identity theory recognizes that not all early Christians consistently 'did this', because of inconsistent identity activation, particularly in times of crisis. Diogmology adds a distinction between individual fathers' ideas of what must be 'done' in the confession of what one should 'be'.

Formation or fabrication?

Candida Moss's assertion that Christians invented martyrdom stories to construct an identity of the persecuted Christian community has been the subject of controversy.[125] Moss dismisses the martyr acts and other early writings as the forgeries, fabrications and fictions of later generations to service their theological agendas. In the same way, she argues, the tradition of Christian martyrdom has been uncritically adopted to service contemporary political agendas. But as Shelton recognizes, such misappropriation has nothing to do with the credibility of ancient Christian persecution.[126] Moss's argument builds on, but departs from, her earlier works[127] which establish regional differences in early martyr traditions, argue persuasively for later dating and redaction of the *Acta*, and illuminate the influence of anachronistic perceptions of 'natural' and 'unnatural death' on the discourse of voluntary

---

[124] Ibid., 204.
[125] Moss, *Myth of Persecution*. Moss extends this fabrication to the Gospel accounts of Jesus' death (pp. 56–61) as well as the martyr acts, which are her primary focus in this work. Two of many reviews which together form a balanced critique are Anne T Thayer, review of *The Myth of Persecution* (by Candida Moss) *Interpretation* 68, no. 1 (2014), 81–3 and W. Brian Shelton, review of *The Myth of Persecution* (by Candida Moss) *Journal of the Evangelical Theological Society* 57, no. 1 (2014), 210–14.
[126] Shelton, review of *Myth of Persecution* (by Candida Moss), 214.
[127] Candida Moss, *Ancient Christian Martyrdom: Diverse Practices, Theologies and Traditions* (New Haven: Yale University Press, 2012); Candida Moss, 'The Discourse of Voluntary Martyrdom: Ancient and Modern', *Church History* 81, no. 3 (2012), 531–51.

martyrdom.[128] It diverges significantly from her earlier more nuanced engagement with 'prosecution' rather than 'persecution'.[129]

The fathers of the church speak from the past, and from different locations and social milieus. The attention given to persecution by Clement, Origen, Tertullian and Cyprian highlights that it was a reality for them and a common feature of their contexts. It is certainly not all that they write about, but it is undeniably there, often in the background, occasionally to the fore. Although the four cannot be considered to have met each other, their collective testimony to a lived experience tells a consistent story. In fact, the absence of opportunity to 'collaborate' makes their testimony the more credible.

I began with an assumption of modified minimalism, the model of intermittent, locally driven animosity occasionally flaring into mob violence, delation to authorities, and potential prosecution according to the discretion of the governor. It is illegitimate to claim to have proven a starting assumption, but it should be evident that the model is a good fit for the situations the fathers describe. There is no need to defend the older 'imperial' or 'top-down' model of persecution. This might be the impression given by a superficial reading of the second-century apologies and the martyr acts, but a consideration of the theological position and testimony of the third-century fathers balances the narrative. It is certainly illegitimate to ignore the fathers' testimony in an effort to dismiss the early church's persecution experience as a myth, based on a negative appraisal of the martyr acts. As Harrison notes,

> Although the conclusions of Moss regarding the limited, local, and sporadic nature of Roman persecution of Christians under the empire, as well as the tendentiousness of the later martyrdom accounts, have long since been accepted by historians, to dismiss the entire tradition of the persecution of the early Christians as a carefully constructed myth is surely an overstatement.[130]

The findings of the present study reinforce this critique. I acknowledge that Moss does not present a theological appraisal of third-century fathers, so we have worked largely from different sources. However, the consistency of the fathers' broad foundational theology of persecution and the explanations of their divergences testify to a significant and real perception that they were part of a persecuted community. They were compelled to make sense of this experience in terms of theological reflection on the Scriptures. They were driven to consider the origins of, reasons for, and endpoint of this experience on a higher plane. They searched for the cosmic reality behind the events, a perceived reality that is by no means foreign to the martyr acts.

In concert with the critiques raised by others, I perceive that Moss strategically errs in targeting the veracity of the early Christian persecution experience in order to

---

[128] Moss, 'Discourse on Voluntary Martyrdom', 548–50.
[129] Moss, *Ancient Christian Martyrdom*, 50–1.
[130] James R. Harrison, 'The Persecutions of Christians from Nero to Hadrian', in *Into all the World: Emergent Christianity in its Jewish and Greco-Roman Context*, ed. Mark Harding and Alanna Nobbs, (Grand Rapids: Eerdmans, 2017), 266–300, at 267.

undermine the basis of contemporary misappropriation of it. A fundamental methodological problem is, having offered a sound argument for the martyr acts to be significantly redacted works dated later than the events they purport to describe, she still treats them as primary formative documents, justifying her dismissal of their historical and theological testimony. However, if they do post-date the reception of Clement's 'middle way' as orthopraxy, then more attention should be paid to what the third-century fathers present as the theology of martyrdom and persecution. I offer this study as evidence that the third-century fathers, independently of the martyr acts,[131] had a coherent and scripturally based theology of persecution, which if Moss is correct (and I believe she is in this respect) predates the *Acta*. This perspective neither dismisses nor legitimizes the rewriting and reinterpretation of the martyr tradition from the fourth century onwards. Something significant was perceived to have happened in the second and third centuries, and it had a significant lasting effect. As Conant explains, 'Scholars routinely acknowledge ... that, whatever its lived realities, the experience of persecution was deeply traumatic to the early church, and that memories of victimization profoundly shaped Christian worldviews for centuries to come'.[132]

Regional differences in martyrology

Moss explores early church martyr literature from Asia Minor, Rome, Gaul, North Africa and Alexandria, concluding that there were ideological distinctives between regions, although they were not absolute.[133] Moss predominantly focuses on martyr acts, but determines that Clement's Alexandrian milieu was influenced by (so-called) Gnosticism and Tertullian's African millieu by an 'apocalyptic' ideology of martyrdom, evident in the Scillitan martyrs and the *Passio Perpetuae*. I recognized the potential for regional diogmological distinctives in determining to compare and contrast two Carthaginians with two Alexandrians in the present work. Whilst acknowledging the significant differences between Moss's study and mine, it is evident that there are indeed regional differences in diogmology. Without discounting the intellectual social, political and historical influences that are Moss's primary interest, I have focused on the interaction between the broader theology and use of Scripture in the two locales.

My study supports Moss's in identifying no significant influence of the martyr acts on Clement, and in her conclusion that 'for Clement, martyrdom is overlaid by the discourse of perfection ... and his ideal Christian – the gnostic'.[134] Further, 'martyrdom, for Clement, is part of living a life in accordance with the knowledge of God, but martyrdom is certainly neither essential to this life, nor qualitatively different from that

---

[131] As Moss herself argues, there is no evidence that Clement knew or used the *Acta*. Tertullian only refers to a version of the *Passio*, the events of which he potentially witnessed. I agree with Moss that the final forms of the *Acta* are redacted and probably post-date the subjects of this thesis.
[132] Jonathan P. Conant, 'Memories of Trauma and the Formation of Christian Identity'. In *Memories of Utopia: The Revision of Histories and Landscapes in Late Antiquity,* edited by Bronwen Neil and Kosta Simic, 36–56, at 36. (London: Routledge, 2020).
[133] Moss, *Ancient Christian Martyrdom*: Moss's interest is in the ideological rather than theological aspects of martyrdom.
[134] Moss, *Ancient Christian Martyrdom*, 147.

life's other parts'.[135] This statement is true with respect to martyrdom, but Moss has not embraced Clement's commitment to confession. Confession is essential to the gnostic life 'in Christ' but it does not have to result in martyrdom. This is what makes Clement not a 'radical martyr' (conflating confession and martyrdom) in contrast to Tertullian. Moss says little about Tertullian in her survey; her African focus is on the Scillitan martyrs and the *Passio Perpetuae*. From these two documents she 'receives the overwhelming impression that North African Christianity was exclusively pro-martyrdom', whilst detecting hints of opposition in the Christian community that Tertullian condemns.[136] Whilst Tertullian's relationship to the *Passio* is controversial, it is fair to say that, of the four fathers, his martyrology has the most in common with martyr acts generally. Nevertheless, this is not a regional influence as much as a diogmological one, as I have shown. Both the Greek and Latin *Acta* unite the act of confession with martyrdom, and consider the victory over the Devil to be in the martyr's death. This same conflation of confession and martyrdom is strongly linked with the idea of Christian identity in the North African writings.

Voluntary martyrdom: yes or no?

I offer a diogmological perspective as a contribution to the discussion of voluntary martyrdom in the early church. Moss contends that it was not a recognized category of martyrdom prior to Clement, and that he developed his three categories in order to position himself, as a Christian gnostic, in the middle way.[137] Whether this was driven by theological conviction or a need to justify his own flight from persecution (as Moss proposes), comes down to his personal integrity and motivation, which we are not in a position to judge. Middleton argues that voluntary martyrdom was common and was accepted as orthodox and not distinguished from other types of martyrdom, until after Clement's time.[138] Both Middleton and Moss identify Clement as a turning point, and both acknowledge that his contemporary Tertullian did not distinguish between types of martyrdom. An appreciation of Clement's diogmology establishes a theological basis for this perceived turning point.

Whether or not Tertullian had read any early versions of the martyr acts (other than the *Passio*) his conflation of confession and martyrdom matches that of the *Acta*. The point of confession of the name in these *Acta* leads immediately to victory in death; the two are inseparable. This, I propose, is at the heart of Middleton's definition. 'Radical martyrs are those Christians who so desired death, that they intentionally sought out arrest and martyrdom.'[139] Perhaps it is conviction that confession to death was *true* confession, rather than an anachronistic descriptor of 'voluteerists' versus orthodox or 'normal' martyrs, that is the real distinguisher. Those who disagreed with

---

[135] Ibid., 147.
[136] Ibid., 145.
[137] Moss, 'Discourse of Voluntary Martyrdom', 544.
[138] Middleton, 'Early Christian Voluntary Martyrdom: A Statement for the Defence', *Journal of Theological Studies* 64, no.2 (2013), 556–73, at 562, 571.
[139] Middleton, *Radical Martyrdom*, 2.

'volunteering' had diogmologies characterized by a broader definition of 'confession'. Again, whether there were personal motives underlying the theology, is impossible to determine. But it is difficult to charge Origen or Cyprian with self-interest or cowardice, even as they broadened the definition of true confession to not necessarily require a martyr's death.

Rather than distinguishing 'voluntary martyrs' as a species of disputed prevalence, who were singled out for condemnation following appropriation of Clement's 'middle way' as orthopraxy, I propose the existence of two diogmological threads or streams within the early church. Firstly, those who conflated confession and martyrdom as the point of victory in the cosmic conflict equate to Middleton's 'radical' martyrs. They emphasized the cosmic conflict and arena motifs and had a high view of martyrdom as a God-ordained good, including its exculpatory benefits. Tertullian and the martyr acts are prime examples. Secondly, there are those who emphasized different forms of confession, and endurance to the end – without denial – as the point of victory in the cosmic conflict. These may still have a high view of martyrdom, such as Cyprian and Origen, but they downplay its exclusivity. They may be even less focused on martyrdom, as was Clement, depending on their views of the role God plays in bringing persecution.

This, I propose, concords with both Moss's and Middleton's positions, although I must disagree with Moss's subsequent conclusion that the whole concept of martyrdom was a fabrication.[140] Middleton concludes that Clement's novel position finds no support in his contemporaries' literature.[141] I suggest this is because he is an outlier in much of his diogmology, which ultimately stems from his idea that persecution is evil and not permitted by God. Origen departs from this, and Tertullian contrasts markedly with it. Moss concludes that the 'discursive production of voluntary martyrdom begins in the early third century with Clement', and considers it unclear whether his predecessors or contemporaries shared it.[142] I propose that they did not. Moss's conclusion on voluntary martyrdom concurs with my own:

> For the Carthaginian Tertullian, the line between forms of martyrdom cuts not between voluntary martyrdom and normative martyrdom but between those who flee from persecution and those who are martyred ... for Clement the point at which martyrdom becomes necessary is the point at which one is forced to confess or deny Christ.[143]

Clement's reticence for martyrdom is grounded in his diogmology. Tertullian's enthusiasm for it is consistent with his diogmology. The 'timing' and distinctiveness of Clement's position make him *appear* to mark a turning point, but the other fathers derive their conclusions from their own diogmologies. The connections between confession and martyrdom evident in the fathers' considerations of persecution thus help to explain, Moss's and Middleton's observations theologically.

---

[140] Moss, *Myth of Persecution*. Her change of position is noted also by Shelton, review of *Myth of Persecution* (by Candida Moss), 211.
[141] Middleton, 'Statement for the Defence', 571.
[142] Moss, 'Discourse of Voluntary Martyrdom', 547.
[143] Moss, 'Discourse of Voluntary Martyrdom', 547.

Contemporary relevance

The four fathers' writings provide evidence for the impact of persecution as a lived experience, which should not be ignored or dismissed, even though the details of the historicity cannot be validated. If contemporary agendas have misappropriated the early church's testimony as a persecuted community, as Moss suggests, the problem can be addressed on two levels. One is the historical evidence, to which the third-century theologians contribute, with arguably less hagiographic redaction than the martyr acts. Even allowing that the four fathers are equally discursive and constructive of 'historical reality', they have an important contribution to make. Critically, if it is alleged that a theological or ideological impropriety is involved in the manipulation of modern Christian identity, then a *theological* engagement is required. Rather than dismissing the textual evidence in a polemical engagement with those who might misrepresent it today, it seems more constructive to offer an appropriately formed diogmology as a corrective.

Concluding reflections

Christians are commonly criticized for engaging in physical and verbal violence and oppression in the defence of their worldview and proselytizing interests. From being a persecuted minority, they became, at times, the persecuting majority. The crusades, the Inquisition and the conflicts between Protestant denominations are well-known examples of conflict and persecution that are fundamentally at odds with that of the early church. Tertullian and Cyprian anticipated an imminent end to the world as they knew it. As persecution shifted from local to empire-wide, and Christians came more to the attention of the imperial authorities, the stage was set for the last great phase of persecution. In 313 the world upended; thereafter Christians were tolerated, even favoured. The church, in a sense, became the world. Ascetics and monks became the new martyrs. As Middleton observes, 'loyalty to the Church, through developing episcopal ecclesiastical structures, created an alternative means of constructing what it meant to be a faithful Christian'.[144]

Middleton traces the changing perspectives on martyrdom in the context of persecution of Christians by other Christians and the consequences for Christian identity. He concludes: 'When Christians eventually began to create other Christian martyrs, Christian identity was transformed from those who suffered to those who inflicted suffering.'[145] It would be a fascinating study to further explore this hypothesis, to trace the development of diogmology into the fourth century and beyond.[146] The

---

[144] Paul Middleton, 'Enemies of the (Church and) State: Martyrdom as a Problem for Early Christianity', *Annali di storia dell'esegesi* 29, no. 2 (2012), 161–81, at 161.
[145] Ibid., 181.
[146] The question of why Christians continue to claim to be persecuted beyond the cessation of state-sponsored persecution/ prosecution after Constantine is explored in the collected essays in Fournier and Mayer, eds, *Heirs of Roman Persecution: Studies on a Christian and Para-Christian Discourse in Late Antiquity,* ed. Éric Fournier and Wendy Mayer (London: Routledge, 2020).

early fathers wrote in the formative period of the church, a period shaped by persecution and their perspective on this experience is worthy of attention. This may be particularly relevant where concerns about the church's role and standing lead to suggestions of imminent defeat or the perceived necessity to defend itself with political and physical aggression.

Would the early church have survived the opposition of society without at least an implicit, if not systematically articulated, diogmology? I suggest not, in terms of its fundamental identity *as Christianity*. This is not such an audacious claim as it might first appear. Let us indulge a brief thought experiment. If the early Christians had not held to the exclusivity of worship of their God, and had embraced syncretism, arguably they would not have been persecuted. Would this have resulted in their survival as a distinct religious entity? Imagine that the early Christians had no clear concept of God's goodness or providential care; perhaps they would espouse an incipient deism, or even a form of Stoic fatalism. Persecution would seem serendipitous, without reason, meaning or restraint. The powers of evil (however they were understood) would have free reign. What reason would there be to hold to Christian distinctiveness rather than capitulate to syncretism? Without a reason, a theological basis for persecution, particularly with an uncertain prospect of good or bad consequences for confession of a given religious ideal, where would be the impetus to withstand opposition? Why confess the name of Christ exclusively, if it meant misery in this life and no clearly articulated recompense in the next? The fact that the early church emerged from this period of tribulation as the *Christian* church testifies that its self-perception as a community of Christ-confessors, not merely its survival in some form or other, was a priority. This in turn required a theological basis for that identity, understood at a fundamental level. The average Christian probably did not work through their diogmology to the same degree as the four fathers, but it was undoubtedly internalized. The church could have responded by active resistance, or by compromise and acquiescence, but had it done either it would not have endured, or if it did it would not have been the church which held to the name of Christ.

In this study, I have endeavoured to set martyrdom within a broader context of persecution. Christian identity is challenged by persecution, but fundamentally, persecution provides the opportunity for confession of that identity in a way that seals and reinforces it and brings it to consummation. Each of the four fathers identifies a conflict at the heart of persecution, a conflict in a cosmic dimension, in which Christians participate. They express different understandings of how victory in that conflict is achieved, of the nature of confession and whether 'bloody' martyrdom is its pinnacle. Yet clearly, the responses the fathers advocated, in terms of attitude and action, reflected their understanding of how that conflict was to be experienced in Christian life. The battle was fought, not with the weapons of violence and hatred directed at them, but through patient endurance and confession (in its various manifestations) unto death (natural or otherwise).

The church was not only involved in 'cosmic conflict', but in 'patient ferment'. Both come together as a lived expression of the Christian's identity in Christ. The identity to be confessed is the identity to be lived. The Christian life of confession and endurance, character and behaviour consistent with the identification with Christ, constitute the weapons of spiritual warfare. As Tertullian insists, Christians must be persecuted for the right reasons, because they bear the name of Christ, not for any misdeeds. Life must reflect conviction, a belief each of the four variously expressed. Distinctiveness confessed, distinctiveness expressed; this was fundamental to the survival and growth of early Christianity.

Bibliography

Primary sources

Acta Proconsularia. Edited by Wilhelm von Hartel. CSEL 3.1. Vienna: Gerold, 1868.
Acts of the Scillitan Martyrs. Edited by Herbert Musurillo. Pages 86–9 in *The Acts of the Christian Martyrs.* Oxford: Clarendon, 1972.
Amat, Jacqueline, *Passion de Perpétue et de Félicité suivi des Actes. Introduction, texte critique, traduction, commentaire et index* Sources Chrétiennes 417 Paris: Les Éditions du Cerf, 1996.
Clément d'Alexandrie. *Le Pédagogue I.* Edited by Henri-Irénée Marrou, translated by Marguerite Harl. SC 70. Paris: Les Éditions du Cerf, 1983
Clément d'Alexandrie. *Le Protreptique.* Edited by Claude Mondésert. SC 2. Paris: Les Éditions du Cerf, 1949.
Clément d'Alexandrie. *Quel riche sera sauvé?* Edited by P. Descourtieux and C. Nardi. SC 537. Paris: Les Éditions du Cerf, 2011.
Clément d'Alexandrie. *Stromate I.* Edited by C. Mondésert and M. Caster. SC 30. Paris: Les Éditions du Cerf, 2013.
Clément d'Alexandrie. *Stromate II.* Edited by P.-T. Camelot and C. Mondésert. SC 38. Paris: Les Éditions du Cerf, 2013.
Clément d'Alexandrie. *Stromate IV.* Edited by A. van den Hoeck and C. Mondésert. SC 463. Paris: Les Éditions du Cerf, 2001.
Clément d'Alexandrie. *Stromate V.* Edited by A. Le Boulluec and P. Voulet. SC 278. Paris: Les Éditions du Cerf, 2006.
Clément d'Alexandrie. *Stromate VI.* Edited by P. Descourtieux. SC 446. Paris: Les Éditions du Cerf, 1999.
Clément d'Alexandrie. *Stromate VII.* Edited by Alain le Boulluec. SC 428. Paris: Les Éditions du Cerf, 1997.
Clementis Alexandrini. *Fragmenta.* Edited by J.-P. Migne. PG 9. Paris: Migne, 1857.
Clementis Alexandrini. *Paedagogos* II. Edited by J.-P. Migne. PG 8. Paris: Migne, 1857.
Clementis Alexandrini. *Stromateis* I, II, III. Edited by J.-P. Migne. PG 8. Paris: Migne, 1857.
Clementis Alexandrini. *Stromateis* VIII. Edited by J.-P. Migne. PG 8. Paris: Migne, 1857.
Cyprian. *Ad Demetrianum.* Edited by M. Simonetti. CCSL 3A. Turnhout: Brepols, 1976.
Cyprian. *Ad Donatum.* Edited by M. Simonetti. CCSL 3A. Turnhout: Brepols, 1976.
Cyprian. *Ad Fortunatum.* Edited by R. Weber. CCSL 3. Turnhout: Brepols, 1972.
Cyprian. *Ad Quirinum.* Edited by R. Weber. CCSL 3. Turnhout: Brepols, 1972.
Cyprian. *De bono patientiae.* Edited by C. Moreschini. CCSL 3A. Turnhout: Brepols, 1976.
Cyprian. *De dominica oratione.* Edited by C. Moreschini. CCSL 3A. Turnhout: Brepols, 1976.
Cyprian. *De ecclesia catholica unitate.* Edited by M. Bévenot. CCSL 3. Turnhout: Brepols, 1972.
Cyprian. *De habitu virginum.* Edited by L. Ciccolini. CCSL 3F. Turnhout: Brepols, 2016.
Cyprian. *De lapsis.* Edited by M. Bévenot. CCSL 3. Turnhout: Brepols, 1972.

Cyprian. *De mortalitate*. Edited by M. Simonetti. CCSL 3A. Turnhout: Brepols, 1976.
Cyprian. *De opere et eleemosynis*. Edited by M. Simonetti. CCSL 3A. Turnhout: Brepols, 1976.
Cyprian. *De zelo et livore*. Edited by M. Simonetti. CCSL 3A. Turnhout: Brepols, 1976.
Cyprian. *Epistulae* 1–57. Edited by G. F. Diercks. CCSL 3B. Turnhout: Brepols, 1994.
Cyprian. *Epistulae* 58–81. Edited by G. F. Diercks. CCSL 3C. Turnhout: Brepols, 1996.
Cyprian. *The Letters of St. Cyprian of Carthage*. 4 vols. Translated and annotated by G. W. Clarke. ACW 43, 44, 46, 47. New York Eusebius: *Historia Ecclesiastica*. Eduard Schwartzin Die Griechischen christlichen Schriftsteller der ersten Jahrhunderte (Leipzig: Hinrichs'sche Buchhandlung, 1897).
Eusebius. Ecclesiastical History. 2 vols. Loeb Classical Library 153, 265. Translated by Kirsopp Lake (I) and J. E. L. Oulton (II) Cambridge MS: Harvard University Press, 1965, 1964.
Eusebius. *The Church History*. Translation and Commentary by Paul L Maier. Grand Rapids: Kregel, 2007.
[Hippolytus]. *Traditio Apostolica*. On the Apostolic Tradition. Translated and edited by Alistair Stewart-Sykes. Crestwood, NY: St Vladimir's Seminary Press, 2001.
Historica Augusta vol. 1. Loeb Classical Library No. 139. Trans. David Magie, rev. David Rohrbacher. Cambridge MS: Harvard University Press, 2022.
Holmes, Michael W., ed. and trans. *The Apostolic Fathers, Greek Texts and English Translations*. Grand Rapids: Baker, 2004.
Jerome. *De viris illustribus*. Edited by J.-P. Migne. PL 23. Paris: Migne/Garnier, 1883.
Julian, *Letter to Arsacius,* trans. Edward J. Chinnock, 1901. http://www.thenagain.info/Classes/Sources/Julian.html
Lactanti. *Diuinae institutiones*. Edited by Samuel Brandt and Georgius Laubman. CSEL 19. Vienna: Tempsky, 1890.
Martyrdom of Perpetua and Felicitas. Edited by Herbert Musurillo. In *The Acts of the Christian Martyrs*, 106–31. Oxford: Clarendon, 1972.
M. Minucii Felicis. *Octavius*. Edited by Carouls Halm. CSEL 2. Vienna, 1867.
Origen. *Commentary on the Gospel according to John*. 2 vols. Translated by Ronald E. Heine. Fathers of the Church 80 and 89. Washington: Catholic University of America Press, 1989, 1993.
Origen. *On First Principles*. 2 vols. Translated and Edited by John Behr. Oxford: Oxford University Press, 2017.
Origen. *The Commentary of Origen on the Gospel of St Matthew*, 2 vols. Translated by Ronald E. Heine. Oxford: Oxford University Press, 2018.
Origen. *Treatise on the Passover and Dialogue with Heraclides and his fellow bishops on the Father, the Son and the Soul*. Ancient Christian Writers: The Works of the Fathers in Translation 54. Translated and annotated by Robert J. Daly. New York: Paulist, 1992.
Origen. *A Letter from Origen to Friends in Alexandria*. H Crouzel, ed. Orientalia Christiana Analecta 195. Roma: Pont. Inst. Or. Stud, 1973, 135–50.
Origène. *Commentaire sur l'Épître aux Romains*, 4 vols. Edited by L. Brésard and M. Fédou (2009), SC 532, 539, 543, 555. Paris: Les Éditions du Cerf, 2009–12.
Origène. *Commentaire sur S. Jean* 1–5. Edited by Cecile Blanc. SC 120, 157, 290, 385. Paris: Les Éditions du Cerf, 1966, 1970, 1982, 1992.
Origène. *Commentaire sur L'Evangile selon Matthieu* I Livres X et XI. Edited by Robert Girod. SC 162. Paris: Les Éditions du Cerf, 1970.
Origène. *Contre Celse*. Edited by Marcel Borret. SC 132, 136, 147, 150. Paris: Les Éditions du Cerf, 1967–9.

Origène. *Entretien avec Héraclide.* Edited by J. Scherer. SC 67. Paris: Les Éditions du Cerf, 2002.
Origène. *Homélies sur la Genèse.* Edited by H. de Lubac and L. Doutreleau. SC 7. Paris: Les Éditions du Cerf, 2011.
Origène. *Homélies sur l'Exode.* Edited by M. Borret. SC 352. Paris: Les Éditions du Cerf, 2011.
Origène. *Homélies sur le Lévitique.* 2 vols. Edited by M. Borret. SC 286, 287. Paris: Les Éditions du Cerf, 1981.
Origène. *Homélies sur Jérémie.* 2 vols. Edited by P. Nautin and P. Husson. SC 232, 238. Paris: Les Éditions du Cerf, 2006.
Origène. *Philocalie 21–7.* Edited by Eric Junod. SC 226. Paris: Les Éditions du Cerf, 2006.
Origène. *Philocalie 1–20 et Lettre à Africanus.* Edited by M. Harl and N. de Lange. SC 302. Paris: Les Éditions du Cerf, 1983.
Origenis. *Commentaria in Evangelium Joannis.* Patrologia Graeca. Edited by J.-P. Migne. PG 14. Paris: Migne, 1862.
Origenis. *Commentaria in Evangelium Secundum Matthaeum.* Patrologia Graeca. Edited by J.-P. Migne. PG 13. Paris: Migne, 1862.
Origenis. *Homiliae in Ezechielem.* Patrologia Graeca. Edited by J.-P. Migne. PG 13. Paris: Migne, 1862.
Origenis. *Homiliae in Genesim.* Patrologia Graeca. Edited by J.-P. Migne. PG 12. Paris: Migne, 1862.
Origenis. *Homiliae in Leviticum.* Patrologia Graeca. Edited by J.-P. Migne. PG 12. Paris: Migne, 1862.
Origenis. *Homiliae in Leviticum.* Patrologia Graeca. Edited by J.-P. Migne. PG 13. Paris: Migne, 1862.
Origenis. *Homiliae in Lucam.* Patrologia Graeca. Edited by J.-P. Migne. PG 12. Paris: Migne, 1862.
Origenis. *Libellus de oratione.* Patrologia Graeca. Edited by J.-P. Migne. PG 11. Paris: Migne, 1857.
Origenous. Ἐις μαρτύριον προτρεπτικός (*Exhortation to martyrdom*). P. Koetschau, ed. Origenes Werke I. Die Schrift vom Martyrium, Buch I–IV gegen Celsus Die Griechischen Schriftsteller (GCS) 2. Leipzig: J. C. Hinrichs'sche Buchhandlung, 1899, 3–47.
Passio sanctarum Perpetuae et Felicitatis. In *Greek and Latin Narratives about the Ancient Martyrs.* Edited by Éric Rebillard. Oxford: Oxford University Press, 2017, 304–49.
Plato, *Republic* vol. 5, books 1–5. Loeb Classical Library no. 237. Edited and translated by Chris Emlyn-Jones and William Preddy. Cambridge MS: Harvard University Press, 2013.
Pliny the Younger, *Letters and Panegyricus* vol. 2. Loeb Classical Library No. 59 Books VIII–X. Translated by Betty Radice. Cambridge MS: Harvard University Press, 1969.
Pontius. *Vita Cypriani.* Edited by Wilhelm von Hartel. CSEL 3.1. Vienna: Gerold, 1868.
Seutonius, *Lives of the Caesars*, vol. 2. Loeb Classical Library no. 38. Trans. J. C. Rolfe (Cambridge MS: Harvard University Press, 1979).
Tacitus, *Annals*, Books XIII–XVI Loeb Classical Library No. 322. Trans. John Jackson. Cambridge MS: Harvard University Press, 1937.
Tertullian. *Ad martyras.* Edited by E. Kroymann. CCSL 1. Turnhout: Brepols, 1954.
Tertullian. *Ad nationes.* Edited by E. Kroymann. CCSL 1. Turnhout: Brepols, 1954.
Tertullian. *Ad Scapulam.* Edited by E. Kroymann. CCSL 2. Turnhout: Brepols, 1954.
Tertullian. *Ad uxorem.* Edited by E. Kroymann. CCSL 1. Turnhout: Brepols, 1954.

Tertullian. *Aduersus Hermogenem.* Edited by E. Kroymann. CCSL 1. Turnhout: Brepols, 1954.
Tertullian. *Aduersus Iudaeos.* Edited by E. Kroymann. CCSL 2. Turnhout: Brepols, 1954.
Tertullian. *Aduersus Marcionem.* Edited by E. Kroymann. CCSL 1. Turnhout: Brepols, 1954.
Tertullian. *Aduersus Praxean.* Edited by E. Kroymann and E. Evans. CCSL 2. Turnhout: Brepols, 1954.
Tertullian. *Aduersus Valentinianos.* Edited by E. Kroymann. CCSL 2. Turnhout: Brepols, 1954.
Tertullian. *Apologeticum.* Edited by E. Kroymann. CCSL 1. Turnhout: Brepols, 1954.
Tertullian. *De anima.* Edited by J. H. Waszink. CCSL 2. Turnhout: Brepols, 1954.
Tertullian. *De baptismo.* Edited by J. G. P. Borleffs. CCSL 1. Turnhout: Brepols, 1954.
Tertullian. *De carne Christi.* Edited by E. Kroymann. CCSL 2. Turnhout: Brepols, 1954.
Tertullian. *De corona.* Edited by E. Kroymann. CCSL 2. Turnhout: Brepols, 1954.
Tertullian. *De cultu feminarum.* Edited by E. Kroymann. CCSL 1. Turnhout: Brepols, 1954. Brepols, 1954.
Tertullian. *De exhortatione castitatis.* Edited by E. Kroymann. CCSL 2. Turnhout: Brepols, 1954.
Tertullian. *De fuga in persecutione.* Edited by E. Kroymann. CCSL 2. Turnhout: Brepols, 1954.
Tertullian. *De idololatria.* Edited by E. Kroymann. CCSL 2. Turnhout: Brepols, 1954.
Tertullian. *De ieiunio adversus Psychicos.* Edited by E. Kroymann. CCSL 2. Turnhout: Brepols, 1954.
Tertullian. *De monogamia.* Edited by E. Kroymann. CCSL 2. Turnhout: Brepols, 1954.
Tertullian. *De oratione.* Edited by E. Kroymann. CCSL 1. Turnhout: Brepols, 1954.
Tertullian. *De paenitentia.* Edited by E. Kroymann. CCSL 1. Turnhout: Brepols, 1954.
Tertullian. *De pallio.* Edited by E. Kroymann. CCSL 2. Turnhout: Brepols, 1954.
Tertullian. *De patientia.* Edited by E. Kroymann. CCSL 1. Turnhout: Brepols, 1954.
Tertullian. *De praescriptione haereticorum.* Edited by E. Kroymann. CCSL 1. Turnhout: Brepols, 1954.
Tertullian. *De pudicitia.* Edited by E. Kroymann. CCSL 2. Turnhout: Brepols, 1954.
Tertullian. *De resurrectione mortuorum.* Edited by E. Kroymann. CCSL 2. Turnhout: Brepols, 1954.
Tertullian. *De spectaculis.* Edited by E. Kroymann. CCSL 1. Turnhout: Brepols, 1954.
Tertullian. *De testimonio animae.* Edited by E. Kroymann. CCSL 1. Turnhout: Brepols, 1954.
Tertullian. *De virginibus velandis.* Edited by E. Kroymann. CCSL 2. Turnhout: Brepols, 1954.
Tertullian. *Scorpiace.* Edited by E. Kroymann. CCSL 2. Turnhout: Brepols, 1954.

Secondary literature

Ashwin-Siejkowski, Piotr. *Clement of Alexandria: A Project of Christian Perfection.* London: T&T Clark, 2008.
Atkinson, Philip C. 'A Study in the Development of Tertullian's Use and Interpretation of Scripture, with Special Reference to his Involvement in the New Prophecy.' PhD diss., University of Hull, 1976. https://hull-repository.worktribe.com/
Barnes, Timothy D. 'Legislation Against the Christians.' *Journal of Roman Studies* 58, nos. 1–2 (1968): 32–50.

Barnes, Timothy D. 'Pagan Perceptions of Christianity.' In *Early Christianity: Origins and Evolution to AD 600*, edited by Ian Hazlett, 231–41. London: SPCK, 1991.
Barnes, Timothy D. *Tertullian: A Historical and Literary Study.* Oxford: Clarendon, 2005.
Bauer, Ferdinand C. *History of Christian Dogma.* Edited by Peter C. Hodgson. Translated by Robert F. Brown and Peter C. Hodgson. Oxford: Oxford University Press, 2014.
Bauer, Walter. *Orthodoxy and Heresy in Earliest Christianity.* London: SCM, 1972.
Baumeister, Theofrid. *Die Anfänge der Theologie des Martyriums*, Münster: Aschendorf, 1980.
Behr, John. Introduction to *Origen, On First Principles.* Translated and edited by John Behr. Oxford: Oxford University Press, 2017.
Benko, Stephen. 'Pagan Criticism of Christianity during the First Two Centuries AD.' *Aufstieg und Niedergang der römischen Welt Asbury* 23, no. 2 (1980): 1054–118.
Bergjan, Silke-Petra. 'Celsus the Epicurean? The Interpretation of an Argument in Origen, Contra Celsum.' *Harvard Theological Review* 94, no. 2 (2001): 179–204.
Bévenot, Maurice. 'The Sacrament of Penance and St. Cyprian's *De lapsis*.' *Theological Studies* 16, no. 2 (1955): 175–213.
Blowers, Paul M. and Peter W. Martens, eds. *The Oxford Handbook of Early Biblical Interpretation.* Oxford: University Press, 2019.
Boardman, John, Jasper Griffin, and Oswyn Murray. *The Oxford History of the Classical World.* Oxford: Oxford University Press, 1986.
Bobertz, Charles Arnold. 'Cyprian of Carthage as Patron: A Social Historical Study of the Role of Bishop in the Ancient Christian Community of North Africa.' PhD diss., Yale University, 1988. https://openlibrary.org/works/OL12295049W/Cyprian_of_Carthage_as_patron
Borret, Marcel. Introduction to *Origène Contre Celse, Introduction, Texte Critique, Traduction et Notes.* 4 vols. Sources Chrétiennes 132 Paris: Cerf, 1967.
Bowersock, Glen. W. *Martyrdom and Rome.* Cambridge: Cambridge University Press, 1995.
Bowlin, John R. 'Tolerance among the Fathers.' *Journal of the Society of Christian Ethics* 26, no. 1 (2006): 3–36.
Boyarin, Daniel. *Dying for God: Martyrdom and the Making of Christianity and Judaism.* Stanford: Stanford University Press, 1999.
Boys-Stones, George R. *Post-Hellenistic Philosophy: A Study of its Development from the Stoics to Origen.* Oxford: Oxford University Press, 2001.
Brakke, David. *The Gnostics: Myth, Ritual and Diversity in Early Christianity.* Cambridge: Harvard University Press, 2010.
Bray, Gerald L. *Holiness and the Will of God: Perspectives on the Theology of Tertullian.* Atlanta: John Knox, 1979.
Bremmer, Jan. 'Religious Violence and its roots: a view from antiquity. In *Reconceiving Religious Conflict: New Views from the Formative Centuries of Christianity,* edited by Wendy Mayer and Chris de Wets. New York: Routledge: 2018, 30–42.
Brent, Allen. 'Cyprian's Reconstruction of the Martyr Tradition.' Journal of Ecclesiastical History 53, no. 2 (2002): 241–68.
Brent, Allen. *Cyprian and Roman Carthage.* Cambridge: Cambridge University Press, 2010.
Bright, Pamela. 'Origenian Understanding of Martyrdom and its Biblical Framework.' In *Origen of Alexandria: His World and His Legacy,* edited by Charles Kannengeisser & William L. Petersen. Christianity und Judaism in Antiquity 1, 180–99. Notre Dame: University of Notre Dame Press, 1988.
Buck, P. Lorraine. 'Athenagoras' *Embassy*: A Literary fiction.' *Harvard Theological Review* 89, no. 3 (1996): 209–26.

Buck, P. Lorraine. 'Justin Martyr's Apologies: Their Number, Destination, and Form.' *Journal of Theological Studies* 54, no. 1 (2003): 45–59.
Burns, J. Patout. 'The Role of Social Structures in Cyprian's Response to the Decian Persecution.' *StPatr* 31 (1997): 260–7.
Burns, J. Patout. 'Confessing the Church: Cyprian on Penance.' *StPatr* 36 (2001): 338–48.
Burns, J. Patout. *Cyprian the Bishop*. London: Routledge, 2002.
Burns, J. Patout, and Robin M. Jensen. *Christianity in Roman Africa: The Development of its Practices and Beliefs*. Grand Rapids: Eerdmans, 2014.
Cain, Emily. 'Medically Modified Eyes: A baptismal cataract surgery in Clement of Alexandria,' *Studies in Late Antiquity* 2 no. 4 (2018) 491–511.
Cameron, Averil. *Christianity and the Rhetoric of Empire: The Development of Christian discourse*. Berkeley: University of California Press, 1991.
Campenhausen, Hans von. *Die Idee des Martyriums in der alten Kirche*. Göttingen: Vandenhoeck & Ruprecht, 1964.
Cernuskova, Veronika, Judith Kovacs and Jana Platova, *Clement's Biblical Exegesis*. Proceedings of the Colloquium on Clement of Alexandria (Olomouc, Czech Republic, May 29–31, 2014). Leiden: Brill, 2016.
Chadwick, Henry. *Heresy and Orthodoxy in the Early Church*. Aldershot UK: Variorum, 1991.
Ciner, Patricia A. Orígenes, *Comentario al Evangelio de Juan/1*, Prólogo, F. García Bazán, Introducción, traducción y notas, Patricia A. Ciner, Biblioteca de Patrística N° 115, Ed. Ciudad Nueva, Madrid 2020.
Clark, Elizabeth A. *The Origenist Controversy: The Cultural Construction of an Early Christian Debate*. Princeton: Princeton University Press, 1992.
Clarke, Graeme W., trans. *The Letters of St. Cyprian of Carthage*. Ancient Christian Writers, vols 43, 44, 46, 47. New York: Newman, 1984, 1984, 1986, 1989.
Cobb, L. Stephanie. *Divine Deliverance: Pain and Painlessness in Early Christian Martyr Texts*. Oakland: University of California Press, 2017.
Cobb, L. Stephanie. 'Martyrdom in Roman Context.' In *The Wiley Blackwell Companion to Christian Martyrdom,* edited by Paul Middleton, 88–101. West Sussex UK: John Wiley & Sons, 2020.
Conant, Jonathan P. 'Memories of Trauma and the Formation of Christian Identity.' In *Memories of Utopia: The Revision of Histories and Landscapes in Late Antiquity,* edited by Bronwen Neil and Kosta Simic, London: Routledge, 2020, 36–56.
Corke-Webster, James. 'Trouble in Pontus: The Pliny-Trajan Correspondence on the Christians Reconsidered.' *Transactions of the American Philological Association* 147, no. 2 (2017): 371–411.
Corke-Webster, James. 'The Early Reception of Pliny the Younger in Tertullian of Carthage and Eusebius of Caesarea.' *The Classical Quarterly* 67, no. 1 (2017): 247–62.
Corke-Webster, James. 'The Roman Persecutions.' In *The Wiley Blackwell Companion to Christian Martyrdom,* edited by Paul Middleton, 33–50. West Sussex UK: John Wiley & Sons, 2020.
Crouzel, Henri. *Origen: The Life and Thought of the First Great Theologian*. Translated by A.S. Worrall. San Francisco: Harper & Row, 1989.
Daley, Brian E. 'Origen's *De Principiis*, A Guide to the Principles of Christian Scriptural Interpretation.' In *Nova and Vereta, Patristic Studies in Honour of Thomas Patrick Hamilton*. Edited by John Petruccione, 3–21. Washington: Catholic University of America Press, 1998.
Daley, Brian E. *The Hope of the Early Church: A Handbook of Patristic Eschatology*. Peabody MS: Hendrickson, 2003.

Daley, Brian E. 'Incorporeality and "Divine Sensibility": The Importance of *De Principiis* 4.4 for Origen's Theology.' *StPat* 41 (2006): 139–44.

Daniel-Hughes, Carly, and Maia Kotrosits. 'Tertullian of Carthage and the Fantasy Life of Power: On Martyrs, Christians and Other Attachments to Juridical Scenes.' *Journal of Early Christian Studies* 28, no. 1 (2020): 1–31.

Daniélou, Jean. *Origène*. Translated by Walter Mitchell. London: Sheed & Ward, 1955.

Daniélou, Jean. *The Origins of Latin Christianity*. Vol. 3 of *A History of Early Christian Doctrine Before the Council of Nicaea*. London: Westminster, 1977.

Danker, Frederick William, editor. *A Greek-English Lexicon of the New Testament and other Early Christian Literature*, (BDAG) 3rd ed. Chicago: Chicago University Press, 2000.

Daugherty, Bradley J. Review of *The Patient Ferment of the Early Church*, by Alan Kreider. *Fides et Histora* 50, no. 2 (2018): 165–7.

Davie, Martin, et al., eds. *New Dictionary of Theology*. 2nd ed. Downers Grove: Inter Varsity Press, 2016.

Davey, Wesley Thomas. 'Sight in the Tempest: Suffering as Participation with Christ in the Pauline Corpus.' PhD diss., SE Baptist Theological Seminary, 2016. https://www.proquest.com/docview/1845889067/615ED1155E64C32PQ/1?accountid=196359

De Labriolle, Pierre. *La péaction païenne: Étude sur la polémique antichrétienne du Ier us VIe siècle*. 2nd ed. Paris: L'Artisan du Livre, 1948.

De Wet, Chris L. *Preaching Bondage: John Chrysostom and the Discourse of Slavery in Early Christianity*. Oakland: University of California Press, 2015.

Dempsey, Michael T. 'The Politics of Providence in the Early Church: Toward a Contemporary Interpretation.' *Didaskalia* 26 (2016): 109–34.

Demura, Miyako. 'Origen after the Origenist Controversy.' In G.D. Dunn and W. Mayer, eds., *Christians Shaping Identity from the Roman Empire to Byzantium: Studies inspired by Pauline Allen*. Supp. *Vigiliae Christianae* 132, 117–39. Leiden: Brill, 2015.

DeVore, Megan. '*Catechumeni*, not 'New Converts': Revisiting the *Passio Perpetuae et Felicitatis*.' *StPatr* 91 (2017): 237–248.

Digeser, Elizabeth De Palma. 'Collaboration and identity in the aftermath of persecution: Religious conflict and its legacy,' In *Reconceiving Religious Conflict: New Views from the Formative Centuries of Christianity*, edited by Wendy Mayer and Chris de Wets. New York: Routledge, 2018: 261–81.

Dijkstra, Jitse H. F. 'Religious Violence in late antique Egypt reconsidered: The cases of Alexandria, Panopolis, and Philae.' In *Reconceiving Religious Conflict: New Views from the Formative Centuries of Christianity*, edited by Wendy Mayer and Chris de Wets, New York: Routledge, 2018: 211–33.

Doumas, François-Régis. 'L'evolution de Tertullien dans son attitude vis-a-vis de la philosophie' Pts. 1 and 2. *Théophilyon* 2, no. 1 (1997): 121–47; 2, no. 2 (1997): 497–521.

Drobner, Hubertus R. *The Fathers of the Church: A Comprehensive Introduction*. Translated by Siegfried S. Schatzmann. Peabody, MS: Hendrickson, 2007.

Dulles, Avery. *A History of Apologetics*. San Francisco: Ignatius, 2005.

Dunn, Geoffrey D. 'Rhetorical Structure in Tertullian's *Ad Scapulam*.' *Vigiliae Christianae* 56, no. 1 (2002): 47–55.

Dunn, Geoffrey D. 'Infected Sheep and Diseased Cattle, or the Pure and Holy Flock: Cyprian's Pastoral Care of Virgins.' *Journal of Early Christian Studies* 11, no. 1 (2003): 1–20.

Dunn, Geoffrey D. *Tertullian*. New York: Routledge, 2004.

Dunn, Geoffrey D. 'The White Crown of Works: Cyprian's Early Pastoral Ministry of Almsgiving in Carthage.' *Church History* 73, no. 4 (2004): 719–26.

Dunn, Geoffrey D. 'Tertullian's Scriptural Exegesis in *De praescriptione haereticorum*.' *Journal of Early Christian Studies* 14, no. 2 (2006): 141–55.
Dunn, Geoffrey D. 'Cyprian and Women in a Time of Persecution.' *Journal of Ecclesiastical History* 57, no. 2 (2006): 205–25.
Edwards, Mark J. *Origen Against Plato*. Aldershot UK: Ashgate, 2002.
Edwards, Mark J. 'Origen's Platonism, Questions and Caveats.' *Zeitschrift für antikes Christentum* 12, no. 1 (2008): 20–38.
Edwards, Mark J. *Catholicity and Heresy in the Early Church*. Surrey: Ashgate, 2009.
Edwards, Mark J. 'The Fate of the Devil in Origen.' *Ephemerides Theologicae Lovanienses* 86, no. 1 (2010): 163–70.
Elliott, Mark W. *Providence Perceived: Divine Action from a Human Point of View*. Berlin: De Gruyter, 2015.
Elm, Eva and Nicole Hartmann, eds. *Demons in Late Antiquity: Their perception and transformation in different literary genres*, Transformationen der Antike, 54. Berlin, Boston: De Gruyter, 2020.
Fahey, Michael A. *Cyprian and the Bible: A Study in 3rd Century Exegesis*. Beiträge zur Geschichte der biblischen Hermeneutik 9. Tübingen: JCB Mohr, 1971.
Fairbairn, Donald. 'Patristic Exegesis and Theology: The Cart and the Horse.' *Westminster Theological Journal* 69, no. 1 (2007): 1–19.
Ferguson, Everett, 'Demonology of the Early Christian World.' In *Lectures presented at the University of Mississippi Feb 1980*. Symposium series vol. 12, 109–15. Lewiston N.Y.: Edwin Mellen, 1984.
Ferguson, Everett. 'Early Christian Martyrdom and Civil Disobedience.' *Journal of Early Christian Studies* 1, no. 1 (1993): 73–83.
Ferguson, Everett. 'Early Church Penance.' *Restoration Quarterly* 36, no. 2 (1994): 81–100.
Ferguson, Everett. *Backgrounds of Early Christianity*. Grand Rapids: Eerdmans, 2003.
Ferguson, Everett. 'Origen's Demonology.' In *Ministry, Initiation and Worship*. Vol. 1 of *The Early Church and Today*. Edited by Everett Ferguson, 193–209. Abiline TX: Christian University Press, 2012.
Ferguson, Everett. 'Tertullian, Scripture, Rule of Faith and Paul.' In *Tertullian and Paul*. Vol. 1 of *Pauline and Patristic Scholars in Debate*. Edited by David E. Wilhite and Todd D. Still, 22–33. New York: T&T Clark, 2013.
Ferguson, Everett. *The Rule of Faith: A Guide*. Eugene OR: Cascade, 2015.
Fisher, George P. *History of the Christian Church*. London: Hodder & Stoughton, 1898.
Floyd, W. E. G. *Clement of Alexandria's Treatment of the Problem of Evil*. Oxford: Oxford University Press, 1971.
Fournier, Éric and Wendy Mayer, eds. *Heirs of Roman Persecution: Studies on a Christian and Para-Christian Discourse in Late Antiquity*. London: Routledge, 2020.
Fournier, Éric. 'The Christian Discourse of Persecution in Late Antiquity: an introduction.' In *Heirs of Roman Persecution: Studies on a Christian and Para-Christian Discourse in Late Antiquity*, edited by Éric Fournier and Wendy Mayer, 1–22. London: Routledge, 2020.
Frend, William H. C. *Martyrdom and Persecution in the Early Church*. Oxford: Blackwell, 1965. Repr., Cambridge: James Clarke, 2008.
Gallagher, Edmon L. and John D. Meade. *The Biblical Canon Lists from Early Christianity: Texts and Analysis*. Oxford: Oxford University Press, 2017.
Gerson, Lloyd. 'Plotinus.' in *Stanford Encyclopedia of Philosophy*, Fall (2018), ed. Edward N. Zalta. https://plato.stanford.edu/archives/fall2018/entries/plotinus/
Gibbon, Edward. *The Decline and Fall of the Roman Empire*. 8 vols. Edinburgh: Ballantyne, 1903–8.

Gibbons, Kathleen. *The Moral Psychology of Clement of Alexandria*. New York: Routledge, 2017.

Gonzalez, Eliezer. 'The Afterlife in the *Passion of Perpetua* and in the Works of Tertullian: A Clash of Traditions.' *StPatr* 65 (2013): 225–38.

Grant, Robert M. *Greek Apologists of the Second Century*. Philadelphia: Westminster SCM, 1988.

Greenberg, L. Arik. '*My Share of God's Reward*': *Exploring the Roles and Formulations of the Afterlife in Early Christian Martyrdom*. New York: Peter Lang, 2009.

Greer, Rowan A. *Origen: An Exhortation to Martyrdom, Prayer and Selected Works*. The Classics of Western Spirituality. London: SPCK, 1979.

Greer, Rowan A. 'The Christian Bible and Its Interpretation.' In *Early Biblical Interpretation*, edited by James L. Kugel and Rowan A. Greer, 107–203. Philadelphia: Westminster, 1986.

Greer, Rowan A., and James L. Kugel. *Early Biblical Interpretation*. Library of Early Christianity 3. Philadelphia: Westminster, 1986.

Griggs, C. Wilfred. *Early Egyptian Christianity: From its Origins to 451 CE*. Leiden: Brill, 1990.

Gwatkin, Henry M. *Early Church History to A.D. 313*. 2 vols. London: MacMillan, 1912.

Hagg, Henny Fiska. 'Deification in Clement of Alexandria with a Special Reference to his use of *Theaetetus* 176B.' *StPatr* 46 (2010): 169–73.

Hall, Christopher A. *Learning Theology with the Church Fathers*. Downers Grove: Inter Varsity Press, 2002.

Hall, Christopher, 'Origen: Exegete, Theologian, Disciple.' In *Sources of the Christian Self: A Cultural History of Christian Identity*, edited by James M. Houston and Jens Zimmerman, 133–45. Grand Rapids: Eerdmans, 2018.

Hampton, Alexander J. B. and John Peter Kenney, eds., *Christian Platonism, A History*. Cambridge: Cambridge University Press, 2021.

Hansen, B. 'Preaching to Seneca: Christ as Stoic Sapiens in *Divinae Institutiones IV*.' *Harvard Theological Review* 111, no. 4 (2018): 541–58.

Hanson, R. P. C. *Allegory and Event*. London: SCM Press, 1959.

Harland, Philip A. *Dynamics of Identity in the World of the Early Christians*. New York: T&T Clark, 2009.

Harrison, James R. 'The Persecutions of Christians from Nero to Hadrian.' In *Into all the World: Emergent Christianity in its Jewish and Greco-Roman Context*, edited by Mark Harding and Alanna Nobbs, 266–300. Grand Rapids: Eerdmans, 2017.

Hartog, Paul. 'The 'Rule of Faith' and Patristic Biblical Exegesis.' *Trinity Journal* 28, no. 1 (2007): 65–86.

Hartog, Paul. 'The Maltreatment of Early Christians, Refinement and Response.' *Southern Baptist Journal of Theology* 18(1) (2014): 49–79.

Hartog, review of *The Patient Ferment of the Early Church* (by Alan Kreider). *Trinity Journal* 38, no. 2 (2017): 255–8.

Hartog, Paul A. 'Themes and Intertextualities in Pre-Nicene Exhortations to Martyrdom.' In *The Wiley Blackwell Companion to Christian Martyrdom*, edited by Paul Middleton, 102–19. West Sussex UK: John Wiley & Sons, 2020.

Heine, Ronald E. 'The Alexandrians.' In *The Cambridge History of Early Christian Literature*. Edited by Frances Young, Lewis Ayers, and Andrew Louth, 117–30. Cambridge: Cambridge University Press, 2004.

Heine, Ronald E. *Reading the Old Testament with the Ancient Church: Exploring the Formation of Early Christian Thought*. Grand Rapids: Baker, 2007.

Heine, Ronald E. *Origen: Scholarship in the Service of the Church*. Christian Theology in Context. Oxford: Oxford University Press, 2010.

Heine, Robert E. Introduction to *The Commentary of Origen on the Gospel of St Matthew*, 2 vols. Translated by Ronalde E. Heine. Oxford: Oxford University Press, 2018.

Hennessey, Lawrence R. 'The Place of Saints and Sinners After Death.' In *Origen of Alexandria: His World and His Legacy*, edited by Charles Kannengeisser and William L. Petersen. Christianity und Judaism in Antiquity 1, 295–312. University of Notre Dame Press, 1988.

Hogg, Michael A., Deborah J. Terry, and Katherine M. White. 'A Tale of Two Theories: A Critical Comparison of Identity Theory with Social Identity Theory.' *Social Psychology Quarterly* 58, no. 4 (1995): 255–69.

Hopkins, Keith. 'Christian Number and its Implications.' *Journal of Early Christian Studies* 6, no. 2 (1998): 185–226.

Hummel, Edelhard L. *The Concept of Martyrdom according to St Cyprian of Carthage*. Catholic University of America Studies in Christian Antiquity 9. Washington: Catholic University of America Press, 1946.

Hyldahl, Jesper. 'Gnostic Critique of Martyrdom.' In *Contextualizing Early Christian Martyrdom*, edited by Jakob Engberg and Uffe Holmsgaard Petersen, 119–38. Frankfurt am Main: Peter Lang, 2011.

Jensen, Michael P. *Martyrdom and Identity: The Self on Trial*. London: T&T Clark, 2010.

Jewett, Robert. *Romans: Hermeneia – A Critical and Historical Commentary on the Bible*. Minneapolis: Fortress, 2007.

Kannengiesser, Charles. 'A Key for the Future of Patristics: The "Senses" of Scripture.' In *In Dominico Eoquio, In Lordly Eloquence, Essays on Patristic Exegesis in Honour of Robert Wilken*, edited by Paul M. Blowers et al., 90–106. Grand Rapids: Eerdmans, 2002.

Kannengiesser, Charles. *Handbook of Patristic Exegesis: The Bible in Ancient Christianity*. Boston: Brill, 2006.

Karamanolis, George. *The Philosophy of Early Christianity*. Durham: Acumen, 2013.

Karavites, Peter. *Evil, Freedom and the Road to Perfection in Clement of Alexandria*. Supp. Vigiliae Christianae 43. Leiden: Brill, 1999.

Kearsley, Roy. *Tertullian's Theology of Divine Power*. Carlisle UK: Paternoster, 1998.

Kelly, J. N. D. *Early Christian Doctrines*. 5th ed. London: Continuum, 1977.

Kenney, John Peter. 'Platonism and Christianity in Late Antiquity.' In *Christian Platonism: A History*, edited by Alexander J.B. Hampton and John Peter Kenney, 162–82. Cambridge: Cambridge University Press, 2021.

Keough, Shawn W. J. 'Eschatology Worthy of God: The Goodness of God and the Groaning of Creation in Origen's De Principiis.' *StPatr* 46 (2010): 189–94.

King, Karen L. *What is Gnosticism?* Cambridge: Harvard University Press, 2003.

Kolbet, Paul R. 'Torture and Origen's Hermeneutic of Non-violence.' *Journal of the American Academy of Religion* 76, no. 3 (2008): 545–72.

Kolbet, Paul R. 'Rethinking the Rationales for Origen's Use of Allegory.' *StPatr* 56 (2013): 41–9.

Koscheski, Jonathan. 'The Earliest Christian War: Second- and Third-Century Martyrdom and the Creation of Cosmic Warriors.' *Journal of Religious Ethics* 39, no. 1 (2011): 100–24.

Kotzé, Annemaré. 'Augustine and the Remaking of Martyrdom.' In *The Wiley Blackwell Companion to Christian Martyrdom*, edited by Paul Middleton, 135–50. West Sussex UK: John Wiley & Sons, 2020.

Kovacs, Judith L. 'Introduction: Clement as Scriptural Exegete: Overview of History and Research.' In *Clement's Biblical Exegesis*. Proceedings of the Colloquium on Clement of

Alexandria, Olomouc, Czech Republic, May 29–31, 2014, edited by Veronika Cernuskova, Judith Kovacs and Jana Platova, 1–37. Leiden: Brill, 2016.

Kreider, Alan. *The Change of Conversion and the Origin of Christendom.* Eugene, OR: Wipf & Stock, 1999.

Kreider, Alan. *The Patient Ferment of the Early Church: The Improbable Rise of Christianity in the Roman Empire.* Grand Rapids: Baker, 2016.

Lanzillotta, Lautaro Roig. 'Greek Philosophy and the Problem of Evil in Clement of Alexandria and Origen.' *Estudios griegos e indoeuropeos* 23 (2013): 207–23.

Lee, Morgan, 'Sorry Tertullian.' *Christianity Today* 58, no. 1 (2014) 18.

Leemans, Johan and Anthony Dupont. 'Scripture and Martyrdom.' In *The Oxford Handbook of Early Christian Interpretation,* edited by Paul M. Blowers and Peter W. Martens, 417–38. Oxford: Oxford University Press, 2019.

Lieu, Judith M. *Christian Identity in the Jewish and Graeco-Roman World.* Oxford: Oxford University Press, 2004.

Lieu, Judith M. 'The audience of apologetics: the problem of the Martyr Acts.' In *Contextualising Early Chirstian Martyrdom,* edited by Jakob Engberg, Uffe Holmsgaard Eriksen, and Anders Klostergaard Petersen, 205–23. Frankfurt am Main: Peter Lang, 2011.

Lilla, Salvatore R. *Clement of Alexandria: A Study in Christian Platonism and Gnosticism.* Eugene OR: Wipf & Stock, 1971.

Litfin, Bryan M. 'Tertullian's Use of the *Regula Fidei* as an Interpretive Device in *Adversus Marcionem.*' *StPatr* 42 (2006): 405–10.

Litfin, Bryan M. 'Was the Early Church 'Patient'?' Oct 2016. https://www.thegospelcoalition.org/reviews/patient-ferment-of-the-early-church/

Livermore, Paul. 'Reasoning with Unbelievers and the Place of the Scriptures in Tertullian's Apology.' *Asbury Theological Journal* 56, no. 1 (2001): 61–75.

Louth, Andrew. 'Hagiography.' In *The Cambridge History of Early Christian Literature,* edited by Frances Young, Lewis Ayers, and Andrew Louth, 358–61. Cambridge: Cambridge University Press, 2004.

Maier, Paul L. *Eusebius: The Church History: Translation and Commentary.* Grand Rapids: Kregel, 2007.

Martens, Peter W. 'On Providence and Inspiration: A Short Commentary on ΠΕΡΙ ΑΡΧΩΝ 4.1.7.' *StPatr* 41 (2006): 201–6.

Martens, Peter W. 'Revisiting the allegory/ typology distinction: the case of Origen.' *Journal of Early Christian Studies* 16, no. 3 (2008): 283–317.

Martens, Peter W. *Origen and Scripture: The Contours of the Exegetical Life.* Oxford Early Christian Studies. Oxford: Oxford University Press, 2012.

Mayer, Wendy and Bronwyn Neil, eds. *Religious Conflict from Early Christianity to the Rise of Islam.* Berlin: De Gruyter, 2013.

Mayer, Wendy. 'Religious Conflict: Definitions, Problems and Theoretical Approaches.' In *Religious Conflict from Early Christianity to the Rise of Islam.* Edited by Wendy Mayer and Bronwyn Neil, 1–20. Berlin: De Gruyter, 2013.

Mayer, Wendy and Chris de Wets, eds. *Reconceiving Religious Conflict: New Views from the Formative Centuries of Christianity.* Routledge studies in the early Christian world. New York: Routledge, 2018.

Mayer, Wendy. 'Heirs of Roman Persecution: Common threads in discursive strategies across Late Antiquity.' In *Heirs of Roman Persecution: Studies on a Christian and Para-Christian Discourse in Late Antiquity,* edited by Éric Fournier and Wendy Mayer, 317–39. London: Routledge, 2020.

McClymond, Michael. *The Devil's Redemption: A New History and Interpretation of Christian Universalism*. 2 vols. Grand Rapids: Baker, 2018–19.

McDonald, Lee Martin. *The Biblical Canon: Its Origin, Transmission and Authority*. Peabody MS: Hendrickson, 2007.

McKim, Donald K. *Theological Turning Points: Major Issues in Christian Thought*. Louisville: Westminster John Knox, 1988.

McLarty, Jane D. 'Early Christian Theologies of Martyrdom.' In *The Wiley Blackwell Companion to Christian Martyrdom*, edited by Paul Middleton, 120–34. West Sussex UK: John Wiley & Sons, 2020.

Middleton, Paul. *Radical Martyrdom and Cosmic Conflict in Early Christianity*. Edinburgh: T&T Clark, 2006.

Middleton, Paul. 'Enemies of the (Church and) State: Martyrdom as a Problem for Early Christianity.' *Annali di storia dell'esegesi* 29, no. 2 (2012): 161–81.

Middleton, Paul. 'Early Christian Voluntary Martyrdom: A Statement for the Defence.' *Journal of Theological Studies* 64, no. 2 (2013): 556–73.

Middleton, Paul, ed. *The Wiley Blackwell Companion to Christian Martyrdom*. West Sussex UK: John Wiley & Sons, 2020.

Middleton, Paul. 'Creating and Contesting Christian Martyrdom.' In *The Wiley Blackwell Companion to Christian Martyrdom*, edited by Paul Middleton, 12–30. West Sussex UK: John Wiley & Sons, 2020.

Middleton, Paul. 'Martyrdom and Persecution in the New Testament.' In *The Wiley Blackwell Companion to Christian Martyrdom*, edited by Paul Middleton, 51–71. West Sussex UK: John Wiley & Sons, 2020.

Migliore, Daniel L. *Faith Seeking Understanding: An Introduction to Christian Theology*. 3rd ed. Grand Rapids: Eerdmans, 2014.

Montgomery, Hugo. 'The Bishop Who Fled: Responsibility and Honour in Saint Cyprian.' *StPatr* 21 (1989): 264–7.

Moss, Candida R. *The Other Christs: Imitating Jesus in Ancient Christian Ideologies of Martyrdom*. Oxford: Oxford University Press, 2010.

Moss, Candida. *Ancient Christian Martyrdom: Diverse Practices, Theologies and Traditions*. New Haven: Yale University Press, 2012.

Moss, Candida. 'The Discourse of Voluntary Martyrdom: Ancient and Modern.' *Church History* 81, no. 3 (2012): 531–51.

Moss, Candida. *The Myth of Persecution: How the Early Christians Invented a Story of Martyrdom*. New York: HarperOne, 2013.

Moss, Candida. 'Justification of the Martyrs.' In *Tertullian and Paul*. Vol. 1 of *Pauline and Patristic Scholars in Debate*, edited by David E. Wilhite and Todd D. Still, 104–18. New York: T&T Clark 2013.

Mullins, Michael. *Called to be Saints: Christian Living in First Century Rome*. Dublin: Veritas, 1991.

Mullins Reaves, Pamela. 'Multiple Martyrdoms and Christian Identity in Clement of Alexandria's *Stromateis*.' *StPatr* 46 (2013): 61–8.

Murphy, Edwina. *The Bishop and the Apostle: Cyprian's Pastoral Exegesis of Paul*. Berlin: de Gruyter, 2018.

Murphy, Edwina. 'Imitating the Devil: Cyprian on Jealousy and Envy.' *Scrinium* 14, no. 1 (2018): 75–91.

Murphy, Edwina. 'Sin No More: Healing, Wholeness and the Absent Adulteress in Cyprian's Use of John.' *Revue des études augustiniennes et patristiques* 64 no. 1 (2018): 1–15.

Murphy, Edwina. 'Cyprian, Scripture and Socialisation: Forming faith in the catechumenate and beyond.' In *The Intellectual World of Christian Late Antiquity: Reshaping Classical Traditions*, edited by Lewis Ayres, Matthew R. Crawford and Michael Champion, 153-65. Cambridge: Cambridge University Press, 2023.

Nagle, D. Brendan and Stanley M. Burstein, *The Ancient World: Readings in Social and Cultural History*. Englewood Cliffs, NJ; Prentice Hall, 1995.

Nicholson, Oliver. 'What Makes a Voluntary Martyr?' *StPatr* 45 (2013): 159-64.

Niehoff, Maren. *Jewish Exegesis and Homeric Scholarship in Alexandria*. Cambridge: University Press, 2011.

Neil, Bronwen and Kosta Simic, eds., *Memories of Utopia: The Revision of Histories and Landscapes in Late Antiquity*. London: Routledge, 2020.

Norris, Richard A. Jr. 'The Apologists.' In *The Cambridge History of Early Christian Literature*, edited by Frances Young, Lewis Ayers, and Andrew Louth, 36-44. Cambridge: Cambridge University Press, 2004.

O'Brien, David P. 'The Pastoral Function of the Second Repentance for Clement of Alexandria.' *StPatr* 41 (2006): 219-24.

O'Keefe, John J. and Russell R. Reno. *Sanctified Vision: An Introduction to Early Christian Interpretation of the Bible*. Baltimore: Johns Hopkins, 2005.

O'Malley, T. P. *Tertullian and the Bible: Language, Imagery, Exegesis*. Utrecht: Dekker & Van de Vegt, 1967.

Osborn, Eric. *The Philosophy of Clement of Alexandria*. Cambridge: Cambridge University Press, 1957.

Osborn, Eric. 'Philo and Clement: Quiet Conversion and Noetic Exegesis.' In *The Studia Philonica Annual* 10, 1988, 108-24.

Osborn, Eric. 'Clement and the Bible.' In *Origeniana sexta Origène et la Bible/ Origen and the Bible: Actes du Colloquium Origenianum Sextum Chantilly*, 30 aout-3 septembre 1993 (1995), 121-32.

Osborn, Eric. 'Was Tertullian a Philosopher?' *StPatr* 31 (1997): 322-34.

Osborn, Eric F. 'Clement and Platonism.' In *Origeniana octava. Origen and the Alexandrian tradition (Origene e la tradizione Alessandrina)*. Papers presented at the 8th international Origen Congress, Pisa, 21-27 August 2001, 419-27.

Osborn, Eric. *Tertullian, First Theologian of the West*. Cambridge: Cambridge University Press, 2003.

Osborn, Eric. *Clement of Alexandria*. Cambridge: Cambridge University Press, 2005.

Osborne, Catherine. 'Clement of Alexandria.' In *The Cambridge History of Philosophy in Late Antiquity* vol. 2. Edited by Lloyd P. Gerson, 270-82. Cambridge: Cambridge University Press, 2000.

Pearson, Birger A. *Ancient Gnosticism: Traditions and Literature*. Minneapolis: Fortress, 2007.

Pelikan, Jaroslav. 'The Eschatology of Tertullian.' *Church History* 21, no. 2 (1952): 108-22.

Perkins, Judith. *The Suffering Self: Pain and Narrative Representation in the Early Christian Era*. London: Routledge, 1995.

Pinckaers, Servais. *Passions and Virtue*. Translated by Benedict M. Guevin. Washington DC: Catholic University of America Press, 2015.

Press, Gerald A. *Plato: A Guide for the Perplexed*. London: Continuum, 2007.

Prince, Andrew J. *Contextualization of the Gospel, Towards an Evangelical Approach in Light of Scripture and the Church Fathers*. Eugene OR: Wipf & Stock, 2017.

Rankin, David I. *Tertullian and the Church*. Cambridge: Cambridge University Press, 1995.

Rankin, David I. 'Class Distinction as a Way of Doing Church: The Early Fathers and the Christian Plebs.' *Vigiliae Christianae* 58, no. 3 (2004): 298-315.

Rankin, David I. *From Clement to Origen: The Social and Historical Context of the Church Fathers*. Hampshire: Ashgate, 2006.

Rankin, David I. *The Early Church and the Afterlife: Post-death Existence in Athenagoras, Tertullian, Origen and the Letter to Rheginos*. London: Routledge, 2018.

Rebillard, Éric. *Christians and their Many Identities in Late Antiquity, North Africa 200–450 CE*. Ithaca: Cornell University Press, 2012.

Rebillard, Éric. *The Early Martyr Narratives: Neither Authentic Accounts nor Forgeries*. Philadelphia: University of Pennsylvania, 2021.

Recla, Matthew. 'Martyrdom and the Creation of Christian Identity. In *The Wiley Blackwell Companion to Christian Martyrdom,* edited by Paul Middleton, 199–214. West Sussex UK: John Wiley & Sons, 2020.

Rives, James B. 'The Decree of Decius and the Religion of Empire.' *Journal of Roman Studies* 89, no. 1 (1999): 135–54.

Rives, James B. 'Animal Sacrifice and the Roman Persecution of Christians (Second to Third Century).' In *Religious Violence in the Ancient World: From Classical Athens to Late Antiquity*, edited by Jitse Dijkstra and Christian Raschle, 177–202. Cambridge: Cambridge University Press, 2020.

Rizzi, Marco. 'Origen on Martyrdom: Theology and Social Practices.' In *Origeniana Nona: Origen and the Religious Practices of his Time*. Papers of the 9th International Origen Congress 2005. Edited by G. Heidl and R. Somos, 469–76. Leuven: Peeters, 2009.

Rizzi, Marco. 'The Work of Clement of Alexandria in the Light of his Contemporary Philosophical Teaching.' *StPatr* 46 (2013): 11–17.

Robinson, James M., Paul Hoffmann, and John S. Kloppenborg, eds. *The Critical Edition of Q*. Leuven: Peeters, 2000.

Rowley-Thomson, Stuart, 'Apostolic Authority: Reading and Writing on Clement of Alexandria.' *StPatr* 46 (2013): 19–31.

Sage, Michael M. *Cyprian*. Patristic Monograph Series 1. Cambridge Mass.: Philadelphia Patristic Foundation, 1975.

Scott, Mark S. M. *Journey Back to God: Origen on the Problem of Evil*. Oxford: Oxford University Press, 2012.

Shelton, W. Brian. Review of *The Myth of Persecution,* by Candida Moss. *Journal of the Evangelical Theological Society* 57, no. 1 (2014): 210–14.

Shelton, W. Brian. Review of *The Patient Ferment of the Early Church,* by Alan Kreider. *Journal of Theological Studies* 68, no. 2 (2017): 772–4.

Sider, Robert D. *Ancient Rhetoric and the Art of Tertullian*. London: Oxford University Press, 1971.

Silva, Gilvan Vista da and Carolline da Silva Soares. 'Protegendo a 'corpo' da igreja: a representaçãi dos lapsi e judaizantes como enfermos por Cipriano e João Crisóstomo', *Revista Jesushistórico*. Revista de Estudios sobre o Jesus Histórico e sua Recepção 10 (2013): 44–61.

Simon, Bernard. *The Essence of the Gnostics*. London: Arcturus, 2004.

Simonetti, Manlio. *Biblical Interpretation in the Early Church: A Historical Introduction to Patristic Exegesis*. Edinburgh: T&T Clark, 1994.

Sittser, Gerald L. 'The Catechumenate and the Rise of Christianity.' *Journal of Spiritual Formation and Soul Care* 6 no. 2 (2013): 179–203.

Spanneut, Michel. *Tertullien et les premiers moralistes africains*. Gembloux: Duculot, 1969.

Ste. Croix, Geoffrey E. M. de. 'Why Were the Early Christians Persecuted?' In *Christian Persecution, Martyrdom and Orthodoxy,* edited by Michael Whitby and Joseph Streeter, 105–52. Oxford: Oxford University Press, 2006.

Ste. Croix, Geoffrey E. M de. 'Voluntary Martyrdom in the Early Church.' In *Christian Persecution, Martyrdom and Orthodoxy,* edited by Michael Whitby and Joseph Streeter, 153–200. Oxford: Oxford University Press, 2006.
Stewart-Sykes, Alistair. 'Ordination Rites and Patronage Systems in Third-Century Africa.' *Vigiliae Christianae* 56 (2002): 115–30.
Stewart-Sykes, Alistair. 'Catechumenate and Contra-Culture: The Social Process of Catechumenate in Third Century Africa and its Development.' *St. Vladimir's Theological Quarterly* 47, nos 3–4 (2003): 289–306.
Studer, Basil and Angelo Di Berardino, eds. *The Patristic Period.* Translated by Matthew J. O'Connell. Vol. 1 of *History of Theology.* Collegeville Minn.: Liturgical, 1997.
Sutcliffe, Ruth. 'To Flee or Not to Flee? Matthew 10:23 and Third Century Flight in Persecution.' *Scrinium* 14, no. 1 (2018): 133–60.
Sutcliffe, Ruth. 'No Need to Apologise? Tertullian and the Paradox of Polemic Against Persecution.' *StPatr,* 23 (2021): 267–78.
Sutcliffe, Ruth. 'Learning Not to Sin: Repentance in Tertullian and Cyprian.' *Colloquium* 53, no. 1 (2021): 73–97.
Tabbernee, William. 'The Opposition to Montanism from Church and State: A Study of the History and Theology of the Montanist Movement as Shown by the Writings and Legislation of the Orthodox Opponents of Montanism.' PhD diss., University of Melbourne, 1978. https://minerva-access.unimelb.edu.au/items/f9778865-5b80-5a7f-98b6-185a04c60100
Tabbernee, William. 'Early Montanism and Voluntary Martyrdom.' *Colloquium* 17, no. 1 (1985): 33–44.
Tabbernee, William. 'Eusebius' "Theology of Persecution": As seen in the various editions of his *Church History.' Journal of Early Christian Studies* 5, no. 3 (1997): 319–34.
Tabbernee, William. '"Keeping the Faith": Montanism and Military Service.' In *Actes du Ier Congres International sur Antioche de Pisidie,* edited by Thomas Drew-Bear, Mehmet Taşlialan, and Christine M. Thomas, 123–36. Paris: de Boccard, 2002.
Tabbernee, William. 'Perpetua, Montanism, and Christian Ministry in Carthage c.203 C.E.' *Perspectives in Religious Studies* 32, no. 4 (2005) 421–41.
Tabbernee, William. *Fake Prophecy and Polluted Sacraments: Ecclesiastical and Imperial Reactions to Montanism.* Vigiliae Christianae 84, Leiden: Brill, 2007.
Tabbernee, William. *Prophets and Gravestones: An Imaginative History of Montanists and other Early Christians.* Peabody MS: Hendrickson, 2009.
Tabbernee, William. 'Montanism and the Cult of the Martyrs in Roman North Africa: Reassessing the Literary and Epigraphic Evidence,' In *Text and the Material World: Essays in Honour of Graeme Clarke,* edited by Elizabeth Minchin and Heather Jackson, 299–313. Studies in Mediterranean Archaeology and Literature 185. Uppsala: Astrom Editions, 2017.
Thate, Michael J. 'Identity Construction as Resistance: Figuring Hegemony, Biopolitics and Martyrdom as an Approach to Clement of Alexandria.' *StPatr* 66 (2013): 69–85.
Thayer, Anne T. 'Review of *The Myth of Persecution,* by Candida Moss.' *Interpretation* 68, no. 1 (2014): 81–3.
Tite, Philip L. 'Voluntary Martyrdom and Gnosticism.' *Journal of Early Christian Studies* 23, no. 1 (2015): 27–54.
Tixeront, J. *A Handbook of Patrology.* Translated by S. A. Raemers. St Lis: Herder, 1920. http://www.earlychristianwritings.com/tixeront/
Tomsick, Richard D. 'Structure and Exegesis in Tertullian's *Ad Uxorem* and *De Exortatione Castitatis.' StPatr* 46 (2010): 9–15.

Torjesen, Karen Jo. *Hermeneutical Procedure and Theological Method in Origen's Exegesis*, Patrische Texte und Studien 28. Berlin: De Gruyter, 1986.

Trevett, Christine. *Montanism: Gender, Authority and the New Prophecy*. Cambridge: Cambridge University Press, 2002.

Trigg, Joseph W. *Origen*. The Early Church Fathers. London: Routledge, 1998.

Trigg, Joseph W. 'Was Origen a Systematic? A reappraisal.' *StPatr* 41 (2006): 139–44.

Ulrich, Eugene. 'Origen's Old Testament Text: The Transmission History of the Septuagint to the Third Century.' In *Origen of Alexandria, his World and his Legacy*, edited by Charles Kannengeisser and William L. Petersen, 3–33. Indiana: University of Notre Dame, 1988.

Van den Hoek, Annewies. *Clement of Alexandria and his use of Philo in the Stromateis: An early Christian reshaping of a Jewish model*. Supp. Vigiliae Christianae 3. Leiden: Brill, 1988.

Van den Hoek, Annewies. 'Clement of Alexandria on Martyrdom.' *StPatr* 26 (1993): 324–41.

Van den Hoek, Annewies. 'The Catechetical School of Early Christian Alexandria and its Philonic Heritage.' *Harvard Theological Review* 90, no. 1 (1997): 59–87.

Van den Hoek, Annewies, Introduction to *Clément d'Alexandrie, Les Stromates, Stromate IV*, Sources Chrétiennes No. 463, Paris: Cerf, 2001, 9–33.

Van der Lans, Birgit and Jan N. Bremmer, 'Tactitus and the Persecution of the Christians: An Invention of Tradition?' *Eirene: Studia Graeca et Latinas* 53 (2017) 299–311.

Van Henten, Jan Willem. 'Early Jewish and Christian Martyrdom.' In *The Wiley Blackwell Companion to Christian Martyrdom,* edited by Paul Middleton, 72–87. West Sussex UK: John Wiley & Sons, 2020.

Vidu, Adonis. *Atonement, Law, and Justice: The Cross in Historical and Cultural Contexts*. Grand Rapids: Baker Academic, 2014.

Vincelette, Alan. 'On the Frequency of Voluntary Martyrdom in the Patristic Era.' *Journal of Theological Studies* 70, no. 2 (2019): 652–79.

Völker, W. 'Der wahre Gnostiker nach Clemens Alexandrinus.' In *Texte und Untersuchungen zur Geschichte der altchristlichen Literatur* 57 (1952): Berlin: n.p. 1952.

Vos, Nienke. 'A Universe of Meaning: Cyprian's Use of Scripture in Letter 58.' In *Cyprian of Carthage: Studies in his Life, Language and Thought*, edited by Henk Bakker, Paul van Geest, and Hans van Loon, 65–93. Leuven: Peeters, 2010.

Westerholm, Stephen, and Martin Westerholm. *Reading Sacred Scripture: Voices from the History of Interpretation*. Grand Rapids: Eerdmans, 2016.

White, L. Michael. 'Transactionalism in the Penitential Thought of Gregory the Great.' *Restoration Quarterly* 21, no. 1 (1978): 33–51.

White, Michael. 'Moral Pathology: Passions, Progress and Protreptic in Clement of Alexandria.' In John T. Fitzgerald, ed., *Passions and Moral Progress in Greco-Roman Thought*, 284–387. London: Routledge, 2007.

Wiles, Maurice F. 'Theological Legacy of St Cyprian.' *Journal of Ecclesiastical History* 14, no. 2 (1963): 139–49.

Wilhite, David E. *Tertullian the African: An anthropological Reading of Tertullian's Context and Identities*. Berlin: de Gruyter, 2007.

Wilhite, David E. 'Cyprian's Scriptural Hermeneutic of Identity: The Laxist "Heresy".' *Horizons in Biblical Theology* 32, no. 1 (2010): 58–98.

Wilhite, David E. 'Rhetoric and Theology in Tertullian: What Tertullian learned from Paul.' *StPatr* 65 (2013): 295–312.

Wilhite, David E. 'The Spirit of Prophecy: Tertullian's Pauline Pneumatology.' In *Tertullian and Paul*. Vol. 1 of *Pauline and Patristic Scholars in Debate*, edited by David E. Wilhite and Todd D. Still, 45–71. New York: T&T Clark, 2013.

Wilhite, David E. 'Marcionites in Africa: What did Tertullian know and when did he invent it?' *Perspectives in Religious Studies* 43, no. 4 (2016): 437–52.
Wilhite, David E. 'Perpetua of History: Recent Questions.' *Journal of Early Christian Studies* 25, no. 2 (2017): 307–19.
Wilhite, David E. *Ancient African Christianity: An introduction to a unique context and tradition*. New York: Routledge, 2017.
Wilhite, David E. 'Tertullian on the Afterlife: 'Only Martyrs are in Heaven' and Other Misunderstandings.' *Zeitschrift für antikes Christentum* 24, no. 3 (2020): 490–508.
Wilhite, David E. and Todd D. Still, eds. *Tertullian and Paul*. Pauline and Patristic Scholars in Debate vol. 1. New York: T&T Clark, 2013.
Wilken, Robert L. *The Christians as the Romans Saw Them*. 2nd ed. Newhaven: Yale University Press, 2003.
Williams, Travis B. *Persecution in 1 Peter: Differentiating and Contextualizing Early Christian Suffering*. Supp. *NovT* 145. Leiden: Brill, 2012.
Wypustek, Andrzej. 'Magic, Montanism, Perpetua and The Severan Persecution.' *Vigiliae Christianae* 51, no. 3 (1997): 276–97.
Wysocki, Marcin R. 'Eschatology of the Time of Persecutions in the Writings of Tertullian and Cyprian.' *StPatr* 65 (2013): 379–93.
Young, Frances. *Biblical Exegesis and the Formation of Christian Culture*. Peabody MS: Hendrickson, 2002.

Scripture index

Exodus		5:10–11	125
1.12	219	5:10–12	20, 28, 56, 90, 96,
6:11–12	219		125, 170, 181, 203
11:2	75	5:11	7, 125
12:35	75	5:11–12	1, 88, 100
		5:12	60, 125
Deuteronomy		5:39	20, 100, 210
6:3	169	5:39–41	7
		5:40	148
1 Samuel		5:42	148
2:15	102	5:44	210
		5:44–5	20, 28, 81, 100, 119,
Psalms			200, 201
4:6	84	5:45	166, 215
27:3–4	219	6:24	188
34:19	94	10	128–9, 143, 203–4,
38	100		215, 216, 221
42:1–2	56	10:12	210
44:22	56	10:16–18	28
118:6	44, 219	10:16–40	20
		10:18–20	63
Isaiah		10:19–20	28, 141, 173,
28:9–11	89		218–20
43:1–3	219	10:21–2	28
45:7	121, 123	10:22	1, 3, 7, 124, 125,
52:11	221		141, 169, 170, 182,
53:10	51		183, 184
		10:23	28, 67–8, 104, 105,
Jeremiah			113, 147, 190, 203,
1:1–10	88		220–1
20:2	89	10:24–5	28, 125
		10:25	7
Zechariah		10:26–8	125, 140, 170
9:9–16	125	10:26–31	28
		10:28–31	81, 101, 119, 165,
2 Maccabees			200–1, 210
6	102	10:32	152, 173, 183
		10:32–3	3, 28, 53–54, 125,
Matthew			135, 170, 197, 203,
4:12	221		204, 216
5:3–12	55, 58	10:33	103
5:10	153	10:37–9	97

10:38	125, 170	12:8–9	28, 53–4, 204, 216
14:13–14	104	12:35–7	182
16:19	193	12:51–3	20
16:24	3	16:19–31	177
16:24–5	125	21:12	125
16:24–7	20, 90	21:14–15	173
16:25	126	21:15	218–20
19:27–9	97	21:17	125
19:29–30	207	21:19	210
20:16	95		
22:21	148	John	
23:34–5	125	1:3	86
23:34–6	20	6:68–70	166
24:9–10	20, 125	7:7	20
24:12–13	94	7:30	105
24:24	94	8:31–2	182
25:36	91	8:41	94
		11:54	101, 104, 221
Mark		14:1–3	95
4:8–20	97	14:1–4	134
4:17	20	14:2	206
5:9–13	120	15:18–21	20, 169
8:29–38	20	15:18–25	126
8:34–5	125, 170	15:19	90
8:34–7	90	15:20	1, 125
8:35	126	15:21	125
8:38	28, 53–4, 125, 152, 170, 204, 216	16:1–3	20
		16:2–4	169
10:16	193	16:33	169, 176
13:9	125	17:14–16	20, 126
13:9–13	20	18:36	88
13:11	218–220		
13:13	125, 170, 210	Acts	
		2:23	51
Luke		5:41	7, 20, 89, 90, 152, 210
6:22	7, 125		
6:22–3	125, 170	7:52	88, 125
6:22–26	215	7:54–6	126
6:22–32	20	8:18	193
6:23	90, 96	8:20	148
6:27–9	100	9:3–5	91
9:23–4	125, 170	9:4–5	20
9:23–25	90	9:17	193
9:23–26	20, 215	15:29	136
9:24	126	23:2	89
9:26	28, 53–4, 103, 152, 204, 216		
		Romans	
11:4–12	20	3:3–4	166
11:49–50	125	5:3–5	131, 206
12:8	152	7:24	90

8:17	126	6:10–17	170
8:17–18	126–7, 131, 206	6:12	53, 92
		6:24	89
8:18	89		
8:28	87, 94, 206	Philippians	
8:29	82	1:29	53
8:35–7	20, 170	3:10	126
8:35–9	89, 93	4:11–13	62
8:36	56, 90		
8:36–37	53	2 Thessalonians	
10:10	102	1:4–7	20
12:12	87, 90, 94	1:4–8	137
12:14	101, 210		
12:14–21	20, 215	1 Timothy	
12:17–21	210	4:12	62
12:19	100	5:22	193
1 Corinthians		2 Timothy	
1:27	123	1:6	193
3:1	89	2:3	126
3:12	102	2:5	89
4:10–13	20	2:11–12	173
4:12–13	101, 210	3:12	88, 91
10:21	187		
10:24	105	Hebrews	
11:27	187	4:14	95
12:3	129	5:12	89
15:3–4	177	6:1–2	193
15:35–44	135	10:32–6	100
15:41	134	10:36–9	62
15:41–2	206	11	62
		11:37–8	89
2 Corinthians		11:35–40	20
1:5	96, 126	12:6	89
4:7–11	20, 61	12:6–8	93, 206
4:8–9	7	13:12–14	20
4:17	89		
4:18	100	James	
5:4	90	1:2–4	210
5:6	135		
12:7–9	179	1 Peter	
12:10	7, 20, 89	1:6	60
		1:6–7	20, 210
Galatians		2:12	7
6:7	189	2:12–15	20, 28
6:12	20	2:15	182
6:14	58, 206	2:19–20	28, 153
		2:19–23	20
Ephesians		2:20	88, 182
4:4	165	2:21–3	175, 206, 215

2:23	210	2:23	173
3:12	182	4:4	168, 219
3:13–18	20, 28	4:18	140
3:15–17	55		
3:17	51, 153, 182	Revelation	
4:12	126	2:9–13	20, 215
4:12–13	53	2:10	141, 182, 219
4:12–14	28, 55, 169	6:9	97
4:12–16	138–9, 206	6:9–10	134, 141
4:12–19	20	6:9–11	20, 28, 153, 177, 179–80, 207, 215
4:13	60		
4:13–14	56, 61, 210	16:6	20
4:15–16	28	17:6	20
5:8–10	20	18:4	221
		18:20	125
1 John		18:24	20
2:19	126, 166	19:2	20

Index of ancient sources

Acts of the Scillitan Martyrs 29

Athenagoras
Embassy
1–2   194

Clement of Alexandria
Frag. 1 Peter   56

Paedagogos I
1.1.2   40
1.1.4   40, 57
1.3.3   57
6.28.1   63
8   201
8.62.3–63.1   43
8.62.3–4   44
8.63.1   43
8.63.1–2   44
8.64.4–65.1   43
8.65.1   57
8.66.1–2   43, 52
8.68.3   43
8.70.3   52
8.71.1   43
9.75.1   45, 52
9.75.2   43
9.76.1   52
9.83.2   43, 57
9.83.3   57
9.88.1   43
9.88.2   43

Protrepticus
1.7.5   48
1.8.4   53
4   201
8.1   20
10.103.1   43
11.112.1–2   40
12.120.3   53
12.122.4   56

Quis Dives Salvetur
1.2   43

Stromateis book I
1.119–20   38
5.121–2   38
17.133–4   50
17.134   44, 52
19.173–4   38
21.146–7   35

Stromateis book II
13.166   60
16.72   41
17   125
19.173   40
20   9, 36
20.174   40, 58, 62
20.178   32, 40, 58, 62

Stromateis book 3
4.89   42
5.190   40

Stromateis book IV
1.1.1   65
3.12.4   65
3.12.5   58
4   32, 63
4.13.1   65
4.14.1   55, 65
4.14.3   60, 63, 65
4.15.4   63, 207
4.16.3   66, 68, 110
4.17.1–3   66
4.17.1   60
4.17.3   65
4.18.3   58
5.23.1   52, 61

6.25.1	60	12.86.2	44, 51
6.25.1–2	58	12.86.2–87.1	52
6.25–7	55	12.86.3–87.1	44
6.28.4	68	12.87.1	49, 51, 52
6.32.1	45	12.95.3	53
6.41.1	56, 58	13.92.2	53
6.41.2	60	13.93.3–94.1	49
6.41.4	58, 59	14.95	200
7.42.3–4	68	14.95.2–3	49
7.46.1	55	14.95–6	61
7.46.1–47.4	56	16.101.1–103.2	62
7.46.3	60, 61	16.103.3–104.1	60
7.47.2	53	17.110.5	59
7.47.4	56	19–21	41
7.47.5	53	19.124.2–3	49
7.52.1	61	21.130.1	60
7.52.2	56	21.130.1–2	58
7.52.2–3	58	21.130.5	58
7.52.3	32	21.131–134	58
7.52.4	44	21.131.1	61
9	42, 54, 218	21.131.1–132.1	62
9.70.4	63	21.132.1	58
9.72–5	203	21.132.2–133.3	58
9.72.1–2	59	22.135.1–4	58
9.72.1–3	54–5	22.137.1–2	57
9.72.3	68	23.147.1	61
9.73.1–3	55	24.153.5–154.2	57
9.73.2–3	58	24.154.3	68
9.73.4	63	26.166.1	61
9.73.5	55, 60, 70		
9.74.1	55, 62, 66	*Stromateis* book V	
9.74.3	55, 60	1.62	44
9.75.3–4	55	1.7.2–3	45
9.73.5–74.1	59	1.7.8	45
9.75.3–4	59	4.25.5	63
10.76.1–77.1	220	9.57.1–2	42
10.76.1–2	68, 203	10.66.2	42
10.76.2	52, 62	12.78	41
10.77.1	52		
10.77.1–2	62	*Stromateis* book VI	
11.78.1–2	55, 203	1.2.1	39
11.78.2–79.1	45	5.42.1	38
11.79	51	6.44.1	38
11.79.2	70	8.62.1	38
11.79.3	70	8.67.1	38
11.80.1	44, 51	13	207
11.80.5	44	13.105.1	59
12.85.1	49	13–14	59
12.85.1–3	51	14.109.3–6	59

14.114.4	59	16	194
15	42	17	194
17.195.9	38	18–19	195
18.166.4	69	20	176
18.167.3	69	21	170, 176
18.167.4	55, 69	23	167, 195
		24	179, 220
Stromateis book VII		24–5	178
2.6.1	53	25	195
2.12.1	49, 51		
2.12.2–3	49	*Ad Donatum*	
2.12.5	59	15	171
3.13.1–2	59		
3.16.2	48	*Ad Fortunatum*	
10–11	59	pref. 1	164, 168, 177
11.64.6–7	63	pref. 2	167, 171, 173
11.66.3	67	pref. 4	178, 179, 190
11.66.3–67.1	60	pref. 4.11	169
11.66.4–67.1	67	pref. 5.10	173
11.67.1	67	2	165
12.74.4	70	5	173, 180
12.74.5	60	5–6	170
12.80.1	61	6	126
13.83	60	9	175, 219
14.84.5	61, 200	10	168, 170, 173, 175, 181, 190, 219
16.95.3–97.2	20		
16.95.3	41	11	168, 169, 194
16.95.4–5	41	12	170, 178, 179, 181
16.95.8	41		
16.96.4	42	12–13	177
16.102.5	52	13	170, 178, 179
17.107.5	69		
		Ad Quirinum testimonia adversus Judaeos book III	
Stromateis book VIII		Intro	20
1	40	10	165
		15	168
Cyprian		16	170, 173, 179, 181, 207
Ad Demetrianum		18	169
2	164	29	169
3	31	80	168
3–4	177	117	170
3–5	164		
5	31, 164, 167, 194	*De bono patientiae*	
6	165	3	166
10	31, 167	4–5	165, 166, 200
12	32	5	165, 175
13	194	9	175, 182

10	175, 182	36	170, 194
12	169, 176, 182	*De mortalitate*	
13	166, 182	2	164, 168, 169, 177, 178
21	176, 179, 207	2–3	178
De ecclesiae catholicae unitate		4	167, 171
1	192	4–5	175
3	192	6	178
4	165	9	167, 171
6	172, 185, 193	11	168
8	172	12	168, 171
14	179, 185	13	166, 175
21	185	13–14	179
De lapsis		15	166, 168
1	166, 190	16	177, 182
2	163, 171, 175, 176, 181, 192	17	166, 183
3	34, 188, 221	17–18	190
4	191	19	166
5	160, 175, 192	20	177
5–6	168	24	177
5–7	160	25	177
7	165, 168, 186	26	177, 178
7–9	162	*De opera et eleemosynis*	
8	166, 167, 171, 186	1	126, 182
8–9	162	2	126, 182
8–12	228	3	193
9	186	4	182
10	166, 189, 190, 221	5	182
10–12	186	26	182
11–12	160	*De oratione Dominica*	
12	170	26	172
13	163, 166, 171, 186		
14	186, 193	*De velandis virginibus*	
15	187, 193	22	178
15–18	228		
16	184, 187, 192	*De zelo et livore*	
17	174, 177, 180, 185	2	167, 172
		3	166, 172
17–18	177	4	167
17–20	187	17	166
18	179, 180, 207		
20	172, 174, 180	*Epistles*	
27	188	5.1.2	192
28	189	5.2	189
35	174, 187, 192	5.2.1	162, 163
35–6	193	6.1.1	181

6.2.1	180, 181	27.3.3	185
6.4	183	28.1.2	163
7	188	28.2.3	185
7.1	32, 162, 189, 190, 221	30.3.1	163, 187
		30.8	163
7.2	189	31.3	177
8.1.1–2.2	189	31.4.1	169
8.2.1	187	33.2.1	192
9.1.2	162	34.4.1	163, 189
10.1	163, 173	36.2.1	185, 187
10.1.1	163, 181	37.1.3	162
10.1–4	183	37.2	178
10.2.2	176	37.3.1	163
10.3	172, 173, 181, 219	37.3.2	178
10.4.4	181	39.1.1–3.3	160
10.5.2	178, 182, 183	40	162
11.1.2	160	41.1.2	163
12.1	183	43.2.2	193
12.1.2	163	43.4.1	32
12.1.2–3	182	43.4.2	162, 189
12.1.3	173	55	172, 190
12.2.2	163, 189	55.4.1–2	174, 184
13.1	176	55.4.3–5	164
13.3.1	176	55.9.1	162
14.2.1	189	55.13.2	192
14.2.1–2	163	55.13.2–14.2	162
14.2.2	169	55.13.2–15.1	188
14.3.1	167	55.14.1	188
15.2.1	187	55.15.1	188
16.2	187	55.16.23	187
16.2.2	174	55.17.3	188
16.4.1	159, 190, 219, 221	55.20.2	193
17.1	187	55.26.1	188
17.1.1	193	55.26.2	193
18	172	55.27.2–3	187
19.1	172	55.29.2	193
19.2.3	174, 184	56	164
20	163	57	164
20.1.2	32, 159, 162, 189, 190, 219, 221	57.1	185
		57.1.1	193
20.2.2	184	57.3.3	193
20.3.2	172, 192	57.4.1–2	185
21.2.2	192	57.4.2	173, 219
21.4.1	192	57.4.3	187
22.2	163	57.4.3–5.2	193
23.3	187	58	164, 160
24.1.1	163	58.1.2	168
25.1.2	174, 184	58.1–2	190
26.1.2	166	58.2	177

58.2.2	168, 169	6.1	73
58.3.2	177	6.1–2	36
58.4	160, 190, 219	6.1–3	73
58.4.2	184	6.3	75
58.5.2	219	6.3.1	37
58.6.3	32	6.6	35, 36, 75
58.7	181	6.11	37
58.10	177, 178	6.13–14	35
59.5.2	165, 201	6.14	37, 73
59.5.3	166	6.14–19	73
59.6.1	164	6.19	74
59.7.2–3	167	6.21	74
59.7.2–4	166	6.23	74
59.12.2	174	6.23–5	74
59.13–14	193	6.23–8	73
60	164	6.28	74
60.2.5	185	6.30–6	73
61	183	6.31–2	74
61.3.2	167	6.34	74
67.1.1	162	6.36	74
67.7	177	6.39	74, 75
68.1.2	164, 192, 193	6.39–40	162
68.4.2	193	6.41–2	163
69.2	193, 215	6.42	164
69.15.1–16.1	167	6.43	164
75.7	193	6.44	164
76	164–5	7.1	73
76.5	173	7.10	164
76.5.1	219	7.11	164
77	165	7.22	175
77.3.2	192		
78	165	*Historia Augusta*	
78.3.1	192	Septimius Severus	16.8–17.1 36
79	165		
79.1.1	192	**Justin**	
80	165	*1 Apology*	
80.1.2	164	4	194
80.1.3	181, 184	7	194
81	165, 181		
81.1	176	**Lactantius**	
81.1.1–3	184	*Divinae institutiones*	
81.1.4	184	5.4	195

Eusebius of Caesarea

Minucius Felix
Octavius
28   194

Historia Ecclesiastica
5.1   29
5.11   36   *Martyrdom of Polycarp*
6–7   160   6–12   30

Origen

Contra Celsum book 1
pref. 2	94
pref. 3	94
pref. 4	107
1.8	94
1.61	103
1.65	103

Contra Celsum book 2
2.13	74, 107
2.13–17	94
2.15	74
2.17	74
2.45	89
2.51	84, 86

Contra Celsum book 3
3.8	95, 107

Contra Celsum book 4
4.28	81
4.32	84, 85
4.40	77
4.62–4	87
4.65	83, 84

Contra Celsum book 5
5.5	84
5.19	95
5.63	101

Contra Celsum book 6
6.56	84, 93

Contra Celsum book 7
7.6.9	201
7.25	100
7.32	95
7.46	101
7.61	100
7.69	84

Contra Celsum book 8
8.3.9	84
8.20	200
8.31	84, 85
8.33	84, 201
8.34	84
8.35	100
8.36	84
8.38	101
8.43	84
8.44	84, 92, 104, 220
8.54.8	32
8.60–3	201
8.67	81
8.70	81, 85
8.72	77, 87, 94

Commentarii in evangelium Joannis
1.71	91
1.104–5	77
2.13.91–4	86
2.13.93	86
2.13.97	84
2.13.99	86
2.96	86
6.53.274	91
6.54.276	207
6.54.281–3	99
6.276	99
6.281–3	97, 106
19.20.136	90
20.17.147	100
20.17.147–8	94, 200
20.17.148	80
20.22.184	84
20.33.292	200
20.34.309	200
20.136	91
20.148	100
20.292	100
20.309	100
28.19.165	91
28.23.192	101, 220
28.23.192–4	104–5
28.23.194–5	101
28.23.196	105
28.23.198	105
28.23.209	105, 220
32.3.26–40	85
32.7, 8	125

Commentarium in evangelium Matthaei
10.31.23	104
13.9	91

on Mt 10:23	98, 220	42	96, 100
on Mt.24	99	44	100
		45	84, 91, 103
Commentarii in Romanos		50	97, 99, 101
1.4.50.2	82		
1.5.52.3	82	*Homiliae in Exodum*	
3.5.236.1	91	5.3	91
5.6.416.6	85	6.1	91
5.10.452.15	85	6.9	91
7.11.3	90	11.1	91
9.1.9	90		
9.23.1	100	*Homiliae in Ezechielem*	
		3.8	94
Dialogus cum Heraclide			
24.10.20	97–8	*Homiliae in Genesim*	
		1.1	77
Epistula ad Gregorium		9.3	89
Thaumaturgum	75		
		Homiliae in Jeremiam	
Exhortatio ad martyrium		1.13.2	88, 100
1	89, 92	4.3.2	36, 94, 95,
1–2	88		106
2	90, 96, 106	14.7	91
2–3	102	14.8.1	91
3	90, 96	14.11.2	84
4	90, 96, 100, 101	14.14.2	89
5	102	14.14.4–5	89
7	102	14.16.3	89
10	102	14.17	88
11	102	19.12.2	89
12	90, 96, 97	19.12.3	89
14	96, 97		
14–15	96, 102, 207	*Homiliae in Leviticum*	
15	97	2.4.6	98
17	102	6.6	91
18	92, 94, 95, 102, 106	7.6.4	75
21	94	9.9.4	90, 98
22	102		
22–29	106	*Homiliae in Lucan*	
28	97, 98, 101, 102	6.9	106
30	97, 98, 101		
32	91	*Homiliae 1 on*	
33	95, 106	*Psalm 38*	100
34	101, 218		
34–5	104	*De oratione*	
37	95, 103	18.8	98
38	99		
39	97, 98	*On the Pascha*	
40	103	27.15	103

Index of Ancient Sources   269

Philocalia	
24.5	94
25.2–3	82
25.3	88
26	87
27.9	93

De principiis book 1	
1	201
1.5	80
1.6	80
2.10	77
2.13	80
3.1	20
3.8	93
4.3	80
5.2	84
5.3	77, 80
5.3–4	83
5.5	77
6.1	95, 99
6.1–3	87
6.2	77, 80
6.2–3	98
6.3	77, 84, 85, 91
7.1	76, 77
8.1	77
8.3	80
8.3–4	86
8.4	82

De principiis book 2	
1.2	77, 83, 86, 96
1.4	80
2.2	76
4	201
5	201
5.1–4	81
5.3	86, 87
8.3–4	95
9.1	76, 77
9.2	86
9.6	77, 82, 201
9.8	82, 98
10.1	95
10.2–4	95
10.4	98
10.4–6	96
10.6	77, 86, 93
11.5–7	95
11.6	77, 93, 98
11.7	95

De principiis book 3	
1.3	86
1.4–6	85
1.6	100
1.12	89, 93
1.13	77, 93
2	201
2.2	84
2.2–3	85
2.5	92
2.6	74, 87, 92
2.7	81, 87, 200
3.2–3	84
3.4	84
4.5	82
5.7	77, 98
5.7–8	93
5.8	77, 81
6.1	77
6.3	77, 86
6.5–6	85
6.6	77, 98
6.8	77

De principiis book 4	
1–3	79
1.1	20
1.1–2	79
1.2	32
2.2	79
2.3	79
2.4	79
2.7	79
2.9	79
3.15	77
4	79
4.8	76
4.9	95

Passio Perpetuae et Felicitatis	
3.7	150
4.3	110
13.8	134

Plato
Republic book II
361–2   61

Pliny the Younger
Epistles
10:96–7   29

Pontius
Vita Cypriani   181

Seutonius
Nero 16   17

Tacitus
Annales
15.44   17, 29

Tertullian

Ad martyras
1	219
1.1	139, 149
1.2, 3	127
1.3	142
2	130
2.7	149
3	131, 142
3.3	134
4.2	32, 131
4.3	84
4.4–8	145
4.9	134

Ad nationes book 1
1	152
1.1–4	122
2	29
7	31
9	31, 194

Ad Scapulam
1.1–2	144, 152
1.2	153
1.3	153
1.3–4	139
2.2	151
2.10	150
3	123
3.1	138, 151, 220
3.3	133
3.5	32, 133, 220
3.5–4.1	145
4	152
4.1	123, 133, 138
4.3	31
4.5–6	110
4.7	151
4.8	123, 134
5	152
5.1–2	145
5.2	153, 226
5.2–3	153
5.3	123, 138, 151
5.4	132, 150, 153

Ad uxorem book 1
3.4–5	147
5	130

Adversus Hermogenem
11	118
16	118, 201

Adversus Marcionem book I
14.3	125
23.3–4	119, 200
26.5	118, 200
27.1–2	124
27.5	111

Adversus Marcionem book II
5–6	119
5.2	118
5.3–7	118
6	121
6.1	119
6.1–2	118
7	121
8.2	119
9.8–9	119
10	121
11	124
13.1–4	124
14	121, 152
17.1	118
28.1	121

Adversus Marcionem book III
9.5	126
22.5	126
24.6	133

Adversus Marcionem book IV
4.5	125
14.17	126
16.1–5	139
20.4–5	126
21.8–9	135
21.10	152
34.14–15	133
36	201
36.1–3	118, 200
39	125
39.8	125

Adversus Marcionem book V
6.1–6	119
10.14–16	133
16.1	137
17.1	126
17.9–10	120
17–18	201
18.12–13	120

Adversus Praxean
8.4–7	142
13.8	30, 111
26.9	152
29.7	142

Adversus Valentinianos
33.1	125

Apologeticum
1	4, 31, 153
1.2	122, 152
1.4–5	123
1.12	139
2	29, 151
4	29
4.4–13	151
6	29
7–8	31
21.3	143
21.25–8	152
22.1–4	120
22.6	120
23.4–5	120
23.19	120
24	151
24.6–10	30
27	120, 152
27.4	122
27.7	84, 127, 153
30, 31	139
31	153
32.1	133
35.4	110
37.1–3	139
39.7	151, 214
40–1	31, 194
40.2	31
46.16–17	139
47.13	135
48.13–15	133
49–50	143, 151
49.4	32
50	146
50.1	127
50.1–3	152
50.2–3	127, 134
50.3	32
50.12	32, 152
50.12–13	153
50.12–16	150
50.13	132, 150
50.14–16	153
50.15–16	137, 207

De anima
2	12
7.3–4	133
9	126
9.4	9, 110
19	126
20.5	119
27	126
35.2	139
39.1, 3	120
40	126
52.11	135
52.11–13	135
52.15	135
55	133
55.2	125
55.3	135

272 *Index of Ancient Sources*

55.4	33, 110, 134, 137, 207	2.1	122, 123
		2.2	123, 127
55.4–5	153	2.5	120
55.5	125, 135, 223	2.6	120, 201
55–6	177	2.7	120, 123
56.7	133	3.1	123, 131
58	133	3.2	119, 123, 200
		4	147
De baptismo		4.1	123, 138, 208
5.6–7	136	4.3	138, 208
6–8	142	4.3–5.3	140
12.7	149	5.1	33, 111, 146, 147, 220, 221
16	137		
20.1	136	5.2	119, 145, 146
		5.3	147
De carne Christi		6.1–2	221
5.3	152	7	140
		7.1	125, 138, 147
De exhortatione castitatis		7.2	33, 129, 131, 141, 147, 152
12	130		
12.3–4	111	8.3	147
		9.1–3	140
De corona		9.3	220
1	111	9.4	147
1.3	134	11	189, 219
1.4	143, 144	11.1	111
1.4–5	150	12	67
1.5	111, 147	12.1	111
2.4	153	12.2–3	126
11.5	125, 152	12.3–4	148
13.4	152	12.5	148
15.1	141	12.6–7	148
15.2–3	132	12.9	133
15.3	141	12.9–10	148
		12–13	163
De cultu feminarum		13.1	148
2.13.4	32, 130	14.3	142, 219, 221
De fuga in persecutione		*De idolatria*	
1	147	12	130
1.1	111, 148	13.6	152
1.2	117, 122	18.7–9	121
1.3	138, 152, 208	21.1–3	121
1.5	127, 133, 141		
1.5–6	152	*De ieiunio adversus psychicos*	
1.6	131	1.1–2	142, 214
1.7	122	11.4–6	142
1–2	223	12	142
2	147	12.2	32, 111, 130

17.9	130	9.21	137, 144, 146, 207
De oratione		11.2	136
5.3	134, 137, 153	12	136
		12.4–6	146
De paenitentia		12.11	136
4.1	136	16.5	136
6.3–4	119	18.18	146
6.17	119	19.25–26	192
7.2	136	19.26	136
7.10	136	21	192, 214
8.3	139	21.11–15	146
12.1–4	133	21.15–17	146
		22	111
De patientia		22.1–5	137
1.6–7	141		
3	132, 141	*De resurrectione mortuorum*	
5	141, 153	8.5	32
5.3–14	119	8.5–6	133
5.21	119	8.6	137, 146
8	125	17	133, 177
8.7–9	139	21	124
9	141	21.3–4	133
10–11	141	25.1	134, 137, 153, 207
10.1–3	139		
11.9	125	25.1–3	133
13	141	35.1–7	140
13.6	131, 147	35.6–7	133
13.6–8	13	38.4	134, 207
13.7	137	40.11–12	127
13.8	32	40.12–15	133
15.2	130	41.2–3	125
16.2–4	119	43.4	134, 135, 207
		56.1	133
De praescriptione haereticorum		62	133
3.6	125, 126, 141		
4	110	*De spectaculis*	
7	112	1.5–6	130
12	125	2.3	130
15–19	113	2.5–7	120
34.5	125	2.12	120
		13	31
De pudicitia		27.1	32
1.14	32	27.1–2	147
2.12	136	28.3–5	130, 131
3	136	29	131
5	192	29.1–3	144
5.5	13	30	133, 138, 153
9.10	136, 146, 192	30.3	139, 140

De testimonio animae
6.1 20

Scorpiace
1	148
1.5	110, 143, 220
1.11–13	9, 110
1.13	144
2.1	144
5	144
5.8–9	126
5.9	130
5.10	135
6	152
6.1	122, 126, 204
6.1–6	126
6.4	134
6.7	144
6.7–8	134
6.9	137, 144, 146, 207
8.1	132, 144
8.8	144
9	143
9–11	204, 221
9.1–3	125
9.1–8	126
9.5	124, 125
9.6	126, 141
9.8	128, 140, 152
9.9	129
9.9–11	204
9.10	129
9.11	129
9.12	129
9.13	129
10.1	124
10.4	152
10.9–17	125
10.14–11.2	143
10.17	141
10.17–11.5	136
11	152
11.1	125
11.1–3	143
11.3	141
12.2–3	139, 153
12.6–9	141
13	126
13.2–4	131

Theophilus of Antioch
To Autolycus
1.1 194

Index of topics

acknowledgement of Christ: *see* confession
Alexandrian school 36–7, 41
almsgiving 182, 192
apokatastasis 77, 82–3, 85, 94
apologetic 69–70, 94, 106–7, 151–4, 195–4
apologies, second century 19, 106, 115
apostasy 68–9, 102–3, 145–6, 186–7, 213
arena metaphor 92, 129, 131, 134
athletic metaphor 92, 127, 133
avoiding martyrdom: *see* martyrdom, avoidance

baptism 146, 179
bishop, role of 149, 189, 191–3, 214–5
blessedness of persecuted 1, 19, 55, 58, 60–1, 100, 125, 170, 181, 203

Carthage 110–11, 116
Christ
    confession of, in and by 53–5, 172–4, 69, 128–9, 152, 170, 203–4
    denial of 203
    imitation of 12, 125–6
    as paedagogue 57, 69
    persecution for the name/ sake of 90–1, 124–6, 152
    unity with 88–90, 91, 126–7, 138, 172–3
Christian identity 23–5, 161, 227–30, 236
Christianity
    growth and spread of 150–1, 225–7
    Roman perspective on 30–1, 161
church: *see* ecclesiology
Clement of Alexandria
    apologetic 69–70
    and apostasy 68–69
    avoidance of martyrdom 67–9, 71–2
    concept of evil 47–51
    concept of God 43–6, 51, 71
    confession 53–5, 59, 62–3, 69
    diogmology, summary 71–2
    ecclesiology 69–71
    gnostic Christian 40, 53, 55–6, 58, 59–60, 61–2
    gnostic martyrdom 55–6, 58, 60, 61–2, 63–7
    life of 35–7
    and martyrdom 58–60, 62–69, 71–2, 211–12
    on perfection 56–60, 61, 71
    and philosophy 37–9, 45–6, 47
    response to persecution 32, 60–71
    and Scripture 40–2
    and theosis: *see* theosis
    universalism 68–9
cognitio extra ordinem 30
confession
    of, in and by Christ 53–5, 172–4, 69, 128–9, 152, 170, 203–4
    completeness of 102
    forms of 55, 62–3, 173, 182–4, 211–13
    and martyrdom, relationship 7, 62–69, 101–2, 128–9, 135, 144–4, 182–6
    necessity of 53–5, 59, 63, 124–6, 128–9, 131
    at trial 17, 55, 59, 62–3, 101–2, 128, 143, 161, 183, 211
    within church communion 172–4
confessors 32, 62–3, 101–2, 129, 141–2, 149–50, 162–3, 173–4, 176, 180, 182–6, 190–1, 218–20
    intercession of 99, 137, 146, 174, 180, 184–5
    support for 149–50, 214
contest: *see* arena metaphor, cosmic conflict
cosmic conflict 91–2, 108, 120–1, 123, 127–8, 133, 138, 152–4, 170–2, 174–5, 179, 204, 206, 211, 222–5, 227
    see also military imagery

Decian persecution 160–3
deification: *see* theosis
demons 48–50, 83–5, 91–2, 102–3, 120, 127
denial of Christ 53–5, 144, 147, 173–4. *See also* apostasy
Devil 48–9, 51–2, 53, 71, 83, 85, 91–2, 102, 108, 119–21, 121–4, 127, 129, 167–9, 171–2, 199
diogmology
  of Clement, summary 71–2
  commonalities 197–8
  of Cyprian, summary 195–6
  definition 5–6
  disparities 198
  of Origen, summary 107–8
  questions 28–9, 197–215, 209
  scope 6–7
  and Scripture 8–9, 28–29, 200–3, 216–222
  of Tertullian, summary 154–5
  as theological locus 7–8, 11
  and theology, relationship 7, 28, 198
discipline 57–8, 130–1, 150, 154, 175–6
dualism 39–40, 47, 81–82, 198

ecclesiology
  Clement 69–71, 214
  Cyprian 172–3, 175, 185, 191–5, 215
  Origen 105–6
  Tertullian 116, 148–51, 214–5
emperors
  persecution by/ under 31, 35–6, 73–4, 110–11, 160–3, 164–5
  worship of 14
  see also Decian persecution, Septimius Severus
encouragement 101–2, 139, 170, 176, 181–2, 183–4
endurance: *see* patience
enemies, love of 61, 100, 139
eschatology
  Alexandrian 96, 130, 149, 179, 202, 206
  Carthaginian 130, 132–3, 137, 149, 202, 205
  see also intermediate state, judgement, parousia, punishment

Eusebius of Caesarea
  history of persecution 73–5, 160
  theology of persecution 11–12
evil 46, 47–51, 82, 86–7, 118, 121. *See also* theodicy
exomologesis: *see* penitence

fall (into sin) 50, 83–5, 119–20
fear 139, 140, 180
flight from persecution 33–34, 52, 67–8, 146–8, 163, 189–90, 220–1
foreknowledge of God 45, 52, 82
forgiveness of sin 60, 98–9, 137, 187, 207
free will 44–45, 50, 82–3, 96, 118–9, 121, 166–7, 199

glory, glorification 126–7
gnostic Christian (Clement) 40, 53, 55–6, 58, 59–60, 61–2, 69, 70–1
Gnosticism 39–40, 47, 63–4
  Valentinian 124, 135
gnostic martyr 55–6, 58, 60, 61–2, 63–7
God
  characteristics of 43–6, 80–83, 118, 166, 199
  foreknowledge of 45, 52, 82
  goodness of 43, 45, 53, 80–82, 86, 118, 199–200
good of persecution: *see* persecution, goodness of

heaven 134–5
heresy 42, 63–66, 143–4. *See also* Gnosticism, Montanism
Holy Spirit 141–3, 149, 173, 181, 218–20

idols, idolatry 120, 121–2
imitatio Christi 12, 125–6
imprisonment 6, 30, 131, 142–3, 162–3
injustice of persecution 121–2, 124, 132
intercession of confessors and martyrs 99, 137, 146, 174, 180, 184–5
intermediate state 133

Jeremiah 88–9
joy in persecution 56, 89, 100, 125, 138–9, 180–1
judgement 18, 132, 135, 205
justice 82, 87, 99–100, 114, 118, 124

Lactantius 195
lapsed 162–4, 174, 184, 186–7, 190–1, 192–4
legal status/ legislation, Christians 29–31, 114–5, 151, 161, 162–3
libellatici 32, 148, 163–4, 187–9
love of enemies 61, 100–1, 139

martyr
  definition 5, 7
  intercession: *see* intercession of confessors and martyrs
  radical: *see* voluntary martyrdom
  types of: 32–3, 63–7, 184–5
martyr acts 18–19, 33, 117, 126, 230–3
martyrdom 58–59, 101–2, 183–4
  avoidance of 67–9, 103–5, 122, 141, 145–148, 187–90
  as conflict: *see* cosmic conflict
  in context of persecution 6–7, 13, 18
  gnostic: *see* gnostic martyrdom
  as good 122, 179
  as sacrifice 99
  as second baptism 146, 179, 207
  voluntary: *see* voluntary martyrdom
military imagery 127, 131, 132, 171–2. *See also* cosmic conflict
Montanism 63–4, 112, 144

Name of Christ, persecution for 90–1, 124–126, 152
New Prophecy: *see* Montanism

Origen of Alexandria
  apologetics 94, 106–7
  on apostasy 102–3
  avoidance of martyrdom 98, 103–5, 108, 212
  ecclesiology 105–6
  eschatology 95–6, 99–100
  influences on 75–7
  life 73–5
  on martyrdom 97–8, 98–9, 101–2, 108, 212
  and philosophy 75–6
  on providence 81–3, 87
  response to persecution 100–8, 212
  and Scripture 78–80, 95–6, 99
  summary of diogmology 107–8
  theological schema 76–7, 86–7, 92–3, 107
  works 74, 76, 78

Paraclete: *see* Holy Spirit, also Montanism
Paradise, under altar 135–6, 207
parousia 133, 154. *See also* eschatology
patience 61–2, 132, 139, 140–1, 175–6, 180–2, 225–7
patristic exegesis 20–3
  allegory 22–3, 95–6
  Christocentricity 88–9
  Clement 40–42
  Cyprian 159–60
  Origen 78–80
  Tertullian 112–4
  and theology 21, 216, 221
penitence 146, 190–1, 192–4. *See also* lapsed.
perfection: *see* theosis
Perpetua 117
persecution
  Christian responses 32–34
  by Christians 234
  and church growth 150–1, 225–7
  contemporary 235
  as contest: *see* cosmic conflict
  definition 4–6
  as evil 51–2, 86–7, 96, 121–2
  extent of 13–15
  goodness of 50–51, 57–8, 87, 93–6, 122, 129–38, 174–80, 204–8
  historical continuity and precedent 88–9, 106
  historical evidence 10, 13–15, 17, 26–7, 29–32, 160–3, 230–33
  injustice of 121–2, 124, 132
  inevitability 55, 69, 88–90, 124–6, 129, 132, 151, 168–80, 202–3
  literary analysis 11
  as myth 15–16, 230
  origin of 42, 51–3, 117, 119–24, 165–8, 198–202
  reason for 53, 55, 87–92, 124–9, 168–74, 202–4
  response to 60–71, 89–91, 138–154, 209–215
  and social identity 23–25, 227–30

telos of 56–60, 204–8 *and see* individual fathers on good of persecution
theology of 5 *and see* diogmology
types of 6, 30–32, 36, 73–5, 89, 110–11, 130–1, 163–3, 164–5, 183, 188, 194
persecutors
　complicity in sin of 62, 145, 167, 206
　prayer for 139, 176
　punishment of 123, 170, 176, 195
　responsibility 44–5, 50, 152–4, 166–7, 195
philosophy, influence 37–39, 45–6
Plato 61
Platonism 37–9, 45–6, 47, 48, 76, 199
Pliny-Trajan correspondence 29
Polycarp 63
prison: *see* imprisonment
providence 44–5, 51–53, 81–3, 87, 101, 105, 119–20, 140, 146–7, 165–8, 200, 202, 226
punishment 43, 52, 57, 87, 93, 96, 119, 123–4, 178–9
　post-mortem 59, 93, 96, 130

Quintus 63

radical martyrdom: *see* voluntary martyrdom
rejoicing: *see* joy
religious conflict literature 26
repentance: *see* penitence
reward
　all Christians 178–9
　degrees of 96–8, 207
　for good works 182
　martyrdom and 96–7, 133–6, 179
　persecution and 92–3, 96–98
righteousness 55–56
Roman power 114–7
rule of faith 76, 79, 112

sacrificati 32, 163–4, 186–7
salvation
　Carthaginian soteriology 126
　of the devil 77, 85
　martyrdom and 136–7
　as theosis 53, 59–60, 93
　universal 68–9, 77, 85, 96, 103

Satan: *see* devil
Scripture: *see* patristic exegesis
Septimius Severus 35–6, 73, 110–1
sin
　and evil 49, 121
　forgiveness of 60, 98–9, 193
　of persecutors: *see* persecutors
social identity of Christians 23–5, 227–30
stantes 32, 146–8, 163, 188–9
suffering 93–4. See also Christ, theodicy

teleosis 56–7 *and see* theosis
Tertullian of Carthage
　apologetic 131, 143, 148–9, 151–4, 195
　attitude to persecution 138–41, 212–3
　on avoidance of persecution 145–9
　on discipline 130–1, 150
　ecclesiology 117, 131, 146, 148–51
　eschatology 132–3, 137–8
　life 109–12
　influences on 111–2, 114–7
　martyrdom, high view of 121, 128, 131, 134–5, 136–7, 141–4, 144–6, 212–3
　and Montanism 112
　origin of persecution 117, 121–4, 154
　on providence 119, 154
　polemic and rhetoric 111–2
　response to persecution 140–54
　rigorism 131, 147–8
　and Scripture 112–4, 116, 132
　summary of diogmology 154–5
　on voluntary martyrdom 144–5
theodicy 6, 47–51
theology
　context of 3
　diogmology relationship 7, 28, 198
　of martyrdom 12–13. *See also* martyrdom
　patristic: *see* patristic theology
　of persecution: *see* diogmology
　and Scripture: 8, 216–22
theosis 38, 40, 53, 56–7, 59–60, 73, 93, 99–100, 205
torture 101, 163, 176, 186, 194

unity with Christ: *see* Christian unity with Christ
universalism: *see* salvation

vengeance 139–40, 226
victory and vindication 91–2, 99, 127, 134, 137

'voluntary' martyrdom 32–4, 63–6, 101, 128, 144–5, 184, 213, 233–4

withdrawal: *see* flight
witness to church 94–5, 131, 176
witness to outsiders 94, 131–2, 176

www.ingramcontent.com/pod-product-compliance
Lightning Source LLC
Chambersburg PA
CBHW071238230426
43668CB00011B/1493